Research Methods in Applied Linguistics

Quantitative, Qualitative, and Mixed Methodologies

ZOLTÁN DÖRNYEI

OXFORD UNIVERSITY PRESS

OXFORD
UNIVERSITY PRESS

Great Clarendon Street, Oxford OX2 6DP

Oxford University Press is a department of the University of Oxford. It furthers the University's objective of excellence in research, scholarship, and education by publishing worldwide in

Oxford New York

Auckland Cape Town Dar es Salaam Hong Kong Karachi Kuala Lumpur Madrid Melbourne Mexico City Nairobi New Delhi Shanghai Taipei Toronto

With offices in

Argentina Austria Brazil Chile Czech Republic France Greece Guatemala Hungary Italy Japan Poland Portugal Singapore South Korea Switzerland Thailand Turkey Ukraine Vietnam

OXFORD and OXFORD ENGLISH are registered trade marks of Oxford University Press in the UK and in certain other countries

First published 2007

2011 2010 2009

10 9 8 7 6 5 4

ISBN: 978 0 19 442258 1

Printed in China

Contents

Preface – *9*

Acknowledgements – *11*

PART ONE **Key issues in research methology** – *13*

1 Introduction: what is research and how does this book approach it? – *15*
- 1.1 The good researcher – *16*
- 1.2 My approach to research methology – *18*
- 1.3 The content of this book – *18*
- 1.4 Further reading – *21*

2 Qualitative, quantitative, and mixed methods research – *24*
- 2.1 The qualitative–quantitative distinction – *25*
- 2.2 Quantitative research – *30*
- 2.3 Qualitative research – *35*
- 2.4 Mixed methods research – *42*
- 2.5 My own paradigmatic stance – *47*

3 Quality criteria, research ethics, and other research issues – *48*
- 3.1 Quality criteria for research – *48*
- 3.2 Research ethics – *63*
- 3.3 Research questions and hypotheses – *72*
- 3.4 Other essentials for launching a study: pilot study, research log, and data management – *75*

4 Longitudinal versus cross-sectional research – *78*
- 4.1 Definition and purpose of longitudinal research – *79*
- 4.2 Longitudinal research in applied linguistics – *80*
- 4.3 Main types of longitudinal designs – *81*
- 4.4 Longitudinal qualitative research – *86*
- 4.5 Longitudinal mixed designs – *88*
- 4.6 Choosing a design: longitudinal or cross-sectional? – *88*
- 4.7 Quantitative longitudinal data analysis – *90*

PART TWO **Data collection** – *93*

5 Quantitative data collection – *95*
5.1 Sampling in quantitative research – *95*
5.2 Questionnaire surveys – *101*
5.3 Experimental and quasi-experimental studies – *115*
5.4 Collecting quantitative data via the Internet – *121*

6 Qualitative data collection – *124*
6.1 Qualitative data – *124*
6.2 Sampling in qualitative research – *125*
6.3 Ethnography – *129*
6.4 Interviews – *134*
6.5 Focus group interviews – *144*
6.6 Introspective methods – *147*
6.7 Case studies – *151*
6.8 Diary studies – *156*
6.9 Research journals – *159*

7 Mixed methods research: purpose and design – *163*
7.1 The purpose of mixed methods research – *164*
7.2 The compatibility of different research paradigms – *166*
7.3 Main types of mixed methods designs – *168*
7.4 Why don't people mix methods more? – *173*

8 Classroom research – *176*
8.1 Origins and main types of classroom research – *177*
8.2 Classroom observation – *178*
8.3 Mixed methods classroom research – *186*
8.4 Difficulties and challenges in classroom research – *187*
8.5 Action research – *191*

PART THREE **Data analysis** – *195*

9 Quantitative data analysis – *197*
9.1 Computerized data analysis and SPSS – *197*
9.2 Preparing the data for analysis – *198*
9.3 Data reduction and reliability analysis – *206*
9.4 Key statistical concepts – *207*
9.5 Descriptive statistics – *213*
9.6 Comparing two groups: t-tests – *215*
9.7 Comparing more than two groups: analysis of variance (ANOVA) – *218*
9.8 Correlation – *223*
9.9 Non-parametric tests – *227*
9.10 Advanced statistical procedures – *230*

10 Qualitative data analysis – *242*
10.1 Main principles of qualitative data analysis – *243*
10.2 Qualitative content analysis – *245*
10.3 Grounded theory – *257*
10.4 Computer-aided qualitative data analysis (CAQDAS) – *262*

11 Data analysis in mixed methods research – *268*
11.1 Data transformation – *269*
11.2 Extreme case analysis – *272*
11.3 Typology/category development – *272*
11.4 Multiple level analysis – *273*
11.5 Computer-aided mixed methods data analysis – *273*

PART FOUR **Reporting research results** – *275*

12 Writing a quantitative report – *277*
12.1 Two functions of academic writing – *278*
12.2 Style manuals – *279*
12.3 The structure of the quantitative research report – *280*
12.4 Reader-friendly data presentation methods – *287*

13 Writing qualitative and mixed methods reports – *290*
13.1 Writing a qualitative report – *290*
13.2 Writing a mixed methods report – *300*

PART FIVE **Summing up** – *305*

14 How to choose the appropriate research method – *307*
14.1 General recommendation I: adopt a pragmatic approach – *307*
14.2 Research content considerations – *308*
14.3 Audience considerations – *309*
14.4 Practical considerations – *309*
14.5 Personal considerations – *310*
14.6 General recommendation II: consider mixing methodologies – *313*
14.7 Final words – *313*

Afterword – *315*

Bibliography – *317*

Index – *329*

Preface

When I started my PhD research in the mid-1980s, I was unaware of the fact that there was a fierce 'paradigm war' raging around me between two camps of research methodologists: the constructivist/interpretists, who used qualitative methods, and the positivist/empiricists, who used quantitative methods. Had I known about this division at the time, I would probably have been inclined, ideologically, to join the constructivist/interpretist camp. However, as it happened, the main research tool employed in the area of my interest—the social psychology of second language acquisition and attitudes/motivation in particular—was the 'attitude questionnaire'. By using this instrument for my PhD research, I now realize that I was irresistibly propelled into the midst of the positivist camp.

I was so ignorant of these issues that when I was first told—in the 1990s—that I was a 'positivist', I needed to find out what 'positivism' actually meant. I learnt that it referred to a scientific paradigm and worldview that assumes the existence of an objective and independent social reality 'out there' that can be researched empirically with standardized scientific instruments. However, I also noticed that the term 'positivist' was almost exclusively used by people who did not themselves align with this paradigm and that their usage of the term was definitely not positive: it seemed to indicate that someone was a bit thick-headed and had definitely lost touch (and probably also had macho leanings).[1] This was not good news and, to add to my sorrows, not only was I a positivist but what many did not know, I was also a 'positivist traitor': in the mid-1990s I started to conduct tentative qualitative research to investigate the concepts of demotivation and group dynamics in SLA, and over the past decade most of my PhD students have been engaged in either qualitative or—even worse—combined qualitative–quantitative research. I was clearly in a mess.

However, my cheerless story seems to have taken a happier turn recently: I have learnt that I now qualify to be a 'pragmatist' as a researcher, that is, a proponent of a respectable philosophical approach, and the research my students and I have been conducting is 'mixed methods research', deemed commendable and highly sought after in some circles. What a fortunate time to be writing this book!

In the light of the above, I can now admit that the approach that guided me in preparing the manuscript of this volume has been pragmatic in every respect. My practical dilemma has been this: research is a complex, multifaceted activity, such that it is not easy to provide novice researchers with relevant procedural knowledge without overwhelming and thus disempowering them. Furthermore, even though acquiring research expertise may well be a life-long process, we simply cannot hold back with our first investigation until we have learnt every relevant detail. Instead, what seems to me the most important thing about doing research is that we get down to it, 'get our feet wet' and as a result get 'hooked' on what is a very exciting activity. So, how can research methodology be taught effectively and what can we do to prevent young scholars from launching investigations that may violate key principles of scientific inquiry?

My answer has been to assume that there exists a basic threshold of research expertise which, once achieved, allows us to embark on the process of doing decent research that we will not be ashamed of when looking back a decade later. We can find an interesting analogy to this idea in the psychoanalytic theory of the 1960s: Winnicott (1965) introduced the concept of the 'good enough mother', which was then extended to parenting in general. The concept of the 'good enough parent' suggests that in order to produce psychological health in the child, we do not need to be perfect; instead, 'good enough parenting' only requires the parent to exceed a certain threshold of quality parenting (including empathic understanding, soothing, protection and love) to promote healthy development (Bettelheim 1987), without necessarily having to be a 'Supermum' or 'Superdad'. Personally, I have always found this notion encouraging and thus, following the 'good enough' analogy, it has been my aim in this book to summarize those key components of research methodology that are necessary to become a 'good enough researcher'.

I strongly believe that the 'good enough researcher' needs to master some knowledge of both qualitative and quantitative research, as well as ways of combining them. In the *Handbook of Mixed Methods in Social and Behavioural Research*, Tashakkori and Teddlie (2003c) point out that perhaps the worst residue of the 'paradigm war' in research methodology has been its impact on students. As they argue, many of our students are as a consequence suffering from a fractured 'dual-lingualism', which represents a split personality in methods of study and ways of thinking. At any given moment, they are asked to be either qualitative or quantitative, and while in each mode to forget that the other exists. This is clearly undesirable and, luckily, applied linguists have by and large steered clear of such extreme positions. I hope that most readers of this book will agree with the need to educate a new generation of 'good enough researchers' who are sufficiently familiar with both qualitative and quantitative methods to be able to understand and appreciate the results coming from each school, and, perhaps, even to vary the methods applied in their own practice according to their particular research topic/question. Thus, I am in full agreement with Duff's (2002: 22) conclusion that 'a greater collective awareness and understanding (and, ideally, genuine appreciation) of different research methods and areas of study would be helpful to the field at large'. Accordingly, the writing of this book has been motivated by the wish to go beyond paradigmatic compartmentalization by highlighting the strengths of both approaches and by introducing ways by which these strengths can be combined in a complementary manner.

Acknowledgements

Writing this book has been an enjoyable journey and I have been encouraged and helped by a number of people along the way. First and foremost, I would like to express my thanks to Cristina Whitecross from Oxford University Press, who has been much more than merely a good editor. Her ongoing support for the project right from the beginning has been invaluable. Special thanks are also due to Simon Murison-Bowie, who has not only done a careful job copy-editing the text but has also provided useful suggestions with regard to the content and the clarity of presentation. Patsy Duff and Jean-Marc Dewaele gave their backing to the book when it was still little more than a proposal—thank you once again and I do hope that in the light of the final version you won't regret your decision.

I have been fortunate to have several friends and colleagues who were willing to read the whole or various parts of the manuscript and give me detailed suggestions on how to improve the book. My warm thanks are due to Kathy Conklin, Judit Kormos, Maggie Kubanyiova, Patsy Lightbown, and Henry Widdowson for their detailed and constructive comments (which, of course, caused me a lot of extra work ...). I have done my best to take as many of the comments on board as possible and I do believe that the manuscript has improved considerably as a result. In the end, however, this is my own personal take on research methodology, with—no doubt—several omissions and flaws. Looking back, this has been a much bigger project than I originally anticipated, but I do hope that I managed to convey some of the fascination that I felt while exploring what makes research work.

1 I was pleased to find out later that Hammersley and Atkinson (1995: 3) shared my perception; as they concluded: 'Today, the term 'positivism' has become little more than a term of abuse among social scientists, and as a result its meaning has become obscured'.

PART ONE
Key issues in research methodology

1

Introduction: what is research and how does this book approach it?

When students first encounter research methodology in the social sciences, they are likely to hear terms such as 'statistics', 'sampling', 'reliability', and 'validity', which make this area look very complex and technical, and also quite intimidating. Indeed, for a normal person the image of a social scientist submitting the results of Likert-scale items obtained from a stratified random sample to structural equation modelling is hardly more real than that of the sombre-looking natural scientist in a white coat doing all sorts of strange things in a laboratory. Such technical terms and images all suggest that research is something that only experts do and ordinary humans should steer clear of. In this book I would like to present a more user-friendly facet of research, trying to show that with a bit of care and lots of common sense all of us can conduct investigations that will yield valuable results. I do hope that by the end of this book most readers will agree that 'You can do it if you really want to'.

So what is research? In the most profound sense 'research' simply means trying to find answers to questions, an activity every one of us does all the time to learn more about the world around us. Let us take a very specific example, say, wanting to find a music CD at the lowest possible price. To do so we can go to several shops to compare prices and nowadays we can also search the Internet for the best price. Throughout all this what we are doing is 'research'. Not necessarily good research, I admit, because our investigation will probably not be comprehensive: even if we find what seems to be a really good price, we will not know whether a shop or a website that we have not visited might have offered the same CD for even cheaper. To do good research we need to be systematic so that by the end we can stand by our results with confidence. That is, research in the scientific sense is 'the organized, systematic search for answers to the questions we ask' (Hatch and Lazaraton 1991: 1). Or in short, research is *disciplined inquiry*.

Following Brown (1988), we can identify two basic ways of finding answers to questions:

1 By looking at what other people have said about a particular issue; this is usually called 'secondary', 'conceptual', or 'library' research and it is an essential form of inquiry because it would be a waste of time and energy to ignore other people's work and 'reinvent the wheel' again and again.

2 By conducting one's own data-based (or in research terms, 'empirical') investigation, which involves collecting some sort of information (or 'data') and then drawing some conclusion from it. This is called 'primary' research.

This book is concerned with the second type of research, the collection of one's own data, particularly as it is applied to the study of languages. But why collect our own data? Isn't it naïve or even arrogant to think that we can contribute something new to the understanding of how languages are acquired or used? After all, people who are far more knowledgeable than us must have surely addressed all the worthwhile questions to be addressed and must have drawn all the conclusions that could be drawn. I would strongly argue that this is not the case for at least two reasons: first, no two language learning/use situations are exactly the same, and therefore the guidelines that we can find in the literature rarely provide the exact answers to one's specific questions. Second, there is *progress* in research, that is, new advances are continuously made by building on the results of past research.

There is also a third reason why I consider doing some primary research important for every language professional: simply put, research can be a great deal of fun and an intellectually highly satisfying activity. Many people enjoy doing crosswords and puzzles, and it is helpful to look at research as something similar but on a larger scale. Furthermore, not only is the process of answering questions, solving puzzles or discovering causes often exciting and illuminating, but it can also be one of the most effective forms of professional development, one that can benefit other people as well. This point has been expressed very clearly in a recent book on research for language teachers by McKay (2006: 1):

> For teachers, a primary reason for doing research is to become more effective teachers. Research contributes to more effective teaching, not by offering definitive answers to pedagogical questions, but rather by providing new insights into the teaching and learning process.

1.1 The good researcher

What kind of characteristics do we need to become good researchers? Let me start by stating that it is my belief that becoming a good researcher does *not* necessarily require decades of gruelling apprenticeship in laboratories, museum archives, or the like. That is, research is not something that can only be done well if we are ready to sacrifice a great deal of our working lives and thus 'pay the price'. (Many applied linguists actually enjoy life!) While experience and academic expertise do undoubtedly help, they are not the main prerequisites to being a successful researcher: For example, it is not unheard of that university seminar papers are published in international journals and more than one important study in applied linguistics has been based on an author's MA dissertation. Thus, in order to be able to produce good research results one does not necessarily have to be old or overly seasoned. In my view, there are four fundamental features of a researcher that will help him/her to achieve excellence: genuine curiosity, a lot of common sense, good ideas, and something that can be best described as a combination of discipline, reliability, and social responsibility. Let us take these one by one.

Over the years I have come to believe that the primary characteristic of good researchers is that they have a genuine and strong curiosity about their topic. Good researchers are always after something that they find intriguing or puzzling or about which they have a hunch (or in research terms, a 'hypothesis'). Serious research will inevitably require some hard work and the only way to maintain our momentum and creativity throughout the laborious parts is to be driven by our passion for the topic. This is why it is advisable for novice researchers to choose a research topic that they are genuinely interested in rather than one that seems sensible from a career point of view.

The second important feature of a good researcher is common sense. When we become intimately involved in pursuing an activity, it is all too easy to lose touch with reality and abandon one's clarity of purpose, to become biased and gradually go astray. Lots of elaborate, costly, and highly 'scientific' investigations have been conducted on trivial and frankly boring topics. Applied linguists are by definition engaged with the real world and I have found that the best researchers in the field tend to be very normal people. They have a high level of common sense that helps to keep their feet firmly on the ground.

The third aspect of successful research that I would like to underline is having good ideas. It seems to me that no amount of sophisticated research design or complex analytical technique can be a substitute for creative thinking that is grounded in reality. Many of the best known studies in applied linguistics are not at all complicated in terms of their research methodology but are based on fairly simple but original insights, making us sigh, 'Why didn't I think of this ...!'

Finally, I strongly believe that a good researcher needs to be disciplined and responsible. This is related to the *systematic* nature of research. During the course of an investigation there are recurring temptations to cut corners, to leave out some necessary steps and to draw conclusions that are not fully supported by the data. It is the researcher's discipline that keeps him/her on the right track, and the lack of discipline or consistency is one of the most frequent sources of inadequate research. An important related characteristic has been pointed out to me by Patsy Duff (personal communication): a good researcher also has a sense of social responsibility, that is, accountability to the field and more broadly, to the world. Research is not done for its own sake, but to generate knowledge and to further our understanding. This means that the good researcher needs to learn to communicate his/her findings with others, which is why Part 4 of this book concerns writing up and reporting our results.

1.2 My approach to research methodology

My approach to research methodology is twofold. On the one hand, I cannot relate well to research texts that are too heavy on discussing the philosophical underpinnings of research methodology. Although, being myself a researcher into motivation, I do accept that our behaviours (and particularly sustained and consistent behaviours such as research efforts) are governed by abstract principles, I get easily disorientated in the midst of discussing research at such an abstract level, and often find myself thinking, 'Can't we just get on with it ...?' I was relieved to find that I am not alone with this feeling; for example, talking about alternative methods in qualitative research, Miles and Huberman (1994: 2) state: 'At times it seems as if the competing, often polemical arguments of different schools of thought about how qualitative research should be done properly use more energy than the actual research does'. I accept, however, that this question is not so simple and therefore we will look at the various stances in more detail in Chapters 2 and 7. (See also the Preface, for a personal account.)

The other side of the coin is, however, that I really dislike *bad* research. Therefore, I firmly believe in the importance of becoming familiar with the 'research lore'—that is, the principles of best practice—that past researchers have accumulated over the decades. There are several technical aspects of research that are certainly worth learning about because the pitfalls that we can fall into if we follow a purely trial-and-error method can be deep and costly in terms of time and energy. Also, there are certain key principles of research methodology that we need to bear in mind or else we risk our results becoming irreparably flawed. Thus, I believe in the usefulness of a straightforward, 'to-the-point' research methodology that offers a great deal of practical help and which also sets clear boundaries for researchers.

1.3 The content of this book

Research methodology covers a very broad range and therefore every overview is inevitably selective. Without wanting to be too technical at this stage, I feel that it is important to describe here some key aspects of my approach in selecting and organizing the content.

Qualitative and quantitative data

As stated before, this book focuses on 'primary research', which involves collecting original data, analysing it and then drawing one's own conclusion from the analysis. Accordingly, the key issue in this book is *data*. Broadly speaking, in applied linguistic research we can find three main types of primary data:

- *Quantitative data* which is most commonly expressed in numbers (for example, the score of a language aptitude test or the number of times a student volunteers in class).
- *Qualitative data* which usually involves recorded spoken data (for example, interview data) that is transcribed to textual form as well as written (field) notes and documents of various sorts.
- *Language data* which involves language samples of various length, elicited from the respondent primarily for the purpose of language analysis (for example, a recorded language task or a solicited student essay that is to be submitted to discourse analysis). We should note here that this type of language data is often subsumed under qualitative data in the literature, but I feel that it is useful to separate the two data types.

This book will focus primarily on the first two types of data and will not be concerned with the third type, language data, unless it is submitted to non-linguistic analysis. The collection and analysis of language data is a highly specialized applied linguistic task, and several sub-disciplines—for example, language testing/assessment, discourse analysis, conversation analysis, and corpus linguistics—have been developed to help to conduct the processing of such data, with a great number of good overviews published in the field (for example, Adolphs 2006; Alderson 2006; Bachman and Palmer 1996; Brown 2005; Carter *et al.* 2001; Chaudron 2003; Ellis and Barkhuizen 2005; Fulcher and Davidson 2006; Markee 2001; Norris and Ortega 2003; Schiffrin *et al.* 2003; Widdowson 2004). Although I will from time to time refer to work in this area, the main intention of this book is to summarize the *generic* aspects of working with qualitative and quantitative data, which can then be transferred to be used in some aspects of language analysis. (This is admittedly a rough classification because there are several 'cross-overs' between data types—for example, both qualitative and language data can be turned quantitative relatively easily—but this broad system is remarkably robust and helpful in clarifying the foundations of research.)

Qualitative, quantitative, and mixed methods research

Due to the different nature of qualitative and quantitative data, different methods have been developed in the past to collect and analyse them, leading to the differentiation between two research paradigms, 'qualitative research' and 'quantitative research'. We should note here that the terms qualitative and quantitative are 'overstated binaries' (Duff 2006: 66) and along with others, Brown (2004a) argues that a more constructive approach is to view qualitative and quantitative research as a matter of degrees or a continuum rather than a clear-cut dichotomy. However, these categories are useful to get us started and we will elaborate on them in the next chapter.

Although the qualitative–quantitative distinction does separate two research approaches, I do not see qualitative and quantitative methodologies as necessarily mutually exclusive, and therefore a special objective of this book is to introduce readers to a third research approach: 'mixed methods research'. This is a new and vigorously growing branch of research methodology, involving the combined use of qualitative and quantitative methods with the hope of offering the best of both worlds. Thus, in this book I will try to break down the barriers between qualitative and quantitative methodologies as much as is practical and highlight the manifold ways of combining them to best effect.

Conservative and canonical approach

Research methodology has reached several interesting crossroads in the past decade. In quantitative research, for example, there is a lively debate concerning applications of certain statistics including significance testing and its alternatives, and in qualitative research there have been some high-profile splits between various schools in ethnographic research and in grounded theory. Such diversity is not unique to these specific issues or areas; because research methodology concerns the principal process of getting to know and coming to terms with the world around us, different scholars with different worldviews are likely to advocate different approaches regarding how to go about doing research. As a consequence, during the past four decades research methodology has become an arena where diverse philosophical and political views have clashed in a spectacular manner over questions such as 'What is the reality around us like?' or 'What is the social responsibility of the researcher?' or 'What evidence do we need to present to be able to argue a point convincingly?'

I do not think that it requires much justification that a basic overview such as that offered by this volume cannot represent all the diverse stances that have been pushing the boundaries, but, instead, needs to focus on the canonical aspects of the accumulated research lore. Therefore, in my summaries I will give priority to the research principles and recommendations that have stood the test of time, which will inevitably result in a somewhat conservative slant of the presentation of the material.

1.4 Further reading

Applied linguists can find useful resources in research methodology in several different areas: first and foremost, there is a healthy body of methodology literature specifically focusing on applied linguistic research. However, because so much in research methodology is sufficiently generic to be transferable, we can also find relevant information in research methodology texts written for social scientists in general and for psychological and educational researchers in particular. Thus, readers interested in more advanced aspects of research issues are advised to consult works from these 'feeder' disciplines, where the accumulated research experience considerably exceeds that in applied linguistics. Qualitative research has traditionally been strong within sociology and anthropology—research texts originating from these traditions are often aimed at the social sciences in general. Quantitative research and statistics have traditionally been driven by psychologists, and the field of psychology subsumes a sub-discipline specialized in assessment issues: 'psychometrics'. Educational research has been creative in adapting a wide range of research methods used in the social sciences to the specific area of student learning, and therefore it can offer unique expertise in specialized areas such as educational intervention research or classroom observation.

In the following I will list a number of research methodology texts that I have found useful in my own research and in writing this book. This is not a comprehensive list and colleagues will probably immediately find some real 'gems' that I have, regrettably, omitted.

Linguistic and applied linguistic resources

The following titles are general research methodology texts for applied linguists. (For recent reviews, see Brown 2004b; Lazaraton 2005; Liskin-Gasparro 2005.) For works that concern narrower research areas, such as specific methods, please see the references in the relevant chapters.

Bachman, L. F. 2004. *Statistical Analyses for Language Assessment.* Cambridge: Cambridge University Press.

Brown, J. D. and **T. S. Rodgers.** 2002. *Doing Second Language Research.* Oxford: Oxford University Press.

Hatch, E. M. and **A. Lazaraton.** 1991. *The Research Manual: Design and Statistics for Applied Linguistics.* New York: Newbury House.

Johnson, D. M. 1992. *Approaches to Research in Second Language Learning.* New York: Longman.

Mackey, A. and **S. M. Gass.** 2005. *Second Language Research: Methodology and Design.* Mahwah, N.J.: Lawrence Erlbaum.

McDonough, J. and **S. McDonough.** 1997. *Research Methods for English Language Teachers.* London: Arnold.

McKay, S. L. 2006. *Researching Second Language Classrooms*. Mahwah, N.J.: Lawrence Erlbaum.

Milroy, L. and **M. Gordon.** 2003. *Sociolinguistics: Method and Interpretation*. Oxford: Blackwell.

Nunan, D. 1992. *Research Methods in Language Learning*. Cambridge: Cambridge University Press.

Richards, K. 2003. *Qualitative Inquiry in TESOL*. Basingstoke, England: Palgrave Macmillan.

Seliger, H. W. and **E. Shohamy.** 1989. *Second Language Research Methods*. Oxford: Oxford University Press.

Wray, A., K. Trott, and **A. Bloomer.** 1998. *Projects in Linguistics: A Practical Guide to Researching Language*. London: Arnold.

Annotated list of selected research texts from the social sciences

Creswell, J. W. 2005. *Planning, Conducting, and Evaluating Quantitative and Qualitative Research*. Upper Saddle River, N.J.: Pearson Prentice Hall. (A balanced coverage of every aspect of research, including mixed methods.)

Denzin, N. K. and **Y. S. Lincoln** (eds.). 2005. *The Sage Handbook of Qualitative Research,* 3rd Edition. Thousand Oaks, CA: Sage. (This is one of the key works in qualitative research, already on its third edition.)

Holliday, A. 2002. *Doing and Writing Qualitative Research*. London: Sage. (A book written by an applied linguist for a general audience, with a special emphasis on writing qualitative reports.)

Johnson, R. B. and **L. Christensen.** 2004. *Education Research: Quantitative, Qualitative, and Mixed Approaches*, 2nd Edition. Boston: Allyn and Bacon. (A comprehensive and balanced research methods text with an educational focus.)

Morse, J. M. and **L. Richards.** 2002. *Readme First for a User's Guide to Qualitative Research*. Thousand Oaks, CA: Sage. (Ideal for novice qualitative researchers.)

Pallant, J. 2005. *SPSS Survival Manual*, 2nd Edition. Maidenhead, England: Open University Press and McGraw-Hill Education. (There are many good SPSS manuals around—I have found this particularly comprehensive and user-friendly.)

Punch, K. F. 2005. *Introduction to Social Research*, 2nd Edition. Thousand Oaks, CA: Sage. (Short, to the point and accessible; highly recommended.)

Richards, L. 2005. *Handling Qualitative Data: A Practical Guide*. London: Sage. (A refreshingly down-to-earth and practical book written by one of the developers of the NUD*IST and NVivo qualitative data analysis software.)

Robson, C. 2002. *Real World Research: A Resource for Social Scientists and Practitioner-Researchers*, 2nd Edition. Oxford: Blackwell. (A comprehensive and very practical overview—there is something in it for everybody.)

Silverman, D. 2005. *Doing Qualitative Research*, 2nd Edition. London: Sage. (Generally accepted to be one of the most useful titles for novice qualitative researchers.)

Tabachnick, B. G. and **L. S. Fidell.** 2001. *Using Multivariate Statistics*, 4th Edition. Needham Heights, MA: Allyn and Bacon. (The ultimate authority when it comes to complex statistical issues.)

Tashakkori, A. and **C. Teddlie** (eds.). 2003. *Handbook of Mixed Methods in Social and Behavioral Research*. Thousands Oaks, CA: Sage. (All you want to know about mixed methods research.)

2

Qualitative, quantitative, and mixed methods research

One of the most general and best-known distinctions in research methodology is that between qualitative and quantitative research. As Davies (1995) emphasizes, the distinction signifies more than merely using figures versus non-quantitative data (such as open-ended interviews or natural data); instead, the dichotomy refers to several things at the same time: the general ideological orientation underlying the study, the method of data collection applied, the nature of the collected data, and the method of data analysis used to process the data and to obtain results. This is clearly a complex issue, so let us start with a preliminary working definition for the two approaches:

- *Quantitative research* involves data collection procedures that result primarily in numerical data which is then analysed primarily by statistical methods. Typical example: survey research using a questionnaire, analysed by statistical software such as SPSS.
- *Qualitative research* involves data collection procedures that result primarily in open-ended, non-numerical data which is then analysed primarily by non-statistical methods. Typical example: interview research, with the transcribed recordings analysed by qualitative content analysis.

I mentioned in Chapter 1 briefly that although the two paradigms represent two different approaches to empirical research, they are not necessarily exclusive. Their principled combination has led to an emerging third research approach:

- *Mixed methods research* involves different combinations of qualitative and quantitative research either at the data collection or at the analysis levels. Typical example: consecutive and interrelated questionnaire and interview studies.

I will discuss the three approaches in detail in separate sections below (in Sections 2.2–2.4), but let us first spend some time examining the qualitative–quantitative distinction to understand what lies at the heart of this methodological schism. In research texts it has become standard usage to refer to the two approaches as QUAL and QUAN when contrasting them, and I will sometimes follow this practice.

2.1 The qualitative–quantitative distinction

Although at first sight the difference between qualitative and quantitative data/research appears to be relatively straightforward, the distinction has been the source of a great deal of discussion in the past at every conceivable level of abstraction. Without dwelling on this issue too long, let me offer a taste of how things can get very complicated when we start discussing the QUAL–QUAN contrast.

To start with, is there really such a contrast? And if so, where exactly does it lie? Richards (2005), for example, points out that the numerical versus non-numerical distinction does not give us clear enough guidelines because qualitative researchers would almost always collect some information in numbers (for example, the age of the participants), and similarly, quantitative researchers usually also collect some non-numerical information (for example, the gender or nationality of the participants). So, as she concludes, 'qualitative and quantitative data do not inhabit different worlds. They are different ways of recording observations of the same world' (p. 36). Arguing in a similar vein, Miles and Huberman (1994) assert that in some sense, all data are qualitative because they refer to 'essences of people, objects and situations' (p. 9); sometimes we convert our raw experiences of the social world into words (i.e. QUAL), at other times into numbers (i.e. QUAN). Therefore, Sandelowski (2003) actually concludes that qualitative research is not clearly distinguishable from quantitative research because there is no consistent manner in which such a comparison can be made.

Even though I agree that QUAL and QUAN are not extremes but rather form a continuum, we still tend to compare them all the time. Why is that? I would suggest that the almost irresistible urge to contrast qualitative and quantitative research goes back to three basic sources of division between the two approaches: (a) an ideological contrast, (b) a contrast in categorization, and (c) a contrast in the perception of individual diversity. Let us look at these contrasts one by one.

2.1.1 Ideological differences

Although scholars in the social sciences (for example, in sociology) have been using both qualitative-like and quantitative-like data since the beginning of the twentieth century, the QUAL–QUAN distinction only emerged after number-based statistical research became dominant in the middle of the twentieth century and some scholars started to challenge this hegemony flying the 'qualitative' banner. (The genesis of the two approaches will be discussed in more detail in separate sections below.) Thus, the terms 'qualitative' and 'quantitative' were originally introduced as part of, or rather for the purpose of, an ideological confrontation. In a thoughtful analysis, Schwandt (2000) describes qualitative inquiry in general as a 'reformist movement', uniting a wide variety of scholars who appear to share very little in common except their general distaste for the mainstream quantitative paradigm. As he writes,

> qualitative inquiry is a 'home' for a wide variety of scholars who often are seriously at odds with one another but who share a general rejection of the blend of scientism, foundationalist epistemology, instrumental reasoning, and the philosophical anthropology of disengagement that has marked 'mainstream' social science. (p. 190)

Having been created in the spirit of antagonism, we should not be surprised that the two terms are still often used to represent contrasting views about the world around us.

2.1.2 Contrasting categorizing/coding practices

One thing that is common to every research approach is that the almost limitless information obtainable from the social world around us needs to be reduced to make it manageable. Researchers typically use 'categories' or 'codes' to structure and shape this information, but this is where the similarities between QUAL and QUAN end. We find that the nature of the categories and the categorization process in QUAL and QUAN are very different. In fact, Bazeley (2003: 414) argues that 'Codes—the way they are generated, what they stand for, and the way they are used—lie at the heart of differences between quantitative and qualitative data and analysis tools'.

Quantitative researchers define the variables they work with well in advance and assign a logical scale of values to them, which can be expressed in numbers. Thus, quantitative research can start a research project with precise *coding tables* for processing the data (for example, within the 'gender' variable, 'male' is to be assigned 1 and 'female' 2). Qualitative researchers also use coding extensively, but the QUAL categories are different in two important ways. First, they are not numerical but verbal, amounting to short textual labels. Second, they are usually not determined a priori but are left open and flexible as long as possible to be able to account for the subtle nuances of meaning uncovered during the process of investigation. For example, if we wanted to draw the boundary between two countries in an unknown terrain, the QUAN approach would be to take the map and after defining the size distribution of the two countries, draw straight lines using a ruler. In contrast, the QUAL approach would resist this top-down decision making but would expect the boundaries to naturally emerge using the inherent geographical properties of the terrain (for example, rivers and mountain ridges).

2.1.3 Different approaches to individual diversity

Most data collected in the social sciences, regardless of whether it is QUAL or QUAN, is related to *people*—what they do, what they are like, what they think or believe in, what they plan to do, etc. Because people differ from each other in the way they perceive, interpret, and remember things, their accounts will show considerable variation across individuals. The problem is that no matter how well-funded our research is, we can never examine all the people whose answers would be relevant to our research question, and therefore we have to face the fact that the final picture unfolding in our research will always be a function of whom we have selected to obtain our data from.

Both QUAL and QUAN researchers acknowledge this link between the specific sample of participants examined and the results obtained by the research, but the two camps consider the issue in a very different light. Quantitative researchers regard the sample-related variation as a problem which needs to be fixed. The QUAN solution is to take a large enough sample in which the idiosyncratic differences associated with the particular individuals are ironed out by the sample size and therefore the pooled results largely reflect the commonalities that exist in the data. Qualitative researchers, on the other hand, question the value of preparing an overall, average description of a larger group of people because in this way we lose the individual stories. They see this as an undesirable reduction process because in QUAL terms the real meaning lies with individual cases who make up our world. Of course, qualitative researchers are not oblivious to the fact that individuals are different, but rather than believing in a higher-level meaning that can be arrived at by summing up individual cases, they hold that there are multiple meanings to discover.

Thus, quantitative researchers follow a 'meaning in the general' strategy, whereas qualitative researchers concentrate on an in-depth understanding of the 'meaning in the particular'. However, the story does not end here because the 'big number' approach of quantitative researchers has offered an additional bonus for QUAN data analysis, *statistics*. We must stop and examine this a bit more before we move on.

2.1.4 Statistics versus researcher sensitivity

Once quantitative researchers had gone down the 'meaning in numbers' path, a welcome bonus emerged. Mathematicians have found that if we have a sufficiently big sample size, the characteristics of the people in this group will approach a very special pattern termed 'normal distribution'. This means that within the sample a few people will display very high values, a few others very low ones, with the bulk of the sample centred around the middle or average range. This is the all-important 'bell-shaped curve' (see Figure 2.1), and it has been found that the greater the sample, the more 'normal' the distribution and the more regular the curve becomes. (For more details, see Section

9.4.2.) What makes this bell-shaped curve so important is that it has unique properties upon which it is possible to build a whole range of mathematical procedures that have led to the development of 'statistics'.

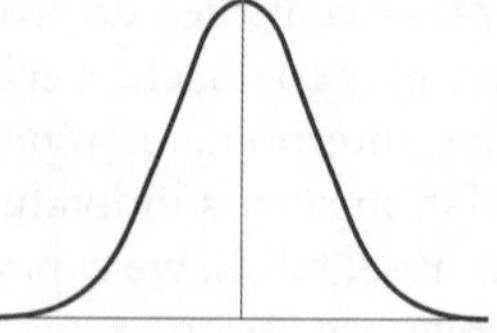

Figure 2.1 The bell-shaped curve of normal distribution

Thus, adopting the 'meaning in numbers' approach has not only offered quantitative researchers a way out of the individual respondent variation dilemma mentioned above, but it has also provided an elaborate set of statistical analytical tools to use to add systematicity to the data analysis phase rather than having to rely on the researcher's subjective interpretations. Thus, quantitative research could eliminate individual variability both at the data collection and the data analysis stages. For many scholars, the major attraction of QUAN is this systematic, 'individual-proof' nature, governed by precise rules and regulations, thus approximating the regularity of the natural sciences.

In contrast, the 'meaning in the particular' approach of qualitative research has not offered any bonus gifts for the analysis phase of qualitative research. Consequently, although qualitative research also applies various data analytical procedures to make the investigations more rigorous and systematic, at the heart of any qualitative analysis is still the researcher's subjective sensitivity, training, and experience. Thus, while no one would deny that by using qualitative methods we can uncover subtle meanings that are inevitably lost in quantitative research, QUAL is linked to two basic sources of variation, associated with the individual respondents and the individual researcher. For many scholars the major attraction of QUAL is exactly this sensitivity to the individual, but we can perhaps start sensing at this point where some of the strong emotions characterizing the QUAL–QUAN debate originate: it is all too easy to present the above contrast as the antagonistic fight between 'callous' versus 'sensitive'; or 'systematic' versus 'fuzzy'; and ultimately, between 'objective' versus 'subjective'.

2.1.5 The QUAL–QUAN contrast and the 'paradigm war'

The inherent QUAL–QUAN differences led to conflicts, which escalated into a fully-fledged 'paradigm war' in the 1970s and 1980s. This clash was almost inevitable because by then all the components were in place for a proper show-down between the two methodological camps: the terms QUAL and QUAN were originally introduced to denote an antagonistic standpoint and, as we have seen in the previous sections, this initial conflicting stance was given substance by the contrasting patterns of the two research paradigms in:

a *Categorizing the world* (QUAN: predetermined numerical category system; QUAL: emergent, flexible verbal coding).

b *Perceiving individual diversity* (QUAN: using large samples to iron out any individual idiosyncrasies; QUAL: focusing on the unique meaning carried by individual organisms).

c *Analysing data* (QUAN: relying on the formalized system of statistics; QUAL: relying on the researcher's individual sensitivity).

Quantitative research was seen to offer a structured and highly regulated way of achieving a *macro-perspective* of the overarching trends in the world, whereas qualitative research was perceived to represent a flexible and highly context-sensitive *micro-perspective* of the everyday realities of the world. In the paradigm war this distinction was extended to two different worldviews and the 'paradigm warriors' contested which level of analysis provided a more valid representation of human life and the social world in general. Many intellectually challenging position papers have been written about these different orientations, arguing that at the end of the day qualitative and quantitative research methodologies are rooted in two strikingly different paradigms and thus, by mixing them, we are likely to lose their very essence. The position I have taken in this book is that this view is incorrect.

2.1.6 Three positions regarding the QUAL–QUAN difference: purist, situationalist, and pragmatist

As we have seen in the previous section, taking theorizing to the level of abstraction of different worldviews, paradigms, and perspectives can logically lead to proposing what Rossman and Wilson (1985) called a 'purist' approach to research methodology, arguing that the qualitative and quantitative methodologies are mutually exclusive. Interestingly, although there is no shortage of convincing intellectual arguments to justify paradigm incompatibility, most researchers have actually stopped short of claiming the inevitability of this conflict and, particularly in the past decade, scholars have started to look for some sort of an interface between the two research traditions. Miles and Huberman (1994: 4–5), for example, pointed out that 'In epistemological debates it is tempting to operate at the poles. But in the actual practice of empirical research, we believe that all of us—realists, interpretivists, critical theorists—are closer to the centre, with multiple overlaps'.

Indeed, if we stop treating QUAL and QUAN research in a very general and contrasting manner and focus on the specific research issues at hand, we find that concrete research topics vary greatly in the extent to which they lend themselves to micro- or macro-level analysis. To take an example from my own research, the concept of 'demotivation' appears to be one where a micro-level qualitative investigation can be beneficial in uncovering the subtle personal processes whereby one's enthusiasm is gradually dampened by a number of internal and external demotivating factors (Dörnyei 2001). On the other hand, the process of 'language globalization' can be investigated particularly well from a quantitative macro-perspective, determining for example how Global English impacts the acquisition and use of local languages in various speech communities (Dörnyei *et al.* 2006). This would suggest that both approaches have value if they are applied in the appropriate research context—a view that has been often referred to as the 'situationalist' approach to research methodology. (See Rossman and Wilson 1985.)

Although the situationalist view accepts the strengths of both research traditions, it still represents an 'either/or' approach. However, we do not necessarily have to stop here. While it is true that particular research questions or topics can be more naturally linked to either QUAL or QUAN methods, in most cases we can also look at the same research question from another angle, using the other approach, thus uncovering new aspects of the issue. For example, when considering student demotivation—which I suggested above can be successfully examined through a qualitative approach—we can also examine how extensive this problem is in our schools or how much impact it has on students' learning achievement, and these questions can be best addressed through quantitative studies. And similarly, even broad trends such as language globalization can be investigated from a micro-perspective by analysing, for example, the day-to-day process whereby bilingual families in multicultural environments shift towards the use of one or the other language. This indicates that some sort of an integration of the two research methodologies can be beneficial to 'corroborate (provide convergence in findings), elaborate (provide richness and detail), or initiate (offer new interpretations) findings from the other method' (Rossman and Wilson 1985: 627). This is the *pragmatist* position underlying mixed methods research, and as stated in the Preface and Chapter 1, it is my personal belief that mixing methods has great potential in most research contexts.

2.2 Quantitative research

Let us set out on a more detailed examination of the three research approaches. The fact that I begin with the analysis of quantitative research is not to be taken as an indication of a hierarchical order. My reason is purely pragmatic: because qualitative research gained paradigmatic status as a reaction against quantitative research, it is practical to get to know quantitative research first, as a kind of baseline. I will follow this practice throughout the whole book.

2.2.1 Brief historical overview

Quantitative social research was originally inspired by the spectacular progress of the natural sciences in the nineteenth century and therefore early social researchers set out to adopt what was called the 'scientific method' in their investigations. This method had been evolving in western thinking since about the mid-sixteenth century (the period of the Enlightenment) through the work of philosophers and scholars such as Copernicus, Bacon, Galilei, Kepler, Newton, Descartes, Hume, Comte, and Peirce. (For overviews, see Garratt and Li 2005; Jordan 2004.) Broadly speaking, the scientific method postulates three key stages in the research process: (a) observing a phenomenon or identifying a problem; (b) generating an initial hypothesis; and (c) testing the hypothesis by collecting and analysing empirical data using standardized procedures. Once the hypothesis has been successfully tested and further validated through replication, it becomes accepted as a scientific theory or law. Thus, the scientific method offered a tool to explore questions in an 'objective' manner, trying to minimize the influence of any researcher bias or prejudice, thereby resulting in what scholars believed was an accurate and reliable description of the world.

The scientific method was closely associated with numerical values and statistics, along the line of Nobel prize winner Lord Rutherford's famous maxim that any knowledge that one cannot measure numerically 'is a poor sort of knowledge'. Being a scientist was ultimately associated with empirically measuring one's subject matter and, preferably, conducting experiments. To serve the mathematical needs of the newly emerging social sciences, statistics became a fully-fledged subdiscipline of mathematics by the end of the nineteenth century. The contribution of one scholar in particular, Francis Galton, was significant in establishing quantitative data collection and analytical methods in psychology at the turn of the twentieth century: amongst other things, Galton initiated psychological testing, introduced the use of questionnaires and created the statistical concepts of regression and correlation.

The first half of the twentieth century saw major developments both in the scientific method (most notably through the work of Karl Popper) and in statistics (for example, by Spearman, Fisher, Neyman, and Pearson), leading to the increased use of quantitative methodology across the whole range of social disciplines. As a result of this progress, the social sciences achieved maturity and earned the reputation of being able to study human beings 'scientifically' both at the individual and the societal levels. Fuelled by the advances in psychometrics (a subdiscipline focusing on measurement in psychology), classical test theory, experimental design, survey research, questionnaire theory, and multivariate statistics, the middle of the twentieth century became dominated by quantitative methodology in the social sciences. This hegemony only started to change in the 1970s as a result of the challenges of qualitative research, leading to a restructuring of research methodology. Currently, in many areas of the social sciences we can see a peaceful coexistence of quantitative and qualitative methods.

In applied linguistics, according to Lazaraton (2005), the period between 1970–1985 saw a significant increase of quantitative research articles, which went hand in hand with the publication of several research methods texts in the 1980s, culminating in Hatch and Lazaraton's (1991) seminal *Research Manual*; this provided a very detailed summary of quantitative research and statistics, richly illustrated with published quantitative studies. Lazaraton (2005) reports on a survey of 524 empirical studies that appeared in four major applied linguistic journals between 1991 and 2001; the results show that as many as 86 per cent of the research papers were quantitative (while 13 per cent qualitative and 1 per cent mixed methods), which led Lazaraton to conclude that quantitative studies 'reign supreme' (p. 219) in our field.

Lazaraton (2005) also highlighted a major change taking place in research orientation in applied linguistics: while in the 1980s there was an 'unquestioned reliance' on quasi-experimental studies, the past 15 years have brought along a broader, multidisciplinary perspective on research methodology, with an increasing number of alternative, often qualitative, designs employed. In an overview of research methods in the field, Duff (2002) also highlights the growing sophistication of quantitative studies in the 1990s, both in terms of their design and their psychometric refinement, which confirms Lazaraton's (2000) conclusion that there has been a 'coming of age' of quantitative research in applied linguistics.

2.2.2 Main characteristics of quantitative research

As we saw in the previous section, quantitative social research had grown out of the desire to emulate the 'objective' procedures in the natural sciences. However, along with many others, Shavelson and Towne (2002) point out that even though several aspects of the 'scientific method' appear to be transferable to social research, there are also some fundamental differences between the natural and social sciences. The most obvious of these is that, unlike atoms or molecules, people show variation over time and across social and cultural contexts. They also display within-individual variation and therefore even if they are placed under similar conditions, their reaction will vary widely, which is something natural scientists working with atoms and molecules do not have to worry about (Dörnyei 2005). Therefore, while quantitative methods in the social sciences by and large align with the general principles of the 'scientific method', they also show certain distinctive features.

Section 2.1 already listed some of the characteristic features of quantitative research. The following summary reiterates those and adds some further characteristics that have not been mentioned before.

- *Using numbers* The single most important feature of quantitative research is, naturally, that it is centred around numbers. This both opens up a range of possibilities and sets some limitations for researchers. Numbers are powerful, as attested to by the discipline of mathematics. Yet numbers are also rather powerless in themselves because in research contexts they do not mean anything without contextual 'backing': they are faceless and meaningless unless we specify exactly the category that we use the specific number for, and also the different values within the variable (i.e. knowing, what '1' or '6' means in a particular category). Thus, for numbers to work, we need precise definitions of the content and the boundaries of the variables we use and we also need exact descriptors for the range of values that are allowed within the variable. However, if we manage to provide all this, numbers *do* work and the development of quantitative research over the last century has been frankly astounding. The level of sophistication that quantitative data analysis has reached is awesome in every sense of the word.

- *A priori categorization* Because the use of numbers already dominates the data collection phase, the work required to specify the categories and values needs to be done *prior to* the actual study. (See also Section 2.1.2.) If, for example, respondents are asked to encircle figures in a questionnaire item, they have to know exactly what those figures represent, and in order to make sure that each respondent gives their numerical answer based on the same understanding, the definitions and value descriptors need to be unambiguous. To achieve this takes time and effort, and although (as will be discussed later) most phases of qualitative research tend to be more labour-intensive than those of quantitative research, the preparation phase is an exception: whereas in a qualitative interview study one can start the first interview soon after the instigation of the project, in a quantitative study several weeks and often months of meticulous preparation and piloting are usually needed before the finalized instrument can be administered. Luckily, after the administration of the instrument, things speed up and even in a large-scale quantitative study it is not unheard of to have preliminary results within a week after the data has been collected. This would be impossible in qualitative research.
- *Variables rather than cases* As discussed in Section 2.1.3, quantitative researchers are less interested in individuals than in the common features of groups of people. Therefore, in contrast to the QUAL emphasis on the individual case, QUAN research is centred around the study of *variables* that capture these common features and which are quantified by counting, scaling, or by assigning values to categorical data. (See Sections 9.2.1 and 9.4.1.) All the various quantitative methods are aimed at identifying the relationships between variables by measuring them and often also manipulating them (as in experimental studies; see Section 5.3); Hammersley and Atkinson (1995) regard the quest for specifying the relationships amongst variables as the defining feature of quantitative social research.
- *Statistics and the language of statistics* Section 2.1.4 discussed the significance of statistics in quantitative research. This is undoubtedly the most salient QUAN feature—as we will see in Chapter 9, statistical analyses can range from calculating the average (or as it is referred to in statistics, the 'mean') of several figures on a pocket calculator to running complex multivariate analyses on a computer. Because of the close link of quantitative research and statistics, much of the statistical terminology has become part

of the QUAN vocabulary, and the resulting unique QUAN language adds further power to the quantitative paradigm. No wonder that qualitative researchers have gone to great lengths to try and replace some of the QUAN research terminology with QUAL-specific language (for example, when defining the QUAL quality criteria—see Section 3.1).

- *Standardized procedures to assess objective reality* Sections 2.1.3 and 2.1.4 highlighted the general QUAN aspiration of eliminating any individual-based subjectivity from the various phases of the research process by developing systematic canons and rules for every facet of data collection and analysis. Quantitative methodology has indeed gone a long way towards standardizing research procedures to ensure that they remain stable across investigators and subjects. This independence of idiosyncratic human variability and bias has been equated with 'objectivity' by quantitative researchers and the results accumulated through such procedures are thought to describe the objective reality that is 'out there', independent of the researcher's subjective perceptions. Of course, as Bachman (2004a) points out, this stance is based on the assumption that there actually exists an objective reality, so that when different researchers observe the same phenomenon using standardized measures, their findings will show agreement and convergence.
- *Quest for generalizability and universal laws* Numbers, variables, standardized procedures, statistics, and scientific reasoning are all part of the ultimate QUAN quest for facts that are generalizable beyond the particular and add up to wide-ranging, ideally universal, laws. Whether such laws actually exist with regard to the social behaviour of humans, and if they do, how universal they are, are fundamental ideological questions that go beyond the scope of this book.

2.2.3 Strengths and weaknesses of quantitative research

The strengths of quantitative research are manifold and most have been discussed in the previous sections. QUAN proponents usually emphasize that at its best the quantitative inquiry is systematic, rigorous, focused, and tightly controlled, involving precise measurement and producing reliable and replicable data that is generalizable to other contexts. The statistical analytical apparatus is refined and far-reaching and it also offers some in-built quality checks and indices (such as statistical significance) that help readers to decide on the validity of quantitative findings. From a practical perspective, even with the longer preparation period discussed earlier, the research process is relatively quick and offers good value for money, particularly because the data analysis can be done using statistical computer software. Finally, quantitative findings tend to enjoy a universally high reputation with almost any audience or stakeholder group.

The downside of quantitative methods is that they average out responses across the whole observed group of participants, and by working with concepts of averages it is impossible to do justice to the subjective variety of an individual life. Similar scores can result from quite different underlying processes, and quantitative methods are generally not very sensitive in uncovering the reasons for particular observations or the dynamics underlying the examined situation or phenomenon. That is, the general exploratory capacity of quantitative research is rather limited. Because of these shortcomings, qualitative researchers often view quantitative research as 'overly simplistic, decontextualized, reductionist in terms of its generalizations, and failing to capture the meanings that actors attach to their lives and circumstances' (Brannen 2005: 7).

2.3 Qualitative research

Describing quantitative research has been a relatively straightforward task because there is a general agreement amongst QUAN practitioners about the main features and principles of the approach. This is not at all the case with QUAL research. In a recent overview of the field, two of the most influential qualitative researchers, Denzin and Lincoln (2005a), concluded that 'qualitative research is difficult to define clearly. It has no theory or paradigm that is distinctly its own. ... Nor does qualitative research have a distinct set of methods or practices that are entirely its own, (p. 6–7). And later they added, 'Qualitative research is many things to many people' (p. 10).

Denzin and Lincoln's view is not at all exaggerated and is shared throughout the profession. For example, another well-known proponent of qualitative research, Silverman (1997), expressed a similar conclusion when he stated that 'there is no agreed doctrine underlying all qualitative social research' (p. 14). Furthermore, Holliday (2004: 731) has added that 'boundaries in current qualitative research are crumbling, and researchers are increasingly doing whatever they can to find out what they want to know'. As seen earlier, the lack of uniformity goes back to the genesis of the qualitative approach when scholars of diverse beliefs united under the qualitative label in their fight against the quantitative paradigm.

Luckily, the overall picture is not as gloomy and fragmented as the above quotes would suggest. Qualitative research is in fact a thriving discipline, and while it is true that some issues have been subject to a lot of, and sometimes heated, discussion, there exists a core set of features that would universally characterize a properly conducted qualitative study. In the next sections we are going to look at these core attributes.

2.3.1 Brief historical overview

Research that can be considered 'qualitative' in retrospect has been around for about a century in the social sciences. Qualitative-like methods were introduced into sociology at the end of the first decade of the twentieth century through the work of the Chicago School for the study of human group life, and during the first third of the century anthropology also produced some seminal qualitative studies by renowned scholars such as Boas and Malinowski, defining the outlines of the fieldwork method (Denzin and Lincoln 2005a). Thus, the basic QUAL ideas and principles are not new at all, yet the first text that tried to define 'qualitative methodology'—Glaser and Strauss's (1967) *The Discovery of Grounded Theory: Strategies for Qualitative Research*—did not appear until the late sixties. In this highly influential book the authors described the use of qualitative procedures by the QUAL pioneers as 'nonsystematic and nonrigorous' (p. 15), and contended that early monographs based on qualitative data consisted of 'lengthy, detailed descriptions which resulted in very small amounts of theory, if any' (ibid.).

After the 1930s and particularly after World War II, quantitative research methodology produced substantial advances (see Section 2.2.1) and qualitative research was relegated to preliminary, exploratory work whose role was seen to provide the 'more serious' quantitative studies with an adequate starting point. The middle of the twentieth century was undoubtedly dominated by quantitative research, and the invaluable merit of Glaser and Strauss's (1967) book was to offer a viable challenge to this hegemony. These authors were explicitly concerned with the 'systematization of the collection, coding and analysis of qualitative data for the generation of theory' (p. 18; see also the discussion of 'grounded theory' in Section 10.3), and for the first time, qualitatively inclined researchers had had an elaborate theoretically based methodology available to them. Qualitative research was on the march.

Recent years have seen an explosion of texts on qualitative methods reflecting a growing interest in the approach across all the disciplines of the social sciences. Seale *et al.* (2004), for example, examined the output of the main publisher of methodology texts, Sage Publications, and found that during the last decade there was a four-fold increase of published qualitative methods textbooks (N = 130+).

In applied linguistics there has been an increasing visibility and acceptance of qualitative research since the mid-1990s (Duff in press). This is related to the growing recognition that almost every aspect of language acquisition and use is determined or significantly shaped by social, cultural, and situational factors, and qualitative research is ideal for providing insights into such contextual conditions and influences. Accordingly, applied linguistics has been offering an increasingly level playing field for both QUAN and QUAL approaches. Having said that, we must also note a serious concern in this respect, highlighted by Lazaraton (2003), namely that there have been too few qualitative studies published in the leading applied linguistics journals, with the possible exception of *TESOL Quarterly*. For example, the editor of *The Modern Language Journal*, Sally Magnan (2000: 2), reported that although there had been an 'increase in ethnographic and case studies submitted for consideration, to the point that their numbers were beginning to approach those of quantitative pieces', during the 1995–2005 period only 19.8 per cent of the research articles in her journal were qualitative (and 6.8 per cent used a mixed methodology) (Magnan 2006). It would be interesting to carry out a systematic analysis of the reasons for the discrepancy between the submission and the publication rates.

Although the frequency of published QUAL studies is still relatively low, the impact of qualitative research in applied linguistics over the past three decades has been profound. Early case studies of the 1970s and 1980s had a groundbreaking effect on our understanding of SLA and generated many of the prevailing principles and models. (See Section 6.7.3.) With regard to contemporary research, we find qualitative studies focusing on topics across the whole research spectrum, even including core quantitative areas such as language testing, and several key areas of applied linguistics (for example, the study of gender, race, ethnicity, and identity) are being driven by qualitative research. (For an overview of qualitative inquiry in applied linguistics, see Richards 2003.)

2.3.2 Main characteristics of qualitative research

The research methodology literature contains several detailed summaries of the core features of qualitative inquiry. Many of the points in the different lists overlap but, as mentioned earlier, there are also some contentious issues. Let us look at the most often mentioned aspects:

- *Emergent research design* In describing the main characteristics of qualitative research, most research texts start with highlighting its *emergent* nature. This means that no aspect of the research design is tightly prefigured and a study is kept open and fluid so that it can respond in a flexible way to new details or openings that may emerge during the process of investigation. This flexibility even applies to the research questions, which may evolve, change, or be refined during the study—see Section 3.3.2. An important aspect of this emergent nature is the fact that, ideally, qualitative researchers enter the research process with a completely open mind and without setting out to test preconceived hypotheses. This means that the research focus is narrowed down only gradually and the analytic categories/concepts are defined during, rather than prior to, the process of the research. For example, in their seminal work, Glaser and Strauss (1967) actively encouraged qualitative researchers to ignore the literature before the investigation in order to assure that 'the emergence of categories will not be contaminated by concepts more suited to different areas' (p. 37). This is a highly controversial issue and for this reason we come back to it in a separate section below.
- *The nature of qualitative data* Qualitative research works with a wide range of data including recorded interviews, various types of texts (for example, field notes, journal and diary entries, documents) and images (photos or

videos). During data processing most data are transformed into a textual form (for example, interview recordings are transcribed) because most qualitative data analysis is done with words—see Section 10.1.1. Although qualitative data is not gathered with the purpose of being directly counted or measured in an objective way, subsequent analysis can define categories through which certain aspects of qualitative data can be quantified—see Section 11.1.1. Because the common objective of all the different types of qualitative methods is to make sense of a set of (cultural or personal) meanings in the observed phenomena, it is indispensable that the data should capture rich and complex details. Therefore, in order to achieve such a 'thick' description, almost any relevant information can be admitted as QUAL data.

- *The characteristics of the research setting* Because of the QUAL objective to describe social phenomena as they occur naturally, qualitative research takes place in the *natural setting*, without any attempts to manipulate the situation under study. In order to capture a sufficient level of detail about the natural context, such investigations are usually conducted through an intense and prolonged contact with, or immersion in, the research setting.
- *Insider meaning* Qualitative research is concerned with subjective opinions, experiences and feelings of individuals and thus the explicit goal of research is to explore the participants' views of the situation being studied. This approach follows from the way qualitative researchers perceive meaning: it is a fundamental QUAL principle that human behaviour is based upon meanings which people attribute to and bring to situations (Punch 2005) and it is only the actual participants themselves who can reveal the meanings and interpretations of their experiences and actions. Therefore, qualitative researchers strive to view social phenomena from the perspectives of the 'insiders' and the term 'insider perspective' has a special place in the qualitative credo.
- *Small sample size* Well-conducted qualitative research is very labour-intensive and therefore qualitative studies typically use, of necessity, much smaller samples of participants than quantitative ones. We will come back to the question of qualitative sampling in Chapter 6 (Section 6.2).
- *Interpretive analysis* Qualitative research is fundamentally interpretive, which means that the research outcome is ultimately the product of the researcher's subjective interpretation of the data. Several alternative interpretations are possible for each dataset, and because QUAL studies utilize relatively limited standardized instrumentation or analytical procedures, in the end it is the researcher who will choose from them. As Miles and Huberman (1994: 7) conclude, 'The researcher is essentially the main "measurement device" in the study'. Accordingly, in qualitative research, the researcher's own values, personal history, and 'position' on characteristics such as gender, culture, class, and age become integral part of the inquiry (Haverkamp 2005).

The emergent/non-emergent debate

One of the most contentious issues amongst qualitative researchers concerns the question as to whether investigators need to enter a QUAL project with only minimal background knowledge so as not to 'contaminate' the emergent nature of the study. As quoted earlier, Glaser and Strauss (1967) were explicit about this requirement and it has become one of the main tenets of the qualitative inquiry that the results 'emerge' naturally, without any biased interference of the researcher. The researcher, therefore, needs to adopt a 'tabula rasa' orientation and Glaser and Strauss proposed that the researcher's 'theoretical sensitivity' is only to appear when the data has already been collected and partially analysed so that the concepts and hypotheses that have emerged from the data can be combined with existing knowledge.

Several scholars have questioned the reality of this prerequisite. Tashakkori and Teddlie (2003b), for example, pointed out that few social scientists would conduct unplanned and unstructured research, with no orientation or point of view to guide them. To the contrary, most established social researchers have extensive backgrounds in the areas that they are studying and therefore the 'tabula rasa' assumption is simply 'naïve' (p. 66). Miles and Huberman (1994) go one step further when they claim that it is the researchers' background knowledge that helps them to see and decipher details, complexities, and subtleties, as well as to decide what kind of questions to ask or which incidents to attend to closely. As they conclude, not to be led by one's conceptual strengths can be self-defeating, which is in contrast with Glaser and Strauss's (1967) warning that if scholars commit themselves exclusively to one specific preconceived theory they become 'doctrinaire'.

2.3.3 Strengths and weaknesses of qualitative research

There is no shortage in the literature of elaborate descriptions of the merits of qualitative research, and I have found the following points particularly significant:

- *Exploratory nature* Qualitative research has traditionally been seen as an effective way of exploring new, uncharted areas. If very little is known about a phenomenon, the detailed study of a few cases is particularly appropriate because it does not rely on previous literature or prior empirical findings (Eisenhardt 1989).
- *Making sense of complexity* Qualitative methods are useful for making sense of highly complex situations. In such cases there is a real danger for researchers in general to produce reduced and simplified interpretations that distort the bigger picture; the participant-sensitivity of qualitative research is very helpful in deciding what aspects of the data require special attention because it offers priority guidelines that are validated by the main actors themselves. That is, the groundedness of qualitative research helps to distinguish real phenomena from intellectual fabrications.

- *Answering 'why' questions* It is not uncommon in quantitative studies to obtain surprising or contradictory results, but in many of these cases the collected data does not offer any real enlightenment as to the causes. This is when researchers include at the end of the research report the well-known statement 'further research is needed to understand ...' (meaning, 'we have no idea why this has occurred ...'). In contrast, the flexible, emergent nature of a qualitative study allows the researcher to conduct the 'further research' straight away, thereby reaching a fuller understanding.

- *Broadening our understanding* Talking about the issue of generalizability in qualitative research, Duff (in press) emphasizes that instead of seeking a generalizable 'correct interpretation', qualitative research aims to broaden the repertoire of *possible interpretations* of human experience. Thus, the rich data obtained about the participants' experience can widen the scope of our understanding and can add data-driven (rather than speculative) depth to the analysis of a phenomenon.

- *Longitudinal examination of dynamic phenomena* Interestingly, one of the main reasons why I have come to appreciate and use qualitative research is rarely mentioned in the literature. I have found that qualitative research is particularly useful for the purpose of longitudinal research. As argued in Chapter 4 (Section 4.2), most of the processes studied by applied linguists are dynamic in nature, and therefore we would need many more longitudinal investigations in the field to explore the sequential patterns and the changes that occur. Qualitative research offers a good starting point in this respect.

- *Flexibility when things go wrong* There is a host of things that can go wrong while doing research in the field, particularly if the research site is within an educational institution. (See Section 8.4 for the various challenges of classroom research.) If we use a purely quantitative research design, some of the unexpected events can render our study meaningless, whereas qualitative methods not only allow us to accommodate the changes but can also enable us to capitalize on them and produce exciting results. Gherardi and Turner (1999) report on a study by Lowe, which examined a series of QUAN investigations carried out by various distinguished scholars. It was found that, with one exception, all the projects reached a point of disruption when the original plan broke down, requiring activities of theoretical 'patchworking' in order to repair the breakdown and to present an appearance of coherence in the work. Gherardi and Turner concluded that if research is recognized to be a journey into the unknown (i.e. QUAL) rather than a task which can be fully specified and planned in advance (i.e. QUAN), then such breakdowns look less surprising and can be handled within the research framework.

- *Rich material for the research report* One disheartening aspect of quantitative studies can be when the results of several months of hard labour are summarized in one or two small tables (of correlations, for example). Gillham (2000) describes this situation well: 'If the basic research questions are complex (when are they not?) then your data are going to look pretty thin and superficial' (p. 121). In contrast, qualitative accounts that use the words and categories of the participants make it much easier to produce a convincing and vivid case for a wide range of audiences.

Weaknesses

In the literature we usually find two types of criticisms of qualitative research. The first consists of quantitatively motivated complaints about certain aspects of qualitative research that are different from quantitative research but which qualitative researchers consider either a strength or a normal feature. The second contains issues raised by qualitative researchers themselves. Let us look at five particularly salient issues:

- *Sample size and generalizability* The most frequent criticism offered by quantitatively minded researchers concerns the idiosyncratic nature of the small participant samples that most qualitative studies investigate. This question was already discussed in Section 2.1.3, where I argued that the two paradigms approach the question of generalizability differently. However, even if we accept that the exploration of personal meaning does not require large samples, Duff (2006) warns us that although the common QUAL practice of examining 'telling' cases may be very helpful in providing insights into a phenomenon, the specific conditions or insights may not apply broadly to others. Yates (2003: 224) calls this issue the 'potential over-reading' of the individual stories.
- *Researcher role* Another contested issue concerns the role played by the researcher in analysing the data. As Miles and Huberman (1994: 10) put it, 'The strengths of qualitative data rest very centrally on the competence with which their analysis is carried out'. Quantitative researchers would like to see some firm safeguards to make sure that results are not influenced by the researcher's personal biases and idiosyncrasies. (For more details, see Section 3.1 on quality criteria.)
- *Lack of methodological rigour* For quantitative researchers, who are used to standardized instruments and procedures and statistical analytical techniques, qualitative research can easily appear unprincipled and 'fuzzy'. It is noteworthy that similar points are also made within the qualitative camp. For example, a group of respected qualitative scholars, Seale *et al.* (2004: 2), argued against the postmodern position within the QUAL movement as follows:

    > These appear to be driven by an anti-methodological tenor that prefers the substance (research topics) to the form (methodology). Such a perspective, born partly in reaction to positivism, waved a flag of the superiority of qualitative research to surveys and experiments and

> considered methodological principles incapable of achieving a deeper understanding of a fragmented and dislocated culture. However, this research style has not always maintained its promise of achieving a deeper kind of research. The consequences are too often exposed to view: low quality qualitative research and research results that are quite stereotypical and close to common sense.

We must note, though, that these comments about a lack of methodological rigour only apply to some qualitative strands because the past two decades have seen a marked shift towards applying rigorous procedures in QUAL studies.

- *Too complex or too narrow theories* Because qualitative researchers have no real means of assessing which of their findings are of more general importance and which are simply idiosyncratic to a particular case, even QUAL scholars (for example, Eisenhardt 1989) point out that there is a real danger of building too narrow theories from the individual cases studied. In a similar way, the intensive use of rich data can also yield a theory which is overly complex.
- *Time consuming and labour-intensive* A final point, which both QUAL and QUAN scholars would agree on, is that QUAL research, particularly the processing of QUAL data, can be rather time-consuming, more so than QUAN research—as mentioned earlier, it is partly this feature which explains the relatively small sample sizes used in QUAL inquiries.

2.4 Mixed methods research

Researchers have been referring to studies that combine qualitative and quantitative methods under a variety of names, such as multitrait-multimethod research, interrelating qualitative and quantitative data, methodological triangulation, multimethodological research, mixed model studies, and mixed methods research (Creswell *et al.* 2003)—as indicated by the title of the recent *Handbook of Mixed Methods Research*, the field appears to have settled with the last term. Over the past 15 years, mixed methods research has been increasingly seen as a third approach in research methodology. The method has been endorsed by some of the most influential methodologists in the social sciences. Miles and Huberman (1994: 310) summarized the new emerging Zeitgeist well:

> Entertain mixed models. We have sought to make a virtue of avoiding polarization, polemics, and life at the extremes. Quantitative and qualitative inquiry can support and inform each other. Narratives and variable-driven analyses need to interpenetrate and inform each other. Realists, idealists, and critical theorists can do better by incorporating other ideas than by remaining pure. Think of it as hybrid vigour.

Let me cite one more illustrative extract from Strauss and Corbin's (1998: 34) book:

> Qualitative and quantitative forms of research both have roles to play in theorising. The issue is not whether to use one form or another but rather how these might work together to foster the development of theory. Although most researchers tend to use qualitative and quantitative methods in supplementary or complementary forms, what we are advocating is a true interplay between the two. The qualitative should direct the quantitative and the quantitative feedback into the qualitative in a circular, but at the same time evolving, process with each method contributing to the theory in ways that only each can.

Let us now examine where the idea of mixing methodologies has come from and what its main principles are.

2.4.1 Brief historical overview

The practice of collecting multiple data types dates back to the earliest social science research at the beginning of the twentieth century, and as Maxwell and Loomis (2003) point out, the practice of mixing very different research approaches—for example naturalistic, contextualized and inductive approaches with experimental manipulation and theory verification—has an even longer history in disciplines such as ethology and animal behaviour, palaeontology and geology. Yet, similarly to qualitative research, an explicit discussion of mixing methodologies had to wait until the second half of the twentieth century, for Campbell and Fiske's (1959) promotion of multitrait-multimethod research as a way of validating research designs by separating trait and method effects. Although Campbell and Fiske focused on collecting multiple types of quantitative data only, their work was instrumental in generally encouraging the use of multiple methods and the collection of multiple forms of data in a single study (Hanson *et al.* 2005).

The real breakthrough in combining qualitative and quantitative research occurred in the 1970s with the introduction of the concept of 'triangulation' into the social sciences. The term was borrowed from naval navigation and land surveying, where it refers to a method for determining the yet unknown position of a certain spatial point through measurement operations from two known points (Erzberger and Kelle 2003), but in social research it became synonymous with combining data sources to study the same social phenomenon. In his famous monograph *The Research Act,* Denzin (1978) advocated triangulation as a way of validating hypotheses by examining them through multiple methods. Although Denzin referred primarily to multiple qualitative methods, he formulated what became the key tenet of mixed methods research, namely that methodological triangulation can help to reduce the inherent weaknesses of individual methods by offsetting them by the strength of another, thereby maximizing both the internal and the external validity of research. (These terms will be further discussed in Section 3.1.1.) For example, Brewer and Hunter (1989: 11) introduced their pioneering book on *Multimethod Research* as follows:

> The social sciences are well known for disputes between proponents of different methods, or styles, of research. In a sense, these methodological debates are a healthy sign. Scepticism is an essential part of scientific inquiry, and different types of methods represent important critical perspectives. Equally important, however, is the fact that different research methods offer possible solutions for one another's problems. This is the central premise of this book.

After the paradigm war had lost its edge in the 1990s and mixed methods researchers gained ideological confidence by drawing on the philosophy of pragmatism (see for example, Cherryholmes 1992), research methodology texts started to include chapters on combined, integrated or mixed methods (one particularly influential work from the time being Creswell 1994). Following this growing momentum, two high profile publications by Tashakkori and Teddlie (1998, 2003a) finally established mixed methods research as a legitimate form of inquiry in the social sciences.

In applied linguistics we find many studies that have combined methodologies; Magnan (2006), for example, reports that over the 1995–2005 period 6.8 per cent of the research papers appearing in *The Modern Language Journal* used mixed methods, which is relatively high if we compare it to the total number of qualitative studies (19.8 per cent). However, we must note that most studies in which some sort of method mixing has taken place have not actually foregrounded the mixed methods approach and hardly any published papers have treated mixed methodology in a principled way. Currently, there is a general call on the part of applied linguists of both QUAL and QUAN orientation for more engagement in this practice, and Lazaraton's (2005: 219) conclusion can be seen as representative: 'I would also hope that we would see more studies that combine qualitative and quantitative research methods, since each highlights "reality" in a different, yet complementary, way'.

2.4.2 Main characteristics of mixed methods research

A straightforward way of describing mixed methods research is to define it as some sort of a combination of qualitative and quantitative methods within a single research project. These two approaches have already been described separately above and so there is no need to reiterate their main features; the real issue in mixed methods research concerns *how* the QUAL–QUAN combination takes place, and scholars have proposed several viable design options in the literature. These are discussed in Chapter 7 in detail; as a preliminary, let me say that the variety of possible combinations is rich, going well beyond simple sequential arrangements (i.e. a research phase is followed by a second phase representing the other approach). Furthermore, qualitative and quantitative principles can also be combined at the data analysis stage by 'quantifying' or 'qualitizing' the data. (See Section 11.1 on data transformation.)

2.4.3 Strengths and weaknesses of mixed methods research

As a result of the growing popularity of mixed methods research, several arguments have been put forward about the value of mixing methods. Let us have a look at the most important ones.

- *Increasing the strengths while eliminating the weaknesses* The main attraction of mixed methods research has been the fact that by using both QUAL and QUAN approaches researchers can bring out the best of both paradigms, thereby combining quantitative and qualitative research strengths (listed in Sections 2.2.3 and 2.3.3). This is further augmented by the potential that the strengths of one method can be utilized to overcome the weaknesses of another method used in the study. For example, as mentioned earlier, QUAN researchers have seen QUAL research as being too context-specific and employing unrepresentative samples—in a mixed methods study the sampling bias can be cancelled out if the selection of the qualitative participants is based on the results of an initial representative survey. (See Section 7.3 on the main types of mixed methods design.) On the other hand, QUAL researchers usually view QUAN research as overly simplistic, decontextualized and reductionist in terms of its generalizations, failing to capture the meanings that actors attach to their lives and circumstances (Brannen 2005)—in a mixed methods study a QUAN phase can be followed by a QUAL component to neutralize this issue by adding depth to the quantitative results and thereby putting flesh on the bones.
- *Multi-level analysis of complex issues* It has been suggested by many that we can gain a better understanding of a complex phenomenon by converging numeric trends from quantitative data and specific details from qualitative data. Words can be used to add meaning to numbers and numbers can be used to add precision to words. It is easy to think of situations in applied linguistics when we are interested at the same time in both the exact nature (i.e. QUAL) and the distribution (i.e. QUAN) of a phenomenon (for example, why do some teenage boys consider modern language learning 'girlish' and how extensive is this perception?). Mixed methods research is particularly appropriate for such multi-level analyses because it allows investigators to obtain data about both the individual and the broader societal context.
- *Improved validity* Mixed methods research has a unique potential to produce evidence for the validity of research outcomes through the convergence and corroboration of the findings. (See Chapter 3 for a detailed discussion of research validity.) Indeed, improving the validity of research has been at the heart of the notion of triangulation ever since its introduction in

the 1970s. Corresponding evidence obtained through multiple methods can also increase the generalizability—that is, external validity—of the results.

- *Reaching multiple audiences* A welcome benefit of combining QUAL and QUAN methods is that the final results are usually acceptable for a larger audience than those of a monomethod study would be. A well-executed mixed methods study has multiple selling points and can offer something to everybody, regardless of the paradigmatic orientation of the person. Of course, there is also the danger that the study might fall through the 'paradigmatic crack' and alienate everybody, but in the current supportive climate this is less likely.

Weaknesses

Mixing qualitative and quantitative methods has come to be seen by many as a forward-pointing and potentially enriching approach, but as Mason (2006) cautions us, the reasoning or logic behind such an assumption is not always as readily expressed as is the sentiment itself. Hesse-Biber and Leavy (2006) go even further when they suggest that the popular belief that the sum may be greater than its parts is not necessarily true. They cite an interview with Janice Morse, who warns about the danger of using mixed methods research as a 'substitute for sharp conceptual thinking and insightful analyses' (p. 334). Indeed, it would be clearly counterproductive to adopt a strategy whereby 'when in doubt, mix methods ...'.

Hesse-Biber and Leavy (2006) also raise the issue of how well-versed any given researcher can be in both types of methodology, which leads to a critical question: Can more harm than good be done when researchers are not adequately trained in both methods? This is a realistic danger because the vast majority of researchers lack methodological skills to handle both QUAL and QUAN data. And even if we can expect this situation to improve with the growing awareness of mixed methods research, the question still remains: Apart from a relatively small number of unique, methodologically ambidextrous specimen, can we assume that the vision of a multimethodologically savvy new breed of researchers is realistic?

Finally, Maxwell and Loomis (2003) highlight a further issue, the diversity of the possible combinations of different methods, which is, as the scholars argue, far greater than any typology can adequately encompass. One cannot help wondering whether there is really a principled approach to guiding the variety of combinations so that we do not end up with an 'anything goes as long as you mix them' mentality. We will come back to this question of 'principled mixing' later in this book (in Section 3.1.3 and Chapter 7).

2.5 My own paradigmatic stance

In accordance with my overall beliefs about research methodology, I try to assume a genuinely unbiased position throughout this book with regard to paradigmatic preferences, emphasizing wherever possible positive aspects and potentials. However, I feel that it is necessary at this point to be a bit more specific about my own background and research orientation.

As already mentioned in the Preface, most colleagues would probably consider me a quantitative researcher because my best-known studies involve the use of research methods associated with quantitative social psychology (attitude/motivation surveys in particular). Indeed, I do appreciate the elaborate technical apparatus involved in quantitative research and I actually like statistics. At the same time, I have also experienced again and again how much richer data we can obtain in a well-conducted and analysed qualitative study than even in a large-scale questionnaire survey. Thus, starting in the mid-1990s, I began to include qualitative components in my research and I have learnt much from the qualitative data my associates and I have collected and analysed over the years.

I do accept that certain issues are best researched using either QUAL or QUAN methods but I have also come to believe that in most cases a mixed methods approach can offer additional benefits for the understanding of the phenomenon in question. Therefore, at the end of the research methodology chapter of a book I have written on L2 motivation (Dörnyei 2001), I included a concluding section called 'Towards a combined use of quantitative and qualitative studies', and over the past decade I have encouraged most of my PhD students to try and integrate QUAL and QUAN methods (investigating a range of topics from acculturation to teacher motivation). Although the generally high quality research findings my students produced have confirmed to me the viability of this approach, I am aware of the fact that most scholars are more naturally inclined towards either QUAL or QUAN research (see Section 14.5 on personal considerations in method selection), a fact that I suspect has to do with our cognitive styles. Therefore, in conducting mixed methods studies I seek to cooperate with researchers who have a qualitative orientation to complement my quantitative background.

3

Quality criteria, research ethics, and other research issues

Before we discuss the collection and analysis of data, we need to address a few basic research issues that have a bearing on our methodological decisions regardless of our paradigmatic choice. First and foremost come the quality criteria for research, because we can only claim that our investigation is indeed a 'disciplined' inquiry if we can set explicit quality standards to achieve. The second topic to cover is research ethics, which is a curiously neglected issue in much applied linguistic research and often surfaces only when researchers realize that they need to produce some 'ethical clearance' for their study if they want to submit the results to obtain a postgraduate degree or to be published in certain journals. Following the analysis of ethical issues we consider the role and significance of research questions and hypotheses—these will be further discussed in Chapter 14. The chapter concludes with the discussion of three topics—piloting the research, research logs, and data management—that are essential issues for launching a research project but which, in my experience, do not receive sufficient attention in applied linguistic research.

3.1 Quality criteria for research

> *'Validity' is another word for truth.*
> (Silverman 2005: 210)

As we have seen, the basic definition of scientific research is that it is a 'disciplined' inquiry, and therefore one thing research cannot afford is to be haphazard or lacking rigour. Accordingly, there is a general consensus amongst researchers that they must continually strive to assess and document the legitimacy of their findings—after all, scholars have to convince their audiences that they should listen to them and, eventually, believe them.

Unfortunately, general agreement about research quality in scholarly circles stops at the recognition of its importance; when it comes to specifying the concrete 'quality criteria' to be applied, the literature is characterized by a host of parallel or alternative views and very little consensus. The fragmented nature of the domain is well reflected by the fact that there does not even exist any universally accepted terminology to describe quality criteria, and the terms that are more widely known—'validity' and 'reliability' in particular—are subject to ongoing criticism, with various authors regularly offering disparate sets of alternatives. Of course, given the huge importance of research quality, this situation is not surprising: representatives of different research traditions understandably emphasize quality parameters that will allow the type of inquiry they pursue to come out in a good light. The problem is that the scope of possible quality criteria is rather wide—ranging from statistical and methodological issues through real world significance and practical values to the benefits to the research participants—and some parameters that seem to do one research approach justice do not really work well with other approaches, thereby leading to tension between camps and to further proliferation of quality criteria.

I mentioned in Chapter 1 (Section 1.3) that an overview such as this book needs to be rather conservative in its approach; in this spirit, I will centre my discussion around the two best-known relevant concepts, 'validity' and 'reliability', and will use these with regard to both qualitative and quantitative research. We must note, however, that both terms were originally introduced in quantitative research, and therefore while the significance of the two concepts is an unquestionable fact of life in the QUAN paradigm, many QUAL researchers deny the relevance of 'validity' and 'reliability' as defined in quantitative terms. In order to introduce quality criteria that are more suitable for QUAL inquiries, several alternative terms have been proposed: validity has been referred to as 'trustworthiness', 'authenticity', 'credibility', 'rigour', and 'veracity', but none of these have reached a consensus and the terminology in general is a highly debated topic. There have also been attempts to match QUAL and QUAN terms (for example, external validity = transferability; reliability = dependability) but, surely, the whole rationale for developing a parallel terminology is the conviction that there are no straightforward parallels in the two research paradigms. I will describe in Section 3.1.2 the most influential alternative validity typology put forward by Lincoln and Guba (1985), but I will then argue in favour of Maxwell's (1992) well-known taxonomy that is built around facets of qualitative validity.

3.1.1 Quality criteria in quantitative research

Although the previous discussion will have given the impression that the terminology used to describe quantitative quality standards and criteria is relatively unproblematic, this is not entirely the case. The concept of 'reliability' is fairly straightforward, but when we look at 'validity' we find two parallel systems in the quantitative literature—one centred around 'construct validity' and its components, the other around the 'internal/external validity' dichotomy—and scholars tend to be surprisingly vague about the relationship between these two systems: the usual practice is that a work either covers one or the other. This dualistic approach is due to the fact that within the quantitative paradigm meaningfulness has been conceptualized from two perspectives: research design and measurement. (See Bachman 2006; Lynch 2003.)

Research validity concerns the whole research process, and following Campbell and Stanley (1963) focuses on the distinction of 'internal validity', which addresses the soundness of the research (i.e. whether the outcome is indeed a function of the various variables and treatment factors measured), and 'external validity', which concerns the generalizability of the results beyond the observed sample.

Measurement validity refers to the meaningfulness and appropriateness of the interpretation of the various test scores or other assessment procedure outcomes. As we will see below, validity here is seen as a unitary concept, expressed in terms of 'construct validity', which can be further broken down to various facets such as content or criterion validity. It is this perspective (going back to Lado's work on testing) that produced the classic tenet that a test is valid if it measures what it is supposed to measure, even though the current view is that it is neither the instrument, nor the actual score that is valid but rather the interpretation of the score with regard to a specific population.

Thus, the discussion of quantitative quality standards is best divided into three parts: (a) reliability, (b) measurement validity, and (c) research validity.

Reliability

The term reliability comes from measurement theory and refers to the 'consistencies of data, scores or observations obtained using elicitation instruments, which can include a range of tools from standardized tests administered in educational settings to tasks completed by participants in a research study' (Chalhoub-Deville 2006: 2). In other words, reliability indicates the extent to which our measurement instruments and procedures produce consistent results in a given population in different circumstances. The variation of the circumstances can involve differences in administrative procedures, changes in test takers over time, differences in various forms of the test and differences in raters (Bachman 2004b). If these variations cause inconsistencies, or measurement error, then our results are unreliable.

It is important to remember that, contrary to much of the usage in the methodological literature, it is not the test or the measuring instrument that is reliable or unreliable. Reliability is a property of the scores on a test for a particular population of testtakers (Wilkinson and TFSI, 1999) and Bachman (2004b) reminds us that, accordingly, all the professional international standards require researchers to estimate and report the reliability of 'each total score, subscore, or combination of scores that is to be interpreted' (AERA,

APA, and NCME 1999: 31). In the light of this, it is surprising that the vast majority of quantitative social scientists do not provide reliability estimates for their own data (Onwuegbuzie and Leech 2005). This is partly due to the false understanding that reliability is a characteristic of the instrument, which would imply that if we use an instrument that has been documented to produce reliable scores before, we do not need to worry about establishing reliability in our sample again.

Bachman (2004b) offers a detailed description of two general approaches whereby classic test theory provides estimates of reliability: (1) we can calculate the correlation between two sets of scores, for example between two halves of a test or two parallel forms, or two different raters' ratings. (2) We can calculate a statistic known as Cronbach alpha (see Section 9.3), which is based on the variances of two or more scores and serves as an 'internal consistency coefficient' indicating how the different scores 'hang together' (for example, more than two raters' scores or several parallel questionnaire items in a scale).

Measurement validity

As mentioned earlier, the concept of validity from a measurement perspective has traditionally been summarized by the simple phrase: a test is valid if it measures what it is supposed to measure. However, the scientific conceptualization of measurement validity has gone through some significant changes over the past decades. According to Chapelle's (1999) description of the development of the concept in applied linguistics, validity was seen in the 1960s as a characteristic of a language test. Several types of validity were distinguished: 'criterion validity' was defined by the test's correlation with another, similar instrument; 'content validity' concerned expert judgement about test content; and 'construct validity' showed how the test results conformed to a theory of which the target construct was a part. This traditional conceptualization is still pervasive today.

In 1985, the main international guidelines for educational and psychological measurement sponsored by the American Educational Research Association, the American Psychological Association, and the National Council on Measurement in Education—the AERA/APA/NCME Standards for Educational and Psychological Testing (AERA, APA, and NCME 1999)—replaced the former definition of three validities with a unitary concept, 'construct validity'. This change was a natural consequence of the shift from seeing validity as an attribute of the test to considering it the truthfulness of the interpretation of the test scores. Lynch (2003: 149) summarizes the new conception clearly: 'When examining the validity of assessment, it is important to remember that validity is a property of the conclusions, interpretations or inferences that we draw from the assessment instruments and procedures, not the instruments and procedures themselves'. Following the new approach, content- and criterion-related evidence came to be seen as contributors to the overall validity construct along with validity considerations of the consequences of score interpretation and use, and even reliability was seen as one type of validity evidence. Validity was portrayed now as the conclusion of a complex validity argument which uses various statistical and theoretical sources as evidence.

Thus, construct validity is now generally accepted as an umbrella term, describing a process for theory validation that subsumes specific test validation operations (Smith 2005). These validation operations are carried out within 'validation studies', and can involve both qualitative and quantitative evidence depending on the specific claims put forward and counterclaims rejected in our validity argument (Bachman 2004b). These arguments are never context-free and McNamara (2006) emphasizes that test score inferences need to be revalidated for every major context of use.

To conclude this brief overview of measurement validity, here is a list of four key points provided by Bachman (2004b) based on Linn and Gronlund's work:

- Validity is a quality of the interpretations and not of the test or the test scores.
- Perfect validity can never be proven—the best we can do is provide evidence that our validity argument is more plausible than other potential competing interpretations.
- Validity is specific to a particular situation and is not automatically transferable to others.
- Validity is a unitary concept that can be supported with many different types of evidence.

Research validity

The second type of validity, 'research validity', is broader than measurement validity as it concerns the overall quality of the whole research project and more specifically (a) the meaningfulness of the interpretations that researchers make on the basis of their observations, and (b) the extent to which these interpretations generalize beyond the research study (Bachman 2004a). These two validity aspects were referred to as *internal validity* and *external validity* by Campbell and Stanley (1963) over four decades ago, and although there have been attempts to fine-tune this typology (for example, by Cook and Campbell 1979), the broadly dichotomous system has stood the test of time:

- A research study or experiment has *internal validity* if the outcome is a function of the variables that are measured, controlled or manipulated in the study. The findings of a study are internally invalid if they have been affected by factors other than those thought to have caused them.
- *External validity* is the extent to which we can generalize our findings to a larger group, to other contexts or to different times. A study is externally invalid if the results apply only to the unique sample or setting in which they were found.

In the quantitative paradigm, research validity is demonstrated by ruling out, or providing evidence against, various 'threats' to validity. These threats concern unintended factors, circumstances, flaws or events that can invalidate the results. Internal validity threats involve the use of inadequate procedures or instruments, any unexpected problems occurring during the study or any uncontrolled factors that can significantly modify the results. The main threat to external validity in experimental studies involves any special interaction between our intervention/treatment and some characteristics of the particular group of participants which causes the experiment to work only in our study (for example, the experiment exploits a special feature of the treatment group that is usually not existent in other groups). In survey studies, external validity threats concern inadequate sampling (to be discussed in Chapter 5).

Main threats to research validity

Let us have a look at the six most salient validity threats. I will not divide them into internal and external categories because a flaw in the research design often affects both aspects of research validity.

- *Participant mortality* or *attrition* In studies where we collect different sets of data from the participants (for example, pre- and post-test or multiple tests and questionnaires), subject dropout is always a serious concern. It reduces the size of the sample that has a complete dataset and, what is more worrying from the perspective of validity, the dropout may not be random but differential (i.e. participants who drop out are different from those who stay), leaving the remaining group with disproportionate characteristics.
- The *Hawthorne effect* The term comes from the name of a research site (in Chicago) where this effect was first documented when researchers investigating an electric company found that work production increased when they were present, regardless of the conditions the workers were subjected to. The reason for such an irrational effect is that participants perform differently when they know they are being studied. Mellow *et al.* (1996: 334) found that this threat is particularly salient in applied linguistic research as it may be 'the single most serious threat to studies of spontaneous language use'.
- *Practice effect* If a study involves repeated testing or repeated tasks (for example, in an experimental or longitudinal study), the participants' performance may improve simply because they are gaining experience in taking the particular test or performing the assessed activity.
- *Maturation* While not a concern in short studies such as a one-off survey, participant maturation—that is, physical or mental change with age—can play a major role in longer-term studies. It is inevitable that subjects change in the course of an experiment or between repeated administration of a questionnaire/test due to the passage of time *per se*—the question is how

much this naturally occurring developmental process affects the target variables in a study.

- *Participant desire to meet expectation (social desirability bias)* The participants of a study are often provided with cues to the anticipated results of the project, and as a result they may begin to exhibit performance that they believe is expected of them. A variation of this threat is when participants try to meet social expectations and over-report desirable attitudes and behaviours while underreporting those that are socially not respected.
- *History* Empirical research does not take place in a vacuum and therefore we might be subject to the effects of unanticipated events while the study is in progress. (See, for example, Section 8.4 on the challenges of classroom research.) Such events are outside the research study, yet they can alter the participants' performance. The best we can do at times like this is to document the impact of the events so that later we may neutralize it by using some kind of statistical control.

3.1.2 Quality criteria in qualitative research

The usual statement we find in the literature about quality in QUAL research is that it is less straightforward to define than quality in QUAN research. (For an insightful analysis from an applied linguistic perspective, see Lazaraton 2003.) While in the previous sections we saw that even quantitative research criteria are not completely unambiguous, it is true that setting explicit quality standards in the qualitative paradigm has been particularly problematic—a claim that even qualitative researchers agree with. Sandelowski and Barroso (2002) summarize the situation well:

> Over the past 20 years, reams of articles and books have been written on the subject of quality in qualitative research. Addressing such concepts as reliability and rigor, value and validity, and criteria and credibility, scholars across the practice and social science disciplines have sought to define what a good, valid, and/or trustworthy qualitative study is, to chart the history of and to categorize efforts to accomplish such a definition, and to describe and codify techniques for both ensuring and recognizing good studies. Yet after all of this effort, we seem to be no closer to establishing a consensus on quality criteria, or even agree on whether it is appropriate to try to establish such a consensus.

One reason for these difficulties lies in the fact that although the terms 'validity' and 'reliability' refer to empirical research in general, in practice they have been associated with quantitative methods and their operationalization has traditionally followed quantitative principles. We saw in Chapter 2 that a qualitative study is inherently subjective, interpretive as well as time- and context-bound; that is, in a qualitative inquiry 'truth' is relative and 'facts' depend upon individual perceptions (Morse and Richards 2002); for this reason several researchers have argued that qualitative research requires its own procedures for attaining validity that are different from those used in quantitative approaches.

The problem is that, although several typologies of 'qualitative validity' have been put forward, none of them have received unequivocal support and therefore at the moment we do not seem to have a straightforward and powerful alternative means of assuring quality and thus confirming the legitimacy of qualitative research. In fact, some scholars have even argued that qualitative research has several built-in criteria for producing valid results by definition, such as the 'thick description' of the targeted phenomenon or the fact that the results are arrived at through an iterative process of going back and forth between the data and the analysis until a 'goodness of fit' is achieved. However, as Lynch (2003: 157) points out, this assumption of automatic quality control 'will not satisfy many people. Evaluation audiences expect explicit evidence in support of validity'. Indeed, the big problem with the 'qualitative-research-is-valid-by-definition' argument is that although it can be made to sound convincing, not all qualitative accounts are equally useful, credible, or legitimate, and in many cases the difference between a more and a less trustworthy account of a phenomenon is not due to the researcher's different perspective but to some methodological factors which distort the results so that these do not reflect the phenomenon in question accurately (Morse and Richards 2002). In short, not every qualitative study is equally stable and correct and therefore we need standards to be able to sift the wheat from the chaff. Let us first look at the 'chaff', that is, some key QUAL quality concerns, before we look at some responses to the quality issue.

Three basic quality concerns in qualitative research

Quantitative researchers sometimes criticize the qualitative paradigm for not following the principles of the 'scientific method' (for example, the objective and formal testing of hypotheses) or having too small sample sizes, but these concerns miss the point as they, in effect, say that the problem with qualitative research is that it is not quantitative enough. There are, however, certain basic quality concerns in QUAL inquiries that are independent of paradigmatic considerations. I have found three such issues particularly salient:

1 *Insipid data* Focusing on 'individual meaning' does not offer any procedures for deciding whether the particular meaning is *interesting* enough (since we are not to judge a respondent's personal perceptions and interpretations), and if it is not sufficiently interesting then no matter how truthfully we reflect this meaning in the analysis we will obtain only low quality results that are 'quite stereotypical and close to common sense' (Seale *et al.* 2004: 2). In other words, the quality of the analysis is dependent on the quality of the original data and I am not sure whether it is possible to develop explicit guidelines for judging one set of complex idiosyncratic meaning as better than another. As Seale *et al.* conclude, past practice in qualitative research

has not always been convincing in this respect, and although taking theoretical sampling seriously does help (see Section 6.2), no qualitative sampling procedure can completely prevent the documentation of the unexciting. This problem is unique to QUAL inquiries because QUAN research addresses the commonality found in larger samples instead of individual meaning.

2 *Quality of the researcher* Morse and Richards (2002) are right when they warn us that any study is only as good as the researcher, and in a qualitative study this issue is particularly prominent because in a way the researcher is the instrument—see Section 2.1.4. This raises a serious question: how can quality criteria address the researcher's skills that are to a large extent responsible for ensuring the quality and scope of the data and the interpretation of the results? Again, quantitative research does not have to face this issue because a great deal of the researcher's role is guided by standardized procedures.

3 *Anecdotalism and the lack of quality safeguards* The final quality concern has been described by Silverman (2005: 211) as follows:

> qualitative researchers, with their in-depth access to single cases, have to overcome a special temptation. How are they to convince themselves (and their audience) that their 'findings' are genuinely based on critical investigation of all their data and do not depend on a few well-chosen 'examples'? This is sometimes known as the problem of anecdotalism.

Indeed, space limitations usually do not allow qualitative researchers to provide more than a few exemplary instances of the data that has led them to their conclusion, a problem that is aggravated by the fact that scholars rarely provide any justification for selecting the specific sample extracts (i.e. do not give any criteria for 'within-case' sampling—see Section 6.2.4). As a result, Miles and Huberman (1994: 2) have concluded: 'We do not really see how the researcher got from 3,600 pages of field notes to the final conclusions, as sprinkled with vivid illustrations as they may be'. Therefore, readers of qualitative studies are usually not in a position to judge the systematicity of the analysis, let alone to produce any possible alternative interpretations. As a consequence, in the absence of any in-built quality safeguards it is unfortunately too easy to abuse the procedure and produce a convincingly qualitative-like report in which the author has chosen a few quotations from a much larger and more complex database that support his/her preconceived argument.

Reliability

Let us start our discussion of specific QUAL quality criteria by examining the notion of 'reliability'. Kirk and Miller (1986) pointed out two decades ago that the main thrust of methodological development in qualitative research had been towards greater validity and therefore reliability had been somewhat overlooked. This situation has not changed greatly over the past two decades.

Reliability refers to the 'degree of consistency with which instances are assigned to the same category by different observers or by the same observer on different occasions' (Silverman 2005: 224). The concept of consistency is also emphasized in Kirk and Miller's (1986: 69) definition of reliability in field work as the degree to which 'an ethnographer would expect to obtain the finding if he or she tried again in the same way', that is, the degree to which 'the finding is independent of accidental circumstances of the research' (p. 20). Morse and Richards' (2002: 168) definition sums up the consistency issue well but at the same time reveals why qualitative reliability has been played down in the past: 'reliability requires that the same results would be obtained if the study were replicated'. The problem is that replication is not something that is easy to achieve in a research paradigm where any conclusion is in the end jointly shaped by the respondents' personal accounts and the researcher's subjective interpretation of these stories. Having said that, it is possible to conduct reliability checks of various sub-processes within a qualitative inquiry, for example of the coding of interview transcripts by asking a second coder to code separately a sizable part of the transcript (either using the researcher's coding template or generating the codes him/herself) and then reviewing the proportion of agreements and disagreements.

Lincoln and Guba's taxonomy of quality criteria

In a spirited denial of the allegations that qualitative research is 'sloppy' and qualitative researchers respond indiscriminately to the 'louder bangs or brightest lights', Lincoln and Guba (1985) introduced the concept of 'trustworthiness' as qualitative researchers' answer to 'validity'. They proposed four components to make up trustworthiness:

a *Credibility*, or the 'truth value' of a study, which is the qualitative counterpart of 'internal validity'.

b *Transferability*, or the 'applicability' of the results to other contexts, which is the qualitative counterpart of 'external validity'.

c *Dependability*, or the 'consistency' of the findings, which is the qualitative counterpart of 'reliability'.

d *Confirmability*, or the neutrality of the findings, which is the qualitative counterpart of 'objectivity'.

These terms are sometimes referred to as 'parallel criteria' because of their corresponding quantitative counterparts. Although these parallel criteria have been embraced by many qualitative scholars, they have also been criticized on several grounds—see Morrow 2005. My personal concern is that the proliferation of terminology is likely to make the picture more confusing; I believe that it is possible to identify standards for qualitative research by identifying various relevant facets of the traditional concepts of validity and reliability, a practice followed by Maxwell (1992), described below.

Maxwell's taxonomy of validity in qualitative research

In the introduction of his influential typology of validity in qualitative research, Maxwell (1992) explicitly stated that he did not think that QUAL and QUAN approaches to validity were incompatible. He even suggested that his analysis might also have implications for the concept of validity in quantitative and experimental research. Let us examine the five components of his proposed system. (For a critical review, see Winter 2000.)

1 *Descriptive validity* concerns the factual accuracy of the researcher's account. Maxwell (1992) regards this as the primary aspect of validity because all the other validity categories are dependent on it. It refers to what the researcher him/herself has experienced and also to 'secondary' accounts of things that could in principle have been observed, but that were inferred from other data. One useful strategy for ensuring this validity is 'investigator triangulation', that is, using multiple investigators to collect and interpret the data.

2 *Interpretive validity* Descriptive validity was called a primary validity dimension because it underlies all other validity aspects and not because Maxwell (1992) considered descriptiveness the main concern for qualitative research. Instead, he argued, good qualitative research focuses on what the various tangible events, behaviours or objects 'mean' to the participants. Interpretive validity, then, focuses on the quality of the portrayal of this participant perspective. An obvious strategy to ensure this validity is to obtain participant feedback or member checking, which involve discussing the findings with the participants. (For more details, see below.)

3 *Theoretical validity* corresponds to some extent to the internal validity of the research as it concerns whether the researcher's account includes an appropriate level of theoretical abstraction and how well this theory explains or describes the phenomenon in question.

4 *Generalizability* It is interesting that in labelling this category Maxwell (1992) did not use a phrase containing the word 'validity', even though there would have been an obvious term to use: external validity. This is because he further divided 'generalizability' into 'internal generalizability' and 'external generalizability' and this division would not have worked with the term 'external validity' (i.e. we cannot really have 'internal external validity'). Both aspects of generalizability refer to the extension of the account to persons, times or settings other than those directly studied, but 'internal generalizability' concerns generalizing within the community or institution observed, whereas 'external generalizability' refers to generalizing to other communities or institutions.

Duff (2006) points out that many QUAL researchers view the term generalizability suspiciously because it is reminiscent of QUAN methodology, in which the capacity to generalize from the sample to some wider population is one of the key concerns. This is where Maxwell's (1992) distinction between internal and external generalizability is enlightening: he agrees that generalizability plays a different role in QUAL research than it does in QUAN research and therefore internal generalizability is far more important for most qualitative researchers than is external generalizability. He further explains that generalization in qualitative research usually takes place through the development of a theory derived from the particular persons or situations studied which helps to make sense of other situations. In other words, even if the particulars of a study do not generalize, the main ideas and the process observed might. This is why even a single specially selected case can be illuminating. A useful strategy to examine generalizability, recommended by Duff, is to include in the qualitative account the participants' own judgments about the generalizability of the targeted issue/phenomenon.

5 *Evaluative validity* refers to the assessment of how the researcher evaluates the phenomenon studied (for example, in terms of usefulness, practicability, desirability), that is, how accurately the research account assigns value judgments to the phenomenon. Thus, this validity aspect concerns the implicit or explicit use of an evaluation framework (for example, ethical or moral judgements) in a qualitative account, examining how the evaluative claims fit the observed phenomenon. Evaluative validity is gaining importance nowadays with various 'critical' theories becoming increasingly prominent in the social sciences and also in applied linguistics.

Strategies to ensure validity in qualitative research

Throughout this chapter I have been uncertain about how much space to devote to describing the various systems of validity and reliability because these typologies are admittedly not too practical in themselves. However, I agree with Maxwell's (1992) argument that such typologies offer a useful framework for thinking about the nature of the threats to validity and the possible ways that specific threats might be addressed. In the following, I list the most common strategies used to eliminate or control validity threats and to generate trustworthiness.

Building up an image of researcher integrity

It is my conviction that the most important strategy to ensure the trustworthiness of a project is to create in the audience an image of the researcher as a scholar with principled standards and integrity. At the end of the day, readers will decide whether they have confidence in one's research not by taking stock of the various validity arguments but by forming an opinion about the investigator's overall research integrity. This image of integrity is made up of several small components but there are certain strategies that are particularly helpful in showing up the researcher's high standards (provided, of course, those exist):

- *Leaving an audit trail* By offering a detailed and reflective account of the steps taken to achieve the results—including the iterative moves in data collection and analysis, the development of the coding frames and the emergence of the main themes—researchers can generate reader confidence in the principled, well-grounded and thorough nature of the research process. (This question is further discussed in Section 6.8 on research journals and in Section 13.1.2 on writing up qualitative reports.) As Holliday (2004: 732) summarizes:

  > As in all research, a major area of accountability must be procedure, and when the choices are more open, the procedure must be more transparent so that the scrutinizers of the research can assess the appropriateness of the researcher 's choices.

- *Contextualization and thick description* Presenting the findings in rich contextualized detail helps the reader to identify with the project and thus come on board.
- *Identifying potential researcher bias* Given the important role of the researcher in every stage of a qualitative study, identifying the researcher's own biases is obviously an important issue in an inquiry, and it also creates an open and honest narrative that will resonate well with the audience (Creswell 2003).
- *Examining outliers, extreme or negative cases and alternative explanations* No research study is perfect and the readers know this. Therefore, explicitly pointing out and discussing aspects of the study that run counter to the final conclusion is usually not seen as a weakness but adds to the credibility of the researcher. Similarly, giving alternative explanations a fair hearing before we dismiss them also helps to build confidence in our results.

Validity/reliability checks

The previous strategies did not actually add to the validity of the data but only helped to convince the audience that the study was valid (provided it was). The following strategies are different in that they involve steps taken by the researcher *during* the project to ensure validity, and it is appropriate to start with the popular technique of building into the study various validity checks.

- *Respondent feedback* (or 'respondent validation' or 'member checking') Because of the emphasis placed in qualitative research on uncovering participant meaning, it is an obvious strategy to involve the participants themselves in commenting on the conclusions of the study. They can, for example, read an early draft of the research report or listen to a presentation of some tentative results or themes, and can then express their views in what is called a 'validation interview'. If there is agreement between the researcher and the participants, the study's validity is indeed reinforced. However, several scholars have raised the question of how any disagreements should be interpreted. In terms of descriptive validity, such checks are undoubtedly useful and as we have seen in the previous section, respondent validation can also enhance generalizability. But whom shall we listen to when there are concerns about the interpretive validity of the results? Even though the participants are clearly the 'insiders', there is no reason to assume that they can interpret their own experiences or circumstances correctly—in family arguments, for example, insiders often have conflicting views about the same phenomena. Thus, the best way of handling such validity checks is to treat them as further data that can contribute to the overall validity argument after proper interpretation.

- *Peer checking* Qualitative studies often include reliability checks performed by peers. They always involve asking a colleague to perform some aspect of the researcher's role—usually developing or testing some coding scheme, but they can also involve performing other activities such as carrying out an observation task—and then comparing the correspondence between the two sets of outcomes. This is a very useful strategy because even low correspondence can serve as useful feedback for the further course of the study, but unfortunately it is often difficult to find someone who is both competent and ready to engage in this time-consuming activity.

Research design-based strategies

Strategies concerning a study's research design can provide the most convincing evidence about the validity of the research as they are an organic part of the project rather than being 'add-ons'. In a way, these practices are not necessarily 'strategic actions' but simply examples of good research practice.

- *Method and data triangulation* The concept of 'triangulation' involves using multiple methods, sources or perspectives in a research project (to be discussed in more detail when describing mixed methods research in Section 3.1.3 and also in Chapter 7). Triangulation has been traditionally seen as one of the most efficient ways of reducing the chance of systematic bias in a qualitative study because if we come to the same conclusion about a phenomenon using a different data collection/analysis method or a different participant sample, the convergence offers strong validity evidence. However, it leaves the same question open as the one already raised with regard to participant feedback: how shall we interpret any emerging disagreement between the corresponding results?
- *Prolonged engagement* and *persistent observation* Research designs that emphasize the quantity of engagement with the target community/phenomenon carry more face validity: most people would, for example, treat an

account by an ethnographer who has spent 15 years studying a community inherently valid, even though this may not necessarily be so (for example, if the observer has 'gone native').

- *Longitudinal research design* Duff (2006) argues that longitudinal studies have the potential to increase the validity of the inferences that can be drawn from them because they can reveal various developmental pathways and can also document different types of interactions over time. (Longitudinal studies are described in Chapter 4.)

3.1.3 Quality criteria in mixed methods research

We have seen in this chapter that qualitative and quantitative research are associated with somewhat different quality criteria, and even though broad quality dimensions might be described using the uniform dichotomy of 'reliability' and 'validity', the specific details in how to operationalize these concepts show variance. So, what shall we do in mixed methods research? How can we satisfy both QUAL and QUAN quality criteria in a single study? This is an important question because mixed methods research is a relatively new approach and therefore researchers adopting mixed designs should be particularly careful to defend the methods they are employing.

Teddlie and Tashakkori (2003) proposed that because mixed methods research is the third main general research approach, it should have its own terminology for quality criteria. As argued earlier, I am not convinced that creating new technical terms will make quality standards clearer or more acceptable; instead, I suggest that we consider three specific aspects of the quality of mixed methods research separately: (a) the rationale for mixing methods in general; (b) the rationale for the specific mixed design applied, including the choice of the particular methods; and (c) the quality of the specific methods making up the study.

The rationale for mixing methods

Mixed methods research as an explicitly marked research approach is still in its infancy and therefore scholars applying the paradigm need to justify their choice clearly. (To a lesser degree, qualitative researchers also face this task, especially in content areas and research environments where there is still a dominance of quantitative methodology.) The general arguments explaining why mixed methods research might be useful were presented in Chapter 2 (Section 2.4), and Chapter 7 provides further details about the possible compatibility of the QUAL and QUAN paradigms. The important point to emphasize is that a mixed methods inquiry offers a potentially more comprehensive means of legitimizing findings than do either QUAL or QUAN methods alone by allowing investigators to assess information from both data types. We saw in the previous section that triangulation has traditionally been seen as a way of ensuring research validity, and therefore the validity argument for mixed methods research can combine the validity evidence offered by the QUAL and the QUAN components separately.

The 'design validity' of the study

Although I have argued above against introducing new nomenclature for quality criteria, the term 'design validity' (Teddlie and Tashakkori 2003) appears to be relevant and necessary because it concerns a new aspect of internal validity, specific to mixed methods research. It refers to the extent to which the QUAL and QUAN components of a mixed methods study are combined or integrated in a way that the overall design displays complementary strengths and nonoverlapping weaknesses of the constituent methods. (See also Brewer and Hunter 1989; Tashakkori and Teddlie 1998.)

In claiming good design validity, researchers need to present evidence for two quality aspects: first, they have to justify the choice of the specific research methods that are combined in the study. In line with the pragmatic nature of mixed methods research, the main rationale here is likely to be centred around the match of the research question/topic with the method, arguing for a 'fitness-for-purpose' selection. (Chapter 14 offers a summary of the considerations that are involved in choosing an appropriate method.) Second, researchers need to demonstrate that the mixed design displays enhanced validity relative to the constituent methods. Chapter 7 presents several mixed methods design options whose explicit purpose is to offer enhanced research characteristics in terms of either internal or external validity. In addition, Chapter 11 describes several data analytical sequences whose aim is to add greater legitimacy to the researcher's conclusions (for example, subjecting 'quantitized' data to statistical analysis in a study which was initially based on qualitative data).

The quality of the specific methods

The specific methods that are combined in mixed methods research are—obviously—either qualitative or quantitative, and therefore the quality principles described earlier in this chapter apply to them. Several mixed methods designs display a dominant method (see Chapter 7), and in such cases most of the evidence included in the validity argument will need to be in accordance with the quality standards of the particular paradigm.

3.2 Research ethics

> *Any qualitative researcher who is not asleep ponders moral and ethical questions.*
> (Miles and Huberman 1994: 288)

Social research—including research in education—concerns people's lives in the social world and therefore it inevitably involves ethical issues. As Punch (2005) points out, such issues are more acute in QUAL than in QUAN approaches because qualitative research often intrudes more into the human private sphere: it is inherently interested in people's personal views and often targets sensitive or intimate matters. Thus, the growing recognition and utilization of qualitative methods in contemporary applied linguistic research raises the 'ethical stakes'. We have to address the issue, particularly because at the heart of the matter lies a basic tension: on the one hand, with our researcher hat on, we cannot deny the fact that ethical issues are often a hindrance to our investigation and in our politically correct age ethical questions can get so out of proportion that it can become virtually impossible to do research in certain contexts. On the other hand, as human beings with moral principles, we cannot deny either that there is more to life than research and if there is a possibility for a clash between the researcher's and the participants' interests, it is clear where the priorities should lie.

Hesse-Biber and Leavy (2006) observe that ethical discussions often remain detached or marginalized from discussions of the 'real' research project, almost as an afterthought. While this might be due to the fact that research publications are usually written for researcher audiences and it is assumed that colleagues are aware of the issues involved, in a research methods text we need to address the various ethical dilemmas that we face when we engage in real world research. As a preliminary, we should note that the international scene displays considerable diversity in terms of the ethical awareness across countries, and the legal regulation of research ethics also shows great differences worldwide. (For more details on ethics in applied linguistics, especially from a North American perspective, see Duff in press; Mackey and Gass 2005.) Yet, even in countries where research ethics have not been formally regulated there is a growing awareness of various data protection issues, which logically lead to the reconsideration of how human research is dealt with. Therefore, I anticipate that within the next decade more and more countries will take the North American example in setting up a strict framework for research ethics that is more participant- than researcher-friendly.

3.2.1 Some key ethical dilemmas and issues

The first ethical dilemma to address is how seriously we should take the various ethical issues in educational contexts. Most research methodology books reiterate broad recommendations of ethical conduct that have been prepared for the social sciences (including psychology) or for medical research, and in these broad contexts there is indeed a danger that misguided or exploitive research can cause real harm. On the other hand, some researchers such as Johnson and Christensen (2004: 111) emphasize that educational research should not be treated similarly to other social disciplines:

> Fortunately, studies conducted by educational researchers seldom if ever run the risk of inflicting such severe mental and physical harm on participants. In fact, educational research has historically engaged in research

that imposes either minimal or no risk to the participants and has enjoyed a special status with respect to formal ethical oversight.

Because this special status has been acknowledged by American lawmakers, a large portion of educational research—for example research on instructional strategies, curricula or classroom management—has been singled out for exempt status in the USA in the Code of Federal Regulations for the Protection of Human Subjects (Johnson and Christensen 2004). This does not mean, however, that ethical principles do not apply to educational research or that we can safely ignore the whole issue; as Johnson and Christensen (2004) point out, certain research practices, especially qualitative ones, include elements that 'muddy the ethical waters' (p. 111) and warrant careful consideration. Some examples of such sensitive aspects of research are:

- *The amount of shared information* As we will see below in Section 3.2.6, one of the basic dilemmas of researchers is to decide how much information should be shared with the participants about the research so as not to cause any response bias or even non-participation. In Cohen *et al.*'s (2000: 63) words: 'What is the proper balance between the interests of science and the thoughtful, humane treatment of people who, innocently, provide the data?'
- *Relationships* Qualitative studies can often result in an intimate relationship between researchers and participants, with the former trying to establish rapport and empathy to gain access to the participants' lives and stories. This relational character of qualitative research raises general ethical questions about the limits of closeness and intimacy with the respondents—Ryen (2004) for example discusses the controversial issue of flirting with (adult) participants—and there is a concrete dilemma about how to *end* a research project without leaving the participants feeling that they were merely used.
- *Data collection methods* Certain methods that remove the participants from their normal activities and involve, for example, one-to-one contact, can fall under the confines of child protection legislation in several countries.
- *Anonymity* A basic dilemma in educational research concerns the fact that although ideally our participants should remain anonymous, we often need to identify the respondents to be able to match their performances on various instruments or tasks.
- *Handling the collected data* The video camera in particular is a very public eye and it allows the identification of the participants long after the research has ended. Audio recordings can similarly be a threat to anonymity.
- *Ownership of the data* Who 'owns' the collected data? Does the researcher, asks Richards (2003), have complete control in editing or releasing information (observing, of course, privacy constraints)?

- *Sensitive information* In deep interviews participants can reveal sensitive information that is not related to the goal of the study (for example, pointing to abuse or criminal activity). How do we react?
- *Testing* Although this book does not cover testing, we need to note that the misuse of test scores carries real dangers.

Such dilemmas and issues show that even in educational research we need to have an ethical framework in place, a need which is also augmented by legal requirements in several countries. Let us consider the main components of such a framework in some detail.

3.2.2 Legal context

In many countries, observing ethical principles is enforced by legal and institutional requirements. In the US, for example, researchers have to submit a detailed research plan for approval to an Institutional Review Board prior to starting their investigations in order to comply with federal regulations that provide protection against human rights violations. These regulations also apply to postgraduate (MA or PhD) research, and only in exceptional circumstances will Graduate Schools accept a thesis or dissertation without some sort of 'human subjects' approval. There are elaborate procedures to go through, including filling in various forms offered by each university's review board. (See Duff in press; Mackey and Gass 2005.)

Legal frameworks and regulations concerning research ethics are usually less developed in countries outside North America (although, as mentioned above, the international tendency is to approximate the US example). In the UK, as Wiles *et al.* (2005) summarize, the British 'Data Protection Act' regulates the need to ensure consent to collecting data (except in very specific circumstances) as well as the use to which data is put. In addition, social research is increasingly being subjected to ethical review from institutional research ethics committees to ensure the ethical scrutiny of research involving human subjects, and undergoing ethical review is set to become a requirement of funding bodies in the future.

3.2.3 Researcher integrity

Curiously, few research methods texts elaborate on the area of research ethics that is, in my view, central to any investigation: the *researcher's integrity*. In Section 1.1 we touched briefly upon the significance of the researcher's reliability and accountability to the field and I believe that at the heart of research ethics lies the moral character of the researcher. In fact, the term 'ethics' derives from the Greek word 'ethos', which means character, and although in our modern world ethical principles can easily be equated simply with 'complying with laws', this is not merely a legalistic issue but concerns basic human honesty and trust. This is fully recognized by the Ethical Standards of the American Educational Research Association (AERA 2002), which starts out with a set of 'guiding standards' describing the researchers' general responsibilities to the field. These include the following points:

- Educational researchers must not fabricate, falsify, or misrepresent authorship, evidence, data, findings, or conclusions.
- Educational researchers must not knowingly or negligently use their professional roles for fraudulent purposes.
- Educational researchers should attempt to report their findings to all relevant stakeholders, and should refrain from keeping secret or selectively communicating their findings.

There are many grey areas in research where not even the most detailed regulations can prevent some undesirable shortcuts or manipulation. Although the general tenor of this book is meant to be highly practical and pragmatic, this is an area where we must firmly draw the line.

3.2.4 Protection from harm and achieving an equitable cost-benefit balance

The primary principle of research ethics is that no mental or physical harm should come to the respondents as a result of their participation in the investigation. This principle overrides all other considerations. Haverkamp (2005) points out that while the primary mechanisms for protecting participants in quantitative research involve a clear division of roles and the minimization of contact between researcher and participants, these mechanisms are incompatible with the highly relational character of most qualitative research. Thus, in qualitative and mixed methods approaches there is an increased likelihood for the occurrence of 'ethically relevant moments'. At this point we need to reiterate that the abuse of test scores poses a similarly relevant ethical issue in quantitative research. Shohamy (2004), for example, reports an occasion when educational authorities used the achievement test results of a study co-authored by her to justify measures against minority students in a way which did not follow from the investigation. Therefore she warns us that researchers must not view their tasks as complete when the research report or the article is published but must 'follow the uses (and misuses) of their research results' (p. 730).

Not only must we prevent our investigation from causing any harm, but we need to try also to make sure that the participants *benefit* from our research in some way. We should never forget that by spending time and energy helping us they are doing us a favour and it is our responsibility to try to make the cost-benefit balance as equitable as possible. Unfortunately, it is all too common to see a 'slash and burn' research strategy whereby investigators use their participants without offering anything in return and as soon as the data has been gathered they disappear. In some cases saying a warm and salient 'thank you' may be enough; in some other cases we can offer the respondents or the participating teachers/schools some feedback on the results if needed. Some researchers go even further by also offering workshops or little gifts. There are many kind gestures that can work—it really is the thought that counts. And it is so important to observe J. D. Brown's (2001: 87) warning: 'Remember, if you make a promise to send them something, you really must remember to do it'.

3.2.5 Privacy, confidentiality, anonymity, and data storage

It is a basic ethical principle that the respondent's right to privacy should always be respected and that respondents are within their rights to refuse to answer questions or to withdraw from the study completely without offering any explanation. It is also the participants' right to remain anonymous, and if the participant's identity is known to the research group, it is the researcher's moral and professional (and in some contexts legal) obligation to maintain the level of confidentiality that was promised at the onset. These straightforward principles have a number of implications:

- We must make sure that we do not promise a higher degree of confidentiality than what we can achieve, and that the guarantees of confidentiality are carried out fully.
- The right to confidentiality should always be respected when no clear understanding to the contrary has been reached.
- We must make sure—especially with recorded/transcribed data—that the respondents are not traceable or identifiable.

At this point we need to realize that qualitative data can include such intimate, personal details of the participants' life and environment that non-traceability is very hard, or almost impossible, to achieve, even in a reasonably disguised account. In such cases the general recommendation in the literature is that we should alter some key elements of the description, but this can actually go counter to the core striving of qualitative research to capture particularity and context. There is no blanket solution here—each individual case should be considered separately, showing sensitivity and exercising caution.

One particular threat to confidentiality is posed by the storage of data, particularly audio and video recording as well as their transcripts. How can we ensure confidentiality 5–10 years down the line? Once the study is over, there is a danger in academic contexts for storage discipline to slacken or for losing count of the number of copies made, which can result in the data falling into unauthorized hands. This issue is augmented if the research team splits up or if the ownership of the data has not been clearly specified right from the start. The best way to prevent the abuse of data storage is to destroy the data after a while.

3.2.6 Informed consent and the issue of deception

The most salient and most often discussed aspect of research ethics is the issue of informed consent. (For relevant guidelines developed for applied linguistics, see the 'Information for Contributors' section of the journal *TESOL Quarterly*.) If there are regulations governing ethical practice in a country or institution, obtaining written consent from the participants is likely to be the first item on the agenda. In the US, for example, federal regulations not only require written consent from the participants but also require informed consent before a researcher can use an individual's existing records for research purposes (Johnson and Christensen 2004). While nobody would question the significance of the fact that research respondents should be willing participants, gaining informed consent from potential study participants is far from being a straightforward issue. There is quite a bit of controversy about (a) how 'informed' the consent should be—that is, how much information do we need to share with the respondents before asking them to participate; and (b) in what form should the consent be given. These are important questions to consider prior to the research because decisions about the styles and means of obtaining informed consent have an impact on the type of people who are likely to agree to participate (Wiles *et al.* 2005).

How 'informed' should the consent be? Of course, when we ask this question what we really mean is 'how little information is enough to share in order to remain ethical?' The reluctance to reveal too much about the nature of our research is a pragmatic one because certain information can influence or bias the participants' responses and may even make them withdraw from the study. So, we need to achieve a trade-off here and the recommendations concerning the minimal level of informedness found in the literature vary; in exceptional circumstances even deception can be acceptable if certain rules are observed—see below. In accordance with the AERA (2002) guidelines, I believe that in a research study the participants (or their guardians—see below) have the right to be informed about the following points:

- As much as possible about the aims of the investigation and the purpose for which he data will be used.
- The tasks the participants will be expected to perform during the study.
- The possible risks and the potential consequences of participating in the research.
- The extent to which answers will be held confidential.
- The basic right of the participants to withdraw from the study at any point.

Deception

It does not require much justification that sometimes researchers cannot provide full disclosure of the nature and purpose of the study without causing participant bias or even invalidating the study, and in some (rare) cases the researcher needs not only to withhold some information but to actively mislead the participants. An ethnographic study of a criminal subculture would be a good example but even in far less extreme cases certain type of information may influence the results. Accordingly, although the AERA (2002) guidelines emphasize the significance of honesty, they do not forbid any engagement in deception if it is absolutely necessary, provided it is minimized and after the study the participants are briefed about the reasons for the deception. In addition, it goes without saying that the deception must not adversely affect the welfare of the participants. While most researchers would accept these general principles, there is considerable debate in the social science literature about the acceptable level of actual deceit.

Forms of consent and the consent forms

There are two basic forms of consent, active and passive. 'Active' consent involves consenting to participate in a research study by signing a consent form, whereas 'passive' consent involves not opting out or not objecting to the study. The most common example of the latter is to send a consent form to the parents of school children and ask them to return it only if they do not want their child to participate in the research. It is clear that obtaining active consent is more explicit in ensuring that the participants know their rights and it also protects the researcher from any later accusations, but in certain types of educational research it may not be necessary or beneficial: a request for consent in such a formalized manner can be off-putting or can raise undue suspicion that something is not quite right about the study, thereby discouraging people from participating. In addition, signed consent is meaningless for some cultural or age groups. Therefore, while I would ask for active consent in a qualitative interview study, I would consider omitting it and obtaining only passive consent—if this does not contradict any legal regulations in the particular context—in an anonymous questionnaire survey.

A written consent form usually contains the following details (Cohen *et al.* 2000; Creswell 2003; Johnson and Christensen 2004):

- A fair explanation of the purpose of the research and the procedures to be followed.
- A description of any risks or discomforts as well as benefits the participant may encounter/receive.
- A statement of the extent to which the results will be kept confidential.
- A statement indicating that participation is voluntary and the participant can withdraw and refuse to participate at any time with no penalty.

- An offer to answer any questions concerning the procedures and (optionally) to receive a copy of the results.
- Signatures of both the participant and the researcher, agreeing to these provisions.

Additional consent from teachers and parents

Many, if not most, educational studies are conducted within schools or other educational institutes and therefore the researcher may need to obtain additional consent from various authority figures such as teachers, head teachers or principals. In some countries consent must be sought even from the local education authorities.

Additional consent must also be obtained when the research is targeting minors who cannot be regarded as fully mature or being on equal terms with the researcher (Cohen *et al.* 2000). They may not be in a position to represent themselves appropriately, which means that someone else needs to be consulted. The question here is to decide who has sufficient authority in such cases: the legal guardian (for example, parent), the children's teacher(s) or both. In this respect the existing legal and ethical research frameworks differ greatly across countries. It is my view that unless there exist legal requirements stating otherwise and if the research is neither aimed at sensitive information nor involves extensive participant engagement (for example, a relatively neutral anonymous questionnaire), permission to conduct the study can be granted by the children's teachers. Teachers are usually aware of the significance of legal matters and therefore if they have any doubts about who should authorize the project, they will seek advice. And even if parental permission for the research is needed, I would favour passive consent whereby parents are advised about the proposed research and parental permission will be assumed unless the parents object before the proposed starting date.

3.2.7 Concluding remarks on research ethics

My personal conclusion about research ethics is that it should be taken more seriously than many researchers do and at the same time it should be taken less seriously than some legislators do. Possibly because applied linguistic research does not usually pose any obvious threat to the participants, researchers in our field often ignore the significance of ethical issues and research ethics are only mentioned within the context of legal requirements to comply with. The problem with this practice is that it does not provide a firm ethical framework that we can rely on when an ethically difficult situation arises. I hope that the previous discussion has shown clearly that research participants need safeguards and researchers need informed answers to ethical dilemmas.

On the other hand, I agree with those (for example, Johnson and Christensen 2004) who emphasize that in educational research we should not simply import ethical guidelines from other fields (for example, psychology or medical research) where the ethical stakes are much higher. If applied mechanically, ethical codes and regulations can easily become too restrictive; ironically, in the field of applied linguistics the most pressing ethical issue I am aware of is the increasing difficulty of conducting research in certain contexts due to the burgeoning constraints of 'ethical correctness'. Seale *et al.* (2004: 8) are right when they conclude, 'Professional ethical codes for researchers are too often constituted as armchair criticism, distanced from the needs of the research practice'. What we need is a contextualized and flexible approach to ethical decision making, relying more on the researchers' professional reflexivity and integrity in maintaining high standards.

3.3 Research questions and hypotheses

> *... many scientists owe their renown less to their ability to solve problems than to their capacity to select insightful questions for investigation ...*
> (Shavelson and Towne 2002: 55)

Most research texts suggest that the proper way to do research involves first generating one or more research questions and then choosing the design, the method, and the instruments that allow the researcher to find answers to these questions. For example, in discussing the principles of scientific research in education, Shavelson and Towne (2002: 99) explicitly state that 'we have to be true to our admonition that the research question drives the design, not vice versa'. While this is a logical position, many novice researchers will attest to the fact that in reality the research process is not so straightforward and the 'research-question-first' principle leaves several questions open. For example, in an investigation that is primarily exploratory, how can we start out by producing a specific research question when we know relatively little of the topic, which is exactly why we want to research into it? How is the research question related to other frequently mentioned terms such as 'research topic' or 'research hypothesis'? What about qualitative research in which the exact theme and angle of the investigation often emerge only during the project? And finally, what is the optimal research question like? Let us briefly discuss these issues; for a more detailed and very practical discussion of the planning stage of a research project, from the generation of initial ideas to narrowing down the focus so that the project is doable, see Richards (2003: Chapter 5).

3.3.1 Research topic, research purpose, and research questions

Every investigation has a starting point and unless we adopt someone else's (for example, the supervisor's) design idea or join an ongoing investigation as a co-researcher, this starting point is a broad 'research topic'. Initially, this is only a general and rather vague area of research interest (for example, a problem or an intriguing phenomenon that we have noticed) and in order to be able to specifically address it we need to develop it into a 'research purpose'. The research purpose is a relatively short statement (not more than a paragraph) that describes the objective of the planned study, explaining why the investigation is undertaken and what its potential significance is.

The next step towards narrowing down and 'operationalizing' the research purpose is to formulate specific 'research questions'. Their role is to translate the research purpose into specific questions that the planned study will aim to answer. Being able to produce good research questions indicates that the researcher is ready to embark on the actual investigation (whereas vague or missing research questions usually send alarm signals to a supervisor or referee), and good research questions also provide orientation to the research methodology that can best achieve the research purpose—see Chapter 14. We should note here that, as Johnson and Christensen (2004) point out, because in some investigations the research question would be, to a great extent, a restatement of the purpose of the study, some scholars actually omit it from the final research report.

What is a good research question like? As we will see in the next section, there is a difference between effective research questions in QUAL and QUAN studies, but in general, good research questions need to address *interesting* issues. When we have thought of some possible questions, we have to ask ourselves: are they worth asking and, more importantly, answering? I believe that one thing we must try and avoid at all cost is to 'run into a "so what" response to our research' (Mackey and Gass 2005: 17). Therefore, I am in agreement with Gall *et al.*'s (2007: 41) conclusion that 'The imagination and insight that goes into defining the research problem usually determines the ultimate value of a research study more than any other factor'.

Where can we receive the inspiration for good research topics and questions? In my experience, most research topics originate from a combination of reading the literature and one's personal history. From time to time something we read 'rings a bell' and we realize that the topic could be further pursued on the basis of relevant experiences we had in the past. In addition, the Conclusion section of most research articles (see Section 12.4.5) tends to contain suggestions for further research, and discussions with friends, colleagues and students can also be very helpful in drawing our attention to potentially fruitful issues. If you decide to keep a research journal (see Section 6.9), the reflections recorded in the journal may contribute to refining the research questions of an ongoing investigation as well as generating ideas for future research.

Sometimes, when we have a hunch or a learned guess about the possible results of our planned investigation, we can narrow down the research purpose into actual 'research hypotheses' instead of, or besides, questions. These hypotheses are statements that formulate specific predictions about the outcomes and the empirical results will either confirm or refute these. If generating research hypotheses is possible in a study, they are very welcome because they are fully in line with the principles of the 'scientific method'—see Section 2.2.1.

Nunan (1992) makes a useful recommendation about how to operationalize an investigation. He has found that asking postgraduate students to create a 'research outline' can greatly facilitate the planning and fine-tuning of a project. Such an outline consists of a series of headings, and students are to add a short statement after each; the headings can be selected in a flexible way, but they would normally include the general research area, research purpose, research question/hypothesis, as well as data collection method, type of data, participants, type of data analysis, and resources required.

3.3.2 Paradigmatic differences in formulating the research questions

Qualitative and quantitative studies differ considerably in terms of how the purpose of the investigation is specified and how it is broken down into specific research questions. In quantitative studies it is generally true that the more specific the research purpose/question, the better. Thus, good quantitative purpose statements often identify the target variables and the causal or descriptive relationship between them that is to be examined. The research questions, then, specify concrete methodological procedures, and research hypotheses are also drawn up containing the researcher's predictions.

One characteristic feature of qualitative studies is their emergent nature and therefore QUAL research purposes and questions are often inevitably vaguer than their QUAN counterparts. Instead of describing a specific issue or problem, the research purpose often contains only the specification of a situated phenomenon or a central idea that will be explored with the aim of developing new insights and possibly forming a theory in the end. In accordance with this, qualitative research questions tend to be broader than quantitative ones, often focusing on the big picture or the main processes that are thought to shape the target phenomenon—usually it is not possible to be more specific at this stage without limiting the inquiry and, therefore, investigators emphasize the exploratory nature of the study instead.

Mixed methods studies present a challenge in terms of specifying the research purpose and questions because they require seemingly contradictory approaches (being specific and vague/broad at the same time). A good strategy in such studies is to start with an overall purpose statement, followed by a rationale for the specific mixed design applied including the choice of the particular methods, and concluded by separate research objectives and questions for the different research components. Creswell (2003) mentions that one useful model found in mixed methods studies involves moving the specific research questions to the introduction of each phase in the study rather than presenting them all at the beginning.

3.4 Other essentials for launching a study: pilot study, research log, and data management

To conclude this chapter, let me address three essential issues to be considered before launching an investigation: (a) piloting the instruments and the various research procedures; (b) keeping a precise research log; and (c) managing and storing data professionally.

3.4.1 Piloting the research

The gist of this section can be summarized in a short sentence: always pilot your research instruments and procedures before launching your project. Just like theatre performances, a research study also needs a dress rehearsal to ensure the high quality (in terms of reliability and validity) of the outcomes in the specific context. And while this tenet is universally endorsed by research methodologists, my personal experience is that all too often piloting either does not happen or is superficial. There are at least three reasons for this omission: first, researchers may simply not realize the significance of the piloting phase. Second, investigators at the preparation stage are usually eager to get down to data collection and see some results. Third, the piloting phase may not have been scheduled in the timeframe of the project because the researchers did not realize that when properly done, this phase can take several weeks to complete.

Piloting is more important in quantitative studies than in qualitative ones, because quantitative studies rely on the psychometric properties of the research instruments. In a questionnaire survey, for example, if we have not covered a variable by sufficient questionnaire items then this variable simply cannot emerge in the results, no matter how important it may be in the particular context. We will come back to the specific stepwise process of piloting questionnaires in Chapter 5 (in Section 5.2.5) but as a preliminary, let me quote two of the best-known experts of questionnaire design, Sudman and Bradburn (1983: 283):'if you do not have the resources to pilot-test your questionnaire, don't do the study'. Thus, piloting is an essential part of quantitative research and any attempt to shortcut the piloting stage will seriously jeopardize the psychometric quality of the study. Furthermore, my personal experience is that by patiently going through the piloting procedures we can avoid a great deal of frustration and possible extra work later on.

In qualitative studies, as Richards (2005) points out, there is normally no real piloting stage in which the research 'tools' are tested. This does not mean that there is no use in trying out certain techniques (for example, interviewing skills), but QUAL piloting differs from QUAN piloting in that we do not have to discard the obtained data after these 'trial runs' but can use it for the final analysis. These early responses may differ from the ones coming from later stages, but differences are 'food for analysis, not a problem for consistency' (p. 78).

3.4.2 Research log

Past research experience has convinced me that it is essential to start a formal 'research log' right at the start of a research project. Data collection and analysis require us to make decisions on an ongoing basis and unless these are properly documented we are likely to soon forget or mix up some of the details. As with any real logbook, all the entries should be properly dated and the consecutive pages of the logbook should be numbered and kept together in a folder. Alternatively, we can keep an electronic log file in our computer that we regularly update. Such a logbook will not only help to sort out any emerging confusion but will also contain invaluable recorded information that is readily usable during the writing-up stage. Indeed, 'research journals'—that is, extended research logs that also contain memos and personal notes—can be an important source of data in qualitative research (see Section 6.9). In quantitative studies the log has more of an organizing and archiving role, containing a wide variety of information such as: dates, records of meetings, exact details of the piloting and data collection phases (when? who? what?), any emerging problems, records of where and in what form the data is stored and finally, all the relevant details of the data analysis process, including records of the statistical procedures tried out (even the dead ends), as well as the main findings and the names and locations of the computer files which contain the supporting statistics. The logbook might even cover the writing-up phase, keeping details of the various drafts and means of backing them up. This organizing/archiving role is vital because numerical details can get easily mixed up and at such times a detailed record to go back to for orientation becomes literally invaluable. So start logging—now!

3.4.3 Techniques to manage and store data records

The significance of good strategies to manage and store the data is twofold, concerning both logistic and ethical issues. First, it is a challenging task to devise a storing and labelling system which will stop us from losing or mixing up data and which will provide an efficient way of locating and accessing information. Researchers need to make a detailed list of all the data sources in a research log (see previous section), organized according to key parameters (for example, type of data, place of data-gathering) and then need to keep these records up-to-date. Audiotapes, video cassettes and any illustrative documents need to be properly labelled and stored in a secure place, and we also need a transparent system for keeping relevant computer files.

Particularly in qualitative research we can quickly gather masses of rather 'unorderly' data ranging from field notes to documents and of course transcripts. It is difficult to imagine now how we used to manage storage before personal computers became widespread: contemporary data analysis software not only helps to process the data but also provides excellent storage facilities. In any case, it is imperative to follow Davidson's (1996: 267) two laws for handling computer data: 'Law 1: Back it up; Law 2: Do it now'. It is also useful to back up audio and video recordings.

The second aspect of data storage has already been touched upon in Section 3.2.5 when discussing the issue of anonymity. Morse and Richards (2002) advise us that when participant anonymity is required it is important that we create and consistently use a system of pseudonyms or codes both in the transcripts and in the labelling system. The list of linking names and codes should be kept in a safe place along with materials that would make the identification of the participants possible (for example, authentic documents, video recordings, etc.).

In sum, in order to be able to remember where things are and in what form, or what certain file names mean, we need to devise a data managing/storing system right from the beginning. It is all too easy to be a bit slapdash when we are in full swing of data collection, but experience suggests that without a foolproof system things will inevitably end up in places where they are not supposed to be. Research is *disciplined inquiry*, and the need to be disciplined must also apply to the area of data management.

4

Longitudinal versus cross-sectional research

For most researchers, longitudinal research is still an unexplored land: fascinating but dangerous.
(Ruspini 2002: 136–7)

Several high-profile strands in applied linguistics focus on developmental aspects of the individual (for example, on the development of L1 literacy or L2 proficiency) and the study of social change is also a prominent area in the field. This salience of development and change highlights the significance of 'longitudinal research', that is, the ongoing examination of people or phenomena over time. Indeed, Abbuhl and Mackey (in press) regard longitudinal research as one of the most promising research directions for applied linguistics to take. Given this importance, it is rather surprising how little longitudinal research we find in the applied linguistics literature and even the available methodology texts have usually little to say about the subject. This warrants devoting a separate chapter to the topic.

The counterpart of longitudinal research is 'cross-sectional research', which refers to a snapshot-like analysis of the target phenomenon at one particular point in time, focusing on a single time interval. It allows us to establish relationships between variables and to find out about the participants' thoughts, attitudes, and emotions as well as various cognitive and personality traits. The epitome of the cross-sectional study is the national census in which a wide range of data is collected from the whole population within a very narrow time period (Cohen *et al.* 2000). Of course, even census data can be turned longitudinal by linking information gathered in two consecutive censuses.

Contemporary applied linguistic research is dominated by cross-sectional studies (which is also true of educational research in general) and therefore the emphasis in this chapter will be on the less familiar approach, longitudinal research. By describing its main types and by exploring its potential benefits relative to cross-sectional studies I would like to present a strong case for the need to experiment more with longitudinal designs in investigations.

4.1 Definition and purpose of longitudinal research

Longitudinal research is a rather imprecise term that refers to a family of methods that share one thing in common: information is gathered about the target of the research (which can include a wide range of units such as people, households, institutions, nations, or conceptual issues) during a series of points in time. While this may seem like a fairly straightforward definition, it is inaccurate in that we may have a single data gathering session that will yield longitudinal information about change over time (for example, an interview focusing on a person's life history) and we may also have a series of deep interviews that last for several weeks or months and yet do not target change but rather some other complex aspect of the interviewee's perception and interpretation of his/her social environment. Accordingly, several scholars point out that there is not necessarily a one-to-one correspondence between the design of a study and the type of data collected (Menard 2002; Taris 2000).

Thus, longitudinal research must be defined in terms of both the data and the design that are used in the research. According to Menard (2002), a longitudinal investigation is research in which (a) data are collected for two or more distinct time periods; (b) the subjects or cases analysed are the same or are comparable (i.e. drawn from the same population) from one period to the next; and (c) the analysis involves some comparison of data between periods. As he concludes, 'as a bare minimum, any truly longitudinal design would permit the measurement of differences or change in a variable from one period to another' (p. 2).

Longitudinal research serves two primary purposes: to *describe* patterns of change, and to *explain* causal relationships. Although these two aims are interrelated, they do not always coincide because we may obtain precise information about the temporal order of events without detecting any causal connection between these events. As Taris (2000) concludes in his accessible introduction to the subject, in order to be able to identify cause–effect links, we need an explicit theory that explains the causal processes underlying the temporal observations.

We should note at this point that although longitudinal research is rather underutilized in our field, it is quite established in some other disciplines within the social sciences. For example, in economics the use of longitudinal data is essential for examining various aspects of economic change (for example, the change of the rate of inflation or the Gross Domestic Product index) and relevant economic information is gathered at very frequent and regular intervals. There are also several ongoing large-scale 'household surveys' in many countries, documenting changes in patterns of social behaviour across nationally representative samples, usually on a yearly basis. In contrast, in the typical practice of longitudinal research in education and applied linguistics, the usual number of data collection points (also called the 'phases' or 'waves' of the study) is much smaller, often only two or three, with the amount of time between the waves being anything from a few weeks to as much as a decade.

Finally, it is also important to point out that longitudinal research has traditionally been associated with the quantitative paradigm, aiming at providing statistical pictures of wider social trends. As Neale and Flowerdew (2003) explain, in such studies societies are studied from the social structure 'downwards' rather than from the individual or personal network 'upwards'. According to these authors, this methodology, then, offers

> a bird's eye view of social life that is panoramic in scope but lacking in any detail. It is an epic movie, offering a grand narrative and herein lies its value, but it is a movie in which the intricacies of the plot and the fluid twists and turns of the individual story lines are hidden from view. (p. 192)

Recently, however, there has been a move in the social sciences to make longitudinal qualitative research more prominent. The distinctiveness of such studies is given by the interplay of the temporal and cultural dimensions of social life, offering a 'bottom-up' understanding of how people move through time and craft the transition processes. Thus, the qualitative movie offers us 'a "close up" of the fabric of real lives as opposed to the quantitative "long shot". The focus is on the plot and detailed story lines of the key actors rather than the grand vistas of the epic picture' (Neale and Flowerdew 2003: 193). Section 4.4 discusses this qualitative movement in some detail and Section 4.5 highlights the fact that longitudinal research also lends itself to mixed methods studies.

4.2 Longitudinal research in applied linguistics

In an insightful study written a decade ago, Mellow *et al.* (1996) argued forcefully that transition theories focusing on the developmental course of language over time are a central aspect of SLA research and that their effective study requires longitudinal research methods such as a time-series design. Mellow *et al.*'s conclusion was reiterated in a recent overview of longitudinal research in SLA by Ortega and Iberri-Shea (2005), who asserted that because language learning happens through and over time, many, if not all, topics about L2 learning that SLA researchers investigate can be most meaningfully interpreted only within a full longitudinal perspective. As they concluded, 'Ultimately, it is through cumulative longitudinal findings that the SLA research community would be able to contribute meaningful characterizations of the gradual process of attaining advanced second language and literacy competencies across various contexts' (p. 28). However, the theoretical centrality of time in SLA research, as the authors pointed out, is in stark contrast with the fact that discussions about longitudinal research are scarce in our field.

Although I am in agreement with Ortega and Iberri-Shea's (2005) conclusion that there is a dearth of principled and professionally executed longitudinal studies in applied linguistic research, if we look at the field more closely, the time element is actually present in many areas. We find, for example, several poststructuralist qualitative investigations, usually framed within sociocultural or language socialization theory, that display longitudinal ethnographic designs (for example, Pavlenko 2002); in fact, both ethnography and case study research emphasize prolonged engagement with the participants (see Sections 6.3 and 6.7), making them inherently longitudinal. However, Ortega and Iberri-Shea are right in pointing out that many of the studies born in this vein are not centred around explicitly formulated longitudinal research goals. A similar situation exists in quantitative research because the common research type, according to Ortega and Iberri-Shea, is the small-scale descriptive quantitative design, without employing any inferential statistics. Thus, we have many 'longitudinal-like' investigations in both paradigms that are simply not designed, conducted and analysed according to modern longitudinal principles. As we will see later in this chapter (in Sections 4.4 and 4.7), this is partly caused by the undeniable fact that to do longitudinal data analysis full justice is no easy task.

Perhaps the most successful area of longitudinal research in applied linguistics has been the investigation of L2 instructional effectiveness using experimental and (more often) quasi-experimental designs—see Section 5.3. However, as Ortega and Iberri-Shea (2005) suggest, even in this area the picture is not entirely rosy because researchers do not seem to take advantage of time-series designs that could enhance the effectiveness of such studies. (For a discussion, see Section 4.7.) The principles of this design and its relevance to SLA were laid out by Mellow *et al.* (1996) a decade ago and yet in their review of the literature Ortega and Iberri-Shea were able to identify only one recent study adopting it.

4.3 Main types of longitudinal designs

The classic longitudinal design involves taking a group of people and following their development by multiple investigations over a period of time. This design is usually labelled a 'panel study' but it is not the only way of gathering empirical data about change. There are as many as three other well-known longitudinal approaches and in many cases they may be more appropriate (and cheaper!) than the panel study. Let us look at the four main design types in some detail. Although the units of measurement in longitudinal studies can be institutions, peoples or nations, longitudinal research is typically targeting people and in the following descriptions I will refer only to human subjects.

4.3.1 Prospective longitudinal studies or 'panel studies'

The design type in which successive measures are taken at different points in time from the same respondents has been called different names, for example 'prospective longitudinal study', 'follow-up study', 'cohort study', or 'panel study', with the latter becoming the standard label. The term was originally coined in the US in the 1940s by sociologist Paul Lazarsfeld when he was studying the long-term marketing effects of radio advertising. The main reason for the popularity of the panel study is the fact that it allows us to collect information about change at the micro level as it really happens. To illustrate the importance of this, let us consider two successive opinion polls regarding two competing political parties, A and B, which examine—unlike a panel study—different samples of the population. Even if the results show that the popularity of Party A increased over time, we cannot tell from the data whether this was a uniform shift from Party B to Party A or whether some people actually changed from Party A to Party B but they were outnumbered by others who changed from Party B to Party A. Thus, successive opinion polls, which are technically speaking 'repeated surveys' (to be discussed below), capture only 'net change', that is, the net effect of all the changes (Firebaugh 1997), whereas proper panel designs enable researchers to observe all the specific changes across time (i.e. it would capture the actual rate of party switching among individuals in our example). Thus, panel studies offer a powerful nonexperimental method for examining development and causality.

Unfortunately, panel studies are rather expensive and time consuming to run, and they also require a committed research team maintained over years. In addition, these designs also suffer from two serious threats to their validity: 'attrition' and 'panel conditioning'.

- *Attrition* The usual pattern of participation in a long-term panel study is that an increasing number of participants drop out of the panel in the successive waves. There can be multiple reasons for this attrition (or 'mortality'); there may be, for example, logistic ones (non-availability, changing address or telephone number, etc.), or panel members may become ill or simply unwilling to continue because of a lack of time or loss of interest. Such attrition is cumulative because once someone has missed a data collection wave, that person is lost for the remainder of the study (Taris 2000). Thus, in a panel study the sample with a full dataset can decrease significantly, and, more worrying from a validity perspective, the reduction may not be random. That is, it may be certain types of participants who give up early or, to turn it round, who stick to the study to the end. The final sample may, therefore, offer a biased representation of the original sample and the population. With proper tracing and staying-in-touch strategies (ranging from sending Christmas cards and research updates to regular telephone contact) the rate of non-response can be reduced but these efforts require substantial human and financial resources. (For a detailed account, see Thomson and Holland 2003.) In education research, panel studies can be particularly difficult to conduct because of the frequent changes in class and staff composition as well as teaching methodology.

- *Panel conditioning* The second problem concerns the fact that when a group of people take part in a longitudinal study, there is a real danger that the regular meetings that the participation involves and the knowledge of being part of the study can alter the panel members' behaviour and responses. They may, for example, lose their inhibition about the data collection format, or the experience of having to focus on certain issues in their lives raises their awareness of, or sensitivity to, these issues. Alternatively, they may also behave differently because they want to please the researchers whom they are getting to know better and better. Thus, the resulting 'panel conditioning' effect can be seen as a combination of 'practice effect' and the 'Hawthorne effect'—see Section 3.1.1.

4.3.2 Repeated cross-sectional studies or 'trend studies'

A popular way of obtaining information about change is by administering repeated questionnaire surveys to different samples of respondents. If the subsequent waves examine samples that are representative of the same population, then the results can be seen to carry longitudinal information at the aggregate level (i.e. for the whole group rather than for the individuals). Such repeated cross-sectional studies are usually called 'trend studies' and if our research topic concerns macro-level aspects of social change (for example, looking at a whole community's evolving beliefs or practices), this level of analysis is appropriate. Furthermore, the design also makes it possible to investigate and compare changes in various subsamples (for example, males and females, ethnic groups, etc.).

Trend studies are not merely 'second best' longitudinal studies—although individual development cannot be traced in them, they have certain advantages over panel studies. First of all, they are usually cheaper and easier to arrange and conduct, which is partly due to the fact that the respondents can remain anonymous and partly that organizing a new sample tends to be simpler than tracking down the participants of the previous survey. A further advantage is that trend studies do not suffer from attrition or conditioning and each wave can be made representative of the population. There is a downside, however: the macro perspective which is characteristic of their design is not particularly suited to resolve issues of causal order or to study developmental patterns (Taris 2000).

A further problem might be caused by the fact that in order to ensure the comparability of the measurements across time, we need to use the same questionnaire in all the waves of the study. However, educational systems and curricula are rarely static for long periods and therefore the further the study gets from the initial phase, the more likely it becomes that some parts of the questionnaire employed will not address the target issues appropriately or that some newly emerging areas will be neglected (Keeves 1994). When we initially design the instrument to be used we may not know what trends we are going to detect and therefore the questionnaire may not be fully suitable for analysing the specific factors associated with it—yet, we cannot change the instrument without compromising its longitudinal capacity.

4.3.3 Retrospective longitudinal studies

A major deterrent of both panel and trend studies is the fact that we have to wait a considerable period of time before we can see results. 'Retrospective longitudinal studies' offer a way around this delay, although not without a cost. Retrospective longitudinal data are gathered during a single investigation in which respondents are asked to think *back* and answer questions about the past. This may sound like a straightforward idea that can save us a lot of time and money but, unfortunately, past retrospective research has revealed that the quality of the recollected data can be very uneven: as much as 50 per cent of the responses may be incorrect or inaccurate in some way (Taris 2000); the retrospective accounts can be simplified or selective, with some important details omitted, suppressed, or simply wrong. Furthermore, by looking at the past through tinted glasses (which we often do) the reconstruction of the participants' experiences might be distorted and past feelings and events might be reinterpreted to match subsequent events or the respondents' current perceptions, or simply to fit some coherent storyline. As a result, retrospective data tends to be more unreliable than prospective data and it is often difficult to separate real from perceived or putative causes (Cohen *et al.* 2000). On the other hand, if our study focuses on a relatively short period (weeks or months rather than years), a retrospective design may be appropriate, especially if the data concerns primarily events or behaviour rather than attitudes or beliefs (Ruspini 2002).

4.3.4 Simultaneous cross-sectional studies

The fourth design introduced here, the 'simultaneous cross-sectional study', is only partially longitudinal, because it does not involve the examination of change over time but rather across age groups. Within this design a cross-sectional survey is conducted with different age groups sampled (for example, investigating four different years in a school). Taris (2000) points out that, in effect, most surveys might be considered an example of this design since nearly all investigations gather some information about the respondents' age. However, in a simultaneous cross-sectional study the respondents' age is the key sampling variable, whereas in 'ordinary' cross-sectional designs age is just another variable to be controlled.

This design is straightforward and economical, and because it yields data about changes across age groups, it can be used to examine developmental issues. One problem, however, is that it measures different cohorts, and the observed changes may not be due to the age difference but to the special experiences of a cohort (which are usually referred to as the 'cohort effects'). Furthermore, similar to trend studies, we need to administer the same questionnaire to all the different subgroups, which may mean that we have to devise generic items that cannot be too age-specific.

4.3.5 Other longitudinal designs

The four basic design types mentioned above have been combined in some ingenious ways to remedy some of the weaknesses inherent to the specific approaches (Ruspini 2002): in 'rotating panels' a certain proportion of the sample is replaced at each wave to correct composition distortions due to attrition or to match the sample to the changing population; such surveys thus combine the features of both panel and repeated cross-sectional studies. 'Split panels' also combine longitudinal and cross-sectional designs by including a 'classic' panel which is accompanied by an additional rotating sample surveyed alongside. This extra group is investigated only once and is therefore not exposed to panel conditioning. 'Linked' or 'administrative panels' are created arbitrarily from existing data which has not been originally collected for longitudinal purposes but which contain identification codes (usually names accompanied by dates and places of birth) that allow the participants to be matched with other data obtained from them (for example, census data).

A further temporal design is the 'cohort study', which is somewhere in between a panel and a trend study: it involves the ongoing investigation of a birth cohort (i.e. the set of people who were born in the same year), but instead of examining each member of the sample in each wave (as the panel study does), a series of repeated cross-sectional surveys are administered to selective members each time. Cohort studies can also incorporate retrospective elements.

Collins (2006) describes an interesting method of obtaining prospective-like data in less time: in the 'accelerated longitudinal design' multiple cohorts of different ages are observed longitudinally for a shorter period of time. The idea is that if the cohorts are slightly overlapping, we can statistically combine the cohorts and estimate a single growth trajectory, extending from the youngest age observed to the oldest.

'Experimental research' (see Section 5.3) is also a type of a panel study in which part of the sample is exposed to some treatment, intervention, manipulation, or some planned learning experience. The study seeks to find out whether or not these participants experienced a change that was different in direction or magnitude from any change experienced by the rest of the sample who did not receive any treatment. Indeed, Johnson and Christensen (2004) argue that when the researcher's objective is to study cause and effect, a panel study with some sort of manipulation can be seen as a more powerful version of the ordinary panel design. One way of achieving this is by applying an 'interrupted time-series design'. As Johnson and Christensen describe, in this design a single group of participants is pre-tested a number of times *before* the treatment (i.e. during the 'baseline phase') and then multiple post-test measures are taken at various points *during* the treatment. If there is a treatment effect, it will be reflected by the differing patterns of the pre-test versus the post-test responses. This discontinuity could be manifested by a change in the level of the pre-test and post-test responses (for example, a change in the slope or direction of the evolving scores).

Finally, 'diary studies', described in Section 6.8, are also inherently longitudinal as they contain data recorded over time.

4.4 Longitudinal qualitative research

Qualitative research studies have often employed longitudinal elements in the past, for example when informants were re-interviewed, research sites revisited or more generally through the researcher's sustained engagement with the project. However, as Thomson *et al.* (2003) explain in the introduction to a special issue of the *International Journal of Social Research Methodology*, 'longitudinal qualitative research' is a distinct new methodological strand because it includes a featured temporal component in the research design to make change a central focus of analytic attention. Thus, the authors conclude, such studies are longitudinal by both design and default.

In principle, designing longitudinal qualitative studies is relatively easy: all we need to do is take one of the quantitative longitudinal designs described earlier and replace the QUAN data collection component with a QUAL method (for example, the questionnaire survey with a qualitative interview). Of course, cross-sectional representativeness is unlikely to be achieved because of the inevitably smaller sample sizes that characterize qualitative research (see Section 2.3.2), but qualitative panel or qualitative retrospective studies are straightforward to devise. Such investigations offer great potential: by placing a participant's accounts and interpretations in a temporal context and reading the responses obtained at different phases of the investigation against each other, a complex and varied picture can be built up that cuts across moods and life stages (McLeod 2003). The individual's story can be understood in terms of individualized notions of *turning points* or *defining moments*, like a movie with an intricate plot that is a true reflection of the twists and turns of the individual story line (Neale and Flowerdew 2003).

If this is so, why have there been so few explicitly longitudinal qualitative investigations to date? (For exceptions, though, see longitudinal case studies in Section 6.7.) Besides the factors that work generally against both qualitative studies and longitudinal research, there are two specific deterrents: (a) the complexity of qualitative data analysis and (b) the increased impact of panel conditioning.

4.4.1 The complexity of qualitative data analysis

As described in Chapter 10, well-conducted qualitative data analysis can be highly complex even without adding a temporal dimension to it. In a detailed and enlightening description of the analytical procedures of a large-scale longitudinal study, Thomson and Holland (2003) admit that adding to the synchronic dimension the temporal element made the data management and analysis highly labour-intensive, to the point that it seemed at times 'intimidating'. In order to do justice to both the breadth and the depth of the data, individual narrative analyses were undertaken by the interviewers shortly after each interview and at the end of each round of interviewing a 'summary narrative analysis' was written. In addition, after the third wave of interviews the researchers drew together the three narrative analyses for each participant to produce a 'case profile', tracing changes and continuities in their narratives over time, thereby adding a prominent diachronic angle. The final interpretations were drawn from the synthesis of the summary narrative analyses and the case profiles. As the authors acknowledge, keeping up this writing schedule was a struggle.

According to Thomson and Holland (2003), ongoing longitudinal investigations also raise the question of when exactly it is appropriate to start making interpretations and writing up the results. After all, there is no real closure of analysis and the next round of data can substantially modify the interpretations. This open-ended nature of the research challenges the authority and stability of the interpretations and the authors reported that by examining the researchers' contemporaneous observations they did indeed observe shifts in their provisional interpretations. As Thomson and Holland concluded, this absence of analytic closure turned out to be the most challenging aspect of their analysis because the new rounds of data always threatened to render the previous interpretations redundant.

4.4.2 Increased panel conditioning

The problematic effects of panel conditioning have already been mentioned with regard to quantitative panel studies. However, the gravity of this issue is much bigger in qualitative studies because of the more intimate relationship between researcher and respondent. A longitudinal qualitative study involves 'journeying together' and Thomson and Holland (2003) point out that in their project they became increasingly aware of the impact of this relationship not only on the respondent but also on the researcher. The normative effects of the repeat interview procedure is thus a very serious threat to the validity of the research.

4.5 Longitudinal mixed designs

We saw in Section 4.3.5 that in order to increase the strengths and reduce the weaknesses of certain longitudinal inquiry types, various creative longitudinal designs combine aspects of cross-sectional and panel studies, thus involving an extensive and an intensive research component. The extensive element is typically quantitative and the intensive component lends itself to qualitative research; accordingly, Neale and Flowerdew (2003) argue that the QUAL and QUAN traditions of longitudinal research are complementary. While I believe that this is true in theory, currently there is a marked imbalance in the social sciences between the relative weight given to these two paradigms, with quantitative studies being dominant. However, because longitudinal studies are inherently concerned both with the micro- and macro-levels of development and change (for example, individual growth and community change), the mixing of approaches is theoretically warranted. In addition, the sheer complexity of various dynamic change patterns also suggests that a combination of qualitative and quantitative methods might be appropriate to do a longitudinal analysis full justice. For these reasons, in their overview of longitudinal SLA research, Ortega and Iberri-Shea (2005) encouraged longitudinal research that capitalizes on the strengths of mixed methods designs.

4.6 Choosing a design: longitudinal or cross-sectional?

Which type of analysis should we prefer: longitudinal or cross-sectional? Given the preponderance of cross-sectional research in applied linguistics (and in the social sciences in general), the fact is that most researchers tend to decide against a longitudinal approach. From a practical and economic point of view it is easy to see why this happens: longitudinal studies take a long time to produce any meaningful results and therefore they may not be appropriate for research students or academics on fixed contracts. Even scholars whose positions are stable are usually under pressure to produce short-term results in the 'publish or perish' spirit of our time. It does not help either that longitudinal projects would need long-term funding to keep the research teams in place, whereas few research grants worldwide cover periods longer than one or two years. Thus, given the multiple pressures and commitments most academics are typically under, as well as the lack of any salient incentives and support structures, nobody can really be blamed for taking the 'easier' way out and conducting a cross-sectional study. After all, one can also produce valuable results in synchronic investigations and by doing so one can possibly have a research report completed and accepted for publication within a year.

Besides the issue of the duration of the project, cross-sectional research offers some further advantages. It is usually easier to recruit respondents on a one-off basis and such designs do not require the considerable cost and energy to keep in touch with the participants over a sustained period. We do not have to worry about panel conditioning or attrition effects either, and the analysis of cross-sectional data is usually less demanding than longitudinal data analysis. Finally, in a cross-sectional study, we are less exposed to the detrimental impact of unforeseen external events that are beyond our control. Thus, as Ruspini (2002) summarizes, longitudinal research can be rightfully seen as a risky 'luxury' that many of us cannot afford.

My general concern with the above arguments is that even though running a several-year-long panel study with a substantial sample may indeed be beyond the means of most researchers, there are several meaningful longitudinal elements that can be added to a research design that do not require huge investments of time or energy. For example, retrospective and simultaneous longitudinal studies require only a single wave of data collection; trend studies can produce meaningful results already after the first phase (because then they can be seen as an 'ordinary' cross-sectional survey); and even panel studies do not necessarily have to take ages—in applied linguistics it might be highly interesting to analyse the micro-processes that occur during, say, a 10-week language course. In short, I have the feeling that when it comes to longitudinal research, where there is a will, there is a way. So the real question is this: when is it more appropriate to use a longitudinal than a cross-sectional design?

In his influential book on longitudinal research, Menard (2002) argues that longitudinal research should be seen as the default when we intend to examine any dynamic processes in the social sciences. Such dynamic processes are obviously involved in human learning/growth or social change, but they can also be associated with various interactions of different levels of an issue (for example, micro or macro) or of different types of variables (for example, learner traits and learning task characteristics). The truth is that there are few (if any) areas in applied linguistics that do not contain some dynamic elements. This would suggest that in many cases a longitudinal design would be more suitable for an investigation than a cross-sectional one and with some research topics adding a temporal dimension to the study would be indispensable.

Cross-sectional research remains useful to describe variables and patterns of relationships as they exist at a particular time. Although such designs are usually inappropriate for establishing cause–effect relationships, sophisticated multivariate statistical procedures (and especially structural equation modelling; see Section 9.10.4) can extend the scope of the possible results obtained from the analysis of cross-sectional data and can even test theoretical models that contain directional paths between the variables. Furthermore, cross-sectional data is also used to compare various groups of people (for example, men and women or intermediate and advanced learners) and it can even compare age groups adequately. Thus, it would be an exaggeration to claim that cross-sectional research is merely a second-best alternative to longitudinal designs. Yet, Menard (2002: 80) is right when he concludes that 'longitudinal research can, in principle, do much that cross-sectional research cannot, but that there is little or nothing that cross-sectional research can, in principle, do that longitudinal research cannot'.

4.7 Quantitative longitudinal data analysis

For most researchers the main deterrent of quantitative longitudinal research is likely to be the complexity of the data analysis required. Change can happen in very different forms and we need different analytical procedures to examine gradual/linear change and curvilinear change, let alone patterns that are more complex than these. Some theoretical models, for example, postulate that there is a discontinuity in continuous change; in other words, there is a distinct change point at which growth accelerates, slows down or levels off —see Collins 2006. And what about growth patterns in which two (or more) changing variables interfere with each other in a systematic way (for example, unemployment and inflation, or to give an applied linguistic example, L2 proficiency and attitudes towards integration/acculturation)? Indeed, the variety of patterns of longitudinal change is wide and, for example, in their study of time-series designs in SLA research, Mellow *et al.* (1996) outline ten possible different learning curves of individuals in response to language instruction. Thus, in order to do quantitative longitudinal data justice, we need to match a theoretical model of change with a corresponding statistical model. As Ortega and Iberri-Shea (2005) report, this is an area where applied linguists have by and large fallen short of the mark because they have typically used descriptive statistics and visual displays to analyse longitudinal data instead of appropriate statistical models.

Regrettably, currently there is no generic statistical procedure for analysing longitudinal change and if we have more than two waves of data collection we cannot avoid using highly advanced statistical techniques such as repeated measures analysis, loglinear analysis or time-series analysis, to name the most well-known methods. (For a recent overview, see Collins 2006.) A further difficulty is posed by the fact that the most cutting-edge statistical procedures are not included in the popular statistical packages such as SPSS or SAS but have to be purchased separately. In spite of these difficulties, in their overview of longitudinal research in SLA, Ortega and Iberri-Shea (2005) highlight the need for applied linguists to become familiar with modern longitudinal analytical procedures. As they conclude,

> In the future more SLA researchers may seek to map the L2 developmental path of a cohort transiting through curricular and instructional time with key turning points, different phases of stagnation and differently-paced development, and nonlinear progress. If this is the case, and more large-size longitudinal quantitative studies are conducted in SLA, it will be important to train ourselves in the use of statistical analytical options that are available specifically for use with longitudinal designs and data. (p. 41)

The description of these specialized statistical options is beyond the scope of this book so here I offer only a general overview for orientation. Menard (2002) provides a rough classification of methods of longitudinal data analysis along two dimensions, the number of cases in our sample and the number of time periods the sample has been assessed at. This simple system offers a good starting point in deciding what kind of analysis we need. Let us examine the two design options that are most relevant to applied linguists who would like to launch a longitudinal investigation:

- *Time series analysis* examines only a few cases (often even a single case) but many assessment points (usually over 20) and the primary interest is in finding patterns of change in individual cases and generalizing the findings across time periods rather than across cases. (See the description of 'interrupted time series analysis' in Section 4.3.5.) Such designs are particularly suited to analysing language development (Mellow *et al.* 1996) and SPSS offers several options for creating and examining time series models (ANALYSE → TIME SERIES), including 'ARIMA' analysis (ANALYSE → TIME SERIES → ARIMA), which has become increasingly popular in the social sciences (Menard 2002).
- The opposite of time series design is a common design in applied linguistic research that involves a large sample (N > 100) and few data periods (preferably not more than three). Data derived from such designs can be analysed by means of 'repeated measures analysis', which is supported by SPSS (ANALYSE → GENERAL LINEAR MODEL → REPEATED MEASURES). The use of 'structural equation modelling' (SEM; see 9.10.4) offers increased flexibility in analysing the results of repeated measures designs (or in SEM terms 'latent growth curved models') as it can handle more than three (up to about seven) time periods.

Although even the basic longitudinal procedures described above may seem too technical for many researchers, longitudinal data analysis is not all bad news: Taris (2000) points out that one of the great virtues of repeated measures data is that it can conveniently be displayed in easy-to-interpret plots on which time is represented on the horizontal axis and the target variable on the vertical axis. Such plots or line diagrams provide a clear visual representation of the underlying trends and help to generate specific hypotheses that can then be tested. With such specific ideas in mind it might be easier to invite expert help to run the necessary statistics.

PART TWO
Data collection

5
Quantitative data collection

Quantitative data can be obtained in a number of ways. The most common instrument used for this purpose is the test, which has several types (for example, language tests or psychological tests such as aptitude tests or personality batteries). As mentioned in Chapter 1, language testing is a complex and highly specialized issue with an extensive literature, and therefore it would go beyond the scope of this book to cover it. A second form of producing quantitative data is to measure some phenomenon objectively by controlled means (for example, assessing response time or behavioural frequency), and we can also quantify data that was originally collected in a non-quantitative way. (This will be discussed in Chapter 10, when we look at mixed methods data analysis.) Finally, a frequent method of collecting quantitative data is through conducting a survey using some sort of a questionnaire. Indeed, besides language tests, questionnaires are the most common data collection instruments in applied linguistics and therefore the bulk of this chapter will be devoted to their description.

In order to achieve a broad understanding of quantitative methods, we need to cover three further topics besides the questionnaire survey: the first one is the different ways of sampling participants to ensure that the results are generalizable. The second topic concerns experimental and quasi-experimental studies, which represent a special research design of data collection and participant manipulation that has been developed—following the model of experiments in the natural sciences—to produce a method of establishing cause–effect relationships. Finally, the chapter will conclude with a section addressing the new and increasingly popular phenomenon of collecting data via the Internet.

5.1 Sampling in quantitative research

The most frequent question asked by novice researchers before starting a quantitative investigation is 'How many people do I need to include in my study?' In measurement terms this question can be rephrased as 'How large should my sample be?' And the second question to follow is usually, 'What sort of people shall I select?'—in other words, 'Who shall my sample consist of?' These questions reflect the recognition that in empirical research issues concerning the participant sample can fundamentally determine the success of a study. Furthermore, it is also clear that in quantitative research sampling decisions must be taken early in the overall planning process because they will considerably affect the necessary initial arrangements, the timing and scheduling of the project as well as the various costs involved. Let us start our discussion by defining the three concepts that lie at the heart of quantitative sampling: *sample, population*, and the notion of *representativeness*.

5.1.1 Sample, population, and representativeness

The *sample* is the group of participants whom the researcher actually examines in an empirical investigation and the *population* is the group of people whom the study is about. For example, the population in a study might be EFL learners in Taiwanese secondary schools and the actual sample might involve three Taiwanese secondary classes. That is, the target population of a study consists of all the people to whom the survey's findings are to be applied or generalized.

A good sample is very similar to the target population in its most important general characteristics (for example, age, gender, ethnicity, educational background, academic capability, social class, or socioeconomic status) as well as all the more specific features that are known to be related to the variables that the study focuses on (for example, L2 learning background or the amount and type of L2 instruction received). That is, the sample is a subset of the population that is *representative* of the whole population. The issue of representativeness is crucial, because as Milroy and Gordon (2003) along with many other scholars point out, the strength of the conclusions we can draw from the results obtained from a selected small group depends on how accurately the particular sample represents the larger population.

Why don't we include every member of the population in a study? This is a valid question and, indeed, there is one particular survey type which does just that: the 'census'. In most other cases, however, investigating the whole population is not necessary and would in fact be a waste of resources. By adopting appropriate *sampling procedures* to select a smaller number of people to be investigated we can save a considerable amount of time, cost, and effort and can still come up with accurate results—opinion polls, for example, succeed in providing national projections based on as few as 1,000–3,000 respondents. The key question, then, is what exactly we mean by 'appropriate sampling procedures'?

5.1.2 Sampling procedures

Broadly speaking, sampling strategies can be divided into two groups: (a) scientifically sound 'probability sampling', which involves complex and expensive procedures that are usually well beyond the means of applied linguists, and (b) 'non-probability sampling', which consists of a number of strategies that try to achieve a trade-off, that is, a reasonably representative sample using resources that are within the means of the ordinary researcher.

Probability sampling

Probability sampling is a generic term used for a number of scientific procedures, the most important of which are the following:

- *Random sampling* The key component of probability sampling is 'random sampling'. This involves selecting members of the population to be included in the sample on a completely random basis, a bit like drawing numbers from a hat (for example, by numbering each member and then asking the computer to generate random numbers). The assumption underlying this procedure is that the selection is based entirely on probability and chance, thus minimizing the effects of any extraneous or subjective factors. As a result, a sufficiently large sample should contain subjects with characteristics similar to the population as a whole. Although this is rarely fully achieved, the rule of thumb is that random samples are almost always more representative than non-random samples.
- *Stratified random sampling* Combining random sampling with some form of rational grouping is a particularly effective method for research with a specific focus. In 'stratified random sampling' the population is divided into groups, or 'strata', and a random sample of a proportionate size is selected from each group. Thus, if we want to apply this strategy, first we need to identify a number of parameters of the wider population that are important from the point of view of the research in a 'sampling frame'—an obvious example would be a division of males and females—and then select participants for each category on a random basis. A stratified random sample is, therefore, a combination of randomization and categorization. In studies following this method, the population is usually stratified on more than one variable and random samples are selected from all the groups defined by the intersections of the various strata (for example, we would sample female learners of Spanish, aged 13–14, who attend a particular type of instructional programme in a particular location).
- *Systematic sampling* In anonymous surveys it can be difficult to make a random selection because we may have no means of identifying the participants in advance and thus their names cannot be 'put in the hat' (Cohen *et al.* 2000). A useful technical shortcut is in such cases to apply 'systematic sampling', which involves selecting every *n*th member of the target group.

- *Cluster sampling* One way of making random sampling more practical, especially when the target population is widely dispersed, is to randomly select some larger groupings or units of the populations (for example, schools) and then examine all the students in those selected units.

It is clear from these brief descriptions that selecting a truly representative sample is a painstaking and costly process, and several highly technical monographs have been written about the topic (for example, Cochran 1977; Levy and Lemeshow 1999). However, it needs to be reiterated that in most applied linguistic research it is unrealistic or simply not feasible to aim for perfect representativeness in the psychometric sense.

Non-probability sampling

Most actual research in applied linguistics employs 'non-probability samples'. In qualitative research such purposive, non-representative samples may not be seen as a problem (see Section 6.2), but in quantitative research, which always aims at representativeness, non-probability samples are regarded as less-than-perfect compromises that reality forces upon the researcher. We can distinguish three main non-probabilistic sampling strategies:

- *Quota sampling* and *dimensional sampling* 'Quota sampling' is similar to proportional stratified random sampling without the 'random' element. That is, we start off with a sampling frame and then determine the main proportions of the subgroups defined by the parameters included in the frame. The actual sample, then, is selected in a way as to reflect these proportions, but within the weighted subgroups no random sampling is used but rather the researcher meets the quotas by selecting participants he/she can have access to. For example, if the sampling frame in a study of 300 language learners specifies that 50 per cent of the participants should come from bilingual and the other 50 per cent from monolingual families, the researcher needs to recruit 150 participants from each group but the selection does not have to be random. 'Dimensional sampling' is a variation of quota sampling: the researcher makes sure that at least one representative of every combination of the various parameters in the sampling frame is included in the sample.

- *Snowball sampling* This involves a 'chain reaction' whereby the researcher identifies a few people who meet the criteria of the particular study and then asks these participants to identify further appropriate members of the population. This technique is useful when studying groups whose membership is not readily identifiable (for example, teenage gang members) or when access to suitable group members is difficult for some reason.

- *Convenience or opportunity sampling* The most common sample type in L2 research is the 'convenience' or 'opportunity sample', where an important criterion of sample selection is the convenience of the researcher: members of the target population are selected for the purpose of the study if they meet certain practical criteria, such as geographical proximity, availability at a certain time, easy accessibility, or the willingness to volunteer. Captive audiences such as students in the researcher's own institution are prime examples of convenience samples. To be fair, convenience samples are rarely completely convenience-based but are usually partially purposeful, which means that besides the relative ease of accessibility, participants also have to possess certain key characteristics that are related to the purpose of the investigation. Thus, convenience sampling often constitutes a less controlled version of the quota sampling strategy described above.

No matter how principled a non-probability sample strives to be, the extent of generalizability in this type of sample is often negligible. It is therefore surprising that the majority of empirical research in the social sciences is not based on random samples. However, Kemper *et al.*'s (2003: 273–4) conclusion is very true:

> Sampling issues are inherently practical. Scholarly decisions may be driven in part by theoretical concerns, but it is in sampling, perhaps more than anywhere else in research, that theory meets the hard realities of time and resources. ... Sampling issues almost invariably force pragmatic choices.

In any case, because of the compromised nature of non-probability sampling we need to describe in sufficient detail the limitations of such samples when we report the results, while also highlighting the characteristics that the particular sample shares with the defined target population. In a similar vein, we also have to be particularly careful about the claims we make about the more general relevance of our findings.

5.1.3 How large should the sample be?

When researchers ask the question, 'How large should the sample be?' what they really mean is 'How small a sample can I get away with?' Therefore, the often quoted 'the larger, the better' principle is singularly unhelpful for them. Unfortunately, there are no hard and fast rules in setting the optimal sample size; the final answer to the 'how large/small?' question should be the outcome of the researcher considering several broad guidelines:

- *Rules of thumb* In the survey research literature a range of between one per cent to ten per cent of the population is usually mentioned as the magic sampling fraction, with a minimum of about 100 participants. However, the more scientific the sampling procedures, the smaller the sample size can be, which is why opinion polls can produce accurate predictions from samples as small as 0.1 per cent of the population. The following rough estimates of sample sizes for specific types of quantitative methods have also been agreed on by several scholars: correlational research—at least 30 participants; comparative and experimental procedures—at least 15 participants in each group; factor analytic and other multivariate procedures—at least 100 participants.

- *Statistical consideration* A basic requirement in quantitative research is that the sample should have a 'normal distribution', and Hatch and Lazaraton (1991) argue that to achieve this the sample needs to include 30 or more people. However, Hatch and Lazaraton also emphasize that smaller sample sizes can be compensated for by using certain special statistical procedures (for example, non-parametric tests—see Section 9.9).
- *Sample composition* A further consideration is whether there are any distinct subgroups within the sample that may be expected to behave differently from the others. If we can identify such subgroups in advance (for example, in most L2 studies of school children, girls have been found to perform differently from boys), we should set the sample size so that the minimum size applies to the *smallest subgroup* in the sample.
- *Safety margin* When setting the final sample size, it is advisable to leave a decent 'margin' to provide for unforeseen or unplanned circumstances. For example, some participants are likely to drop out of at least some phases of the project; some questionnaires will always have to be disqualified for one reason or another; and we may also detect unexpected subgroups that need to be treated separately.
- *Reverse approach* Because statistical significance (see Section 9.4.4) depends on the sample size, our principle concern should be to sample enough learners for the expected results to be able to reach statistical significance. That is, we can take a 'reverse approach': first we approximate the expected magnitude or power of the expected results and then determine the sample size that is necessary to detect this effect if it actually exists in the population. For example, at a $p < .05$ significance level an expected correlation of .40 requires at least 25 participants. (These figures can be looked up in correlational tables available in most texts on statistics; see, for example, http://www.uwe.ac.uk/hlss/llas/statistics-in-linguistics/Appenix1.pdf.) Researchers can also use a more complex procedure, 'power analysis', to decide on the necessary sample size. (For a free, Internet-based power analysis software see Buchner *et al.* 1997.)

5.1.4 The problem of respondent self-selection

To conclude the discussion of the various sampling issues, let me highlight a potential pitfall that might put the validity of an investigation at risk: the problem of participant self-selection. This refers to cases when for various reasons the actual composition of the sample is not only the function of some systematic selection process but also of factors related to the respondents' own willingness to participate. Problems can arise, for example, when:

- Researchers invite volunteers to take part in a study (occasionally even offering money to compensate for their time).
- The design allows for a high degree of dropout (or 'mortality'), in which case participants self-select themselves *out* of the sample.
- Participants are free to choose whether they participate in a study or not (for example, in postal questionnaire surveys).

Self-selection is inevitable to some extent because few investigations can be made compulsory; however, in some cases—for example, in the examples above—it can reach such a degree that there is a good chance that the resulting sample will not be similar to the target population. For example, volunteers may be different from non-volunteers in their aptitude, motivation or some other basic characteristics, and dropouts may also share some common features that will be underrepresented in the sample with their departure (for example, dropouts may be more unmotivated than their peers and therefore their departure might make the remaining participants' general level of motivation unnaturally high). Consequently, the sample may lose its representative character, which of course would prevent any meaningful generalizability. Brown (2001: 85) explains this well with regard to questionnaire surveys:

> The problem is that the types of respondents who return questionnaires may be a specific type of 'eager-beaver' or 'gung-ho' respondent. Thus the results of the survey can only be generalized to 'eager-beaver' or 'gung-ho' people in the population rather than to the entire population.

5.2 Questionnaire surveys

Survey studies aim at describing the characteristics of a population by examining a sample of that group. Although survey data can be collected by means of structured interviews (for example, in market research or opinion polls), the main data collection method in surveys is the use of questionnaires; in this section I focus only on this option. The results of a questionnaire survey are typically quantitative, although the instrument may also contain some open-ended questions that will require a qualitative analysis. The main methodological issues concerning surveys are (a) how to sample the participants, which has been discussed above, and (b) how to design and administer the research tool, the 'self-report questionnaire'.

As stated in Chapter 1, the essence of scientific research is trying to find answers to questions in a systematic and disciplined manner and it is therefore no wonder that the questionnaire has become one of the most popular research instruments applied in the social sciences. The popularity of questionnaires is due to the fact that they are relatively easy to construct, extremely versatile and uniquely capable of gathering a large amount of information quickly in a form that is readily processible. Indeed, the frequency of use of self-completed questionnaires as a research tool in applied linguistics is surpassed only by that of language proficiency tests. (For reviews, see Baker in press; Dörnyei 2003.) Yet, in spite of the wide application of questionnaires in our field, there does not seem to be sufficient awareness in the profession about the theory of questionnaire design and processing; the usual perception is that anybody with a bit of common sense and good word processing software can construct a fine questionnaire. Unfortunately, this perception is not true: Just as in everyday life, where not every question elicits the right answer, it is all too common in scientific investigations to come across questionnaires that fail. In fact, I believe that *most* questionnaires used in applied linguistic research are somewhat *ad hoc* instruments, and questionnaires that yield scores with sufficient (and well-documented) reliability and validity are not that easy to come by in our field. So, let us see how questionnaire theory can help us to devise better instruments.

5.2.1 What are questionnaires and what do they measure?

Although the term 'questionnaire' is one that most of us are familiar with, it is not a straightforward task to provide a precise definition of it. To start with, the term is partly a misnomer because many questionnaires do not contain any real questions that end with a question mark. Indeed, questionnaires are also often referred to under different names, such as 'inventories', 'forms', 'opinionnaires', 'tests', 'batteries', 'checklists', 'scales', 'surveys', 'schedules', 'studies', 'profiles', 'indexes/indicators', or even simply 'sheets'.

Second, even in the research community the general rubric of 'questionnaire' has been used in at least two broad senses: (a) interview schedules/guides—described in detail in Section 6.4.2; and (b) self-administered pencil-and-paper questionnaires. In this chapter, I cover this second type of questionnaire, defining it as 'any written instruments that present respondents with a series of questions or statements to which they are to react either by writing out their answers or selecting from among existing answers' (Brown 2001: 6).

What do questionnaires measure? Broadly speaking, questionnaires can yield three types of data about the respondent:

Factual questions which are used to find out certain facts about the respondents, such as demographic characteristics (for example, age, gender, and race), residential location, marital and socio-economic status, level of education, occupation, language learning history, amount of time spent in an L2 environment, etc.

Behavioural questions which are used to find out what the respondents are doing or have done in the past, focusing on actions, life-styles, habits, and personal history.

Attitudinal questions which are used to find out what people think, covering attitudes, opinions, beliefs, interests, and values.

We should note at this point that although questionnaires are often very similar to written tests, there is a basic difference between the two instrument types. A test takes a sample of the respondent's behaviour/knowledge for the purpose of *evaluating* the individual's more general underlying competence/abilities/skills (for example, overall L2 proficiency). Thus, a test measures how well someone can do something. In contrast, questionnaire items do not have good or bad answers; they elicit information about the respondents in a *non-evaluative* manner, without gauging their performance against a set of criteria. Thus, although some commercially available questionnaires are actually called 'tests', these are not tests in the same sense as achievement or aptitude tests.

In a similar vein, 'production questionnaires'—or as they have been traditionally been called, 'discourse completion tasks' (DCTs)—are not questionnaires proper either. These pencil-and-paper instruments, commonly used in interlanguage pragmatics research, require the informant to produce some sort of authentic language data as a response to situational prompts. Thus, they are structured language elicitation instruments and, as such, they sample the respondent's competence in performing certain tasks, which makes them similar to language tests.

5.2.2 Multi-item scales

One central issue about questionnaire design concerns how the items to be responded to are actually worded. When it comes to assessing non-factual matters such as the respondents' attitudes, beliefs and other personal or mental variables, the actual wording of the items can assume an unexpected importance. Minor differences in how a question is formulated and framed can often produce radically different levels of agreement or disagreement. For example, Converse and Presser (1986: 41) report on a survey in which simply changing 'forbid' to 'not allow' in the wording of the item 'Do you think the United States should [forbid/not allow] public speeches against democracy?' produced drastically different responses. Significantly more people were willing to 'not allow' speeches against democracy than were willing to 'forbid' them even though 'allow' and 'forbid' are exact logical opposites. Given that in this example only one word was changed and that the alternative version had an almost identical meaning, this is a good illustration that item wording in general has a substantial impact on the responses.

So, how can we deal with the seemingly unpredictable impact of item wording? Do we have to conclude that questionnaires simply cannot achieve the kind of accuracy that is needed for scientific measurement purposes? We would have to if measurement theoreticians—and particularly American psychologist Rensis Likert in his PhD dissertation in 1932—had not discovered an ingenious way of getting around the problem: by using 'multi-item scales'. These scales refer to a cluster of several differently worded items that focus on the same target. The item scores for the similar questions are summed, resulting in a total scale score, and the underlying assumption is that any idiosyncratic interpretation of an item will be averaged out during the summation of the item scores. In other words, if we use multi-item scales, 'no individual item carries an excessive load and an inconsistent response to one item would cause limited damage' (Skehan 1989: 11). By way of illustration, Table 5.1 contains four items belonging to the 'Satiation control' scale in Tseng *et al.*'s (2006) Self-Regulatory Capacity in Vocabulary Learning questionnaire, concerning eliminating boredom and adding extra attraction to vocabulary learning tasks.

Satiation control

- Once the novelty of learning vocabulary is gone, I easily become impatient with it. [REVERSED CODING]
- During the process of learning vocabulary, I feel satisfied with the ways I eliminate boredom.
- During the process of learning vocabulary, I am confident that I can overcome any sense of boredom.
- When feeling bored with learning vocabulary, I know how to regulate my mood in order to invigorate the learning process.

Table 5.1 The four items making up the 'Satiation control' scale in Tseng et al.'s (2006) Self-Regulatory Capacity in Vocabulary Learning questionnaire

Thus, multi-item scales maximize the stable component that the items share and reduce the extraneous influences unique to the individual items. Accordingly, there is a general consensus among survey specialists that more than one item (usually 4–10) is needed to address each identified content area, all aimed at the same target but drawing upon slightly different aspects of it. An obvious point that is nevertheless often overlooked by novice researchers is that in the final version of the questionnaire the items of the various multi-item scales have to be mixed up to create a sense of variety and to prevent respondents from simply repeating previous answers.

5.2.3 Writing questionnaire items

The typical questionnaire is a highly structured data collection instrument, with most items either asking about very specific pieces of information (for example, one's address or food preference) or giving various response options for the respondent to choose from, for example by ticking a box or circling the most appropriate option. This makes questionnaire data particularly suited for quantitative, statistical analysis. It is, of course, possible to devise a questionnaire that is made up of open-ended items (for example, 'Please describe your dreams for the future ...'), thereby providing data that is qualitative and exploratory in nature, but this practice is usually discouraged by theoreticians. The problem with questionnaires from a qualitative perspective is that they inherently involve a somewhat superficial and relatively brief engagement with the topic on the part of the respondent. Therefore, no matter how creatively we formulate the items, they are unlikely to yield the kind of rich and sensitive description of events and participant perspectives that qualitative interpretations are grounded in. If we are seeking long and detailed personal accounts, other research methods such as interviews (see Section 6.4) are likely to be more suitable for our purpose. Robson (1993: 243) has summarized this point well: 'The desire to use open-ended questions appears to be almost universal in novice researchers, but is usually rapidly extinguished with experience'.

Thus, most professional questionnaires are primarily made up of 'closed-ended' items, which do not require the respondents to produce any free writing; instead, respondents are to choose one of the given alternatives (regardless of whether their preferred answer is among them). The selected response options can, then, easily be numerically coded and entered into a computer database. Having said that, most questionnaires do contain certain partially open-ended items, and these will be summarized after an overview of the most common closed-ended item formats. (For a more detailed description of the item types with illustrations, see Dörnyei 2003.)

Likert scales

The most famous type of closed-ended items is undoubtedly the 'Likert scale' (named after its inventor), which consists of a characteristic statement and respondents are asked to indicate the extent to which they 'agree' or 'disagree' with it by marking (for example, circling) one of the responses ranging from 'strongly agree' to 'strongly disagree'. For example:

Hungarians are genuinely nice people.

Strongly agree	Agree	Neither agree nor disagree	Disagree	Strongly disagree

After the item has been administered, each response option is assigned a number for scoring purposes (for example, 'strongly agree' = 5 ... 'strongly disagree' = 1) and the scores for the items addressing the same target are summed up or averaged.

Semantic differential scales

Another frequently applied way of eliciting a graduated response is the 'semantic differential scale'. This technique is popular because by using it researchers can avoid writing statements (which is not always easy); instead, respondents are asked to indicate their answers by marking a continuum (with a tick or an 'X') between two bipolar adjectives at the extremes. For example:

Research methodology texts are:
difficult ___:___:___:___:___:_X_:___ easy
useless ___:_X_:___:___:___:___:___ useful

Semantic differential scales are similar to Likert scales in that several items are used to evaluate the same target, and multi-item scores are computed by summing up the individual item scores. An important technical point concerning the construction of such bipolar scales is that the position of the 'negative' and 'positive' poles, if they can be designated as such, should be varied (i.e. the positive pole should alternate between being on the right and the left hand sides) to avoid superficial responding or a position response set (Aiken 1996).

Numerical rating scales

'Numerical rating scales' involve 'giving so many marks out of so many', that is, assigning one of several numbers (which correspond to a series of ordered categories) to describe a feature of the target. We use this technique in everyday life when we say, for example, that on a scale from one to five something (for example, a film) was worth three or four. The popularity of this scaling technique is due to the fact that the rating continuum can refer to a wide range of adjectives (for example, excellent → poor; conscientious → slapdash) or adverbs (for example, always → never); in fact, numerical ratings can easily be turned into semantic differential scales and vice versa.

Other closed-ended item types

Depending on the purpose and the topic of the questionnaire, as well as on the age and other characteristics of the respondents, questionnaire designers have also used a variety of other closed-ended item types, the most common of which are as follows:

- *True–false items* While generally it is true that the more response options an item contains, the more accurate evaluation it yields, there might be cases when only a polarized yes–no decision can be considered reliable. For example, little children are sometimes seen as incapable of providing more elaborate ratings, and some personality test items also follow a true–false rating to ensure reliability in domains where the respondent may not be able to properly evaluate the degree to which a particular feature is present/true or not. The problem with this forced-choice format is that it can simplify things too much, resulting in highly reduced and occasionally even distorted data.

- *Multiple-choice items* Most applied linguists are familiar with this format because of its popularity in standardized L2 proficiency testing. In questionnaires they are often used when asking about personal information, such as the level of education of the respondents.

- *Rank order items* It is a common human mental activity to rank order people, objects, or even abstract concepts according to some criterion, and rank order items in questionnaires capitalize on our familiarity with this process. As the name suggests, these items contain some sort of a list and respondents are asked to order the items by assigning a number to them according to their preferences. A short list of, say, three items can then be quantified by assigning three points to the top ranked option, two to the middle and one to the lowest ranked item.

Open-ended questions

'Open-ended questions' include items where the actual question is not followed by response options for the respondent to choose from but rather by some blank space (for example, dotted lines) for the respondent to fill in. As mentioned earlier, questionnaires are not particularly suited for truly qualitative, exploratory research, but some open-ended questions can still have merit. By permitting greater freedom of expression, open-format items can provide a far greater richness than fully quantitative data. The open responses can offer graphic examples, illustrative quotes, and can also lead us to identify issues not previously anticipated. Furthermore, sometimes we need open-ended items for the simple reason that we do not know the range of possible answers and therefore cannot provide pre-prepared response categories.

In my experience, open-ended questions work particularly well if they are not completely open but contain certain guidance, as illustrated by the following four question types:

- *Specific open questions* ask about concrete pieces of information, such as facts about the respondent, past activities, or preferences.
- *Clarification questions* can be attached to answers that have some special importance, and such questions are also appropriate after the 'Other' category in a multiple-choice item (for example, by stating '*Please specify* ...').
- *Sentence completion* where an unfinished sentence beginning is presented for the respondents to complete (for example, 'The thing I liked most about the course is ...'). This can elicit a more meaningful answer than a simple question. I have successfully used this technique on various feedback forms.
- *Short-answer questions* are different from 'essay questions' (which are not recommended in ordinary questionnaires and therefore will not be discussed) in that they are worded in such a focused way that the question can be answered succinctly, with a 'short answer'—this is usually more than a phrase and less than a paragraph.

Rules about item wording

Over the past 50 years, survey researchers have accumulated a considerable body of knowledge and experience about what makes a questionnaire item work and what the potential pitfalls are. However, it needs to be pointed out that item design is not a 100 per cent scientific activity because in order to write good items one also needs a certain amount of creativity and lots of common sense. In the absence of hard and fast rules, it is the rigorous piloting of the questionnaire that will produce good psychometric properties—see Section 5.2.5. Here is a list of practical advice on item wording concerning clarity and accessibility:

Aim for short and simple items Whenever possible, questionnaire items should be short, rarely exceeding 20 words. They should preferably be written in simple sentences rather than compound or complex sentences, and each should contain only one complete thought.

Use simple and natural language As a rule, in questionnaire items we should always choose the simplest way to say something. Items need to be kept clear and direct, without any acronyms, abbreviations, colloquialisms, proverbs, jargon, or technical terms. We should try to speak the 'common language'—the best items are the ones that sound like being taken from an actual interview.

Avoid ambiguous or loaded words and sentences It goes without saying that any elements that might make the language of the items unclear or ambiguous need to be avoided. The most notorious of such elements are:

Nonspecific adjectives or adverbs (for example, 'good', 'easy', 'many', 'sometimes', 'often').

Items containing universals such as 'all', 'none', 'never'.

Modifying words such as 'only', 'just', 'merely'.

Words having more than one meaning.

Loaded words (for example, 'democratic', 'modern', 'natural', 'free', etc.), because they may elicit an emotional reaction that may bias the answer.

It is also obvious that loaded questions such as 'Isn't it reasonable to suppose that ...?' or 'Don't you believe that ...?' are likely to bias the respondent towards giving a desired answer and should be rephrased in a neutral way.

Avoid negative constructions Items that contain a negative construction (i.e. including 'no' or 'not') are deceptive because although they read satisfactorily, responding to them can be problematic. For example, what does a negative response to a negative question mean? In order to avoid any possible difficulties, the best solution is to avoid the use of negatives altogether. In most cases negative items can be restated in a positive way by using verbs or adjectives that express the opposite meaning (for example, 'dislike' instead of 'not like').

Avoid double-barrelled questions 'Double-barrelled' questions are those that ask two (or more) questions in one while expecting a single answer. For example, the question 'How are your parents?' asks about one's mother and father, and cannot be answered simply if one of them is well and the other unwell. Indeed, questions dealing with pluralisms (children, students) often yield double-barrelled questions, but compound questions also often fall into this category (for example, 'Do you always write your homework and do it thoroughly?'). With double-barrelled questions even if respondents do provide an answer, there is no way of knowing which part of the question the answer responded to.

Avoid items that are likely to be answered the same way by everybody In rating scales we should avoid statements that are likely to be endorsed by almost everyone or almost no one. In most cases these items are not informative and they are certainly difficult if not impossible to process statistically (because of insufficient variance).

Include both positively and negatively worded items In order to avoid a response set in which the respondents mark only one side of a rating scale, it is worth including in the questionnaire both positively and negatively worded items. We should note, however, that it is all too easy to fall into the trap of trying to create a negatively worded item by using some sort of a negative construction (for example, 'don't'), which has been previously warned against. Instead, negatively worded items should focus on negative rather than positive aspects of the target (for example, instead of writing 'I don't enjoy learning English' we can write 'Learning English is a burden for me').

5.2.4 The format of the questionnaire

Main parts

Questionnaires have a fairly standard component structure that consists of the following elements:

- *Title* Just like any other piece of writing, a questionnaire should have a title to identify the domain of the investigation, to provide the respondent with initial orientation and to activate relevant background knowledge and content expectations.
- *General introduction* The 'opening greeting' usually describes the purpose of the study and the organization conducting/sponsoring it. Further important functions of this section involve emphasizing that there are no right or wrong answers; promising confidentiality or anonymity and requesting honest answers; and saying 'thank you'.
- *Specific instructions* These explain and demonstrate (with examples) how respondents should go about answering the questions.

- *Questionnaire items* These constitute the main body of the questionnaire. They need to be very clearly separated from the instructions. This is where different typefaces and font styles are useful.
- *Additional information* At the end of the questionnaire we may include a contact name (for example, the researcher's or an administrator's) with a telephone number or address and some explicit encouragement to get in touch if there are any questions. It is a nice gesture (unfortunately too rarely used) to include a brief note promising to send the respondent a summary of the findings if interested. Sometimes questionnaires can also end with an invitation to volunteer for a follow-up interview.
- *Final 'thank you'* It is surprising how often this is omitted!

Length

How long is the optimal length of a questionnaire? It depends on how important the topic of the questionnaire is for the respondent. If we feel very strongly about something, we are usually willing to spend several hours answering questions. However, most questionnaires in applied linguistics concern topics that have a low salience from the respondents' perspective, and in such cases the optimal length is rather short. Most researchers agree that anything that is more than 4–6 pages long and requires over half an hour to complete may be considered too much of an imposition. As a principle, I have always tried to stay within a four-page limit. It is remarkable how many items can be included within four well-designed pages and I have also found that a questionnaire of 3–4 pages does not tend to exceed the 30-minute completion limit.

Layout

It is my experience that the layout of the questionnaire is frequently overlooked as an important aspect of the development of the instrument. This is a mistake: over the past 20 years I have increasingly observed that producing an attractive and professional design is half the battle in motivating respondents to produce reliable and valid data. After all, as will be discussed in more detail in Section 5.2.6 (on administering the questionnaire), people usually do not mind expressing their opinions and answering questions as long as they think that the survey is serious and professionally conducted. Three points in particular are worth bearing in mind:

- *Booklet format* Not only does the questionnaire have to be short but it also has to *look* short. I have found that the format that feels most compact is that of a *booklet* (for example, an A3 sheet folded into two to make a four-page A4 booklet). This format also makes it easy to read and to turn pages (and what is just as important, it also prevents lost pages ...).
- *Appropriate density* With regard to how much material we put on a page, a compromise needs to be achieved. On the one hand, we want to make the

pages full because respondents are much more willing to fill in a two-page rather than a four-page questionnaire even if the two instruments have exactly the same number of items. On the other hand, we must not make the pages look crowded (for example by economizing on the spaces separating different sections of the questionnaire). Effective ways of achieving this trade-off involve reducing the margins, using a space-economical font and utilizing the whole width of the page, for example by printing the response options next to each question rather than below it.

- *Sequence marking* I normally mark each main section of the questionnaire with Roman numbers, each question with consecutive Arab figures, and then letter all the subparts of a question; as a result, I may have Question 1a or 27d within Section I or III. This creates a sense of structuredness. It is also beneficial to include a phrase such as 'Continued on back' at the bottom of the first side of a sheet that is printed on both sides.

Item sequence

Once all the items to be included in the questionnaire have been written or collected, we need to decide on their order. Item sequence is a significant factor because the context of a question can have an impact on its interpretation and the response given to it. There are four principles in particular that we need to bear in mind:

Mixing up the scales The items from different scales need to be mixed up as much as possible to create a sense of variety and to prevent respondents from simply repeating previous answers.

Opening questions To set the right tone, the opening questions need to be interesting, relatively simple yet at the same time focused on important and salient aspects. We need to be careful not to force the respondents to take a fundamental decision at such an early stage because that would affect all the subsequent answers. So the initial questions need to be relatively mild or neutral.

Factual (or 'personal' or 'classification') questions As Oppenheim (1992) concludes, novice researchers typically start to design a questionnaire by putting a rather forbidding set of questions at the top of a blank sheet of paper, asking for name, address, marital status, number of children, religion, and so on. These personal/classification questions resemble the many bureaucratic forms we have to fill in and are best left at the end of the questionnaire. Also, in many cultures issues like age, level of education, or marital status are considered personal and private matters, and if we ask them near the beginning of the questionnaire they might create some resistance in the respondents, or, in cases where respondents are asked to provide their name, this might remind them of the non-anonymous nature of the survey, which in turn may inhibit some of their answers.

Open-ended questions at the end If we include real open-ended questions that require substantial and creative writing, it is preferable to place them near the end rather than at the beginning of the questionnaire. In this way, the other items will not be affected by the potential negative consequences of the open-ended question (for example, the required work can put some people off; others might get bogged down and spend most of the available time and mental energy agonizing over what they should write). In addition, some people find it psychologically more acceptable to put in the necessary work if they have already invested in the questionnaire and if they know that this is the final task.

5.2.5 Developing and piloting the questionnaire

The general importance of piloting research tools and procedures was already highlighted in Section 3.4.1. Because, as we have seen earlier, in questionnaires so much depends on the actual wording of the items, an integral part of questionnaire construction is 'field testing', that is, piloting the questionnaire at various stages of its development on a sample of people who are similar to the target sample for which the instrument has been designed. The developing and piloting of a questionnaire is a stepwise process:

Drawing up an item pool The first step is to let our imagination go free and create as many potential items for each scale as we can think of—this collection is referred to as the 'item pool'. In doing so we can draw inspiration/ideas from two sources: (a) qualitative, exploratory data gathered in interviews (one-to-one or focus group) or student essays focusing on the content of the questionnaire; and (b) established/published questionnaires in the area (borrowing questionnaire items is an acceptable practice if the sources are properly acknowledged).

Initial piloting of the item pool In order to reduce the large list of questions in the item pool to the intended final number, it is useful to first ask 3–4 trusted and helpful colleagues or friends to go through the items and provide feedback.

Final piloting (dress rehearsal) Based on the feedback received from the initial pilot group we can normally put together a near-final version of the questionnaire that 'feels' satisfactory and that does not have any obvious glitches. However, we still do not know how the items will work in actual practice, that is, whether the respondents will reply to the items in the manner intended by the questionnaire designers. There is only one way to find out: by administering the questionnaire to a group of about 50 respondents who are in every way similar to the target population the instrument was designed for.

Item analysis The answers of the pilot group are submitted to statistical analyses to fine-tune and finalize the questionnaire. The procedure usually involves checking three aspects of the response pattern: (a) missing responses and possible signs that the instructions were not understood correctly; (b) the range of the responses elicited by each item. We should exclude items that are endorsed by almost everyone or by almost no one because they are difficult if not impossible to process statistically (since statistical procedures require a certain amount of variation in the scores); and (c) the internal consistency of multi-item scales. Multi-item scales are only effective if the items within a scale work together in a homogeneous manner, that is, if they measure the same target area. In psychometric terms this means that each item on a scale should correlate with the other items and with the total scale score, which has been referred to as Likert's criterion of 'internal consistency'. Statistical packages like SPSS (see Section 9.1) offer a very useful procedure, 'reliability analysis', which provides a straightforward technique to exclude items that do not work (see Section 9.3) and to select the best items up to the predetermined length of the instrument.

Post hoc item analysis After the administration of the final questionnaire researchers usually conduct a final item analysis following the same procedures as described above to screen out any items that have not worked properly.

5.2.6 Administering the questionnaire

One area in which a questionnaire study can go very wrong concerns the procedures used to administer the questionnaire. Strangely enough, this aspect of survey research has hardly ever been discussed in the L2 literature—questionnaire administration is often considered a mere technical issue relegated to the discretion of the research assistants. This is mistaken; there is ample evidence in the measurement literature that questionnaire administration procedures play a significant role in affecting the quality of the elicited responses.

In social research the most common form of administering questionnaires is by mail, but educational research is different in this respect because administration by hand is typically more prominent than postal surveys. In applied linguistic research, group administration is the most common method of having questionnaires completed, partly because the typical targets of the surveys are language learners studying within institutional contexts, and it is often possible to arrange to administer the instrument to them while they are assembled together, for example, as part of a lesson. In this format a few questionnaire administrators can collect a very large number of data within a relatively short time.

Why would the respondents take the survey seriously when they have usually nothing to gain from participating in the research? School children are often willing to work hard on a task simply because it is assigned to them, and in my experience people in general do not mind expressing their opinions and answering questions as long as they think that the survey is related to a worthy cause and that their opinion matters. Thus, if we take sufficient care planning and executing the administration process, we can successfully build on this human characteristic and can secure the cooperation of our informants. The following strategies have been found effective in achieving this objective:

Advance notice Announcing the questionnaire a few days in advance and sending each participant a printed leaflet that invites their participation, explains the purpose and nature of the questionnaire, and offers some sample items is an effective method of generating a positive climate for the administration and of raising the 'professional' feel of the survey.

Attitudes conveyed by teachers, parents, and other authority figures Participants are quick to pick up their superiors' (for example, teachers', bosses', or parents') attitude towards the survey and only acquiesce if the message they receive is positive. It is therefore an imperative to win the support of all these authority figures in advance.

Respectable sponsorship If we represent an organization that is esteemed highly by the respondents, the positive reputation is likely to be projected onto the survey.

The behaviour of the survey administrator The administrators of the questionnaire are, in many ways, identified with the whole survey and therefore everything about them matters: their clothes should be business-like but certainly not more formal than what is typical in the given environment; the way they introduce themselves is important: friendliness is imperative and smiling usually breaks the ice effectively; their overall conduct should be professional to represent the serious character of the survey without being stiff and unnatural.

Administrator attitudes A crucial aspect of the survey administrators' behaviour is that it should exhibit keen involvement in the project and show an obvious *interest* in the outcome.

Communicating the purpose and significance of the survey An important element in selling the survey to the participants is communicating to them the purpose of the survey and conveying to them the potential significance of the results. The introductory speech of the questionnaire administrator needs to be carefully designed to cover the following points: greeting and thanking; the purpose of the survey and its potential usefulness; why the particular participants have been selected; assurance of confidentiality/anonymity; the duration of completing the questionnaire; 'Any questions?'; final 'thank you'.

5.2.7 Strengths and weaknesses of questionnaires

The main attraction of questionnaires is their efficiency in terms of researcher time and effort and financial resources: by administering a questionnaire to a group of people, one can collect a huge amount of information in less than an hour, and the personal investment required will be a fraction of what would have been needed for, say, interviewing the same number of people. Furthermore, if the questionnaire is well constructed, processing the data can also be fast and relatively straightforward, especially by using some computer software. Questionnaires are also very versatile, which means that they can be used successfully with a variety of people in a variety of situations targeting a variety of topics. Respondents usually do not mind the process of filling in questionnaires and the survey method can offer them anonymity if needed. As a result of these strengths, the vast majority of research projects in the behavioural and social sciences involve at one stage or another collecting some sort of questionnaire data.

On the other hand, questionnaires also have some serious limitations, and it is all too easy to produce unreliable and invalid data by means of an ill-constructed questionnaire. In fact, as Gillham (2000: 1) points out, in research methodology 'no single method has been so much abused'. The weakest aspect of questionnaires is the fact that the items need to be sufficiently simple and straightforward to be understood by everybody. Thus, this method is unsuitable for probing deeply into an issue (Moser and Kalton 1971) and it usually results in rather superficial data. The necessary simplicity of the questions is further augmented by the fact that the amount of time respondents tend to be willing to spend working on a questionnaire is rather short, which again limits the depth of the investigation. Thus, questionnaire surveys usually provide a rather 'thin' description of the target phenomena. Other issues include possible respondent literacy problems and the social desirability bias—see Section 3.1.1.

5.3 Experimental and quasi-experimental studies

Having talked about one of the most popular quantitative data collection tools, the questionnaire, let us now turn to a special quantitative data collection design, the experimental study, which many people would claim to represent quantitative research at its most scientific because it can establish unambiguous cause–effect relationships.

Many research studies in applied linguistics are intended to uncover causal links by answering questions such as 'What's the reason for ...?' 'What happens if/when ...?' and 'What effect does something have on ...?' However, to establish firm cause–effect relationships is surprisingly difficult because in real life nothing happens in isolation and it is hard to disentangle the interferences of various related factors. For example, if we want to compare the effects of using two different coursebooks in language teaching, how do we measure their impact? If we simply compare two learner groups which use the two coursebooks and find some marked differences between their learning achievement, can we really claim that this difference was due to the difference in the coursebook they used? Not necessarily, because there can be a host of other factors contributing to the difference, for example, the composition of the learners in the two groups or the different learning environments (and possibly the different teachers). Indeed, in their seminal work, Campbell and Stanley (1963) point out that unless we apply special research designs, we have no way of discriminating among numerous possible alternative explanations for such outcomes.

The answer to the cause–effect dilemma has been provided by a simple but ingenious methodological idea that has been labelled 'experimental design': first, take a group of learners and do something special with/to them, while measuring their progress. Then compare their results with data obtained from another group that is similar in every respect to the first group except for the fact that it did not receive the special treatment. If there is any discrepancy in the results of the two groups, these can be attributed to the only difference between them, the treatment variable. Thus, the common feature of experimental designs is the fact that certain consciously manipulated processes take place in a tightly controlled environment in which only the target variables are varied while others are kept constant (Johnson and Christensen 2004).

A typical experimental design would be an intervention study which contains at least two groups: the 'treatment' or 'experimental group', which receives the treatment or which is exposed to some special conditions, and the 'control group', whose role is to provide a baseline for comparison. From a theoretical perspective, the ultimate challenge is to find a way of making the control group as similar to the treatment group as possible. As Cook and Campbell (1979) summarize, one of the great breakthroughs in experimental design was the realization that with sufficient participants the random assignment of the participants to experimental and control groups can provide a way of making the average participant in one group comparable to the average participant in the other group before the treatment is applied.

While the experimental group is receiving the treatment, the control group is also receiving instruction, which is usually the standard, that is, the unmarked form of tuition in the particular learning context. Progress is measured by administering pre-tests before the intervention and post-tests after the treatment has been completed. The comparison of the two groups in such a 'pre-test–post-test control-group design' is carried out by using statistical procedures that will be described in Section 5.3.2 below.

Thus, the main difference between experimental designs and survey research lies in the fact that in the former the researcher does not only look at the relations between different observed variables, but actually *alters* one (or more) variable and determines the effects of this change on other variables. The addition of a control group, then, allows us to isolate the specific effect of the target variable in an unequivocal manner, which is why many scholars consider experimental design the optimal model for rigorous research.

Unfortunately, in educational contexts true experimental designs with random group assignments are very rarely feasible and therefore the common method applied uses intact class groups. This design is obviously a less-than-perfect compromise and has been called accordingly the 'quasi-experimental design'. Before we look at the characteristics of such studies, let me briefly warn against an inadequate variation of the true experimental design that should be avoided if possible: the 'one-group pre-test–post-test design'. When wanting to try out the impact of a special treatment (for example, strategy training), novice researchers often speculate that it is enough to take a learner group, administer the treatment, and if the difference between the pre-test and the post-test is significant, then the treatment has obviously worked. The problem is that even if the speculation is correct, the design cannot exclude other possible sources of change, such as the maturation effect, the practice effect, or the Hawthorne effect—see Section 3.1.1. Therefore, I would suggest that researchers always include a control group in their experimental designs.

5.3.1 Quasi-experimental design

In most educational settings random assignment of students by the researcher is rarely possible and therefore researchers often have to resort to a 'quasi-experimental design'. Quasi-experiments are similar to true experiments in every respect except that they do not use random assignment to create the comparisons from which treatment-caused change is inferred (Cook and Campbell 1979). Because of the practical constraints, working with 'non-equivalent groups' has become an accepted research methodology in field studies where randomization is impossible or impractical. However, in such cases we cannot rely on the neat and automatic way the true experiment deals with various threats to validity but have to deal with these threats ourselves. In practical terms, in order to be able to make causal claims based on a quasi-experimental study, the effects of the initial group-differences need to be taken into account.

In a meta-analysis comparing full experimental and quasi-experimental designs, Heinsman and Shadish (1996) found that if the two research methods were equally well designed, they yielded comparable results. However, the authors also pointed out that it is no easy task to design a quasi-experimental study as well as an experimental study. The results of the meta-analysis pointed to two specific ways of improving the design of quasi-experimental studies: (a) avoiding any situations whereby the students self-select themselves (for example, volunteer) to be in the treatment group; and (b) minimizing pre-test differences between the treatment and the control groups as much as possible. There are two frequently used methods for achieving this latter goal:

Matching participants in the treatment and control groups The most common matching procedure involves equating the control and treatment groups on a case-by-case basis on one or more variables. If we know that some learner characteristics are likely to have an impact on the target variable we are examining in the study (i.e. the 'dependent variable'), we first need to determine or measure the particular individual difference variables (for example, sex or IQ) and then identify participants in the two comparison groups with very similar parameters (for example, a girl with an IQ of around 102 in both groups). In a quasi-experimental study we are unlikely to be able achieve perfect matching even if we omit some participants who do not have a close counterpart, but the resultant group compositions will be considerably more compatible than the initial one without matching.

Using analysis of covariance (ANCOVA) ANCOVA offers a statistical method for adjusting the post-test scores for any pre-test differences; in other words, we can statistically screen the unwanted effects out of the outcome measure. (The procedure is described in Section 9.7.3.)

There is no doubt that a quasi-experimental design leaves a study more vulnerable to threats to validity than a full experimental design, but as Johnson and Christensen (2004) emphasize, just because a threat is possible, it does not mean that it is necessarily plausible. Furthermore, we can significantly reduce this plausibility by applying the above techniques. As a result, it is generally accepted that properly designed and executed quasi-experimental studies yield scientifically credible results.

5.3.2 Analysing the results of experimental and quasi-experimental studies

Data obtained from a study with a 'pre-test–post-test control-group design' can be analysed in two ways. The simpler method involves first computing 'gain scores' separately in the treatment and the control groups by subtracting the pre-test scores from the post-test scores, and then comparing these gain scores by using t-tests or 'analysis of variance' (ANOVA) (see Sections 9.6 and 9.7) to see whether the gain in the treatment condition was significantly bigger than that in the ordinary (control) condition.

A slightly more complicated method is using ANCOVA in which we compare the post-test scores by controlling for the pre-test scores—see Section 9.7.3. Both methods are acceptable and used in contemporary studies, but there is a growing recognition that ANCOVA offers more precise results (Johnson and Christensen 2004) for at least two reasons: first, several (but not all) methodologists claim that gain scores are not sufficiently reliable as they are systematically related to any random error of measurement. (See Menard 2002.) Second, especially in quasi-experimental studies, ANCOVA helps to reduce the initial group differences (as described above).

5.3.3 Experimental studies in educational and applied linguistic research

In educational research, experimental studies have typically been called 'intervention research', and as Hsieh *et al.* (2005) describe, such investigations have been evident since the beginning of the twentieth century. The method was reinvigorated in the 1960s by the publication of Campbell and Stanley's (1963) classic text on experimental research. Over the past two decades, however, the use of experimental methodology in educational research has been be on the decline: In a survey of research studies published in four leading educational psychological journals as well as the flagship journal of American educational research, the *American Educational Research Journal* (AERJ), Hsieh *et al.* found that between 1983 and 2004 the proportion of intervention studies dropped from 55 per cent (educational psychology) and 37 per cent (AERJ) to 35 per cent and 14 per cent, respectively. Furthermore, as the authors report, not only has educational intervention research been decreasing in quantity but there has also been a decline in quality, with the interventions becoming shorter. For example, in the four educational psychology journals in 1995, 26 per cent of the interventions lasted more than one day, whereas the same figure in 2004 was only 16 per cent. One important reason for this decline is the increased use of structural equation modelling (see Section 9.10.4), which makes it possible to make 'quasi-causal' claims about outcomes based on non-experimental, correlational research. Thus, by using this procedure, researchers can sometimes (but not always!) circumvent the laborious and lengthy procedure of running a full experimental study.

In applied linguistics there was a steady stream of intervention studies in the 1960s as part of the 'methods comparison studies' in classroom research (see Section 8.1), but over the subsequent decades experiments became less popular for at least two reasons: (a) many of the topics applied linguists are interested in are not directly related to 'treatment' or 'intervention', that is, they do not easily lend themselves to manipulation (for example, gender differences, personality traits, ethnolinguistic variation); and (b) experimental research is rather narrow in scope as only one or a few variables can be altered at a time. On the other hand, typical applied linguistic venues such as language classrooms are complex environments where many factors operate simultaneously, and significant changes can often only be achieved if several variables work *in concert* or in *special combinations*. An experimental design, targeting one or two variables, is inadequate to address such multivariate patterns.

While these limitations are valid, let me also emphasize that in many situations experimental studies would be feasible (for example, in studies that look at the impact of any language-related processes) and undoubtedly superior to the less labour-intensive correlational or survey studies that are usually conducted. A welcome recent trend in this direction has been the emergence of longitudinal investigations of L2 instructional effectiveness, focusing on specific instructional techniques such as corrective feedback—as Ortega and Iberri-Shea (2005) summarize, the quality of the quasi-experimental design that is typically employed in these studies has shown a considerable improvement in recent years, featuring longer treatment periods and immediate as well as delayed post-tests.

5.3.4 Strengths and weaknesses of experimental and quasi-experimental designs

The main strength of the experimental design is that it is the best method—and some would claim the *only* fully compelling method—of establishing cause–effect relationships and evaluating educational innovations. A full 'pre-test–post-test control-group design' does an excellent job at controlling for the various threats to the internal validity of the experiment. However, as Clarke (2004) points out, the price that has to be paid for doing this can sometimes be high. His main concern is that in order to control all the variables tightly we may end up with artificial frameworks in laboratory conditions which reduce the external validity (i.e. the generalizability) of the study. In other words, experimental studies can sacrifice external validity for enhanced internal validity, which is one reason why the merits of their use in education have been seriously questioned. (See Shavelson and Towne 2002.) And even properly conducted experimental studies can be affected by the Hawthorne effect, in which the outcome of an otherwise solid experiment is not caused by the treatment variable but by the fact that a treatment has been applied, regardless of its nature—see Section 3.1.1.

In quasi-experimental studies we do not have to worry so much about reduced external validity because these investigations take place in authentic learning environments using genuine class groups, but such designs open up the study to a number of new threats due to the inequality of the initial treatment and control groups. This problem is referred to as the 'selection bias', and it involves outcome differences that are not due to the treatment but are artefacts of the differences in pre-existing characteristics of the groups being compared. (See Larzelere *et al.* 2004.) As a result of this bias, such non-randomized designs are less effective in eliminating competing plausible hypotheses with the same authority as a true experiment. McDonough and McDonough (1997) also draw attention to the fact that in most language instructional situations the list of possible confounding variables is so large that achieving satisfactory control is a real challenge. While this is undoubtedly so, well designed and executed quasi-experimental studies that control for the effects of the main initial group differences are usually seen to deliver scientifically credible results.

A final problem rarely mentioned in research texts is that, even though intervention studies are rather labour-intensive, they can examine only one or two target variables at a time. In educational research we often have a whole range of potential independent variables to test (for example, the impact of various instructional conditions and strategies) and in such cases experimental or quasi-experimental designs are simply not feasible.

5.4 Collecting quantitative data via the Internet

With the growing use of the Internet it was inevitable that researchers would start collecting data by means of web-based procedures. Indeed, given the increasingly available and continuously improving computer hardware and software, it is becoming relatively easy to set up an Internet survey or experiment, and a web-based study offers some tempting benefits (for reviews, including information on free software, see Birnbaum 2004; Fox *et al.* 2003):

- *Reduced costs* Since most universities or research institutes have the necessary facilities, setting up an Internet-based project is not more expensive than initiating traditional research, whereas the running costs are significantly lower (see below).
- *Convenience of administration* The main attraction of web-based research is that it does not require administration of the materials in person; once the recruitment posting had been made, administration is self-running.
- *Automatic coding* Using a so-called 'CGI script' to record responses to disc makes the coding and recording of the answers automatic, which, coupled with self-running administration, is a real bonus.
- *High level of anonymity* The perception is that web-based research is truly anonymous, which enhances the level of honesty. However, because the machine number of a submission is traceable and the security of the data during transit over the Internet cannot be guaranteed by the researcher, it is in principle possible to identify respondents by authorities.
- *International access* The Internet does not have boundaries and therefore scholars can reach much larger and more diverse samples worldwide than would have been possible before. This is good news for cross-cultural research, even though the language barriers are still there.
- *Access to specialized populations* Web-based recruiting allows access to small, scattered, or specialized populations which would otherwise be difficult to reach.

Enamoured of these benefits and possibilities, an increasing number of investigators has already begun experimenting with web-based research, and it seems that the initial experiences and the public acceptance of the findings have been sufficiently positive for this method to become established. It is not hard to see that web-based research will play a major role in future research methodology. While this is understandable, we must also consider the limitations of this approach to be able to decide whether it is appropriate for our purposes. Two particularly important areas in this respect concern technical and sampling issues.

5.4.1 Technical issues

The new standard of 'Hypertext markup language' (HTML) introduced in 1994 allows a person viewing a web page to easily send data back to a designated server, which can process, code, and save the data electronically (Birnbaum 2004). However, Internet users have different computers, systems, browsers, and monitors, so the actual stimulus received may differ quite a bit from what the investigator has intended. For this reason, in a survey on self-harm, Fox *et al.* (2003) decided to employ a single HTML page only. As the authors explain, while it may have been possible to improve the user interface through the use of other technologies (for example, JavaScript and various other plug-ins), it was felt that the benefits would have been outweighed by the potential adverse effects of the questionnaire not being available in the same format to as wide a population. Currently, participation in more complex web-based surveys and experiments is limited by technical issues such as connection speed to the Internet and quality of installed software, but given the speed of progress in these areas such restrictions are likely to be temporary.

5.4.2 Sampling issues

The most acute problem associated with Internet-based research is that it is not possible to apply any systematic, purposive sampling strategy. What normally happens in such research is that once the instrument (typically but not always a survey) has been constructed and tested, the investigators contact various Internet discussion groups, bulletin boards, and lists, and/or initiate some sort of snowball sampling by emailing potential participants and then hope for a sizeable sample. This is obviously far from being systematic, but before we decide that this lack of control over who will eventually participate in the study should disqualify such projects from the category of scientific inquiry, we should recall that non-probability sampling (and especially convenience sampling) is the most common sampling 'strategy' even in non-web-based research—see Section 5.1.2. So, the main problem does not necessarily concern the unprincipled selection procedures but rather the fact that the actual sample that completes the web-based survey or experiment may be much more heterogeneous than in traditional research, consisting totally of self-selected participants. As a result, even if we have thousands of responses, it may be very difficult to decide how to generalize the findings.

While there are no known solutions to the sampling problem, Birnbaum (2004) mentions two strategies that might offer at least a partial solution.

In the first approach we analyse the research question separately within each substratum of the sample (for example, age, education, gender, and other demographic variables). If the same conclusions are reached in each subgroup, this might lend some external validity to the results. The second approach also involves the comparison of subsamples, but this time the investigators compare the web-based results with the outcomes of a similar, non-web-based survey or experiment. Again, the convergence of the findings can help to validate the results. Finally, we can also imagine combined studies in which a sample of respondents is approached in some traditional way, but instead of administering some research instrument to them they are asked to log on and complete the survey or experiment online. This can happen at home (which would be basically the same as a take-away questionnaire) or in more controlled circumstances such as a computer lab.

6

Qualitative data collection

Qualitative data are sexy.
(Miles and Huberman 1994: 1)

Quantitative inquiry can be divided into two distinct phases—data collection and data analysis—quite easily because they typically follow each other in a linear manner. This is not the case with qualitative research because, as we saw in Chapter 2, in accordance with the flexible and emergent nature of the qualitative research process, qualitative data collection and analysis are often circular and frequently overlap. Furthermore, it is sometimes problematic to decide whether a certain qualitative method refers primarily to data collection, data analysis or a unique, combined design—grounded theory and the case study are good examples of this ambiguity. Indeed, it is fair to say that research methodology texts in general have been inconsistent in how they have broken down the broad umbrella term 'qualitative research' into specific data collection and data analytical methods, techniques, and designs.

In this chapter I will largely disregard the various terminological inconsistencies concerning the distinctions of method versus design and data collection versus data analysis, and will cover all the important qualitative procedures that lead to the generation of a dataset, including ethnography, one-to-one interviews, focus group interviews, introspection, case studies, diary studies, and research journals. Grounded theory will be discussed in Chapter 10 (which focuses on qualitative data analysis) because its most salient aspect in contemporary research is the special three-phase coding system it offers. Before examining the specific data collection procedures, let us first look at two basic issues, the characteristics of qualitative data in general and the description of qualitative sampling.

6.1 Qualitative data

We saw in Chapter 2 that although qualitative data can come from many sources, it is usually transformed into textual form (see also Section 10.1.1), resulting in hundreds (if not thousands) of pages of transcripts and field notes. I believe it is important to highlight at the beginning of this chapter two main characteristics of a typical qualitative dataset: its tendency to become increasingly long and its rather unfocused and heterogeneous nature. To put it broadly, qualitative data tends to be bulky and messy.

In qualitative research there are no explicit restrictions on what can be considered 'data' and as Richards (2005) concludes, the researcher in a qualitative project often starts out by treating everything around a topic as potential data. Thus, qualitative data expands quickly, and novice researchers often find that the real challenge is not to generate *enough* data but rather to generate *useful* data. In fact, a serious problem in qualitative research can be *too much* data, which is augmented by the fact that 'qualitative data are messy records' (p. 34), usually consisting of a mixture of field notes, transcripts of various recordings as well as documents of a diverse nature and length. This does not mean that qualitative data cannot produce valuable results, but it does mean that processing such sizeable and heterogeneous datasets can involve a lot of work. The case of a recent research student of mine is not at all unusual: on a three-week data collection field trip back to her home country she gathered so much data that she spent the next eight months translating, transcribing, and preliminarily coding it, which cut dangerously into her remaining time for follow-up data collection and second-order analysis. Thus, a somewhat unfocused exploration of the social world can be, in Silverman's (2005: 79) words, 'a recipe for disaster'. In such cases everything looks important and it may be over-optimistic to expect that the truth will miraculously emerge from the tons of data collected.

The other side of the coin is that although we need to be careful to be selective during data collection, we must not forget either that qualitative research is *by definition* less systematic and standardized in its data collection approach than quantitative research and that the messiness of the rich data that we are aiming for is often merely a reflection of the complex real-life situations that the data concerns. In order to tap into core participant meanings, we often need to follow multiple strategies into multiple directions at multiple levels. Accordingly, the design of most qualitative data collection is fluid and open-ended, and researchers are not required to plan all elements of the project at the outset. While this is in line with the discovery-oriented character of qualitative inquiry, Richards (2005) also stresses that possibly the most common cause of problems in qualitative data collection is the lack of any plans for data reduction. As she argues, 'Novice researchers can very easily frame the scale of a project in terms of how widely they might need to spread their net, rather than how wide, realistically, the spread can be' (p. 20).

6.2 Sampling in qualitative research

We saw in Section 2.1.3 that QUAN and QUAL research differ greatly in how they approach participant sampling. In quantitative studies the principle is straightforward: we need a sizeable sample to be able to iron out idiosyncratic individual differences. Qualitative research, on the other hand, focuses on describing, understanding, and clarifying a human experience and therefore qualitative studies are directed at describing the aspects that make up an idiosyncratic experience rather than determining the most likely, or mean experience, within a group (Polkinghorne 2005). Accordingly, at least in theory, qualitative inquiry is not concerned with how representative the respondent sample is or how the experience is distributed in the population. Instead, the main goal of sampling is to find individuals who can provide rich and varied insights into the phenomenon under investigation so as to maximize what we can learn. This goal is best achieved by means of some sort of 'purposeful' or 'purposive' sampling.

6.2.1 Purposive and theoretical sampling

Because there is always a limit to how many respondents we can contact or how many sites we can visit, we have to make some principled decisions on how to select our respondents, at which point to add additional participants to the sample and when to stop gathering more data. Even when our sample consists of one case only, we need to select the aspects of that case that we will focus on. (See 'within-case sampling' in Section 6.2.4.) Therefore, a qualitative study must have a sampling plan describing the sampling parameters (participants, settings, events, processes), and this plan should line up with the purposes of the study. Punch (2005) suggests that if it is not clear to us which cases, aspects, or incidents to study, it is usually worth devoting more work to developing the initial research questions.

In their influential work on grounded theory, Glaser and Strauss (1967) spoke about 'theoretical sampling', highlighting the fact that sampling should be a flexible, ongoing, evolving process of selecting successive respondents or sites, directed by our earlier discoveries so that the emerging ideas and theoretical concepts can be tested and further refined. Silverman (2005) explains that the term 'theoretical sampling' has been transferred from grounded theory to qualitative research in general, and in current practice it is typically used synonymously with 'purposive' sampling.

6.2.2 Iteration, saturation, and sample size

Researchers are in agreement that the participant selection process should remain open in a qualitative study as long as possible so that after initial accounts are gathered and analysed, additional participants can be added who can fill gaps in the initial description or can expand or even challenge it. This cyclical process of moving back and forth between data collection and analysis is often referred to as 'iteration'.

Although iteration is a key process in qualitative sampling, it cannot go on for ever. When do we stop it? There are no rigid guidelines, but scholars agree that ideally the iterative process should go on until we reach *saturation.* Glaser and Strauss (1967) defined this as the point when additional data do not seem to develop the concepts any further but simply repeat what previous informants have already revealed. In other words, saturation is the point when the researcher becomes 'empirically confident' (p. 61) that he/she has all the data needed to answer the research question. In practice, however, researchers usually decide when to stop adding cases to a study based on a combination of theoretical saturation and pragmatic considerations such as available time and money (Eisenhardt 1989).

Finally let us address the fundamental question: how big should the sample size be in a qualitative study? After all, we can talk about the flexibility of the process of iteration but in reality most researchers need to make some sort of an initial plan about the sample size to schedule their investigation. The pragmatic answer is that, in my experience, an interview study with an initial sample size of 6–10 might work well. Using computer-aided data analysis we can increase the sample size to as many as 30, although that would probably be pushing the limits and would be barely manageable for a single researcher such as a postgraduate student. The point, though, is that a well-designed qualitative study usually requires a relatively small number of respondents to yield the saturated and rich data that is needed to understand even subtle meanings in the phenomenon under focus.

6.2.3 Specific sampling strategies

Purposive sampling can follow a number of different strategies depending on the research topic and setting. When designing the sampling plan, we also need to take into account feasibility issues (in terms of time, money, respondent availability) and—what is often ignored—saturation considerations. The more cohesive/homogeneous the sample, the faster the saturation, but at the same time, the narrower the scope of the project. The following list of the most common qualitative sampling strategies offers a sense of how wide we need to throw the net to be able to reach saturation in different research areas. As a preliminary, let me emphasize that it is very important to make the sampling strategy explicit right from the start so that we can convey the underlying logic to the readers of the final research report.

Relatively quick saturation can be achieved by the following three interrelated sampling strategies because they all aim at selecting participants who are similar in some respect:

- *Homogeneous sampling* The researcher selects participants from a particular subgroup who share some important experience relevant to our study (for example, they have participated in a study-abroad programme). In this way, this strategy allows us to conduct an in-depth analysis to identify common patterns in a group with similar characteristics.

- *Typical sampling* The researcher selects participants whose experience is typical with regard to the research focus (for example, they all study a foreign language as a school subject at an intermediate level with moderate success). This strategy assumes that we have a profile of the targeted attributes possessed by an 'average' learner. Although we cannot generalize from the results because we cannot claim that everybody will have the same experience, we can list the typical or normal features of the experience.
- *Criterion sampling* The researcher selects participants who meet some specific predetermined criteria (for example, company executives who failed an important language exam).

We can also gain valuable insight into an issue if, rather than selecting typical participants, we intentionally look at the whole range of possible responses, including very special cases. While this approach certainly increases the scope of the analysis, Duff (2006: 71) mentions that it also carries the potential problem of placing 'over-emphasis on possibly atypical, critical, extreme, ideal, unique or pathological cases, rather than typical or representative cases'. The following three strategies overlap to some extent:

- *Maximum variation sampling* The researcher selects cases with markedly different forms of experience (for example, L2 learners from all developmental levels). This process will allow us to explore the variation within the respondents and it will also underscore any commonalities that we find: if a pattern holds across the sampled diversity, we can assume that it is reasonably stable.
- *Extreme or deviant case sampling* Following the same logic as maximum variation sampling the researcher selects the most extreme cases (for example, the most motivated and demotivated learners). On the one hand, this allows us to find the limits of the experience; on the other hand, if even such cases share common elements, they are likely to be real core components of the experience.
- *Critical case sampling* The researcher deliberately targets cases which offer a dramatic or full representation of the phenomenon, either by their intensity or by their uniqueness (for example, in a language attrition study examining people who have completely forgotten an L2 they used to speak). Their case may be taken as the most salient or comprehensive manifestation of the phenomenon under scrutiny; in such situations researchers are not only interested in what they find but also in what they do not, because something that does not occur in such salient cases is unlikely to happen elsewhere.

As it often happens, the most practical and feasible (and of course most common) sampling strategies are the least sound from a theoretical point of view. Three such 'less principled' strategies are particularly well known:

- *Snowball or chain sampling* The starting point of this strategy is a principled list of key respondents, who are then asked to recruit further participants who are similar to them in some respect central to the investigation. This chain reaction can reach far, which is ideal in situations where the experience in question is rare.
- *Opportunistic sampling* This is an unplanned and potentially haphazard procedure in the sense that it is followed on the spur of the moment: while working in the field, the researcher sometimes comes across respondents who are 'too good to miss' and a decision to include them is made on the spot. The problem is that they are not always exactly what is needed, yet their selection is very much in line with the emergent nature of the qualitative inquiry.
- *Convenience sampling* This is the least desirable but the most common sampling strategy, at least at the postgraduate research level. It is not purposive but largely practical: the researcher uses those who are available. Of course, in an ideal world nobody would employ a convenience sample, but research (and particularly postgraduate research) all too often happens in less-than-ideal circumstances, under considerable time or financial constraints. One redeeming feature of this sampling strategy is that it usually results in willing participants, which is a prerequisite to having a rich dataset. On the other hand, saturation may not happen at all. Thus, this strategy may save time, money, and effort, but at the expense of credibility (Miles and Huberman 1994).

6.2.4 Within-case sampling

Although qualitative researchers are becoming aware of the importance of principled, purposive sampling, the process is usually applied only to selecting respondents, that is, to 'between-case sampling'. In some qualitative methods (for example, ethnography or case study) we need to extend our sampling plan to also include 'within-case sampling' (i.e. selecting data from the potentially available data pool concerning a participant), because we have to make regular decisions about when and how to collect data from a particular respondent, what aspects of the case to direct our attention to and which activities, locations, or events to focus on. In these decisions we need to be just as purposive with our choices as with the selection of informants.

6.3 Ethnography

A good starting point in our exploration of the specific qualitative methods of discovery is ethnography, because this approach embodies in many ways the essence of the qualitative inquiry. In fact, 'ethnography' has frequently been used as a synonym for 'qualitative research' and Hammersley and Atkinson (1995: 1), for example, started their influential monograph on ethnography by stating, 'For the purposes of this book we shall interpret the term "ethnography" in a liberal way, not worrying much about what does and does not count as examples of it'. They then added, 'the boundaries around ethnography are necessarily unclear. In particular, we would not want to make any hard-and-fast distinction between ethnography and other sorts of qualitative inquiry' (p. 2). We should note, however, Duff's (in press) warning that equating ethnography with qualitative research in general confuses the picture because certain qualitative methods, such as the case study, often display characteristics that are different from those of ethnography.

Originating in cultural anthropology, ethnographic research aims at describing and analysing the practices and beliefs of cultures. 'Culture' is not limited to ethnic groups but can be related to any 'bounded units' (Harklau 2005) such as organizations, programmes, and even distinct communities. Thus, we can talk about the ethnography of the language classroom, or the ethnographic analysis of specific schools, or other language learning contexts. The classic image of the ethnographer is a researcher who enters into the community and becomes immersed in its culture, for example, by living among 'natives' on a remote island for several years. For this reason, ethnography has been criticized in the past for representing a colonialist attitude, but since we are looking at the educational applications of the method, we do not have to review this debate here. Neither will we examine the current divide in various schools and styles of ethnographic theory, partly precipitated by postmodernism. (See Harklau 2005.)

The main goal of most ethnographic research is to provide a 'thick description' of the target culture, that is, a narrative that describes richly and in great detail the daily life of the community as well as the cultural meanings and beliefs the participants attach to their activities, events, and behaviours. For this purpose ethnography uses an eclectic range of data collection techniques, including participant and nonparticipant observation (see Section 8.2), interviewing (Section 6.4), and the ethnographer's own diary with field notes and journal entries (Section 6.9). These data sources are further supplemented by film or audio recordings as well as authentic documents and physical artefacts, and ethnographers may even use structured questionnaires that have been developed during the course of the fieldwork.

Applied linguistics as a field has an inherent interest in intercultural communication and therefore ethnographic research has been embraced by scholars who look at language learning as a profoundly social practice and see 'second language learning', 'second culture learning', and 'language socialization' as inextricably bound (for example, Roberts *et al.* 2001; Schieffelin and Ochs 1986). In addition, because of the increasingly situated nature of much recent SLA research, ethnography has also been utilized for the contextualized analysis of classroom discourse and school learning (for example, Duff 2002; Rampton 1995; van Lier 1988; Watson-Gegeo 1997; for recent overviews, see Harklau 2005 and Toohey in press). Thus, as Duff (2002) summarizes, ethnography has been consistently gaining prominence within applied linguistics since the appearance of Watson-Gegeo's (1988) influential article on the topic, and this importance is well reflected by the fact that the journal *TESOL Quarterly* has published separate '(Critical) Ethnography Guidelines' (Chapelle and Duff 2003) for its contributors. Toohey (in press) also confirms that the number of ethnographic language education studies has dramatically increased over the past ten years, with much of the work examining specific linkages among negotiations of identities, practices, and language learning both in local contexts and on a wider societal scale. (For details, see Section 6.7.3 discussing case studies, since case study research often utilizes ethnographic methodology.)

6.3.1 Main features of an ethnographic study

According to Harklau (2005), a hallmark of classic ethnographic research is that it involves firsthand 'participant observation' in a natural setting, and most studies that frame themselves as 'ethnographic' include some degree of this method. However, we saw that ethnographers also utilize several other data collection techniques and, in fact, Harklau points out that multiple data sources are usually considered desirable. So, if the method of data collection is not a key determinant of the ethnographic approach, what are the features that define it? The following three points are emphasized most frequently in the literature; they will need little elaboration here because they have been described earlier when discussing the qualitative approach in general. (See Section 2.3.2.)

- *Focusing on participant meaning* In ethnographic studies the participants' subjective interpretation of their own behaviours and customs is seen as crucial to understanding the specific culture. Therefore, a central aspect of ethnography is to find ways of looking at events through the eyes of an insider.
- *Prolonged engagement in the natural setting* The subtleties of the participants' meaning (and most often, multiple meanings) cannot be uncovered unless the researcher immerses him/herself in the culture and spends an extended period living there, observing the participants and collecting data. Therefore, a minimum stay of 6–12 months is usually recommended to achieve the necessary prolonged engagement.
- *Emergent nature* Because the ethnographer is entering a new culture, the exact focus of the research will evolve contextually and 'emerge' *in situ* only after some fieldwork has been done.

6.3.2 Main phases of an ethnographic study

An ethnographic study involves a complex process of 'getting in' and 'coming out' which can be described as a sequence of four relatively distinct phases (Morse and Richards 2002; see also Richards 2003):

- The first phase involves entering what is for the researcher a strange environment. The ethnographer needs to negotiate the entry with the gatekeepers and then find a way, reason, or adequate role for fitting in. In L2 research, gatekeepers are likely to be head teachers, school managers/principals, various education officials, who, as Richards (2003: 121) points out, all have 'their own particular axes to grind and territories to protect'. Therefore, this is a rather delicate phase; the researcher is understandably somewhat lost and does not understand the setting or the participants, as a consequence of which data collection in this phase largely involves 'mapping the terrain', deciding who's who and, in general, keeping a diary with field notes.
- The second phase is easier in many ways than the first because by now the ice has been broken and the researcher has become familiar with the participants and the routines in the setting. Nonparticipant observation is now in full swing and the critical task of finding key informants begins along with conducting initial interviews with them. At this stage the ethnographer also needs to start analysing the preliminary data to develop some initial ideas and concepts.
- The third phase is the most productive research phase. Acculturation has been completed and the researcher has been accepted and now feels 'at home' in the setting. This allows him/her to employ a variety of techniques to collect increasingly focused data, which is used to verify initial hypotheses and ideas and to develop broader theoretical concepts. Data analysis at this stage is characterized by 'progressive focusing', involving sifting, sorting, and reviewing the data (Cohen *et al.* 2000).
- The final phase is the necessary withdrawal. This may be an emotionally taxing closure phase evoking a feeling of loss, and the ethnographer needs to make sure that he/she disengages from the field in a way that brings as little disruption to the group or situation as possible. The focus is on data analysis and additional data is collected only to fill gaps, to resolve ambiguities, and to validate previous findings.

6.3.3 Strengths and weaknesses of ethnographic research

The ethnographic approach is particularly useful for exploring uncharted territories and understanding social processes from the participants' perspective. It is an excellent way of 'crossing cultures' and gaining insight into the life of organizations, institutions and communities. In short, ethnography is ideal for generating initial hypotheses about something totally unknown. Hornberger (1994: 688) also highlights the capacity of ethnography to take a holistic view and focus on the whole picture that 'leaves nothing unaccounted for and that reveals the interrelatedness of all the component parts'. As she goes on to argue,

> The value here is that the approach allows, indeed, it is the very essence of the approach to ensure, comparison and contrast between what people say and what people do in a given context and across contexts in order to arrive at a fuller representation of what is going on. It is not enough for ethnographers to ask teachers about their communicative approach to ESL teaching; they must also observe it in action. It is not enough to surmise that student participation patterns in class are different from those the children experience in home socialization; ethnographers seek to observe both contexts for themselves. It is by comparing and contrasting these dimensions that a realistic and multilayered description can begin to emerge. (pp. 688–9)

The main drawback of the approach is that the need for prolonged engagement with the participants in their natural setting requires an extensive time investment that few academic researchers can afford. Hornberger (1994) also mentions a further limitation, the 'insider/outsider dilemma', which concerns the difficulty of striking a balance between insider and outsider perspectives. As she argues, this tension surfaces in several guises (for example, in the extent of researcher participation versus nonparticipant observation and closeness versus detachment) and it is particularly acute in ethnographic research by teachers in their own classrooms and by minority researchers in their own communities. Widdowson (personal communication) adds that the insider/outsider dilemma is further manifested in reporting the research results to external audiences, because this process inherently involves presenting insider perspectives in outsider terms and this translation is likely to involve alterations.

Finally, Harklau (2005) draws attention to a peculiarity concerning ethnography in applied linguistics, namely that ethnographic work remains largely limited to white anglophone researchers in English-speaking countries, with English remaining the target language in the vast majority of studies. While this may indeed be true of the current practice, the situation is likely to change in the future because ethnographic research is in the process of gaining further ground in applied linguistics both in terms of scope and quantity. Furthermore, ethnography has also been playing an important role in influencing several aspects of qualitative research in general, producing various fruitful 'quasi-ethnographic' approaches.

6.4 Interviews

The second qualitative method of inquiry to be described in this chapter is conducting interviews. Interviewing is a frequent part of the social life surrounding most of us: we can hear interviews on the radio, watch people being interviewed on television, and we ourselves often participate in interviews of various types either as interviewers or interviewees. As Miller and Crabtree (1999) point out, the interview genre with its turn-taking conventions and expectations for participant roles, etiquettes, and even linguistic phrases is usually shared cultural knowledge. It is exactly because interviewing is a known communication routine that the method works so well as a versatile research instrument—in fact, although there is a range of qualitative research techniques available for researchers, the interview is the most often used method in qualitative inquiries. It is regularly applied in a variety of applied linguistic contexts for diverse purposes. (See for example, Block 2000; Richards 2003; Rubio 1997.)

There are different types of interviews: the highly structured version shares many similarities with quantitative written questionnaires and therefore it will be discussed here only very briefly. The typical qualitative interview is a one-to-one 'professional conversation' (Kvale 1996: 5) that has a structure and a purpose 'to obtain descriptions of the life world of the interviewee with respect to interpreting the meaning of the described phenomena' (pp. 5–6)—this section will concern primarily this interview type. In subsequent sections (Sections 6.5 and 6.6.2) we will also look at two specialized interviewing techniques: 'focus group interviews', which involve a group format, and 'retrospective interviews', which come under the umbrella term of 'introspective methods'.

After reviewing the main interview types, this section will focus largely on the two practical aspects of conducting interview research: (a) how to prepare the 'interview guide' (i.e. the list of questions to use during the interview), and (b) how to conduct the actual interview. (For further discussions, see Kvale 1996; Patton 2002; Richards 2003.)

6.4.1 Main types of interviews

One-to-one interviews can be divided into different types according to the degree of structure in the process and whether there are single or multiple interview sessions. Let us start with the latter, less often mentioned aspect.

Single or multiple sessions

The typical qualitative interview is a one-off event lasting about 30–60 minutes. However, as Polkinghorne (2005) argues, one-shot interviews are rarely able to produce the full and rich descriptions necessary for worthwhile findings. Drawing on Seidman's work he recommends that researchers administer a sequence of three interviews with the same participant to obtain sufficient depth and breadth. The first interview breaks the ice and develops rapport, while also providing a quick sweep of the areas to be investigated later. The interval between the first and the second interviews allows the interviewer to prepare a more made-to-measure interview guide for the second session and it also offers the interviewee the chance to think more deeply about the experience. As a result, the second interview is more focused than the first. Finally, having analysed the transcripts of the first two sessions, in the third interview the researcher can ask any 'mop-up' or follow-up questions to fill in and to clarify the account.

It must be noted that the multiple session format outlined here is not the same as a longitudinal interview study (see Section 4.4) because the purpose of the three sessions is not to document temporal changes but to arrive at a full account. In a longitudinal interview study the multiple sessions would need to be organized differently, with the first one or two interviews creating the baseline knowledge and the subsequent, regularly occurring interviews focusing on how and why the particular phenomenon under study changes.

Structured interviews

The second main categorizing principle of interviews is the degree of structure in them, with one extreme being the 'structured interview'. In this format, the researcher follows a pre-prepared, elaborate 'interview schedule/guide', which contains a list of questions to be covered closely with every interviewee, and the elicited information shares many of the advantages (for example, comparability across participants) and disadvantages (for example, limited richness) of questionnaire data. Such tightly controlled interviews ensure that the interviewee focuses on the target topic area and that the interview covers a well-defined domain, which makes the answers comparable across different respondents. The other side of the coin is, however, that in a structured interview there is generally little room for variation or spontaneity in the responses because the interviewer is to record the responses according to a coding scheme. There is also very little flexibility in the way questions are asked because by adopting a standardized format it is hoped that nothing will be left to chance. This interview type is appropriate when the researcher is aware of what he/she does not know and can frame questions that will yield the needed answers. That is, structured interviews are used in situations where a written questionnaire would in theory be adequate except that for some reason the written format is not feasible (for example, because of the low level of literacy amongst the participants or the need for tighter control as in some market research surveys or opinion polls).

Unstructured interviews

The other extreme, the 'unstructured interview' (sometimes also referred to as the 'ethnographic interview'), allows maximum flexibility to follow the interviewee in unpredictable directions, with only minimal interference from the research agenda. The intention is to create a relaxed atmosphere in which the respondent may reveal more than he/she would in formal contexts, with the interviewer assuming a listening role. No detailed interview guide is prepared in advance, although the researcher usually thinks of a few (1–6) opening questions (sometimes called 'grand tour' questions) to elicit the interviewee's story. During the interview, the researcher may ask an occasional question for clarification and may give reinforcement feedback as any good communication partner would to keep the interview moving, but interruptions are kept to a minimum.

It is easy to see that for an unstructured interview to be successful it is indispensable that the interviewer establishes very good rapport with the interviewee. This kind of interview is most appropriate when a study focuses on the deep meaning of particular phenomena or when some personal historical account of how a particular phenomenon has developed is required. In-depth interviews can also be used where exploratory work is required before a more focused (for example, quantitative) study can be carried out.

Semi-structured interviews

In applied linguistic research most interviews conducted belong to the 'semi-structured interview' type, which offers a compromise between the two extremes: Although there is a set of pre-prepared guiding questions and prompts, the format is open-ended and the interviewee is encouraged to elaborate on the issues raised in an exploratory manner. In other words, the interviewer provides guidance and direction (hence the '-structured' part in the name), but is also keen to follow up interesting developments and to let the interviewee elaborate on certain issues (hence the 'semi-' part). Because of the great popularity of this interview format, most of the following recommendations on question wording and interview conduct will be geared at semi-structured interviews in particular.

The semi-structured interview is suitable for cases when the researcher has a good enough overview of the phenomenon or domain in question and is able to develop broad questions about the topic in advance but does not want to use ready-made response categories that would limit the depth and breadth of the respondent's story. This format therefore needs an 'interview guide' which has to be made and piloted in advance. Usually, the interviewer will ask the same questions of all of the participants, although not necessarily in the same order or wording, and would supplement the main questions with various probes—see below.

6.4.2 Preparing for the interview and designing the interview guide

The complete interview process involves a series of carefully designed steps, with the preparation starting well before the first interview session. After the initial sampling plan has been finalized and ethical issues such as informed consent have been considered, the researcher needs to prepare a detailed interview guide, which will serve as the main research instrument. Although we may believe that this is a straightforward and quick job—after all, all we need to do is jot down a few relevant questions—a good interview guide requires careful planning followed by some piloting. A few trial runs can ensure that the questions elicit sufficiently rich data and do not dominate the flow of the conversation.

The main function of the interview guide (or 'interview schedule/protocol') is to help the interviewer in a number of areas: (a) by ensuring that the domain is properly covered and nothing important is left out by accident; (b) by suggesting appropriate question wordings; (c) by offering a list of useful probe questions to be used if needed; (d) by offering a template for the opening statement; and (e) by listing some comments to bear in mind. It might be advisable to combine this guide with an 'interview log' and thus leave space in it for recording the details of the interview (for example, participant, setting, length) as well as for the interviewer's comments and notes. As McCracken (1988) points out, the use of an interview guide is sometimes regarded as a discretionary matter in qualitative interviews; this, he argues, is wrong because due to the demanding objectives we want to achieve and the multiple factors we have to attend to during the interview, the interview guide is indispensable. Indeed, as anybody who has done interviewing will confirm, the interviewer can do with every bit of help during the interviewing process and the interview guide offers us the best possible help in this respect.

Question types and wording issues

There are a variety of questions we can include in the interview guide, but we need to bear in mind that these only provide the framework and the real meaning is so often uncovered through exploratory and unstructured responses that deviate from the interview schedule.

- *The first few questions* These are particularly important in an interview, not so much from the content point of view but rather because they set the tone and create initial rapport. If the interviewees feel that they can do themselves justice when answering these initial questions, this will make them feel competent, help them to relax and consequently encourage them to open up. This is why researchers often start with easy personal or factual questions (for example, about the respondent's family or job). The quality of the subsequent responses will to a large extent depend on the climate of trust that we create in this initial ice-breaking period.

- *Content questions* Patton (2002) points out that on any given topic, it is possible to ask any of six main types of question focusing on: (a) experiences and behaviours, (b) opinions and values, (c) feelings, (d) knowledge, (e) sensory information (i.e. what someone has seen, heard, tasted, smelled, etc., and even what the interviewer would have seen or heard if he/she had been in a particular place), and (f) background or demographic information. These six categories concern different aspects of the participant's overall view/experience of the phenomenon and therefore we can get a rounded picture by including in our interview guide questions that tap into each dimension.

- *Probes* The emergent nature of qualitative interview data can be enhanced by applying various probes that use what the interviewee has said as a starting point to go further and to increase the richness and depth of the responses. Probes may include detail-oriented and clarification questions but a technique often used in person-centred psychotherapy is to simply take a salient content word used by the respondent and ask to elaborate ('You have used the word "freedom" twice—what exactly does it mean to you/do you mean by that ...?'). Patton (2002) also mentions an interesting probe, the 'contrast probe' which asks about how a particular experience/feeling/action/term compares to some other, similar concept.
- *The final closing question* This permits the interviewee to have the final say. Several scholars have noted in the literature the richness of the data that simple closing questions such as the following ones can yield: 'Is there anything else you would like to add?' or 'What should I have asked you that I didn't think to ask?'

With regard to the wording of the questions asked in a qualitative interview, the literature contains a great deal of advice. Some of this advice is self-evident (for example, 'Don't use words that the interviewee does not understand'), but some other suggestions are truly practical and useful—Patton (2002), for example, offers particularly detailed guidelines. Similar to the wording of written questionnaire items (see Section 5.2.3), there are some rules of thumb about how to formulate our questions. Two particularly important rules are that we should avoid (a) leading questions ('It was frustrating, wasn't it ...?') and (b) loaded or ambiguous words and jargon. In general, short and relatively simple questions that contain only one idea work best. Using words that make sense to the interviewee and reflect his/her worldview help to connect to the respondent and improve the quality of the interview data.

6.4.3 Conducting the interview

While it is true that practice usually makes us more relaxed and polished interviewers, I have found that simply being familiar with certain key issues regarding interview conduct is already helpful and there are several techniques that we can implement right from the start with good effect. So let us examine key components of the interviewing process. (See also Richards

2003: Chapter 2, for a very practical account aimed at applied linguists, also including suggestions on how to develop interviewing skills.)

Recording the interview

There is general agreement in the literature that if we want to use the content of a semi-structured or unstructured interview as research data, we need to record it—taking notes is simply not enough as we are unlikely to be able to catch all the details of the nuances of personal meaning; furthermore, note-taking also disrupts the interviewing process. However, we must be aware of the fact that many people do not like to be recorded, and therefore we must discuss this aspect with the interviewee in advance.

Recording has a technical and a theoretical aspect. The technical is straightforward: we must make sure that the technology works so that we end up with good quality recordings. Although this may sound self-evident, it is amazing how frequently researchers do *not* end up with good quality recordings. The importance of this technical aspect is reflected by the fact that in the appendix of his monograph on *Linguistic Anthropology*, Duranti (1997) devoted seven pages to discussing recording issues, ranging from how to position the microphone to how to label the cassettes.

The best precaution is to take Murphy's Law very seriously: 'If it can go wrong, it will'. So, if possible we should have a spare recorder with us, always use new batteries (and cassettes if applicable), and test that the equipment works at the beginning of the interview by doing a trial recording. One notorious problem with recording is that unless we label the recorded cassettes/discs/digital files immediately and precisely, they will get mixed up. Because we are likely to end up with a lot of these recordings, it is important to keep a precise log of their content right from the start. (See also Sections 3.4.2 and 3.4.3 on research logs and data storage.) Duranti (1997) also recommends that after we have finished recording, we make copies of the original tapes for listening and transcribing—in digital terms this would mean making backup files.

The theoretical issue about recording concerns the fact that by doing audio recording we inevitably lose some information, for example nonverbal cues such as eye movements, facial expressions or gestures. This would suggest that a video recording is always preferable but many researchers do not accept this claim. Although video data is obviously richer than audio recordings, the video recording process is much more difficult and obtrusive than switching on a small dictaphone, and analysing video data is not an easy task either. (See Section 10.2.1.) So my recommendation is that we should use video data for our research only if we really need it.

Starting the interview

The first few minutes of the interview session are important because this is the time when we set the tone/climate of the interview and 'sell ourselves', that is, establish our credentials and make ourselves accepted. We must demonstrate that we are really interested in what the interviewee has got to say and also that we are a reasonably nice and non-threatening person. As McCracken (1988: 38) concludes, it is better to appear 'slightly dim and too agreeable than to give any sign of a critical or sardonic attitude'. As he further argues, an effective manner of presenting ourselves is striking a balance between formality and informality: a certain formality in dress and style is useful because it creates a 'serious' and 'professional' image (after all, 'real' scientists wear white coats and use Latin words that few people can understand), and it also indicates that the investigator can be trusted to maintain the confidentiality that has been promised the respondent. On the other hand, a certain amount of informality is useful because it reassures the respondent that we are also imperfect human beings, not indifferent to the complexities and difficulties of the respondent's life.

Before starting the recording, we need to explain again the reason for the interview—understanding the purpose of the questions will increase the motivation of the interviewee to respond openly and in detail. We should also summarize briefly what will happen to the interview data and it may be worth reassuring the respondent again on the issue of confidentiality. Already at this stage we need to facilitate a relaxed, non-threatening atmosphere in which the interviewee can feel comfortable to express him/herself. Some small talk is also helpful to build rapport with the interviewee. When we think that the interviewee is at ease, we should ask if it is all right to switch on the recorder and to test that it works. Then get on with the first questions—as described in the previous section (Section 6.4.2), these should be such that they can be easily answered.

Conducting the interview

A good qualitative interview has two key features: (a) it flows naturally, with the various parts connecting seamlessly. We must remember that we are there primarily to listen (and not speak!)—this is, in fact, the first of Robson's (2002) general recommendations on interviewing (presented in Table 6.1). We must let the interviewee dictate the pace without being rushed or interrupted. Even if there is a silence, we need to be patient and resist stepping in too quickly with a new question; and (b) it is rich in detail. Accordingly, Richards (2003: 53) points out that a golden rule for all interviewing is: 'Always seek the particular'. It is clear that meeting this second requirement can come at the expense of the first because at times we may need to interrupt the natural flow of an account (particularly if it drifts into rambling mode) and focus on specific details. This is an area where the skilful use of various probes can make a real difference. I will come back to this question below, but first we need to address an issue that is central to the interviewer's conduct: the *neutrality* of the researcher.

It has been a key principle in interview methodology that the interviewer should try to be neutral, without imposing any personal bias. But what does this neutrality mean in practical terms? I believe that it involves creating appropriate space for the interviewees to share their experience with us freely, regardless of any social, moral, or political content. The point to stress here is that simply not expressing any personal bias ourselves may not be enough to create this neutral space because respondents will be inevitably influenced by what is usually termed the 'social desirability bias'. (See Section 3.1.1.) That is, they may feel that some response would meet with disapproval not necessarily because we have given any indication that this might be so but because the response clashes with some social conventions or norms. Inevitably, respondents enter the interview session with some ideas of what may constitute preferred and dispreferred responses and if we do not deal with this issue head-on, we may end up with a neat, self-censored, and rather sterile narrative. After all, as Oppenheim (1992) warns us, even factual questions can be loaded with desirability issues: people might claim, for example, that they read more than they do, bathe more often than is true or spend more time with their children than actually happens. The truly neutral interview space encourages the sharing of even the socially less-than-desirable.

How can such neutrality be achieved? Rapport is indispensable and not presenting ourselves in a perfect light is also helpful. There are also some practical techniques to mitigate the undesirable (see also Dörnyei 2003), such as wording the question in a way that it suggests that the behaviour is rather common (for example, 'Even the most conscientious teachers sometimes ...'); using authority to make the sensitive issue/behaviour appear to be justifiable (for example, 'Many researchers now think that ...'); including reasons that explain the behaviour (for example, 'Does your busy schedule sometimes prevent you from ...?'); or simply adopting a casual approach (for example, 'Did you happen to ...?').

It must be noted that there is a debate in the qualitative literature concerning the neutrality issue (for a recent analysis, see Kvale 2006), and for example Fontana and Frey (2005) advocate 'empathetic interviewing' in which the interviewer takes a stance. The authors argue that the goal of scientific neutrality in an interview session is 'largely mythical' (p. 696) because interviewing is not merely the neutral exchange of asking questions and getting answers but rather a co-constructed social exchange in which taking a stance becomes unavoidable. This empathic stance is undoubtedly helpful in dealing with sensitive topics and eliciting more honesty because the interviewer is seen as an ally, but I am not quite sure how one is to handle an interview if one's personal stance does not fully coincide (or even clashes) with that of the interviewee. Obviously, some delicate balancing act is needed here between non-judgemental neutrality and empathetic understanding and approval.

- Listen more than you speak. Most interviewers talk too much. The interview is not a platform for the interviewer's personal experiences and opinions.
- Put questions in a straightforward, clear and non-threatening way. If people are confused or defensive, you will not get the information you seek.
- Eliminate cues which lead interviewees to respond in a particular way (for example, 'Are you against sin?'). Many interviewees will seek to please the interviewer by giving 'correct' responses.
- Enjoy it (or at least look as though you do). Don't give the message that you are bored or scared. Vary your voice and facial expression.

Table 6.1 Robson's (2002: 274) general advice for interviewers

Once we have successfully established the flow of the interview, we need to sustain it in an unobtrusive way. There are a number of useful techniques to keep the interview on track:

- *Carry-on feedback* Backchannelling signals (for example, nods, 'uh-huh' noises, one-word utterances like 'yeah') are offered by any sympathetic listener as part of normal communication and the interviewer must appear to be a particularly sympathetic listener. Miller and Crabtree (1999) also highlight the important role of small gestures such as the 'attentive lean' and the 'eyebrow flash', and we can add here the 'sympathetic smile'.
- *Reinforcement feedback* Just as in a normal conversation, we need to provide from time to time reinforcement, indicating that we are pleased with the way the interview is going and confirming that the interviewee's efforts are worthwhile. Everybody likes to be praised!
- *Negative reinforcement* What shall we do when the interview is not going as well as we think it could? After all, people often like to talk and go off at a tangent in a way which is not 'spontaneously emerging personal meaning' but merely waffling. If we give regular short reinforcement feedback (for example, nodding, uh-huhs) then simply withholding these and replacing them with an interjected question or a shift in our position might be enough of a nudge to get back on track. Alternatively, as Patton (2002) points out, some clever phrases might be used for inoffensive interruption and refocusing (for example, 'Let me stop you here for a moment and go back to what you said earlier to make sure that I understood you well').
- *Encouraging elaboration* In cases when the interviewee is not very forthcoming about a certain topic, we can use various probes (discussed in Section 6.4.2), including 'silent probes' that involve remaining quiet to indicate that we are waiting for more. More direct calls for elaboration include the 'echo prompt' (repeating the last word spoken by the respondent), low-inference paraphrasing or reflective summary and clarification questions. As mentioned earlier, a common technique is to take a salient

content word used by the respondent and repeat it with an interrogative tone or ask the interviewee to elaborate on it.

- *Attention focusing devices* In a long interview we need from time to time to rekindle the respondent's interest and refocus the responses. An attention-getting comment that precedes the question can achieve this; it may concern the question's importance, difficulty or any other characteristics ('Can I ask you now about an issue that is very important but not easy to talk about ...'). It is also useful to have transition announcements and introductory statements before a new issue is addressed because this advance notice will help to create the appropriate mindset or schema.

Ending the interview

We can signal that the interview is nearing the end by using pre-closing moves such as summarizing or recapping the main points of the discussion. These also have a significance content-wise because they allow the interviewee to correct anything that we may have misunderstood and to make any additional points. In fact, as discussed in connection to the interview guide (Section 6.4.2), we may wish to give the respondent an explicit opportunity to make any comments that might be relevant/important but which have not been covered in the rest of the interview ('I have no further questions. Do you have anything more you want to bring up, or ask about, before we finish the interview?' Kvale 1996: 128). Whether we do this or not, we need to be careful not to end the interview on a difficult topic—just like in oral language exams, we need to include a final winding down phase by steering the interview towards positive experiences. Kvale calls this function 'debriefing' and considers it vital given that the interviewee has opened him/herself up and may have disclosed deeply personal information. Therefore, in this final phase we need to re-express our gratefulness and respect, and discuss the ways by which the material will be used and the logistics of how to keep in touch in the future.

6.4.4 Strengths and weaknesses of interviews

The interview is a natural and socially acceptable way of collecting information that most people feel comfortable with and which can be used in a variety of situations and focusing on diverse topics to yield in-depth data. The interviewer's presence allows for flexible approaches, probing into any emerging new issue, while the interview guide helps to maintain a systematic coverage of the domain. Because of the high social profile of interviewing most of us will have several good interviewer models in our minds and therefore even beginning researchers are likely to be able to obtain rich data in their very first interviews.

The main weakness of the interview is that it is time-consuming to set up and conduct, and that it requires good communication skills on the part of the interviewer, which not all of us have naturally. Because the interview format does not allow for anonymity, there is a chance that the respondent will try to display him/herself in a better than real light. Interviewees can also be too shy and inarticulate to produce sufficient data, or at the other extreme, they can be too verbose, generating a lot of less-than-useful data.

6.5 Focus group interviews

Focus group interviews are sometimes treated as a subtype of interviewing but because both the format and the interviewer's role are considerably different in the interviewing process, I find it more appropriate to keep the two methods separate. Focus group interviews—as the name suggests—involve a group format whereby an interviewer records the responses of a small group (usually 6–12 members). This is obviously an economical way to gather a relatively large amount of qualitative data and therefore focus groups are used for a variety of purposes in many different fields. The name originally comes from market research but now the terms 'focus group interview' and 'group interview' are used interchangeably. The method has become familiar to the larger public when political parties have started to use it to gauge voter reaction to some planned policies and group interviews also feature frequently on television.

The focus group format is based on the collective experience of group brainstorming, that is, participants thinking together, inspiring and challenging each other, and reacting to the emerging issues and points. This within-group interaction can yield high-quality data as it can create a synergistic environment that results in a deep and insightful discussion. The format also allows for various degrees of structure, depending on the extent to which the researcher relies on an interview guide/protocol rather than giving the participants freedom to discuss some broad topics. Just like with one-to-one interviews, the semi-structured type of focus group is the most common format because it includes both open- and closed-ended questions posed by the researcher.

6.5.1 Characteristics of the focus groups

The size of a focus group ranges between 6–10 (sometimes 12) people. Fewer than six people would limit the potential of the 'collective wisdom' whereas too large a size makes it difficult for everyone to participate. When designing a focus group study, the two key technical questions to decide are (a) whether to have homogeneous or heterogeneous people in a group; and (b) how many groups to have.

- *Composition* Although, in line with the principles of maximum variation sampling (see Section 6.2.3), heterogeneous samples consisting of dissimilar people could in theory be useful in providing varied and rich data that covers all angles, it has been found that the dynamics of the focus group works better with homogeneous samples. Therefore, in order to obtain a wide range of information, the usual strategy is to have several groups which, as a whole, are different from each but each of which is made up of similar people; this is usually referred to as 'segmentation' and it involves within-group homogeneity and intergroup heterogeneity in the sample.

- *Number or parallel focus groups* The standard practice is to run several focus groups in any research project. In this way we can mitigate any idiosyncratic results that occur because of some unexpected internal or external factor that affects the dynamics of a group. Thus, in order to achieve adequate breadth and depth of information, it is usually recommended that a project involve 4–5 groups as a minimum, with a few more if possible.

6.5.2 Conducting the focus group interview

In focus group interviews the interviewer is usually referred to as the 'moderator', and this special name reflects the fact that the researcher's role differs from that in one-to-one interviews. Although they still need to ask questions, during the session they need to function more as facilitators of the discussion than as interviewers in the traditional sense. Because the dynamic of the focus group is one of the unique features of this method, the researcher's role inevitably involves some group leadership functions, including making sure that nobody dominates the floor and that even the shyer participants have a chance to express their views. In addition, moderators need to prevent any dominating and inhibiting group opinion—or 'groupthink'—from emerging by actively encouraging group members to think critically (Dörnyei and Murphey 2003). It is because of these multiple responsibilities that research methodologists usually agree that a focus group is only as good as its moderator.

Thus, focus group moderation can be a challenging task, particularly in the light of the fact that a focus group interview can last as long as three hours (although the usual length is between 1–2 hours). The process starts with an introductory phase, in which the moderator welcomes the participants, outlines the purpose of the discussion and sets the parameters of the interview in terms of length and confidentiality. Researchers should at this point also spend some time explaining why they record the interview and what sort of technical issues this raises in a group discussion (particularly talking one at a time). Finally, it is important to emphasize that the discussion is about personal views and experiences and therefore there are no right or wrong answers.

The actual discussion follows broadly the interview guide but even a semi-structured guide does not usually contain more than 5–10 broad, open-ended questions accompanied by a few closed-ended questions. After all, the strength of this format is the discussion that emerges about a broad topic. The moderator can steer the discussion by using probes, and body language and gesturing are effective devices to control the flow and keeping the group focused. Particular care must be taken to also allow socially less desirable views to be voiced because in a group session respondents may be more reluctant to share dispreferred answers than in a one-to-one interview.

In the concluding phase, the moderator needs to ask if there are any issues or concerns that require further discussion or have not yet been addressed. Because of the group nature of the session we also need to include a short winding down phase and some positive feedback so that nobody leaves the session being dissatisfied with themselves or with the social image they may have projected.

6.5.3 Strengths and weaknesses of focus group interviewing

Focus groups are highly versatile: as mentioned earlier, they can be used in a wide range of areas, from market research to political opinion probing, and in educational contexts they are also often used for programme evaluation to assess the effectiveness of a particular course to understand what was or was not working and why. People do not usually mind participating in focus groups—in fact, they tend to find the sessions enjoyable and stimulating—and the interviews typically yield rich data. These merits, coupled with the quick turnaround, make the method popular.

Because of the flexible and information-rich nature of the method, focus groups are often used in mixed methods research. Although they can be used as a stand-alone method of inquiry, this is not that common except for some areas where focus groups are well established (most notably market research) because researchers often feel that they have more control over the content and can elicit deeper and more 'unedited' personal meaning in one-to-one interviews. In applied linguistic research they have been widely used for generating ideas to inform the development of questionnaires and subsequent deep interviews.

The downside of focus group interviews is that they need quite a bit of preparation to set up, and to do them well the moderator needs to be able to carry out several functions simultaneously. There is also more need to improvise because the number of questions to be asked following the interview guide is relatively low and a lot of the content emerges from well-managed group discussion facilitated by probe questions. With regard to the content of the elicited material, Smithson (2000) mentions two possible limitations: the tendency for certain types of socially acceptable opinion to emerge and for certain types of participant to dominate the research process. Finally, an important technical point is that transcribing such an interview can be rather difficult because of the number of people (i.e. voices) involved. For this reason, researchers sometimes also prepare a video recording of the interviews—ancillary to audiotaping—so that they can identify who is speaking at any one time.

6.6 Introspective methods

Ever since the beginnings of psychological research at the end of the nineteenth century, psychologists have been trying to find ways of obtaining information about unobservable mental processes such as thoughts, feelings, and motives. One obvious source of information about these processes is the individual him/herself, and the various ways of eliciting self-reflections from respondents is usually referred to under the umbrella term 'introspective method'. It subsumes several different approaches that all aim at helping the respondents to vocalize what is/was going through their minds when making a judgement, solving a problem or performing a task. The data generated by this methodology is called a 'verbal report' or 'verbal protocol' and therefore introspective methods are also referred to as 'verbal reporting' or 'protocol analysis'.

We must note here that there is some inconsistency in the terminology in the area, because sometimes 'introspection' is used as a higher-order term that includes any form of self-report such as diaries, interviews, and even surveys, and when the term is applied so broadly, verbal reporting is seen only as a subset. (See Gass and Mackey 2000.) However, typically when we talk about introspective methods we usually imply two specific techniques: 'think-aloud' and 'retrospective reports/interviews', the latter also called 'stimulated recall'. The main difference between these two types of introspection lies in the timing: the think-aloud technique is applied real-time, concurrently to the examined task/process, whereas the retrospective interview, as the name suggests, happens after the task/process has been completed.

As Gass and Mackey (2000) explain, the assumption underlying introspection is that it is possible to observe internal processes, that is, what is going on in one's consciousness, in much the same way as one can observe external real-world events. Of course, this 'observation' requires the active cooperation of the person whose thought processes we are examining, and a subsequent assumption is, therefore, that humans have access to their internal thought processes at some level and can verbalize them.

Ericsson (2002; see also Ericsson and Simon 1987) observes that introspection has been present in western thought for a long time, but appeared as a method of scientific inquiry at the end of the nineteenth century when psychology first emerged as a scientific discipline. In fact, early psychologists relied heavily on introspective analysis of thoughts and memories but the method soon lost favour because it came to be regarded as unreliable and reactive (i.e. interfering with the actual thought processes rather than purely reporting them). It was only after cognitive psychology gradually replaced the dominance of behaviourism in the 1960s that verbal reporting, especially think-aloud techniques, were reintroduced into scientific research and the methodology was systematically refined.

Because of the significance of various mental operations in producing language, introspective methods have been seen to have considerable relevance to applied linguistics for several decades. (See Færch and Kasper 1987.) Kormos (1998) points out that the method is particularly important in second language research because it can help to uncover the cognitive and psycholinguistic processes underlying language performance. Because introspective methods can be used to supplement almost any other research method, I believe there is a large scope for increasing its application in our field.

6.6.1 Think-aloud technique

One of the main proponents of introspective methods in psychology, Ericsson (2002), explains that the closest connection between thinking processes and verbal reports are found when participants are instructed to verbalize their ongoing thoughts while focusing on a task. This technique has come to be known as 'think-aloud' and it involves the concurrent vocalization of one's 'inner speech' without offering any analysis or explanation. Thus, respondents are asked to verbalize only the thoughts that enter their attention while still in the respondent's short-term memory. In this way, the procedure does not alter the sequence of thoughts mediating the completion of a task and, according to Ericsson, can therefore be accepted as valid data on thinking. The resulting verbal protocol is recorded and then analysed.

It is clear that providing think-aloud commentary is not a natural process and therefore participants need precise instructions and some training before they can be expected to produce useful data. They need to be told to focus on their task performance rather than on the 'think-aloud' and they usually need to be reminded to keep on talking while carrying out an activity (for example, 'What made you do that?' or 'What are you thinking about now?'). In terms of training, the researcher needs first to demonstrate the procedures on a similar task (or show a video that models the required behaviour) and then respondents are given trials on warm-up tasks until they get the feel of reporting without explaining or justifying. (See Cohen 1998.) Gass and Mackey (2000) point out that it is still an unresolved issue how such training affects the validity of the verbal report because verbalizations can be influenced by the preceding input (i.e. confounding variables can be introduced).

6.6.2 Retrospective interview or stimulated recall

In 'retrospection', the respondents verbalize their thoughts after they have performed a task or mental operation. In such cases, the relevant information needs to be retrieved from long-term memory and thus the validity of retrospective protocols depends on the time interval between the occurrence of a thought and its verbal report. Ericsson (2002) concludes that for tasks with relatively short response latencies (less than 5–10 seconds), subjects are able to produce accurate recollections, but for cognitive processes of longer duration, the difficulty of accurate recall of prior thoughts increases. Although Mackey and Gass (2005) report some immediate recall studies in applied linguistic research, they point out that this type of retrospection is difficult to implement in areas such as interaction research. Instead, they recommend another type of retrospection that is often referred to as 'stimulated recall' or 'retrospective interview'.

Stimulated recall takes place some time after the occurrence of the targeted thought processes and in order to help the respondents to retrieve their relevant thoughts, some sort of stimulus is used as a support for the recall (hence the term 'stimulated recall'), such as watching the respondent's own task performance on video, listening to a recording of what the person has said, or showing the person a written work that he/she has produced. Thus, the underlying idea is that some tangible (visual or aural) reminder of an event will stimulate recall to an extent that the respondents can retrieve and then verbalize what was going on in their minds during the event (Gass and Mackey 2000).

While the quality of the recall inevitably suffers with the time lapse regardless of the nature of the stimulus prompt, Ericsson (2002) also highlights a merit of this approach: it is the least reactive of all the introspective techniques, because the targeted thought processes are not affected by the procedure in any way, particularly if we do not even tell the respondents during the task that we would like to ask them to give a running commentary afterwards.

How can we improve the quality of the retrospective data? Based on Gass and Mackey (2000), Mackey and Gass (2005), the studies in Færch and Kasper (1987) as well as my own experience, the following recommendations can be made:

- We need to try and keep the interval between the task and the retrospective interview as short as possible. Often (for example, in strategy research) the researcher first needs to transcribe and analyse the respondent's speech to make the retrospective session really meaningful because only such a thorough engagement with the text can reveal certain subtle issues that require clarification; however, even in such cases the time lapse should not exceed two days (and should preferably be less than 24 hours).

- The richer the contextual information and stimulus about the target event, the better. Therefore, listening to a recording is better than merely looking at the transcript, and watching a video recording is superior to listening to an audio recording.

- We should only encourage the recall of directly retrievable information (for example, 'What were you thinking of?') rather than explanations or interpretations.

- If possible, the respondents should not be informed of the subsequent retrospective interview (or the exact details of what it will involve) before the completion of the task so that the foreknowledge does not affect their performance.

- Gass and Mackey (2000) point out that stimulated recall does not require extensive participant training because simple instructions and a direct model are often enough. We need to be careful not to cue the respondents into any aspects of the study that are unnecessary and might affect their responses.
- During the retrospective interview we should try and involve the respondents as much as possible in volunteering data (for example, ask them to stop the cassette recorder when they remember something that might be useful) and even when we highlight parts to comment on (for example, by stopping the playing of the tape at critical points), we should avoid leading questions or any other researcher interference.
- If possible, the retrospective interview should be in the respondent's L1 (or in the language the respondent chooses).
- The whole retrospective procedure needs to be piloted. Gass and Mackey (2000) offer complete sample protocols for stimulated recall procedures in oral interaction settings.

6.6.3 Analysing introspective data

Just because introspective reports come 'straight from the horse's mouth', they cannot be taken as the ultimate revelations about thought processes. Rather, as Kasper (1998) emphasizes, they represent information about what is going through someone's mind when addressing a task or issue and the underlying cognitive processes need to be inferred from these verbal reports just as with other types of data. In other words, verbal reports must be seen only as one valuable source of data that needs to be subjected to qualitative data analysis similar to all the other qualitative data types. (See Chapter 10.) Swain (2006) further argues that verbal protocols not only report cognitive processes but have the power to influence cognition as well, and although given the intensive participant engagement required by most qualitative techniques it is not unique to have the threat of some sort of an interaction between respondent data and design parameters in general (for example, 'researcher effect', 'practice effect', or 'panel conditioning'; see Section 3.1.1), we need to bear in mind that introspective data is very sensitive to this because the articulation of thoughts can easily (and Swain argues, inevitably) mediate development. This adds further weight to the fact that we need to exercise caution when interpreting introspective data.

6.6.4 Strengths and weaknesses of introspective methods

The major advantage of the use of introspective methods is obvious: by applying them we can potentially gain access to mental processes that are central, for example, to language processing and production but which are inaccessible by any other means. Verbal reports are also versatile as they can b in a variety of domains—retrospective interviews can utilize diverse s from video recordings to written products and even test or questic responses. Introspection can be combined with most other research methods (see Section 7.3.2) and it has been generally found to greatly enhance the richness of the data obtained and can also increase to a considerable extent the reliability of the data analysis (Kormos 1998).

Although the reliability and the validity of introspective measures has been questioned in psychology, it appears that properly designed and conducted introspective studies meet the requirements of scientific research. (See Cohen 1998; Ericsson 2002; Gass and Mackey 2000.) As Ericsson concludes, the theoretical and methodological questions raised about verbal reports have never cast doubt on people's ability to recall part of their thought sequences and all major theoretical frameworks concerned with thinking have advocated the use of verbally reported sequences of thoughts.

On the negative side, as Cohen (1998) summarizes, critics of introspective methods note that much of cognitive processing is inaccessible because it is unconscious, and even certain conscious processes can be argued to be too complex to be captured in verbal protocols. Furthermore, verbal reports are not immune to the social desirability bias and there is a danger that the background knowledge or 'folk psychology' of the respondent might contaminate the data. In addition, in stimulated recall studies there is an inevitable information loss due to the time lapse between the task and the retrospective interview.

One of the most serious concerns about introspective data is the reactive effects of producing verbal reports. The procedure can interfere with task completion and thought processes and in a study by Stratman and Hamp-Lyons (1994) on the reactivity of think-alouds in writing, the researchers found some (but not conclusive) evidence that think-aloud protocols influenced the correction of organizational-level errors as well as the amount and kind of micro-structural meaning changes. In addition, I have already mentioned Swain's (2006) concern that verbal reports are not neutral 'brain dumps' but rather processes of comprehending and reshaping experience.

6.7 Case studies

The 'case study'—as the term suggests—is the study of the 'particularity and complexity of a single case' (Stake 1995: xi). What is a 'case'? Cases are primarily people, but researchers can also explore in depth a programme, an institution, an organization, or a community. In fact, almost anything can serve as a case as long as it constitutes a single entity with clearly defined boundaries. Research studies sometimes describe a series of 'multiple cases'; this is fine as long as each individual case is considered the target of a separate study. For example, Duff (in press) describes her ethnographic case study of bilingual education in Hungary as having at least three levels: the first level was one case, the country itself; the second level involved three cases, the three schools studied, and the third level included as many as eight cases, the teacher participants.

How are the selected cases studied? Case study researchers usually combine a variety of data collection methods such as interviews, observation and document archives. Although case studies are typically discussed under the label of qualitative research (because a single case cannot be representative of a population), actual case studies often include quantitative data collection instruments as well such as questionnaires (Verschuren 2003). Thus, the case study is not a specific technique but rather a method of collecting and organizing data so as to maximize our understanding of the unitary character of the social being or object studied. In many ways, it is the ultimate qualitative method focusing on the 'Particular One'.

6.7.1 Main features of a case study

Stake (1995, 2005) distinguishes three types of case study: (a) the 'intrinsic case study' is undertaken to understand the intriguing nature of a particular case. That is, the case is of interest not because it illustrates something or represents other cases but because of its own value or speciality; (b) the 'instrumental case study' is intended to provide insight into a wider issue while the actual case is of secondary interest; it facilitates our understanding of something else; and (c) the 'multiple or collective case study' where there

is even less interest in one particular case, and a number of cases are studied jointly in order to investigate a phenomenon or general condition. Thus, a multiple case study is, in effect, an instrumental case study extended to several cases. As one of the leading case study researchers in applied linguistics, Duff (2006), describes, most of her students conduct case studies with 4–6 focal participants in one or more sites, and this multiple case study format can be seen as fairly typical. Duff explains that choosing six cases initially means that even if there is attrition among the participants (and there usually is), there will likely be 3–4 cases remaining.

Because of the detailed information we wish to gather about the case, researchers usually spend an extended period of time examining the case in its natural surroundings. Therefore, case studies are often at least partially longitudinal in nature. During this period—as mentioned above—almost any type of research method can be used that can yield case-specific data. Especially if the case is not an individual but, say, an institution, this can lead to an overabundance of data, and in order to remain on top of all the details, it may be useful to have a 'data-gathering plan', which defines the case, the research questions, the data sources, and the allocation of time.

6.7.2 The generalizability issue

The main reservation about case studies, particularly if they concern individuals rather than social objects, is their generalizability: how can knowledge coming from one inevitably idiosyncratic source be of wider relevance? In Section 2.1.3 we saw that qualitative research is not overly concerned with generalizability as long as the researcher believes that the specific individual meaning obtained from the sample is insightful and enlightening. Yet, there is admittedly a great psychological difference between trusting a small-scale qualitative study (regardless of the sample size) and a single-case study. As a result, this issue has been the subject of heated discussions in the literature and warrants further attention here too.

As we saw above, in intrinsic case studies the case represents some unique or not-yet-understood feature which might explain not only to the researcher but also to the research audience the relevance of the case to our general understanding of a wider domain. For example, few people would question that a case study of a 'language savant' (an individual with less-than-average mental skills but with very special language abilities) or a uniquely gifted language learner would be a worthwhile and a widely sought-after investigation in applied linguistics. Multiple case studies again have satisfactory face validity because of their comparative nature. (See for example, Wong-Fillmore 1979, which has been a particularly influential study in applied linguistics regardless of the fact that it only involved five cases.) The real issue, then, is what Stake (1995, 2005) has termed the instrumental case study, where we examine a case to gain insights into a more general matter. There are two points to consider here:

- *Analytic generalization* Duff (in press) points out that although the concept of 'generalization' is usually understood as generalizing to populations, it can also refer to the generalization to *theoretical models*, resulting in 'analytic generalization'. The early case studies in applied linguistics (see Section 6.7.3 below), many of which fall under the instrumental category, represent this approach well because they led to the formulation of several theoretical principles and models that are still considered relevant today.
- *Purposive sampling* In instrumental case studies a key issue underlying the broader relevance of the investigation is the sampling strategy that results in the selection of the particular case. Indeed, Duff (in press) confirms that case selection and sampling are 'among the most crucial considerations in case study research'. Section 6.2.3 presents various qualitative sampling strategies that fall under the broader category of 'purposive sampling'; I would argue that if conducted well, several of these strategies—such as typical, criterion, extreme/deviant, and critical case sampling—will lead to cases whose study can have a lot to offer to the wider research community, particularly in terms of new conceptualizations and novel propositions.

This is especially true, as Punch (2005) emphasizes, in areas where our knowledge is shallow, fragmentary, incomplete, or nonexistent.

Thus, case studies following purposive sampling and combined with analytic generalization can offer (and have proved to be able to offer) as valid results as any other research method. On the other hand, Punch (2005) also emphasizes that the potential value of in-depth case studies does not mean that we should not be critical of some stand-alone studies that are too descriptive or insufficiently integrated into the broader study of the subject matter, or which claim more from their findings than the data can bear.

6.7.3 Case studies in applied linguistic research

Two recent reviews of case studies, by Duff (in press) and van Lier (2005), provide convincing evidence that the case study approach has been productive and highly influential in applied linguistics. In fact, as both scholars point out, the foundations of the whole discipline were based on the results of the first wave of case studies of language learners in the 1970s and 1980s (by researchers such as Hatch, Schmidt, Schumann, and Wong-Fillmore). These studies are still widely cited in the literature because they helped to shape our collective thinking in substantial ways.

Case studies did not lose their significance after the foundations had been laid and applied linguistic research entered into a new phase of fine-tuning the broad observations made by the first generation scholars. As described in Chapter 2, qualitative research is uniquely capable of documenting and analysing the situated, contextual influences on language acquisition and use, as well as the subtle variations in learner and teacher identities that emerge during the language learning/teaching process. Case study researchers (for example, Duff, Han, Lam, McKay, Norton, Sarangi, Toohey and colleagues), have embraced a wide range of related topics, from race and gender to community membership and social status; by exploiting the inherently longitudinal nature of case study methodology they succeeded in generating a new understanding of how SLA is experienced and perceived by the participants, and what effects their agency has on their specific language development. Van Lier (2005) points out that an area which is currently much in need of case study research is the role of technology in SLA, for example CALL.

To illustrate the variety of case study research, let me list some typical participants of these studies (Duff in press): infants, children in monolingual and bilingual homes/schools, minority students, adolescent and adult immigrants, study-abroad students, adults learning an additional language or losing an existing language, exceptional learners, etc. The domains addressed have also been far-ranging as demonstrated by the following selection of prominent topics covered by Duff (in press): child language acquisition, bilingualism, bilingual families, biculturalism, language loss, developmental order, identity, investment, gender, fossilization, pragmatic development, language socialization, virtual discourse communities, teacher agency, etc. Thus, it is obvious that case study methodology has been suitable to be utilized in relation to diverse contexts and topics throughout the evolution of the field of applied linguistics up to the most current research interests.

6.7.4 Strengths and weaknesses of case studies

The case study is an excellent method for obtaining a thick description of a complex social issue embedded within a cultural context. It offers rich and in-depth insights that no other method can yield, allowing researchers to examine how an intricate set of circumstances come together and interact in shaping the social world around us. When done well, as Duff (in press) concludes, case studies display a high degree of completeness, depth of analysis and readability, and they are effective in generating new hypotheses, models, and understandings about the target phenomena. Thus, the method is highly recommended for exploring uncharted territories or making sense of a particularly problematic research area, and it can provide an unparalleled understanding of longitudinal processes. As van Lier (2005: 195) summarizes, 'Case study research has become a key method for researching changes in complex phenomena over time. Many of the processes investigated in case studies cannot be adequately researched in any of the other common research methods'.

In addition, what is particularly noteworthy from the perspective of this book, the case study is ideally suited for being combined with other research approaches (for example, a subsequent survey) in mixed methods studies. Indeed, Duff (in press) reports that case studies have been increasingly used in mixed methods studies such as programme evaluations.

With regard to its weaknesses, Duff (in press) points out that case study methodology is often contrasted negatively with large-scale experimental methods, with the strengths of one approach being the weaknesses of the other. This contrast is inappropriate and rather unfair because the two types of methodologies are intended to achieve different goals. Yet, having a single case presents certain limitations, and with the case study being a prototype of qualitative research, many of the potential shortcomings of the qualitative approach mentioned in Chapter 2 (Section 2.3.3) could be listed here. My personal feeling is that because of the heightened vulnerability of this method in terms of idiosyncratic unpredictability and audience criticality, in most cases it may be worth using (a) multiple-case designs or (b) case studies in some combination with other methods.

6.8 Diary studies

Diary-writing is a pervasive narrative form.
(McDonough and McDonough 1997: 121)

Diaries have been used for hundreds of years to record the events of people's everyday lives, but the diary study as a data collection method has been employed by social researchers only since the 1970s. Diary methods were initiated in the field of psychology to study emotions and moods across situations in daily experience and they have also been used in family psychology to obtain data about intimate aspects of the life of couples (Laurenceau and Bolger 2005). In general, diaries offer the opportunity to investigate social, psychological, and physiological processes within everyday situations and, as Bolger *et al.* (2003) summarize, asking research participants to keep regular records of certain aspects of their daily lives allows the researcher to capture the particulars of experience in a way that is not possible using other methods.

It is important to note at this point that the term 'diary studies' usually refers to data obtained from 'solicited diaries' only, that is, from accounts produced specifically at the researcher's request, by an informant or informants (Bell 1999). Of course, personal diaries may also contain data that is relevant for some research purposes, but using such data raises research ethical and validity questions, and in any case, finding such spontaneous diaries is usually not practical for most research studies. Solicited diaries offer the possibility to capture the autobiographical aspect of private diaries in a more systematic and controlled way, thereby letting 'people be heard on their own terms' (p. 266).

In applied linguistics, diaries have been used since the beginning of the 1980s to obtain personal accounts of the experience of language learning both by learners themselves and by parents documenting their (mainly bilingual) children's L2 development, and diary studies have also been used in teacher education programmes. (For overviews, see for example, Bailey 1990; Duff in press; McDonough and McDonough 1997: Chapter 8.)

6.8.1 Recording diary entries

Diary studies have often been classified into three categories depending on when the diary entries are to be made: 'interval-', 'signal-', and 'event-contingent' designs (Bolger *et al.* 2003). The interval-contingent design requires participants to report on their experiences at regular, predetermined intervals (for example, every afternoon at 4 pm). Signal-contingent designs rely on some signalling device such as a pager, a programmed wristwatch or a phone call to prompt participants to provide diary reports. This design is often used when studying momentary experiences of people such as psychological states (for example, happiness or stress). Event-contingent studies require participants to provide a self-report each time a specific event (such as a meeting with an L2 speaker) occurs.

The most commonly used approach in diary studies is giving the respondents traditional paper and pencil diaries. The entries can involve filling in a short questionnaire or entering a short verbal account. The former is, in fact, a repeated-measures quantitative questionnaire study and will not be discussed here. Over the last decade, paper and pencil diaries have been gradually replaced by electronic data collection methods of various forms, utilizing handheld computers equipped with special software. (For a detailed technical introduction that also includes software descriptions, see Bolger *et al.* 2003.) These allow for specific signalling and also provide time- and date-stamps for the responses.

6.8.2 Strengths of diary studies

Diaries offer a range of special features that are difficult or impossible to replicate using other data collection methods The most important ones are as follows:

- Diaries allow the researcher an unobtrusive way of tapping into areas of people's lives that may otherwise be inaccessible (Gibson 1995). We have seen in Chapter 2 that qualitative research involves the study of people in their natural contexts, with as little obtrusion as possible—diary studies can satisfy this requirement to a large extent.
- A further element of the qualitative inquiry is to try and elicit the participants' own descriptions and interpretations of events and behaviours—in diary studies the participants inevitably become co-researchers as they keep records of their own feelings, thoughts, or activities. Diary data is by definition an insider account.
- Diary methods enable the researcher to study time-related evolution or fluctuation within individuals by collecting data on many occasions from the same individuals. Thus, diary studies are appropriate for looking at temporal variation in dynamic processes, investigating for example how people change or respond to certain stimuli. Diary studies are more sensitive to such questions than many other longitudinal designs (see Section 4.3) because they typically involve more frequent data recording that can capture changes with increased fidelity.
- Diary studies can provide ongoing background information that can help resolve ambiguity regarding causal direction between variables. In applied linguistics, Schmidt and Frota (1986) reported, for example, that diary entries helped them to confirm the existence of certain acquisitional orders.

- Diary studies offer a self-report format that reduces inaccuracies stemming from not remembering something correctly, because when writing their entries participants recall recent rather than distant events (van Eerde *et al.* 2005).

6.8.3 Weaknesses of diary studies

If diary studies have as much potential as described in the previous section, why don't we use them more? There are at least two main reasons for the dearth of diary studies in applied linguistics. One is simply that this method is rather novel and therefore it is not yet covered in standard methodology courses and texts. Thus, many scholars are simply not familiar with it sufficiently to consider it a realistic option when preparing a research design. The other reason is that the method has some serious weaknesses which make researchers think twice before attempting to use it. Let us have a look at these:

- The first and most obvious limitation of diary studies is that the informant needs to be not only literate but actually comfortable at writing diary entries. As Gibson (1995) points out, one way of overcoming the problem of illiteracy would be to allow the informant to keep an audio or video diary.
- The second source of weakness is that a diary study is very demanding on the part of the informant. First of all, it requires a detailed training session to ensure that participants fully understand the protocol. Second, to produce regular, high quality data, diary studies must achieve a level of participant commitment and dedication rarely required in other types of research (Bolger *et al.* 2003). Rossiter's (2001: 36) experience, for example, appears to be quite typical: 'Students were also asked to complete learning journals and motivation graphs in addition to their assigned homework, but, as there was no incentive for them to do so, many did not'. One way of addressing the problem is to reduce the time necessary to use the diary instrument, but this is obviously at the expense of the richness of the resulting dataset.
- A further, seemingly trivial but in actual practice rather serious shortcoming of diary studies is that they are vulnerable to honest forgetfulness, where participants fail to remember the scheduled response times or fail to have the diaries at hand (Bolger *et al.* 2003); alternatively, they may be too tired or simply not in the mood to prepare their scheduled entry. This, of course, can defeat the main benefit of diaries, their ability to obtain accurate, real-time information.
- It has also been found that the length and depth of diary entries show considerable variation. Gibson (1995), for example, reviews studies that report a consistent decline in the recounting of events with the passage of

time. Also, and for obvious reasons, there is a decline in the diary entries during stressful events, even though from the researcher's perspective these events may be of particular interest.

6.8.4 Practical suggestions to facilitate diary studies

Despite all the problems they might be associated with, diary studies could be used to good effect more often in applied linguistic research. Therefore, let me make some practical points to facilitate this practice:

- The multiple benefits of diary studies would warrant in many cases at least an attempt to implement a diary study. I have seen encouraging examples of successful diary studies in educational contexts where the researchers were in regular touch with the informants (for example, they or their research assistants/associates were teaching the respondents).
- Researchers have tried different ways of increasing the informants' motivation to persist with the study and make high quality entries at the scheduled time. (See Bolger *et al.* 2003; Gibson 1995.) First, the procedures can be made as convenient and user-friendly as possible, with making portable, pocket-size diaries and preprint the dates and times of expected responses onto the diary sheets in order to keep participants on track. In certain studies the diary can be further structured by adding, for example, key questions—When? Where? What? Who?—on the diary pages. Second, a regular gentle check-up and, if needed, 'nudge' by a research assistant with whom the informant has developed good rapport has been found to be beneficial. Third, in some instances researchers have used rewards as an incentive to boost compliance—this can either be money or some gift token.
- Finally, even if there are gaps in the diary entries, these can be filled in by follow-up interviews. In this case the diary entries have a similar function to the written or auditory recall prompts used in stimulated recall methodology. (See Section 6.6.2.)

6.9 Research journals

> *One of the best ways to begin to define what interests you and your thoughts about what you already know is with a research journal.*
> (Hatch and Lazaraton 1991: 10)

Research journals are diaries kept by the researchers themselves during the course of a research project rather than by the participants of a study concerning the topic of the investigation (which was discussed in the previous section); to make this distinction clear, I will refer to these researcher notes as 'journals' even though in the literature the terms 'diary' and 'journal' are often used synonymously. It is a common recommendation in social research that the researcher should keep a journal, and we find a mention of the use of the author's research journal in many research publications. (For a recent overview of using research journals in educational research, see Altrichter and Holly 2005.) However, apart from ethnographic studies where field notes are an integral part of the inquiry, qualitative investigations typically provide few details on the nature of the journal data, that is, what sort of information was recorded and how. In fact, as Hammersley and Atkinson (1995) point out, even ethnographic field notes are characterized by 'relative invisibility' (p. 176), and my personal experience is that novice researchers who do not specialize in ethnography are often unaware of the fact that if they keep their research journal 'orderly' by using some standardized format, then it can be entered as a valuable source of data.

It was said in Chapter 2 that in qualitative research almost anything can be perceived as potential data, and there is no reason why the researcher's field notes, real-time comments, memos, and annotations would be exceptions. Personal agency is an important part of qualitative inquiries and the 'meta-data' generated by the researcher offer valuable insights into the project. In Section 3.4.2 we discussed the importance of the 'research log', but whereas in quantitative studies such a log plays largely an administrative role, the log trail of a qualitative study can become an important part of the dataset. As Hammersley and Atkinson (1995: 191–2) comment, 'The construction of analytic notes ... constitutes precisely the sort of internal dialogue, or thinking aloud, that is the essence of reflexive ethnography'. And the vehicle to transform private knowledge, by reflection and analysis, into potential public knowledge is the researcher's journal. Silverman (2005: 252) also recommends keeping a research journal as in this 'you can show your readers the development of your thinking; help your own reflection; improve your time management; and provide ideas for the future direction of your work'.

Richards (2005) emphasizes a further significance of an appropriately maintained 'log trail'. She argues that in order to make claims credible, qualitative researchers need to account for each step in the project and document where the ideas and theories came from. Thus, such accounts are central in fending off challenges to validity and reliability in qualitative research. (See also the discussion on 'audit trails' in Section 3.1.2.)

Despite these obvious advantages, few researchers actually maintain a systematic research journal. One reason for this may be simply not realizing the significance of the journal, but Duff (in press) points out a second possible reason, namely that keeping a systematic account of one's research activities and reflections takes considerable discipline, 'especially when juggling many kinds of tasks (including data collection and analysis) at once'. Yet, she recommends having a research journal because it not only helps in remembering important details later on, but 'journal-keeping becomes part of the analysis and interpretation process itself as researchers start to mull over new data and themes'. She cites Schmidt's famous research journal (Schmidt and Frota

1986) as a good example of how the journal can become a 'platform for conceptualizing, noticing, articulating, or testing out new hypotheses or ideas'.

6.9.1 How to keep research records

Scientific data needs to meet certain requirements of reliability and validity, and therefore if we decide to use our research journal as a data source, we need to pay attention to some technical details. If we keep a pencil and paper journal, the minimal requirement is to have a properly pre-bound folder with each page numbered and each entry dated, but some researchers recommend a more formalized approach. Silverman (2005), for example, outlines an organization framework consisting of four categories: (1) observation notes about experiences, (2) methodological notes about how and what kind of data were collected, (3) theoretical notes describing hunches, hypotheses and ideas, and (4) personal notes containing feeling statements (concerning for example, satisfaction, surprise, shock, etc.) and other subjective comments. Cryer (2000: 99) recommends that research students should record in their logbooks and journals the following:

- What you do, and where, how, when, and why you do it.
- What you read.
- What data you collect and how you process it.
- Any outcomes of the data analysis.
- Particular achievements, dead ends, and surprises.
- What you think or feel about what is happening, and any ideas that may be relevant for your research.
- Anything else that is influencing you.

With the increasing availability and use of personal, and especially portable, computers more and more scholars transfer some of the traditional paper and pencil records to electronic files. Qualitative data analysis software fully supports such electronic logging and memoing (see Richards 2005 and Section 10.4 in this volume) and they make it easy to integrate the entries of the electronic research journal with the rest of the transcribed data. In this way, our own reflections and ideas can become more than analytic tools—they can become data that can be submitted to further analysis.

Altrichter and Holly (2005) emphasize that an important aspect of the research journal as a data source is to include 'descriptive sequences' such as accounts of activities and events, or reconstructions of dialogues. In such accounts, the authors stress, details are more important than summaries and we need to focus on the particular rather than the general. Exact quotes (marked with quotation marks) are welcome, particularly words and phrases that are typical of a person. Altrichter and Holly also make some practical points, on the basis of which the following six journal writing strategies can be formulated:

1 Write regularly.
2 Persist through the initial difficult period that occurs to many new writers.
3 Consider the journal *private* so that you don't have to censor yourself or worry about style and punctuation (you can decide about disclosing some parts later).
4 Introduce a regular structure and format in your entries.
5 Include relevant illustrative materials such as photos, notes, documents, lesson plans, student works, etc.
6 From time to time do a provisional analysis of the journal entries to check whether the balance and amount of the different type of notes is right.

7

Mixed methods research: purpose and design

> *... it is important to note that we see no chasm between qualitative and quantitative techniques. It is our experience that many qualitative projects involve counting at some stage, and many questions are best answered by quantification.*
> (Morse and Richards 2002: 27)

A mixed methods study involves the collection or analysis of both quantitative and qualitative data in a single study with some attempts to integrate the two approaches at one or more stages of the research process. In other words, mixed methods research involves the mixing of quantitative and qualitative research methods or paradigm characteristics (Johnson and Christensen 2004). As mentioned in Section 2.4, various labels have been used to describe this methodology—multitrait-multimethod research, interrelating qualitative and quantitative data, methodological triangulation, multimethodological research, mixed model studies, and mixed methods research—with 'mixed methods research' becoming the widely accepted standard term.

We saw in Chapter 2 that after the 'paradigm war' in the 1970s and 1980s, which emphasized the ideological differences between qualitative and quantitative research, a period of reconciliation followed, as a result of which QUAL and QUAN researchers have not only started to accept each other but have even begun to integrate the two approaches. In fact, as Sandelowski (2003) concludes, mixed methods research has by now become somewhat of a fad, a way to be methodologically fashionable and to exercise methodological ecumenicism. It has its enthusiasts and, for example, Onwuegbuzie and Leech (2005: 375) go as far as to claim that 'Monomethod research is the biggest threat to the advancement of the social sciences'. Such committed believers in mixed methodology not only view the use of multiple perspectives, theories, and research methods as a strength in educational research, but they would claim that mixed methods studies can be superior to investigations produced by either quantitative or qualitative research alone. This is admittedly an extreme view, but there is now ample evidence in the literature that combining methods can open up fruitful new avenues for research in the social sciences.

In order to present a convincing case for mixed methods research, three basic questions need to be answered: (1) Why do we want to mix methods? (2) Isn't there a danger that the paradigmatic collision cancels out any potential benefits? (3) What are the best ways of mixing methods? Each of these questions will be addressed in a separate section and the chapter is concluded by examining a final, add-on question: why don't people mix methods more?

7.1 The purpose of mixed methods research

According to Sandelowski (2003), there are two main and somewhat conflicting purposes for combining methods: (a) to achieve a fuller understanding of a target phenomenon and (b) to verify one set of findings against the other. In the first instance the goal is to achieve an elaborate and comprehensive understanding of a complex matter, looking at it from different angles. The second purpose is the traditional goal of triangulation, namely to validate one's conclusion by presenting converging results obtained through different methods. (For a detailed discussion of the different functions with actual examples from educational research, see Hammond 2005.) We can add a very practical third purpose to the list of the main rationales for mixing: to reach audiences that would not be sympathetic to one of the approaches if applied alone. Let us have a look at these three objectives in more detail.

7.1.1 Expanding the understanding of a complex issue

According to Mertens (2005), mixed methods have particular value when we want to examine an issue that is embedded in a complex educational or social context. She argues that many researchers have used mixed methods because it seemed intuitively obvious to them that combining and increasing the number of research strategies used within a particular project would broaden the scope of the investigation and enrich the scholars' ability to draw conclusions about the problem under study. In an important paper in 1989, Greene, Caracelli and Graham listed four specific functions by which mixed methods research can produce a fuller picture of an issue:

- *Complementarity function* Qualitative and quantitative methods are used to measure overlapping but also different facets of a phenomenon, yielding an enriched understanding by illustrating, clarifying, or elaborating on certain aspects. The assumption therefore is that supplementary findings can produce a fuller portrait of the social world, similarly to pieces of a jigsaw puzzle when put together in the correct way (Erzberger and Kelle 2003). This idea underlies the often mentioned conception about the QUAL–QUAN 'division of labour' (for example, McCracken 1988) whereby qualitative research is used to *explore* a new phenomenon and develop an initial hypothesis, which is then *tested* in terms of the breadth of its distribution in the population by a quantitative method (for example, a survey).

- *Development function* Qualitative and quantitative methods are used sequentially so that the results of the first method inform the development of the second. For example, a focus group interview is used to develop items for a quantitative questionnaire. 'Development' can also be understood here to inform sampling decisions (for example, a questionnaire is used to select participants for a follow-up interview study).
- *Initiation function* Results obtained by multiple methods do not always produce corroborating or complementary results; however, divergent results can also be illuminating. Therefore, researchers may intentionally utilize varied methods to generate discrepancies, paradoxes, or contradictions, which are meant to be provocative through the recasting of questions, leading hopefully to new perspectives.
- *Expansion function* It is a frequent desire of researchers to expand the scope and breadth of a study by including multiple components. For example, qualitative methods can be used to explore the processes of a certain instructional programme and quantitative methods to assess the programme outcomes.

7.1.2 Corroborating findings through 'triangulation'

In Section 2.4.1 we saw that the introduction of 'triangulation' in the social sciences played a key role in initiating the combined use of qualitative and quantitative research in the 1970s. Transforming Campbell and Fiske's (1959) original concept into a broader research framework, Denzin (1978) applied the term to refer to the generation of multiple perspectives on a phenomenon by using a variety of data sources, investigators, theories, or research methods with the purpose of corroborating an overall interpretation. Since then triangulation has been seen as an effective strategy to ensure research validity: if a finding survives a series of tests with different methods, it can be regarded as more valid than a hypothesis tested only with the help of a single method (Erzberger and Kelle 2003).

It is important to note at this point that although it is indeed reassuring when a conclusion is confirmed from a different vantage point, the real question is how we should interpret any *divergence* in the triangulated findings. Exploring the conflicting results can lead to enhanced understanding, especially if it also involves further data collection, but this process is already not part of 'triangulation' in the strict sense but becomes an example of the 'initiation function' discussed above.

We should note further that whereas in the technical sense 'triangulation' only refers to 'validation-through-convergence', it has been used very broadly in research methodology texts, often as a synonym for mixing methods. Thus, 'triangulation' has become a popular umbrella term with different possible meanings that can be related to a variety of problems, which made Tashakkori and Teddlie (2003c) argue against the use of the term by mixed methods researchers. (For a recent overview of the triangulation issue, see Moran-Ellis *et al.* 2006.).

7.1.3 Reaching multiple audiences

I mentioned already in Section 2.4.1 that, because of the combination of methods in mixed methods research, the final results can be more palatable for certain audiences than the outcomes of a monomethod study. To put it broadly, a well-executed mixed methods study has multiple selling points. For example, if a PhD dissertation panel consists primarily of scholars working in the quantitative paradigm, they will be better able to relate to a qualitative study if it is accompanied by some quantitative component. This is not simply a case of validation through triangulation as described in the previous section but rather generating an overall level of trustworthiness for the researcher. Todd *et al.* (2004) also maintain that making findings more presentable this way also increases the chances of getting the results of largely qualitative work published in a more traditionally quantitative journal. (See also Section 13.2.1 on the 'Challenges and advantages of mixed methods reports'.)

7.2 The compatibility of different research paradigms

> *... much research in the 'real world' does not fit into neat categorizations of 'qualitative' and 'quantitative' and also does not appear to be too concerned with the epistemological issues that so exercise some commentators.*
> (Harden and Thomas 2005: 257)

Before looking at the main types of mixed methods designs, let us address the key issue underlying mixed methods research: can different forms of data and knowledge about the world be integrated? After all, we saw in Chapter 2 that quantitative researchers aspire to objectivity and universal truths, while qualitative advocates emphasize the 'interpretive, value-laden, contextual, and contingent nature of social knowledge' (Greene *et al.* 2005: 274). Were the 'paradigm warriors' engaging in the paradigm war of the 1970s and 1980s all overreacting? Or is there some truth in the claim that differing world views and contrasting explanatory logics can only be mixed superficially, resulting in an eclectic mish-mash?

I believe that there is no correct answer if we ask the questions this way, because everything depends on what exactly we are after in our research. Different scholars look at the world through different lenses, regard different things as important to know, and express themselves best within different research paradigms. Yet, this multi-coloured research scene is not to be mistaken for an 'anything goes' disposition; the crucial point is that one's world view, research methodology, and nature of interpretation should be *consistent*.

If we achieve this consistency we can produce high quality research results both in qualitative and quantitative ways—and mixed methods research has been advocated as a third principled approach to pursuing this objective. This has been clearly expressed by Johnson and Onwuegbuzie (2004: 14–15) in a position paper entitled 'Mixed methods research: A research paradigm whose time has come':

> Our purpose in writing this article is to present mixed methods research as the third research paradigm in educational research. We hope the field will move beyond quantitative *versus* qualitative research arguments because, as recognized by mixed methods research, *both* quantitative *and* qualitative research are important and useful. The goal of mixed methods research is not to replace either of these approaches but rather to draw from the strengths and minimize the weaknesses of both in single research studies and across studies. If you visualize a continuum with qualitative research anchored at one pole and quantitative research anchored at the other, mixed methods research covers the large set of points in the middle area. If one prefers to think categorically, mixed methods research sits in a new third chair, with qualitative research sitting on the left side and quantitative research sitting on the right side.

How can we achieve consistency in an approach that is based on mixing up very different components? The key process is 'principled mixing'. Mixing methods is not good per se and, in fact, it can be a distraction to serious research. However, certain mixtures can combine different methods in such a way that their strengths aggregate, thereby making the sum greater than the parts. This 'additive mixing' is at the heart of mixed methods research, which is why Johnson and Turner (2003) concluded that the *fundamental principle of mixed methods research* is that researchers should collect multiple data using different strategies, approaches, and methods in such a way that the resulting mixture or combination is likely to result in complementary strengths and non-overlapping weaknesses.

In accordance with the pragmatic foundation of mixed methods research, the mixing process is centred around the purpose of the investigation, that is, the research topic or question. Johnson and Onwuegbuzie (2004) argue that today's research scene is becoming increasingly interdisciplinary and complex, as a result of which many researchers feel the need to complement one method with another. Brannen (2005) adds a further research dimension that works in favour of the transcendence of paradigms: the growing desire of social researchers to link micro- and macro-level analyses. In the past, social scientists exploring the relationship between the individual and the surrounding social world have typically adopted one of two perspectives: an individualistic or a societal.

- In the 'individualistic perspective', the complexity of the social environment is only important inasmuch as it is reflected in the individual's mental processes and the resulting attitudes, beliefs, and values; that is, this perspective views the social world through the individual's eyes (for example, in social cognition theory).

- The 'societal perspective' focuses on broad social processes and macro-contextual factors, such as sociocultural norms, intergroup relations, acculturation/assimilation processes, and interethnic conflicts; from this perspective, the individual's behaviour is seen to be determined by the more powerful forces at large (for example, in social identity theory).

The tension between the two perspectives has been one of the most basic dilemmas in social research and over the past decades there have been calls for developing integrative theoretical frameworks that can create links between the two paradigms to understand individuals *in* society. (For an overview, see Abrams and Hogg 1999.) Mixed methods research seems ideally suited to operationalize the theoretical transcendence of the micro and macro perspectives at the research level.

To conclude, let us return to the starting question of this section: can different research paradigms be integrated? The general answer emerging in the field is 'yes' and often to very good effect. Greene and Caracelli (2003) even claim that in actual research, paradigms do not matter that much and therefore the philosophical discussions about paradigm compatibility have little relevance to empirical research: 'applied social inquirers appear to ground inquiry decisions primarily in the nature of the phenomena being investigated and the contexts in which the studies are conducted. Inquiry decisions are rarely, if ever, consciously rooted in philosophical assumptions or beliefs' (p. 107). From this perspective, mixed methods research offers researchers the advantage of being able to choose from the full repertoire of methodological options, producing as a result many different kinds of creative mixes. We are going to survey these next.

7.3 Main types of mixed methods designs

Several complex taxonomies have been proposed to cover all the possibilities whereby different components of qualitative and quantitative research can be integrated into a single study. (For reviews, see Creswell 2003; Creswell *et al.* 2003; Johnson and Onwuegbuzie 2004; Maxwell and Loomis 2003.) While such typologies can be beneficial in organizing and labelling varied practices and thus conveying a sense of rigour (Creswell *et al.* 2003), it is not clear how far it is worth pursuing such a formalized typological approach. The problem is twofold: on the one hand, the actual or potential diversity in mixed methods studies is far greater than any typology can adequately encompass and therefore not even the most detailed typologies are exhaustive (Maxwell and Loomis 2003; Teddlie and Tashakkori 2003). On the other hand, the typological approach seems to have developed a life of its own, detached from the actual research practice: although we can think of a range of sophisticated mixed models, Bryman's (2006) large-scale review of the research literature demonstrates that in actual research far fewer combinations have been used, with the combination of two methods in particular—questionnaires and semi-structured interviews—dominating.

In the light of the above, the bulk of the following material describing various research designs will be organized around an 'exemplar-based' typology that emphasizes the most frequent method combinations. Although this chapter focuses on data collection and Chapter 11 on data analysis, the material in the two chapters overlaps somewhat because mixed designs often display combinations at various levels at the same time.

7.3.1 Typological organization

According to Tashakkori and Teddlie's (2003c: 682) summary, the terminology currently describing mixed methods designs is 'chaotic'. In order to create some order, a number of different typologies have been proposed, centred around various organizing principles. The two most widely accepted typological principles have been the *sequence* and the *dominance* of the method constituents and scholars have also developed a simple symbol system to produce a straightforward visual representation (for example, Johnson and Christensen 2004: 418):

- 'QUAL' or 'qual' stand for qualitative research.
- 'QUAN' or 'quan' stand for quantitative research.
- Capital letters denote priority or increased weight.
- Lowercase letters denote lower priority or weight.
- A plus sign (+) represents a concurrent collection of data.
- An arrow (→) represents a sequential collection of data.

Thus, for example, 'qual → QUAN' indicates a study that consists of two phases, with the second, quantitative phase dominating; this symbol combination would describe, for example, a questionnaire survey where initial focus-group interviews were used to facilitate the development of the instrument.

If a study has only two components, a qualitative and a quantitative, both the sequence and the dominance dimensions have three categories (qualitative first, quantitative first or concurrent; and qualitative dominant, quantitative dominant or equal status), resulting in nine possible combinations:

1 QUAL + QUAN
2 QUAL + quan
3 QUAN + qual
4 QUAL → QUAN
5 QUAN → QUAL
6 QUAL → quan
7 qual → QUAN
8 QUAN → qual
9 quan → QUAL

This list becomes more extensive if we take more than two possible research phases into consideration, and the possible design types proliferate almost unstoppably if we add further organizing categories following the suggestions of several scholars. Punch (2005), for example, also recommended considering whether or not the methods influence the operationalization of each other; Creswell (2003; Creswell *et al.* 2003) divided the function of integration into three classes: triangulation, explanation, or exploration. Tashakkori and Teddlie (1998) highlighted the importance of deciding at what stage(s) in the research process the integration occurs: research objectives formulation, data collection, data analysis, or data interpretation. These are all important classification dimensions but if we include all their permutations in a typology, it will become far too large to serve any practical purpose. At the same time, as Johnson and Onwuegbuzie (2004) conclude, this variety illustrates the fact that mixed methods research truly opens up an exciting and almost unlimited potential for future research.

7.3.2 Exemplar-based typology

As seen above, the typological approach tends to be rather abstract and although it is possible to think of concrete examples for most of the different categories, such theoretically conceived typologies are more useful for the purpose of post-hoc classification of studies than for designing new research projects. Therefore, in the following I will follow a more pragmatic approach in presenting various mixed designs that are organized around the actual data collection methods applied and the main functions of the mixing. Listing design types in this way has a positive and a negative side: on the positive side, it uses descriptive labels to facilitate understanding (for example, 'Questionnaire survey facilitated by preceding interview' instead of 'qual → QUAN'). On the negative side, the list is selective rather than comprehensive; that is, it only includes the most prominent basic combinations. I believe that such a selective approach is useful to familiarize researchers with the concept of mixing so that they can then produce their own made-to-measure variations.

Questionnaire survey with follow-up interview or retrospection (QUAN → qual)

We saw in Chapter 5 that although the questionnaire survey is a versatile technique that allows us to collect a large amount of data in a relatively short time, it also suffers from an inherent weakness: the respondents' engagement tends to be rather shallow and therefore we cannot explore complex meaning directly with this technique: The use of sophisticated statistical procedures allows us to examine the interrelationship of the variables measured but if we find some unexpected results (and there are always some unexpected results!) we cannot usually interpret those on the basis of the questionnaire data. And even if an observed relationship makes sense, the questionnaire data usually reveals little about the exact nature of the relationship. Adding a subsequent qualitative component to the study can remedy this weakness. In a follow-up interview (either in an individual or group format) we can ask the respondents to explain or illustrate the obtained patterns, thereby adding flesh to the bones. In a study investigating the effect of class size differences on classroom processes, Blatchford (2005: 203) expressed this complementary function very clearly:

> There may be research questions best addressed with just one technique, but there are times, and we would cite our study of relations between class size and teaching as one such, when results from the integration of different techniques add up to more than the sum of the parts. This is seen, for example, in the way that numerical evidence on the way small classes leads to more individual attention, was strengthened and made more complete by detailed information on how this was expressed in particular classrooms (case studies) and perceived by individual teachers (questionnaires).

Creswell *et al.* (2003) labelled this combination a 'sequential explanatory design', which expresses its rationale well. This is a straightforward design that is easy to implement and analyse, yet which enriches the final findings considerably. It can benefit almost every quantitative study.

An important variation of this design that highlights its explanatory nature involves conducting a 'retrospective interview' (see Section 6.6.2) with some of the survey participants, using the respondents' own survey responses as the retrospective prompts for further open-ended reflection about what they really meant. This design pattern can also be used for validating test results with a newly developed test.

Questionnaire survey facilitated by preceding interview (qual → QUAN)

A frequently recommended procedure for designing a new questionnaire involves conducting a small-scale exploratory qualitative study first (usually focus group interviews but one-to-one interviews can also serve the purpose) to provide background information on the context, to identify or narrow down the focus of the possible variables and to act as a valuable source of ideas for preparing the item pool for the purpose of questionnaire scale construction. Such a design is effective in improving the content representation of the survey and thus the internal validity of the study. It is routinely used when a researcher is building a new instrument.

Interview study with follow-up questionnaire survey (QUAL → quan)

A broad generalization in research methodology that is by and large true is that one of the strengths of qualitative research is its *exploratory* nature, allowing us to gain new insights and formulate new theories. However, because of the non-representativeness of the typical samples, qualitative data cannot inform us about how widely what is discovered exists in the rest of the world—examining the distribution of a phenomenon in a population is a typical quantitative objective. Combining a qualitative interview study with a follow-up survey can offer the best of both worlds, as the questionnaire can specifically target the issues uncovered in the first phase of the research and investigate the generalizability of the new hypotheses in wider populations. Alternatively, or in addition to this, the questionnaire can also be used to test certain elements of the theory emerging from the qualitative phase.

Interview study facilitated by preceding questionnaire survey (quan → QUAL)

It was pointed out in Chapter 2 (Section 2.1.3) that an area where qualitative research shows vulnerability is the usually small sample sizes of the respondents examined. One way of dealing with this issue is to apply purposive sampling (see Section 6.2) and this procedure can be made more principled if we include an initial questionnaire in the study whose role is to help to select the participants for the subsequent qualitative phase systematically. Thus, as Duff (in press) points out, the design can help to establish the representativeness of the cases presented. The strength of this design is its flexibility because it can be used for most theoretical sampling purposes (for example, to choose extreme or typical cases or to highlight individuals with certain traits). However, the design also has one possible drawback: it does not work if the initial questionnaire is anonymous because then we cannot identify the appropriate survey participants.

Concurrent combinations of qualitative and quantitative research (QUAL/qual + QUAN/quan)

So far we have looked at sequential designs in which a dominant phase was accompanied by a secondary component to enhance certain strengths or reduce certain weaknesses of the main method. An alternative to sequential designs is the variety of 'concurrent designs', in which we use two methods in a separate and parallel manner (i.e. they do not influence the operationalization of each other) and the results are integrated in the interpretation phase. The main purpose of this design is to broaden the research perspective and thus provide a general picture or to test how the different findings complement or corroborate each other. Depending on how much weight is assigned to the contribution of the various methods, a study can be (a) QUAL + quan, which is frequent in case studies where the primarily qualitative data can be supplemented by questionnaire or testing data; (b) QUAN + qual, which is useful, for example, to describe an aspect of a quantitative study that cannot be quantified or to embed a qualitative component within a larger, primarily quantitative study such as a programme evaluation; and (c) QUAL + QUAN, which is employed, for example in a traditional triangulation design conducted for validation purposes.

In general, concurrent designs are invaluable when we examine a phenomenon that has several levels. For example, the impact of teacher cognition can be studied at the teacher's level using interviews and at the class (i.e. students') level using questionnaires. Concurrent designs are also useful for combining micro and macro perspectives: for example, quantitative research can tap large-scale trends in social life, while qualitative research can provide a micro-analysis of how the broad trends affect or are perceived by the individuals.

Experiments with parallel interviews (QUAN + qual)

The mixed methods patterns described above have involved the use of the two most common research methods, the questionnaire survey and the interview study, as the key research components, but method mixing is not confined to these. Johnson and Christensen (2004), for example, point out that we can sometimes improve experiments even further by conducting interviews (one-to-one or focus groups) to get at the research participants' perspectives and meanings that lie behind the experimental research findings. In fact, because experiments involve featured process elements (i.e. the development of the participants as a result of the treatment), including a qualitative phase to explore the nature of such processes is a natural and potentially highly fruitful design that can greatly enhance the study's internal validity.

Longitudinal study with mixed methods components (QUAN + QUAL)

The experimental design described above is already an example of a longitudinal study and we can conclude in general that longitudinal designs lend themselves to various combinations of qualitative and quantitative methods at different stages of the project. This has been explained in more detail in Chapter 4 (Section 4.5).

Combining self-report and observational data (QUAL + QUAN)

Two fundamental ways of gaining information about people are: (a) through self-report, that is, through the individuals' own accounts (for example, in interviews or questionnaires) and (b) through external observation of the individual. (A third way involves assessing the performance of the individual on an instrument or a task, but this falls under the auspices of testing and is therefore outside the scope of this book.) Both methods have advantages and disadvantages, and combining them offers the classic merit of mixed methods research, namely to increase the strengths and mitigate the weaknesses of the study. Indeed, classroom observation studies are often accompanied by various self-report measures, with researchers being interested in both the convergent and divergent results. (For more details on mixed methods classroom research, see Section 8.3.)

7.4 Why don't people mix methods more?

The list of the most common combinations of QUAL and QUAN methods in the previous section has provided (I hope) convincing evidence that method mixing can be beneficial and often requires relatively little investment on the part of the researcher. Also, the viable examples mentioned will have succeeded (again, I hope) in defusing the philosophical concern that by mixing different worldviews we might end up in 'paradigmatic vacuum' or in an irresolvable 'paradigmatic schism'. Mixed methods research can be seen in many situations as an attractive option and, as explained earlier, the approach has recently acquired a good reputation. Yet, we do not see many published studies that feature any principled use of method mixing. So, why don't people mix methods more?

Although this is a complex issue with undoubtedly several explanations, I believe that there are two main factors at the heart of it: a lack of sufficient knowledge about method mixing and a lack of expertise to implement a mixed design. The first factor is relatively easy to deal with: mixed methods research is a new phenomenon on the research palette and therefore it is likely to take a while for it to be fully integrated into methodology texts and courses. However, on the basis of the rate of its growing popularity it is safe to conclude that the full emancipation of the approach is not too far away. But when this happens, will people actually use it? Will established researchers change their monomethodological stance and will young scholars embrace the challenges of methods mixing? It is not easy to answer these questions because mixed methods research has a severe 'shortcoming': it requires the competent handling of both qualitative and quantitative research. Let us examine this question.

Most established researchers are not equally well-versed in both QUAL and QUAN methodologies and this is not simply due to insufficient or imbalanced research training. As I will further discuss in Chapter 14, I believe that most researchers have a natural inclination towards either qualitative or quantitative research, which is most probably related to differences in their cognitive styles and certain personality traits. Taking my own case, although I genuinely appreciate qualitatively oriented colleagues' skills in teasing meaningful patterns out of masses of rather fluid and messy data, my attraction to well-structured systems, clear-cut boundaries, standardized procedures, and statistical analyses make me more naturally a quantitative researcher. Similarly, there are many people who would feel that they are less able to do themselves justice using one approach than the other. In addition, it requires considerable effort to study a phenomenon with two (or more) separate methods, and in the light of all this it is understandable that many (if not most) researchers may prefer to remain on safe monomethodological grounds.

Along with others (for example, Hanson *et al.* 2005; Johnson and Christensen 2004), I believe that the real potential for the implementation of mixed methods research lies in working in teams that consist of members with different research orientations. Duff (2002: 22) is right when she concludes that 'Combining the expertise of applied linguists espousing different research paradigms in complementary types of analysis of the same phenomenon would also yield richer analyses of complex issues'. As evidenced by the number of co-authored publications in applied linguistics, collaborative research is widespread; setting up such 'mixed' teams is, therefore, not at all inconceivable. It may well be the case that part of the reason for the insufficient cooperation between qualitative and quantitative researchers in the past has been the lack of any obvious blueprints for such collaboration. Mixed methods designs now offer attractive action plans that can facilitate the formation of teams. Greene *et al.* (2005) provide a detailed description of how such teamwork was initiated and structured as part of the 'Harvard Family Research Project'; as the authors conclude, by mixing methods they arrived at a unique, complex, and nuanced understanding of their research topic (the relationship between low-income mothers' employment and their family educational involvement) and they 'also arrived at an appreciation of mixing methods as a challenging but eminently worthwhile approach' (p. 279).

Finally, there may be a third reason for the paucity of mixed methods studies. The publication pressures of the current research climate promote piecemeal publications in general and therefore even when a project involves methods mixing, the authors might choose to try and publish the results of the different phases separately (Judit Kormos, personal communication).

8

Classroom research

Classroom research is a broad umbrella-term for empirical investigations that use the classroom as the main research site. Thus, the term concerns any study that examines how teaching and learning takes place in context. Although given the variety of possible teaching spaces (for example, seminar rooms, language labs, computer rooms, lecture theatres) it may not be absolutely straightforward to define what a 'classroom' is, the best thing is to rely on our common sense and include any physical space in which scheduled teaching takes place. In a recent overview of the field, Nunan (2005) has pointed out that such a definition has recently come under challenge because of the rapid spread of information technology in education and the subsequent development of 'virtual' classrooms, but in this chapter I do not extend the notion of classroom research to Internet-based learning environments.

Why do we need a separate chapter on classroom research? After all, I am in agreement with Mackey and Gass (2005), who point out that although classrooms constitute a distinct context for research, many of the methodological practices applied in researching classrooms are not unique to classroom settings. Yet these authors also devote a whole chapter to the topic, for the same reason as I do: the classroom—and most often the foreign/second language classroom—is a primary research site in applied linguistic investigations and the unique features of this context have a strong bearing on the way we can conduct research in it. This does not mean that everything about classroom research is distinctive; as we will see, classroom researchers use several methods that have already been described (for example, surveys, quasi-experiments, ethnographic research). Yet there are three unique aspects of conducting research in a classroom context that require special attention:

1 The research method of *classroom observation*, which is a highly developed data collection approach typical of examining learning environments.

2 The prominence that most classroom researchers place on conducting *mixed methods research* to be able to understand the intricate tapestry of classroom events. I argue throughout this book that in many research

situations combining quantitative and qualitative methodologies can be beneficial, and several scholars claim that in classroom research mixing methods is indispensable.

3 Doing high-quality classroom research poses special *challenges*. Although doing good research is never easy, it appears that the inherent difficulties of classroom investigations are a salient feature of this particular research type, usually underplayed by research reports and methodology texts. Schachter and Gass (1996: viii) summarize this point so well: 

> Reports of research projects make it all look so simple. ... There is no indication of the blood, sweat, and tears that go into getting permission to undertake the project, that go into actual data collection, that go into transcription, and so forth.

The situation, according to Schachter and Gass (1996), is a bit like going to the theatre: the performance all looks so easy and so professional but we rarely think about what has gone on behind the scenes during the preparation phase. Talking about her classroom-based PhD work, Rossiter (2001) also emphasized that none of the research manuals she had reviewed provided a truly comprehensive treatment of the many complexities of the research process; she called for research texts to reflect the realities of the contexts in which the research was conducted better. Duff and Early (1996) agree that the dismissal or downplaying of difficulties associated with the actual conduct of classroom research constitutes a 'disservice to other researchers, and particularly those with less experience' (p. 26) and they encourage more open discussion of research problems that may impede productive classroom research.

In the following, I will discuss the three issues outlined above, and conclude the chapter with a section on a special and somewhat controversial type of classroom research that is usually referred to as 'action research'. Let us first, however, start our exploration with a short overview of the origins and the main types of classroom research.

8.1 Origins and main types of classroom research

As Wragg (1999) describes, early classroom research was initiated in the 1920s and 1930s in the United States, investigating the effectiveness of teacher behaviour and teacher talk, and producing rather 'tendentious' value statements about the various teacher acts. Modern classroom research started in earnest much later, in the 1950s, as part of teacher training courses when trainers realized that they needed appropriate observation instruments and quality standards to be able to evaluate effective teaching. The area was given further impetus in the 1960s by the so-called 'methods comparison studies' (Nunan 2005), which involved large-scale investigations that compared various teaching methods, for example the audiolingual method to more traditional approaches in the language teaching area. The move from teacher training to more basic research resulted in a refinement of the instruments used (Allwright and Bailey 1991): observation schedules/schemes that initially contained rather broad and prescriptive categories were replaced by more elaborate checklists that served descriptive purposes, and a number of standardized observation schemes were published, the most famous being Flanders' Interaction Analysis Categories (FIAC) scheme (included, for example, in the Appendix of Allwright and Bailey 1991).

Contemporary classroom research, both in educational psychology and in applied linguistics, is striving for a situated understanding of learning, documenting, and analysing the dynamic interplay of various classroom processes and conditions that contribute to variation in learning outcomes. As Lightbown (2000: 438) summarizes in her comprehensive overview of classroom SLA research, the various classroom research projects share the unifying desire to 'identify and better understand the roles of the different participants in classroom interaction, the impact that certain type of instruction may have on FL/SL learning, and the factors which promote or inhibit learning'. For this purpose, investigators employ the whole repertoire of available research methodological techniques: while structured classroom observation has maintained a prominent position in classroom research, information about classrooms is also gathered by self-report techniques such as surveys, interviews, and diary studies. In addition, the role of specific instructional features and practices is often examined by means of conscious manipulation within quasi-experimental designs. A prominent area of classroom research involves ethnographic studies which treat classrooms as subcultures whose complexities need to be uncovered through sustained qualitative engagement, based on insider accounts (van Lier 1988). These latter methods have been described in Chapters 5 and 6 and will not be further discussed here. A final domain in classroom research involves the discourse analysis of classroom interaction but as described in Chapter 1, language analysis falls outside the scope of this book. (For a review, see for example the special issue of *Applied Linguistics* edited by Zuengler and Mori 2002.)

8.2 Classroom observation

> *Classrooms are exceptionally busy places, so observers need to be on their toes.*
> (Wragg 1999: 2)

Besides asking questions, *observing* the world around us is the other basic human activity that all of us have been involved in since babyhood to learn and gain understanding. From a research perspective, observation is fundamentally different from questioning because it provides direct information rather than self-report accounts, and thus it is one of the three basic data sources for empirical research (with testing being the third). Although observation is an integral part of the research repertoire of ethnography, the typical type of classroom observation that this section focuses on is not intended to provide a full ethnographic account but focuses on details of specific areas; for this reason, Polio (1996) called this type of research 'nonethnographic, nonexperimental research'.

To organize the many different ways in which we can observe classrooms, two dichotomies are usually offered: 'participant' versus 'nonparticipant observation' and 'structured' versus 'unstructured observation'. The participant-observer becomes a full member of the group, taking part in all the activities. This is the usual form of observation in ethnographic studies. In classroom observation, however, the researcher is usually not or only minimally involved in the setting and therefore he/she can be described as a 'nonparticipant-observer'. While this distinction may be helpful in some cases, Morse and Richards (2002) warn us that it simplifies the myriad ways of watching and listening; as they argue, no observer is entirely a participant, and it is impossible to observe in almost every nonexperimental situation without some participation.

The 'structured/unstructured' distinction is similar to the 'quantitative/qualitative' distinction in observational terms. Highly structured observation involves going into the classroom with a specific focus and with concrete observation categories (QUAN), whereas unstructured observation is less clear on what it is looking for and the researcher needs to observe first what is taking place before deciding on its significance for the research (QUAL) (Cohen *et al.* 2000). The former approach involves completing an observation scheme, while the latter completing narrative field notes, often supplemented by maps or diagrams. This is, of course, a continuum, and in practice usually some combination of the two approaches takes place.

In the following, I will focus primarily on structured, quantitative observation that utilizes 'observation schemes' because this is the unique data collection method associated with classroom research. However, let me stress as a preliminary that regardless of how sophisticated an observation protocol might be, it will fail to tell the whole story of classroom life. As Allwright and Bailey (1991) warned us, structured, 'closed' techniques may easily miss the insights that could be provided by the participants themselves. To capture such insights we need to combine structured observation with alternative forms of data collection by means of mixed methods research, which will be described in Section 8.3.

8.2.1 Observation schemes

If we decide to use a structured 'observation scheme' (also called 'observational schedule' or 'protocol'), we can choose from a number of readily available instruments, but in most cases they will need to be adapted to our specific research focus and classroom situation. Allwright and Bailey (1991) provide examples of seven different published coding schemes and useful information on existing schemes can also be found in Chaudron (1988) and Mackey and Gass (2005).

The main principle of observation schemes is—similar to questionnaires—to have a range of systematic categories which allow the observer to record events quickly by using tally marks. There is usually no time during the observation to enter lengthy open-ended comments so the observation scheme needs to be carefully piloted in advance. There are two main methods for recording events:

- In *event sampling* we enter a tally mark against a category every time it occurs (for example, every time the teacher asks a question). Thus, this method provides an accurate description of the total frequency of the events or procedures observed.
- In *time sampling* a category is recorded at a fixed interval, most often every 30 seconds or one minute. The researcher either notes what is happening on the stroke of the interval or charts what has happened during the preceding interval. Thus, time sampling does not provide an exhaustive record of the occurrence of an event but rather gives a chronological representation of the flow of the whole class, that is, the distribution of the particular phenomenon throughout the class.

Whatever the exact coding convention employed, the final scores are usually obtained by adding up the tally marks for each category and standardizing the sums for time to compensate for unequal lesson lengths (for example, by dividing the sum by the total length of the lesson in minutes and multiplying it by 100). We should note here that observation schemes may also contain 'rating scales' (often 'semantic differential scales'—see Section 5.2.3) for the researcher to make some overall judgements about some aspects of the class observed either during or immediately after the observation.

What kind of categories can an observation scheme contain? Because classroom processes are extremely varied and involve different and continuously changing combinations of participants, the range of categories used in the past has been broad, from aspects of teacher talk and body language through task organization to student behaviours such as volunteering. The only criterion is that the category should refer to an *observable* phenomenon in one of two ways:

- A *low-inference* category is so straightforward that even in real-time coding (i.e. ongoing coding during observation) the observer can reach almost perfect reliability in recording instances of it (for example, teacher writing on the board).
- A *high-inference* category is based on what the observer can see but it also requires some judgement about the function or meaning of the observed

behaviour (for example, type of feedback or praise). With such categories, consistent recording cannot be achieved without some training.

Mackey and Gass (2005) point out that although classroom observation schemes vary considerably, we can identify some common elements which seem to be central to the description of classroom processes, regardless of the specific focus of the study. Such common categories include the 'grouping format' of the participants (for example, individual, pair, or group work), 'content/topic' of the task/lesson, main characteristics of the 'interaction' (for example, who initiated it or what language is used), and the targeted 'linguistic area'. By way of illustration, let me describe three rather different schemes, Gertrude Moskowitz's Flint; Spada and Fröhlich's COLT; and Guilloteaux and Dörnyei's MOLT.

The Flint (Foreign Language Interaction Analysis) is Moskowitz's (1971; reprinted in Chaudron 1988 and Allwright and Bailey 1991) modification of Flanders' famous Interaction Analysis Categories (FIAS) scheme for use in second language studies. The Flint requires real-time coding in three-second intervals according to 22 categories. These are divided into three groups: (a) teacher talk (six categories related to 'indirect influence' such as 'praises' or 'jokes'; and six categories related to 'direct influence' such as 'gives direction' or 'criticizes student response'), (b) student talk (three categories: 'student response, specific', 'student response, choral', and 'student response, open-ended or student-initiated'), and (c) a miscellaneous category containing seven categories such as 'silence', 'confusion, work-oriented', and 'laughter'.

COLT (Communication Orientation of Language Teaching; Spada and Fröhlich 1985) was developed as part of a large-scale investigation of communicative competence and language teaching at the Ontario Institute of Studies in Education (Toronto, Canada). The scheme is divided into two parts: Part A focuses on classroom events and requires real-time coding at one-minute intervals, using a very detailed grid, with 48 category columns (see Figure 8.1). These concern various aspects of activity type, participant organization, content, student modality (i.e. language skills involved), and materials. Organized into 30+ categories, Part B is designed for non-real-time, post-hoc analysis of the communicative language features of each activity (based on tape recordings). Usually only certain activities selected on the basis of Part A are subjected to the very detailed micro-level analysis of Part B. Due to its elaborate category system and the high-profile research it has been used in, COLT has been highly influential in L2 classroom research.

Communicative Orientation of Language Teaching (COLT): Part A

School | **Grades** | **Date**
Teacher | **Lessons** | **Observer**
Subject

Col 1	2	3	4	5	6	7	8	9	10	11	12	13	14	15	16	17	18	19	20	21	22	23	24	25	26	27	28	29	30	31	32	33	34	35	36	37	38	39	40	41	42	43	44	45	46	47	48
Time	Activities	Participating organization							Content																								Student					Materials									
		Class			Group		Comb.		Man.			Language				Other topics														Topic control			modality					Type							Use		
																narrow				limited					broad													Text									
		T s/c	S s/c	Choral	Same	Different	Individual	Gr/Ind.	Procedure	Discipline		Form	Function	Discourse	Socioling.	Classroom	Stereotyp.	Pers/Bio.	Other	Personal	Rout./Soc.	Fam./Com.	School T.	Other	Abstract	Pers./Ref.	Imagination	World T.	Other	Teacher	Teacher/Stud.	Student	Listening	Speaking	Reading	Writing	Other	Minimal	Extended	Audio	Visual	Pedagogic	Semi-Pedagog.	Non-Pedagog.	High Control	Semi Control	Mini Control

MOLT (Motivation Orientation in Language Teaching; Guilloteaux and Dörnyei in press) has been developed modelled on COLT but focusing on aspects of the teacher's motivational practice and the students' motivated behaviour in language classes. The real-time interval sampling format is similar to Part A of the COLT scheme and several of the 41 categories it contains coincide with those in COLT. The categories that describe the teacher's motivational practice follow Dörnyei's (2001) system of motivational strategies. Figure 8.2 provides a sample extract from the scheme.

Minute	Generating, maintaining, and protecting situation-specific task motivation																		Encouraging positive retrospective self-evaluation				Motivated behaviour		
	Teacher discourse										Activity design														
	Signposting	Stating the communicative purpose/utility of activity	Establishing relevance	Promoting integrative values	Promotes instrumental values	Arousing curiosity or attention	Scaffolding	Promoting cooperation	Promoting autonomy	Referential Questions	Pair work	Group work	+ tangible reward	+ personalization	+ creative/interesting/fantasy element	+ intellectual challenge	+ team competition	+ tangible task product	Process feedback session	Elicitation of self/peer correction session	Effective praise	Class applause	Attention (>⅔ of the class)	Participating (>⅔ of the class)	Eager volunteering (at least ⅓)
1																									
2																									
3																									
4																									
5																									

Figure 8.2 Extract from the MOLT observation scheme (motivation-specific categories only) (Guilloteaux and Dörnyei in press)

8.2.2 Video recording classrooms

'Video recording' has provided a technology that might be considered ideal for classroom research as it can replace the need for real-time coding. Indeed, nowadays even most postgraduate students can arrange to borrow good quality equipment for their research in observational settings, and many universities and research centres have not only got video cameras available for research purposes but can even provide technicians to help. Regrettably, including video recording in our research design does not eliminate all the difficulties associated with classroom observation because videotaping as a classroom research tool is far from being perfect. As Mackey and Gass (2005) point out, in a laboratory setting video recording can be a relatively straightforward matter, but in classrooms it can present a unique set of problems, ranging from technical issues such as using microphones that pick up every detail (video equipment is usually stronger on image than sound) to ethical issues of how to arrange students if some of them have not consented to be videotaped.

In a detailed analysis of the differences between the 'analyst eyes' and 'camera eyes', Zuengler *et al.* (1998) argue that while technology can enhance our ability to see certain things, it can also create 'literal and figurative blind spots' (p. 4). The researchers have highlighted two problems in particular:

- *Literal blind spots* A fixed camera can only see what it is pointing at and usually we cannot back the camera up far enough to capture the entire class and the instructor. Zuengler and her colleagues (1998) first tried to compensate for this by using the 'pan and scan' technique offered by a movable camera, but this simply did not work for two reasons: first, the camera was always lagging behind the action because of the unpredictable nature of classroom events and second, the technique introduced a strong subjective component because the camera operator was forced to continually make instantaneous decisions about who or what was worthy of the camera's 'precious focus'. The solution that the team arrived at involved using two cameras, a moving camera with an operator in the back covering the teacher, and a static camera in the front capturing the faces of the students. While this arrangement produced a satisfactory video coverage, the need for extra equipment considerably increased the research costs and the overall upheaval in the classroom. Even the subsequent analysis of the two recorded parallel accounts was not straightforward; the best solution they found was the 'picture-in-picture' technique for combining video images: they synchronized the two tapes and the teacher's image was superimposed in the corner of the larger, static image of the classroom.
- *Distraction caused by the camera* Even in our age when video cameras are common, the process of videotaping in the classroom may distract the participants and may elicit out-of-the-ordinary behaviour on the part of both the teacher and the students. Zuengler *et al.* (1998) found that even in their longitudinal study, where it was hoped the participants would be so familiar with the procedures that they would forget about the presence of the researchers, there were regular references in the data to the fact that the participants were being videotaped, and Duff (in press) reports a similar experience. Indeed, in an experimental study on the impact of anxiety on SLA by MacIntyre and Gardner (1994), a video camera was successfully

used to intentionally generate the anxiety condition amongst the participants. Yet, as Zuengler *et al.* argue, a large part of classroom interaction and behaviour is beyond the ability of most people to alter significantly for extended periods of time, and therefore it is only one-off recordings that are particularly vulnerable to obtaining distorted and unnatural data.

In spite of the above (and other) shortcomings, Zuengler and her colleagues (1998) concluded that the advantages of video recording are compelling. They likened the current situation to when the microscope was introduced to the life sciences, causing a revolution in biology by making visible previously unseen details. In a similar vein, the video can help us uncover the subtle reality of classroom life. Furthermore, video recordings can also be used as a helpful ancillary to audiotaping: Murison-Bowie (personal communication) points out the usefulness of video in disambiguating audio recordings, particularly in identifying who is speaking at any one time. In such cases a fixed position video camera is set up to take an overview of the class group and the recording is used solely to facilitate the transcription process. Once the audio transcription has been completed, the video recording can be discarded, which helps to eliminate some of the ethical problems associated with video.

8.2.3 Strengths and weaknesses of observational data

The main merit of observational data is that it allows researchers to see directly what people do without having to rely on what they say they do. Therefore, such data can provide a more objective account of events and behaviours than second-hand self-report data. Observation is also versatile and can be used with participants with weak verbal skills. It is invaluable for providing descriptive contextual information about the setting of the targeted phenomenon.

Adding structure to observation by means of using observation schemes makes the process more reliable and produces results that are comparable across classrooms and over time. Structured observational guidelines make the formidable task of documenting the complexity of classroom reality doable, and help to focus on certain key events and phenomena. Thus, coding schemes introduce systematicity into the research process. Moreover, processing structured observational data is relatively straightforward and can be further analysed by means of statistical procedures.

On the negative side, we must start with the obvious, namely that only observable phenomena can be observed, whereas in applied linguistics so many of the key variables and processes that researchers investigate are mental and thus unobservable. A second problem is that recording a phenomenon does not necessarily lead to understanding the reasons why it has happened, particularly when low-inference categories are used. A more technical issue that has already been discussed earlier with regard to videotaping also applies to observations in general, namely that the presence of the investigator can affect and bias the participants' behaviour. Indeed, the quality of observational data is dependent on the skill with which the researcher conducts the observation.

Finally, a serious concern with structured observation is that regardless of the coding convention applied it involves a reduction of the complexity of the observed situation, and by focusing on the target categories the observer can miss some more important features. Highly structured schemes also share the general weakness of quantitative measures, namely that the examined categories are preconceived and the instrument is not sensitive to context-specific emergent information.

8.3 Mixed methods classroom research

The classroom is a highly complex environment and therefore, as Turner and Meyer (2000) summarize, it has been variously studied in terms of the 'beliefs, goals, values, perceptions, behaviours, classroom management, social relations, physical space, and social-emotional and evaluative climates that contribute to the participants' understanding of the classroom' (p. 70). It is common to distinguish at least two broad dimensions of the classroom environment, the 'instructional context', which concerns the influences of the teacher, students, curriculum, learning tasks, and teaching method, amongst other things, and the 'social context', which is related to the fact that the classroom is also the main social arena for students, offering deeply intensive personal experiences such as friendship, love, or identity formation. These two contexts are interdependent and also interact with the complex process of *learning*, resulting in plenty of food for thought for several disciplines and research directions within the broad areas of education, psychology, sociology, and anthropology.

I argued in Section 7.1.1 that the understanding of the operation of complex environments—such as classrooms—lends itself to mixed methods research, because combining several research strategies can broaden the scope of the investigation and enrich the researcher's ability to draw conclusions. This recognition has been echoed by many classroom researchers in the past. For example, Allwright and Bailey (1991: 67) stated:

> From all that we have said on the topic, it should be clear that we see most value in investigations that combine objective and subjective elements, that quantify only what can be usefully quantified, and that utilize qualitative data collection and analysis procedures wherever they are appropriate.

Mackey and Gass (2005) also emphasize the necessity of 'using multiple methods and techniques' (p. 196) in classroom research, and according to Nunan (2005: 237), 'Classroom researchers appear to be increasingly reluctant to restrict themselves to a single data collection technique, or even a single research paradigm'. In a similar vein, Chaudron (1988: 13) begins his detailed review of classroom research by stating:

> In the survey of L2 classroom research that follows, the reader will recognize a continuous give-and-take between the successes and failures of quantitative or qualitative approaches to portray and explain adequately the processes and products of classroom interaction.

We should note, however, that in actual practice, mixing methods in classroom research may not be an unambiguous process, and this has been explicitly expressed in the self-reflections of two highly experienced classroom ethnographers, Duff and Early (1996: 18): '... despite prescriptions and assurances to the contrary ... both our studies found it challenging to attempt to strike a meaningful balance between quantitative and qualitative approaches to studying classroom phenomena'.

I started this section referring to a study by educational psychologists Turner and Meyer (2000: 79); let us return to their account to see how they tried to deal with the QUAL–QUAN tension:

> We have allowed our data and the contradictions among our different methods to inform our analyses, and we have changed our coding categories and re-visited conclusions based on inductive reasoning. As a result, we have developed new and more contextualized understandings of the theories used to frame our questions.

In the end, the fruitfulness of this iterative process has led Turner and Meyer (2000) to call for more multimethod approaches to achieving a description and explanation of what is happening in classrooms. As they concluded, methodologies directed at the measurement of classroom variables in educational psychology have been mostly deductive and quantitative with little exploration of the how and why of learning; based on their experience, discerning what the various constructs mean in a particular setting necessitates qualitative methods that can uncover participant interpretations—an argument that has been stated more than once in this book.

8.4 Difficulties and challenges in classroom research

There is no doubt in my mind that Mr Murphy (from 'Murphy's Laws') was originally a classroom researcher and it was this experience which originally generated his rather gloomy worldview. Indeed, I fully share Rossiter's (2001: 36) experience:

> Faced with developing constraints related to non-equivalent groups, student and teacher participants, data collection, data analysis, task differences, and ethical considerations, the temptation for many classroom-oriented researchers in my position might be to curtail or even abandon their study. I maintain, however, that what are often perceived

> as problems by researchers are in fact the daily realities of the contexts in which most teachers practise. The limitations in these research settings may frustrate investigators ... they are, however, part and parcel of the classroom context.

Thus, the main purpose of the following catalogue of difficulties and challenges is to forewarn researchers and to reassure them that the problems they might encounter in classroom research do not necessarily constitute evidence of their total inadequacy, requiring a career change. So let us look at ten particularly salient trouble spots—regrettably, this list may not be exhaustive:

1 *Meeting different needs and standards* Perhaps the greatest challenge of conducting research in classrooms is, as Pica (2005: 341) points out, the fact that the researcher must deal with standards for methodological rigour in a complex educational setting with participants who have important work to do and have responsibilities and goals that may not be compatible with those of the researcher. As she asks, 'Is it possible to develop a methodology that can satisfy the needs and expectations of learners, teachers and researchers?' The honest answer is that it *has* been done in the past but it is not always easy and can sometimes turn out to be outright undoable.

2 *Fluidity of the student body* For rigorous research we need a well-defined participant sample. This seemingly basic condition can be surprisingly difficult to achieve in school settings if the study involves more than a one-off cross-sectional survey. Rossiter (2001), for example, gives a detailed account of how her quasi-experimental design was disrupted by student attrition, newcomers, students repeating a course as well as participants withdrawing from the project for various reasons. These changes not only reduced her sample with a complete dataset (i.e. without any missing values) but also affected the classroom dynamics of the participating groups and caused considerable turmoil. Duff and Early (1996) also report very similar experiences.

3 *Time-consuming nature* Research carried out in classrooms takes up a lot of time, not just because of the data collection procedures (which are predictable) but because of the necessity of meeting school administrators, teachers, students, and sometimes even the parents regularly to sell the project to them and to keep them engaged. Furthermore, the researcher's job is not over even after the field work has been completed because we need to report back to the participants with the results. Indeed, Spada (2005: 336) is right when she concludes that 'the time-consuming nature of classroom research is not a minor factor'.

4 *Working with teachers* Classroom research typically involves working with a number of teachers for an extended period. This can be taxing: teachers can be very busy and stressed out, and they have their own distinctive beliefs and styles as well as professional and personal agendas. Thus,

it may not be easy to bring them on board, and it is a real challenge in almost every case to keep up their commitment. This is understandable because, let's face it, the research project is often a major nuisance for the classroom practitioners and it may require great social skills to keep them motivated. (For a detailed account of how to achieve this, see Spada *et al.* 1996.) Rounds (1996: 45) summarizes the conflicting situation well:

> Researchers often describe the teachers they study as uncooperative, unhelpful, inflexible, untrusting, and even just plain obstructionist. How is it that researchers are sometimes seen by these same teachers as being demanding, intrusive, unhelpful, inflexible, and dogmatic?

It does not help either that the turnover of teachers in almost every type of school system is high and even if the teachers do not actually leave the school, the frequent reorganizations that characterize the educational system of many countries nowadays may also disrupt the continuity and design of the project. In addition, a special source of difficulty arises if we need to involve the teachers to deliver some instructional treatment for us in their classes. Even if we prepare complete packages of teaching materials with detailed guidelines to try to ensure a uniform implementation of the materials, this may not necessarily happen and 'the fact remains that we can never know everything that takes place in a classroom during an instructional intervention' (Spada 2005: 334).

5 *Working with students* Even if we have the full support and cooperation of the teachers, this may not mean that all the students will follow suit. Learners may have varying native languages and cultures, proficiency levels, learning styles, motivations, and attitudes, and the dynamics of the different participating learner groups may also be dissimilar. In fact, it is highly unlikely that every student will do his/her best for a project in which they have little interest and which has no direct bearing on their school grades. In a large-scale task-based study, for example, we have found (Dörnyei and Kormos 2000) that the results only started to make sense once we separated the students who did and who did not take the tasks seriously. Duff and Early (1996) also reported that test results that seemed irregular (suggesting, for example, cheating or apathy) had to be analysed separately or dropped in their study.

6 *Unexpected events and interruptions* Almost every classroom researcher has a story about arriving at the school on 'D-day' with all the technical equipment only to find out that the students are away on a class trip or skiing holiday which nobody has remembered to tell them about. O'Connor and Sharkey's (2004: 338) experience is, sadly, universal:

> Although we anticipated that sick days, snow days, school holidays, and parent-teacher conferences would crowd our schedules, we did not and perhaps could not have foreseen the series of well-meaning events

that disrupted our process and project. These events, often called within a week or even a day's notice, included politicians' visits, schoolwide meetings, district ESOL meetings, guest speakers, and professional development workshops that teachers were encouraged to attend.

7 *Obtrusive researcher effect* One source of problems has got to do with us, the researchers: we have already mentioned the negative impact of the 'observer effect', and regardless of how low a profile we strive to keep we must face it: classroom researchers are intruders who are inevitably obtrusive. It is a real challenge in most situations to find ways of minimizing the intrusion so that classroom events are as natural and unstaged as possible while we are present, which of course is the prerequisite for obtaining valid data.

8 *Ethical considerations* In Chapter 3 we talked about various ethical issues, and for many applied linguists it is during classroom research that such concerns actually become tangible. The disruptions mentioned above may not only affect negatively the purity of our data, but more generally, the whole learning process. Not only may students *not* benefit from participating in our research, but in fact the project may have *harmful effects* on their development. In addition, there is the question of privacy and confidentiality. Duff and Early (1996) are right when they point out that the common advice of disguising the identity of our participants is not very useful in situations where there is usually just one principal and maybe only one or two language teachers in the school that is our research site. How can we report data from/about them without it being obvious who we are talking about?

9 *Technical difficulties* Murphy's universal law states that if something can go wrong, it will. I can only add to this that classroom equipment will fail particularly at those times when we have forgotten to bring spare equipment. But even if the electrical devices do work, the voices in a recording can be drowned by environmental noises from sources such as corridors, traffic, and playgrounds (Rossiter 2001).

10 *Multisite design* Finally, Duff and Early (1996) draw attention to the possible drawbacks of multisite designs, that is, studies that include several research sites for the sake of participant variety. These researchers have found that the disadvantages associated with the inability to maintain a presence at any one site over a long period of time and thus having to conduct the research from afar or by proxy may exceed the benefits of having a wider range of situations and pool of participants.

8.5 Action research

It is difficult to decide how to present 'action research': on the one hand, in an ideal world it ought to be a viable research area with a powerful impact. On the other hand, although it is undoubtedly a noble idea, it just does not seem to work in practice, regardless of continuous efforts to keep it going ever since the notion was first introduced by social psychologist Kurt Levin in the mid-1940s. (For an informative historical overview, see Burns 2005.) Let us examine this enigma.

8.5.1 Definition

'Action research' is a generic term for a family of related methods that share some important common principles. The most important tenet concerns the close link between research and teaching as well as the researcher and the teacher: action research is conducted by or in cooperation with teachers for the purpose of gaining a better understanding of their educational environment and improving the effectiveness of their teaching. Thus, the enhancement of practice and the introduction of change into the social enterprise are central characteristics of action research (Burns 2005).

Traditionally, the teacher–researcher link was taken so seriously in this area that only research done by the teacher him/herself was considered action research proper. However, after it was realized that it is often unrealistic to expect teachers to have the expertise to conduct rigorous research, scholars started to emphasize the collaboration between teachers and researchers. Burns (2005) explains that this collaboration can take several forms, from the researcher owning the project and co-opting a participating teacher to real collaboration where researchers and teachers participate equally in the research agenda.

8.5.2 Problematic issues

There is one big problem with action research: there is too little of it. Published studies of action research in applied linguistics are small in number and as far as my personal experience is concerned, I am still to meet a teacher who has been voluntarily involved in an action research project. So, ironically, even though one of the stated goals of action research has been to 'democratize' research, that is, to oppose a 'professional expert model' and avoid the pitfalls of 'the "top-down technology transfer model" of academic intervention, policy formation and policy implementation' (David 2002: 12), the movement is rather 'top-down' itself with primarily researchers trying to promote it. Interestingly, Bartels (2002) provides some evidence that even applied linguists themselves fail to conduct action research in their own teaching, which suggests the possibility of double standards.

There are at least three reasons for action research not becoming more prominent: teachers usually lack (a) the time, (b) the incentives, and (c) the expertise or professional support to get meaningfully engaged with research. Let us start with the time issue. Language teachers usually have a very high workload and they often complain of not having sufficient time even to prepare for their classes, let alone to do extra research. It is noteworthy that even one of the original promoters of action research, Dick Allwright, started to have serious doubts about the viability of a high-profile project that he had initiated in Brazil:

> The classroom-based SLA research project was clearly taking up far too much staff time to be worth pursuing, and it was also requiring staff to learn research skills that were not likely to be helpful in their lives as teachers. So it was heavily parasitic upon their normal working lives, rather than supportive of them ...
> (Allwright 2005: 354)

And later Allwright (2005: 355) added, 'Looking at Action Research in action in various parts of the world at that time, it seemed to me it had the same potential to lead to burnout as my academic model of research'. Such a pessimistic view has been echoed by many authors working in other parts of the world (for example, O'Connor and Sharkey 2004); talking about Canadian ESL contexts Rossiter (2001: 40) for example concluded:

> The majority of teachers have minimal time for course preparation and reflection and even less opportunity to read the journals or research manuals to which they might have access. Without a clear understanding of the research process and relevant literature, however, aspiring teacher-researchers chance wasting their time and energy on fruitless endeavours.

Although, classroom practitioners tend to be very busy, if not overworked, my experience is that many of them could be motivated to engage in some meaningful exploration activity, even spending some of their free time on it, if there was some institutional *incentive* for it in the form of, for example, official recognition, financial reward, or release time. This, however, hardly ever happens, and even in contexts where teachers are provided with in-service training, this tends to involve lectures or workshops rather than some form of action research.

Finally, as Nunan (2005) summarizes, the average classroom practitioner may not have the research knowledge and skills to conduct an inquiry in a way that would guard it against threats to reliability and validity. The danger is that even if teachers decide to initiate an action research project, the chances are that with little background knowledge and insufficient research expertise they will produce questionable or trivial results. Ideally, they would need the support of a trained supervisor or at least access to some sort of a 'research clinic' but, regrettably, in most contexts these are less-than-realistic wishes.

8.5.3 Concluding words about action research

As I said at the beginning of this section, it is difficult to decid
the summary of a research movement that is highly commend
I do not consider viable for the time being. I fully agree wit
251) claim that action research 'offers a means for teachers to become ag
rather than recipients of knowledge about second language teaching and learning, and thus to contribute toward the building of educational theories of practice'. I can also see why action research can evoke ideology-driven passion, well expressed by Crookes (1993: 137):

> So long as research is only presented as something that other people—not teachers—do, and so long as it seems to teachers that research reports must necessarily be written in a language they do not read or speak, we will be accommodating the exploitative pressures of the institutions teachers work in. Action against such pressures can take many forms. The conducting of action research as a means of critical reflection on teaching and on the sociopolitical context in which teachers find themselves has the potential to be a major component in the continuing struggle to improve SL [second language] teaching.

However, it seems to be the case that action research is not fulfilling these hopes because in the current unsupportive teaching climate it is simply not happening extensively enough to have an impact. Allwright has come to terms with this fact and moved on to suggest a more teacher-friendly version of action research, 'exploratory practice'. (See Allwright 2005; Allwright and Bailey 1991.) The purpose of this approach is similar to action research in that it offers ways for teachers to understand classroom events, but instead of rigorous research methods it uses a sequence of reflective pedagogical practices (for example, experimenting with classroom procedures and interpreting the outcomes) to achieve this purpose. As such, it falls outside the remit of this book.

In conclusion, I believe that it is fair to make the following three claims: (a) many, if not most, language teachers would like to gain a more thorough understanding of the teaching and learning process as well as the various classroom events; (b) one main purpose of applied linguistic research is to provide answers to questions that concern these issues; and (c) currently there is a wide gap between teachers and researchers in most countries, which needs to be bridged. As Lightbown (2000: 453) summarizes, it is essential for researchers 'to enter into dialogue with classroom teachers—not only so that teachers can know what researchers are saying, but also so that researchers can hear what teachers are saying'.

The question, then, is how to make the teacher–researcher link viable and active. Simply considering teachers as passive recipients of researcher knowledge has not been successful in the past, but neither has the other extreme, namely trying to get teachers to generate their own knowledge and theories.

The challenge is to find some doable form of teacher–researcher partnership between these two extremes that is embraced (and supported!) by educational managers and which teachers will not consider merely an additional burden on their already busy daily lives. The most obvious place to start would be in pre-service and in-service teacher training courses, and as Burns (2005) and McDonough (2006) summarize, there are indeed some hopeful initiatives in these areas. The action research programme described by McDonough amongst postgraduate Teaching Assistants appears to be particularly useful and viable.

Let me finish the discussion of action research on a positive note with an extract from Richards (2003: 232) that is at the heart of any optimistic beliefs that teachers can be integrated somehow into the research process:

> Most ESOL [i.e. EFL/ESL] teachers are natural researchers. We're used to working out the needs of our students, evaluating the effects of particular approaches, spotting things that work or don't work and adjusting our teaching accordingly. Very few teachers approach their work mechanically and nearly all of us reflect on what we do in the classroom.

PART THREE
Data analysis

9

Quantitative data analysis

Having collected quantitative data, the next step is to analyse it using a set of mathematical procedures, called 'statistics'. These range from simple descriptive statistics such as calculating the mean (i.e. the average) of the scores in a group to complex multivariate procedures such as structural equation modelling. The selection of the exact procedure will depend on the research question and the type of data collected, and once the analysis is completed the results will provide information on the basis of which we can answer the research questions and accept or reject the research hypotheses. We saw in Chapter 2 that quantitative analysis is more straightforward in this respect than qualitative analysis because here there are well defined procedures, guided by universally accepted canons, to address research issues and the computer will do most of the detailed mathematical work for us, producing relatively straightforward results.

Most of this chapter will be devoted to describing the main statistical procedures used in applied linguistics. However, there are two prerequisites for getting down to data analysis that need to be discussed first: (1) we need to select and learn to use a statistical program to run the statistical procedures; 
and (2) the data need to be prepared for analysis.

9.1 Computerized data analysis and SPSS

In the early days most statistics were calculated manually on paper, filling reams of paper with equations, with only simple calculators to help with basic arithmetic. This situation has completely changed. Nowadays the mathematical aspects of quantitative data analysis are largely left to the computer, and several statistical programs have been developed to direct the computer's work. These software packages have become increasingly user-friendly, to the extent that researchers do not need to have any mathematical training to use them and most of the procedures are fully interactive (i.e. we do not even have to write commands but only choose options that suit our purposes from ready-made menus). What we do need is an understanding of the purpose of the various statistical procedures so that we can select the appropriate procedure for analysing the data and then instruct the computer to run the analysis.

There are many statistical packages on the market, and even spreadsheets such as Microsoft's Excel can do a fair amount of statistics. However, my recommendation is that novice researchers start working with one of the major software packages right from the beginning. Considerable efforts have been made to make these computer programs user-friendly, so their use is hardly more difficult than that of the smaller packages and the range of analyses they are capable of running is incomparably superior. The question then is, which program shall we choose? The software package most commonly used in applied linguistic and educational research is 'SPSS' (Statistical Package for the Social Sciences), produced by SPSS, Inc. in Chicago, USA, and it makes sense to adopt this program. Therefore, all the specific advice on statistical applications in this chapter will concern SPSS. It should be able to perform all the statistical operations that one needs at this stage, and if your research requires further, more specialized statistical analyses at a later stage (for example structural equation modelling), you can find appropriate software that is compatible with SPSS.

SPSS is not a beginners' software package, yet it is appropriate for people who have little experience in statistics and programming because of its user-friendly interactive features. It has been around for over 35 years and therefore the current version (at the time of writing this, Version 14) is highly refined and by and large bug-free. SPSS is easy to install and start. If you decide to use it in your research, you will need some sort of a guide or manual to help to run the software, although one can go a long way by simply relying on the software's own 'Help' system. Furthermore, because SPSS is being taught at so many universities, even a quick search on the Internet will result in a number of very useful online tutorials and user-friendly overviews. Because of the widespread use of SPSS, most of the serious academic publishers offer their own 'How to ...' manuals—I would suggest choosing one which (a) does not include any mathematical equations; (b) also offers statistical explanations besides the instructions on how to run the software; (c) has step-by-step guidelines and extensive illustrations; and (d) offers templates of how to present the results. (I have found Pallant 2005 very useful.)

9.2 Preparing the data for analysis

As Brown (2001) rightly points out, having collected our data is half the battle, and now we must address the other half, the processing of the stacks of completed questionnaires or tests or multiple pages of our notes of various quantitative scores. Davidson (1996: ix) remarks that it is surprising how few of the statistics texts describe the 'painful experience of going from a stack of disorganized hard copy to online data that are trustworthy'. This is quite true, so let us spend some time going through the initial procedures that are usually referred to as 'data preparation'.

The first principle of preparing our data for analysis is that quantitative data need to be stored in a computer file. This requires the systematic coding of the data, creating a data file, and then inputting the coded data. Once we have our data online, we need to screen, clean, and possibly manipulate it before it is ready for analysis.

9.2.1 Coding quantitative data

Quantitative data analysis software handles data in a numerical rather than an alphabetic form, and even though SPSS allows the storage of information recorded as letters (for example, words or proper names), the procedures that are available for handling such textual data are limited compared to the vast arsenal of statistical techniques to be used with numerical responses. Therefore, the first step of data processing involves converting the respondents' answers to numbers by means of 'coding procedures'. Because numbers are meaningless in themselves and are all too easy to mix up, a major element of the coding phase is to define each variable and then to compile coding specifications for every possible 'value' that the particular variable can take. (We should note here that 'value' is a technical term used in statistics, referring to the numbers assigned to the response options of the variable). For example, gender data is usually labelled 'sex' and it can take two numerical values: 'male' is usually coded '1' and 'female' '2.'

With numerical variables such as test scores, the coding is simple because the value range of the variable will be the same as the possible scores for the test (for example, the value of the variable 'TOEFL' for a person is, say, 580). With closed-ended questionnaire items, such as Likert scales (see Section 5.2.3), the coding frame is similarly straightforward: each pre-determined response option is assigned a number (for example, 'strongly disagree' = 1, 'disagree' = 2, 'neutral' = 3, 'agree' = 4, 'strongly agree' = 5). For simple open-ended questionnaire items (for example, a background information question such as 'What foreign languages have you learnt in the past?') the coding frame is more complex because it can have many categories (for example, German = 1, French = 2, etc.), in fact, as many as the number of the different answers in all the questionnaires. Thus, with such items the coding frame is continuously extended during the processing of the data, with every new language mentioned by the respondents being assigned a new number.

The coding of other open-ended questionnaire items that elicit more diverse or longer responses, however, may go beyond the mechanical conversion of a category into a number and may require a certain amount of subjective interpretation and summary on the part of the coder. For example, with a question such as 'What is your favourite leisure activity?' the task is to condense the diverse information contained in the responses into a limited number of categories; ongoing decisions will need to be made about whether to label two similar but not completely identical responses (for example, 'walking the dog' and 'going for a walk') as the same or whether to mark the difference somehow.

In the past, researchers have had to compile a 'codebook' that included the coding frames for each variable in their investigation. However, the data files in the latest versions of SPSS offer such convenient facilities to include detailed descriptions of all the variables and values that many researchers nowadays simply incorporate the codebook into the data file. This practice is further supported by the fact that, starting with Version 12, variable names can be as long as 64 characters, allowing for meaningful descriptors (whereas in the earlier versions eight characters were the maximum, which often forced us to produce strange abbreviations for the variable names).

9.2.2 Inputting the data

Entering the data into a computer file requires three steps: (1) creating the data file, (2) defining the coding frames for the variables, and (3) keying in the data.

Creating and naming the data file

Creating a new data file is easy in modern statistical software such as SPSS. However, the nature of data files is such that we regularly make changes in them during the process of data analysis (for example, recode variables or compute new composite variables) and one of the recurring problems I have encountered with novice (and not-so-novice) researchers is that multiple versions of the data files are stored next to each other, with the file names becoming confusing and the files getting mixed up. Furthermore, in most studies we are likely to return to the dataset at later stages, and without a foolproof naming/labelling system and a properly maintained research log (see Section 3.4.2) it might be a daunting task to sort out which file is what. Therefore, it is worth adopting the following filing process (though please consult an SPSS guide on how exactly to carry out the following steps):

1. Give the data file a simple generic name (for example, 'Motivation_data'), to which SPSS will add the extension 'sav'; whenever you make any changes in the data file, save the modified file under a new version name (for example, 'Motivation_data1.sav', 'Motivation_data2.sav', etc.). My rule of thumb is that no change in the data file should be saved under the old file name because this would make it very difficult (if not impossible) at a later stage to trace back what we have done.

2. The first version of the data file ('Motivation_data1.sav') should contain the raw data, without any modifications.

3. When we make any change in the data file, we need to have a permanent record of this change in the form of a 'command file', which in SPSS is

called a 'syntax file' and carries the extension of 'sps'. Such syntax files can be formed in the interactive mode by using the 'PASTE' command.

4 Name the syntax file that creates a new version of the data file in a way that it corresponds to the newly created data file's name. For example, the file that creates 'Motivation_data2.sav' should be named 'Motivation_data2.sps'.

5 If you follow this procedure consistently, you will always know which is the latest version of the data file—the one with the highest version number—and you can always trace back what has changed from one version to the other by looking at the series of corresponding syntax files. Table 9.1 offers an example of the process.

Initial data file containing the raw data:	*Motivation_data1.sav*
Syntax file creating a new version of the data file:	*Motivation_data2.sps*

Example of Motivation_data2.sps:

```
GET FILE='C:\My Documents\Motivation_data1.sav'.

RECODE quest1 quest5 quest10 (1=6) (2=5) (3=4) (4=3) (5=2) (6=1).

SAVE OUTFILE='C:\My Documents\Motivation_data2.sav'

/COMPRESSED.
```

(This syntax file first opens the last version of the data file, then recodes the values of three variables—quest1, quest5, and quest10—and finally saves the new, modified data file under the consecutive version number.)

Table 9.1 Example of creating a new version of an SPSS data file

Defining the coding frames

When the data file has been created and properly named, we need to decide on the 'coding frames' for all the variables. The SPSS Data Editor screen has a 'data' and a 'variable' view (indicated in the bottom left corner). In the 'variable' view we must first specify the name of each variable (the best thing is to choose one word up to 64 characters for each variable, but the shorter the name, the better), and we may also want to create a 'variable label' (this is optional) to accompany each variable name—this is a longer definition or description (for example, the whole questionnaire item that generated the particular variable). I would suggest that after specifying the variables we create 'value labels' for each variable (this again is optional) to describe the possible numbers that the variable can take and what each number stands for. Proper labelling will help us to remember the details when we come back to the data file at a later stage.

Keying in the data

Keying in the data is a rather tedious and time-consuming process. All of us involved in quantitative research have spent countless hours in front of a computer screen typing seemingly endless rows of figures. However boring and mechanical this job may be, it is essential that we maintain concentration because every mis-typed number will be a contamination of the dataset. In agreement with Brown (2001), I have found that one way of making the task more interesting and more accurate is to work with a partner, taking turns at dictating and typing. The SPSS Data Editor screen offers a number of user-friendly shortcuts and options (for example, cutting and pasting) to help the data entry process—please consult the manual.

When we come across missing data—for example, we do not have the proficiency test score for a person because he/she was absent when the test was administered—the best option is to leave the particular cell empty (rather than following the traditional practice of typing in a set number such as '99'). This ensures that we do not mix up real values with missing data values by accident, and there will be opportunities later for each statistical analysis to decide how to handle the missing data.

9.2.3 Data screening and cleaning

In my experience, the initial data file will always contain mistakes. Some of these are the result of human error occurring during the data entry phase (for example, typing the wrong number) and some are mistakes made by the respondents when filling in the questionnaire. 'Data screening and cleaning' involves spotting and correcting as many of these errors and inaccuracies as possible before starting the actual analyses. This is an indispensable phase of preparing the data because some mistakes can completely distort our results. The main screening techniques are as follows:

- *Correcting impossible data* Most items have a specific range, determined by the given response options or by the inherent logic of the item. A quick frequency listing of all the items (in SPSS: ANALYSE → DESCRIPTIVE STATISTICS → FREQUENCIES) can expose out-of-range values; for example, with a six-point Likert scale a value of 7 is obviously incorrect, and if someone's age is entered as 110, we can also suspect human error. Once such impossible values have been detected, we need to check the hard copy of the particular questionnaire or record sheet and then enter the correct values.
- *Correcting incorrectly entered values that conform to the permissible range* It is easy to detect and correct a value of 7 with a six-point Likert scale. But what about a typing error in the same scale when '5' has been recorded instead of '4'? The only way of detecting such a mistake is by means of a very laborious procedure, whereby the entire data bank is re-entered in a second data file and then the two data files (which ought to be identical) are computer-checked for correspondence with each other.

- *Correcting contradicting data* Some questionnaires have 'routed' items, which means that some questions are to be answered only if the respondent gave a particular answer to a previous question. For example, if a language learner gives a negative answer to the question 'Have you ever stayed in the L2 environment for an extended period?' and then answers 'six months' to the subsequent question 'If so, for how long?', something is obviously wrong. Depending on the type of questions asked, several other logical checks are also conceivable. In any case, when such inconsistencies are found, a closer inspection of the questionnaire can usually help to remedy these, but sometimes the only way of getting rid of the contamination is to eliminate both parts of the contradicting or illogical combination.

Dealing with outliers

The data check may highlight values that are inconsistent with the rest of the dataset, for example, because they are way out of the usual range (for example, the size of the speech produced by a language learner in a task is twice as big as the second largest score). These suspicious values are referred to as *outliers* and they are often the result of incorrect data entry. The problem with outliers is that they can seriously distort the statistical results by having an undue impact on the outcome. Therefore, an important aspect of data screening/cleaning is to check the data for outliers and then deal with the identified extreme cases (if there are any). A visual way of spotting these is by using 'scatterplots' (GRAPHS → SCATTER/DOT). The EXPLORE procedure in SPSS (ANALYSE → DESCRIPTIVE STATISTICS → EXPLORE) is particularly suitable for checking for outliers because it not only provides a variety of plots (for example, histograms and boxplots) but also displays extreme values (the five largest and the five smallest values) for each variable. Figure 9.1 presents outputs of the EXPLORE procedure (by ticking 'Outliers' in the 'Statistics' option) of the number of words L2 learners used in a communicative task. In the boxplot any score that SPSS considers an outlier appears as a little circle with its case number written next to it. In our example, Case 34 has an extreme value and the Extreme Values table confirms indeed that this student used more than 20 per cent more words in her performance than the second most talkative speaker.

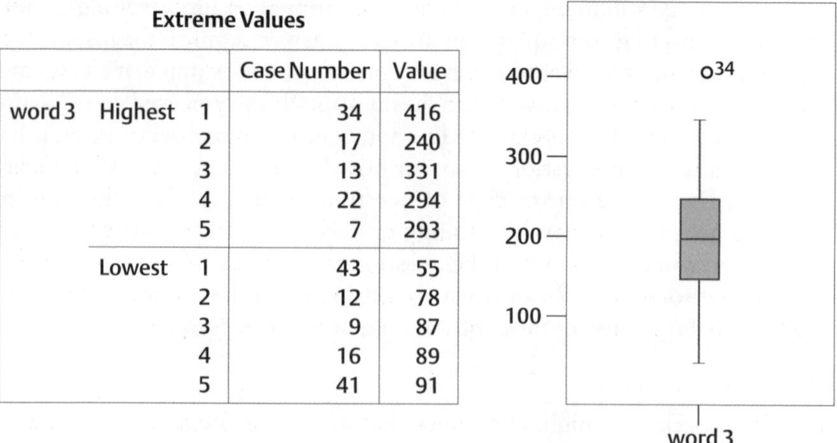

Extreme Values

			Case Number	Value
word 3	Highest	1	34	416
		2	17	240
		3	13	331
		4	22	294
		5	7	293
	Lowest	1	43	55
		2	12	78
		3	9	87
		4	16	89
		5	41	91

Figure 9.1 Output of the 'Outlier' option of the SPSS EXPLORE procedure: extreme values and boxplot

How shall we 'deal' with outliers? First we need to check in the original questionnaire or data record whether the extreme value is simply the result of a mistake we made when entering the data. If so, it can be easily corrected. However, outliers can also indicate an out-of-the-ordinary but true response, respondent carelessness, and even intentional silliness on the part of the participants (which does happen with some participants such as teenage kids). If a close analysis of the response patterns in the particular questionnaire/record points to one of the latter options, we should consider deleting the spurious information so that it does not bias the results. If we cannot make an unambiguous decision as to whether the outlier reflects a true or an unreal case, we may conduct the main analyses twice, with and without the outlier, and see if the outcomes will provide a clue about how to handle the outlier.

9.2.4 Data manipulation

'Data manipulation' involves making changes in the dataset prior to the analyses in order to make it more appropriate for certain statistical procedures; it does *not* involve biasing the results one way or another. At this stage there are three particular issues to attend to: (a) handling missing data, (b) recoding certain values, and (c) considering standardizing the data.

Handling missing data

Missing data are a nuisance for at least two reasons. First, it is not always clear whether the lack of any response is meaningful or not, that is, whether the omission was deliberate or merely an accident. Second, for the purpose of certain statistical procedures a single missing value can invalidate an otherwise complete dataset for a person. For example, in multivariate statistics when many variables are examined at the same time, it can be a basic requirement to have valid values for *every* variable for a person, or else the person will be automatically excluded from the analyses. Given that, regrettably, it is quite common to have a few missing values in every questionnaire, we can end up losing as much as half of our sample this way, which is clearly undesirable. In such cases the program might offer some ways of inputting the missing data that are unlikely to change the results, for example by including item means or maximum likelihood estimates. Luckily, several statistical procedures allow for a choice between 'listwise deletion' and 'pairwise deletion' of cases with missing values: the former refers to the 'hard line' solution whereby one missing value deletes a whole case from all the analyses even if some of the available data could be used for certain calculations. The latter option—which would be my recommendation for most cases—refers to the temporary deletion of a case from an analysis only when specific statistics are computed that would involve the particular missing value, while including the case in all the other analyses for which it has sufficient information.

Recoding negatively worded values

In order to avoid a response set in questionnaires whereby the respondents mark only one side of a rating scale, questionnaire designers often include both positively and negatively worded items (this may also reduce the harmful effects of the 'acquiescence bias'); for example, a scale that targets positive attitudes towards the L2 class may include the item 'I find my language classes boring'. If we have such negatively worded items, we must not forget to reverse the scoring for these before including them in multi-item scales (TRANSFORM → RECODE → INTO SAME VARIABLES; see Table 9.1 for an example). This may sound like an obvious and trivial recommendation, but unless you make the recoding of such scores a compulsory step in the data preparation phase, it is all too easy to forget about it.

Standardizing the data

When we use pooled results from various subsamples (for example, several schools or class groups), one way of controlling for the heterogeneous nature of the subgroups is to use standardized scores. The standardization of raw scores involves the conversion of the distribution within a sample in a way that the mean will be 0 and the standard deviation 1. (For an explanation of these terms, see Section 9.5 on descriptive statistics.) Thus, standard scores express how much each raw value is different from the group mean, and by equalizing the means, scores obtained from different subsamples are readily comparable. Such a transformation is permissible with correlation-based analyses (for example, correlation analysis, factor analysis, and structural equation modelling) because when we compute correlations we can carry out certain mechanical conversions of the raw scores without these affecting the resulting coefficients. For a detailed argument in favour of standardizing heterogeneous questionnaire data, see Gardner (1985: 78–80), who also provides a hypothetical illustration in which a motivation measure shows significant positive correlation with learning achievement in two school classes when computed separately, but the same correlation becomes non-significant when the data are pooled without standardization. Standard scores can be computed in SPSS by ticking the 'Save standardized values as variables' box in DESCRIPTIVES (ANALYSE → DESCRIPTIVE STATISTICS → DESCRIPTIVES).

9.3 Data reduction and reliability analysis

'Data reduction' is somewhere between data manipulation and data analysis in the sense that although this procedure already affects the results, its impact is kept minimal and the main objective of the procedure is to prepare the data for analysis by reducing the number of variables to a manageable size. Every initial quantitative dataset has many more variables than necessary. For example, a well-designed questionnaire contains multiple items focusing on each content area (see Section 5.2.2) and therefore the parallel items need to be summed up in 'multi-item scales' for the purpose of analysis. Thus, data reduction involves creating fewer but broader variables that carry almost as much information as the original variables. The most common procedure to achieve this is to calculate the mean of the parallel or interrelated items (TRANSFORM → COMPUTE). In order to decide which items hang together and how much, we can apply a useful procedure: 'factor analysis' (Section 9.10.2).

It does not require much justification that composite variables such as multi-item scales are only effective if the constituent items that make up the variable work together in a homogeneous manner, that is, if they measure the same target area. In psychometric terms this means that each item on a multi-item scale should correlate with the other items and with the total scale score, which has been referred to as Likert's criterion of 'internal consistency'. Indeed, 'internal consistency reliability' is generally seen as the psychometric prerequisite for any multi-item scale in a questionnaire that is to be used as a research instrument. Surprisingly, the internal consistency reliability of a scale does not only depend on the internal consistency of the items but also on the *number of items* making up the scale. That is, it is easier to achieve appropriate internal consistency reliability with 20 items than with three. This, of course, makes good sense: in a short scale consisting of 3–4 items a divergent item can make much more of a disruption than in a scale of 20, and therefore short scales need to display more evidence of homogeneity than long ones if they are to be seen as trustworthy.

Internal consistency reliability is measured by the Cronbach Alpha coefficient (named after its introducer, L. J. Cronbach). This is a figure ranging between 0 and +1 (although in extreme cases—for example with very small samples and with items that measure different things—it can also be negative), and if it proves to be very low, either the particular scale is too short or the items have very little in common. Internal consistency estimates for well-developed scales containing about 10 items ought to approach 0.80. Because of the complexity of the second language acquisition process, L2 researchers typically want to measure many different areas in one questionnaire, and therefore cannot use very long scales (or the completion of the questionnaire would take several hours). This means that somewhat lower Cronbach Alpha coefficients are to be expected, but even with short scales of 3–4 items we should aim at reliability coefficients in excess of 0.70; if the Cronbach Alpha of a scale does not reach 0.60, this should sound warning bells.

How do we obtain Cronbach Alpha coefficients? SPSS makes it relatively easy to conduct reliability analysis. The 'Reliability' procedure of SPSS (ANALYSIS → SCALE → RELIABILITY ANALYSIS) not only provides the Cronbach Alpha for any given scale but, by choosing a statistics option, it also computes what the alpha coefficient would be if a particular item were deleted from the scale. By looking at the list of these 'would-be' alphas for each item, we can immediately see which item reduces the internal consistency of the scale and should therefore be considered for omission.

9.4 Key statistical concepts

Before we start exploring the range of statistical techniques at our disposal, there are certain key statistical concepts that we need to understand to be able to choose the right procedure and interpret the results correctly. In this section I will discuss the main types of quantitative data, the importance of a normal distribution of the data, the distinction between descriptive and inferential statistics, and the notions of statistical significance, confidence interval, and effect size.

9.4.1 Main types of quantitative data

Although quantitative research has several possible data sources, the final numerically coded data is only of three types: 'nominal' (or 'categorical'), 'ordinal', and 'interval'. The difference between the three main types lies in the precision of the measurement and this distinction determines the type of statistical procedures that we can use to analyse the data.

- *Nominal* or *categorical* data is the least precise data type. It is associated with variables that have no numerical values, such as gender or race. Here the assigned values are completely arbitrary; for example as already mentioned, for the gender variable male is usually coded '1' and female '2,' which does not indicate any difference in size or salience.
- *Ordinal* data involves ranked numbers. For example, a multiple-choice item with options such as 'never', 'once a day', 'once a week', and 'once a month' will produce ordinal data because the answers can be placed on

a 'frequency' continuum, but the values do not correspond to any regular measurement on a scale (as would 'once a day', 'twice a day', 'three times a day', etc.).

- *Interval* data is the most precise type; it can be seen as ordinal data in which the various values are at an equal distance—or intervals—from each other on a continuum. Test scores, for example, usually provide a series of values which correspond to equal differences in the degree/size of the variable measured.

The separation of these three types of measures becomes important when we select the statistical techniques to be used with our data. The big dividing line is between 'parametric procedures', which require interval data, and 'non-parametric procedures', which can be applied to ordinal and even nominal data. (We will come back to this question in Section 9.9.)

9.4.2 Normal distribution of the data

A second characteristic of the data that has a special statistical significance is whether it is 'normally distributed'. This means that if we plot the data we get a symmetrical, bell-shaped curve, which has the greatest frequency of scores in the middle, with smaller frequencies towards the extremes, just like the illustration below. In practical terms a normal distribution means that some of the values are low, some high, and the bulk of the values are centred around the middle, that is, around the mean.

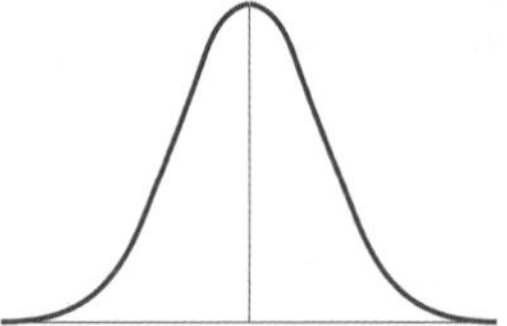

In the previous section I mentioned that 'parametric' tests require interval data and now we can add that in order to be able to use parametric procedures the interval data also needs to be normally distributed. This is an important assumption of the data because most of the statistical procedures discussed in this chapter are parametric. (For non-parametric tests, see Section 9.9.) Fortunately, normality does not have to be perfect because most procedures work well with data that is only approximately normally distributed.

How can we decide whether our data is normally distributed? The EXPLORE procedure of SPSS (ANALYSE → DESCRIPTIVE STATISTICS → EXPLORE) offers a special 'Normality plots with tests' function under the 'Plots' option, producing various plots as well as the results of the 'Kolmogorov-Smirnov' statistic, which is a test of normality. This latter works well with smaller samples but it can be too sensitive with large samples—however, with samples of 100 or more cases the impact of any deviations from normality diminishes and with such large datasets examining the visual appearance of the distribution is usually sufficient (Tabachnick and Fidell 2001: 74).

9.4.3 Descriptive versus inferential statistics

Statistics can be divided into two principal areas, 'descriptive statistics' and 'inferential statistics'. This distinction lies at the heart of statistics and failure to understand statistics is often caused by the fact that insufficient attention has been paid to this difference. Descriptive statistics are used to summarize sets of numerical data in order to conserve time and space. It is obvious that providing the mean and the range (i.e. minimum and maximum values) of a variable is a more professional way of describing the respondents' answers than listing all the scores that we have obtained. And if we also include the 'standard deviation' of the results (which, as we will see in Section 9.5 on descriptive statistics, is an index of the average disparity among the scores), we have achieved a well-rounded description of the scores that would satisfy most purposes. Thus, descriptive statistics offer a tidy way of presenting the data we have. The important thing, however, is to note that these statistics do not allow drawing any general conclusions that would go beyond the sample. In practice this means that when we report descriptive results we ought to start every sentence which describes descriptive features with 'In my sample ...'. If we want to say something about possible general lessons that may be drawn from our study—which is what we usually do when we conduct research—we need to compute inferential statistics. Broadly speaking, inferential statistics are the same as descriptive statistics except that the computer also tests whether the results that we observed in our sample (for example, differences or correlations) are powerful enough to generalize to the whole population. It makes intuitive sense that what we find needs to pass a certain threshold of magnitude to be of general significance—inferential statistics basically evaluates the results against such a threshold.

Descriptive statistics are useful, for example, to describe the achievement of a particular class of learners. What happens, however, if we notice that, say, the L2 learning achievement of boys and girls shows a remarkable difference in our sample, with girls outperforming boys (which is often the case)? Can we draw the inference that girls are better language learners? No. Based on descriptive statistics all we can say is that in this class girls did better than boys. In order to venture any generalization concerning the wider population and not just the particular sample, we need to show that the difference between girls and boys is significant in the statistical sense. To achieve this, as discussed above, we need to employ inferential statistical procedures.

9.4.4 Statistical significance

The main concern of inferential statistics has traditionally been the testing of 'statistical significance'. Statistical significance denotes whether a particular result observed in a sample is 'true' for the whole population and is therefore generalizable. If a result is non-significant, this means that we cannot be certain that it did not occur in the particular sample only because of chance (for example, because of the unique composition of the learners examined). In other words, even if we feel that the particular descriptive data reveals some true and more general tendencies, if the results are not significant we cannot exclude the possibility of a mere coincidence. For this reason, statistically non-significant results *must* be ignored in research studies.

One important feature of statistical significance is that it is the function of not only the *magnitude* of the result but also the *size of the sample* investigated. It is easy to see why this is so: if we assess, say, millions of people, even a relatively weak tendency can be regarded as typical of the whole population, whereas with only a handful of people we cannot be certain even about far stronger tendencies. Therefore, the computer takes the combined effect of magnitude and sample size into account when it calculates the significance of a result. If a particular result is marked as significant, we can utter a sigh of relief as this means that the observed phenomenon represents a significant departure from what might be expected by chance alone. That is, it can be assumed to be real and we can report it. However, if a particular result is not significant, we must not report it (for example, if the mean scores of two groups are not significantly different, we *must not* say that one is larger than the other even if the descriptive statistics do show some difference!).

Significance is measured by a probability coefficient (p), which can range from 0 to +1. A p figure of, say, 0.25 means that the obtained result might be due to pure chance in 25 per cent of the cases. In social sciences we typically consider a result significant if $p < 0.05$, that is, if the probability of the result not being real but only due to chance (for example, sampling peculiarity) is less then 5 per cent (i.e. five times out of a hundred). Significance is typically marked in tables as follows:

* indicates $p < .05$
** indicates $p < .01$
*** indicates $p < .001$

It is important to stress here that statistical significance is *not* the final answer because even though a result may be statistically significant (i.e. reliable and true to the larger population), it may not be valuable. 'Significance' in the statistical sense only means 'probably true' rather than 'important'. To examine the importance of an observed score we need to consider the notions of 'confidence intervals' and 'effect size'—see below. And finally a technical point: I suggest that researchers always set the computer to compute 'two-tailed' significance (which is the default in SPSS), which is appropriate when we are not sure about whether the results will be negative or positive (i.e. in t-tests—see Section 9.6—we are not sure which of the compared means is larger and in correlation we do not know whether the coefficient will be positive or negative). In my experience only very rarely can we predict with certainty the direction of the results in advance, in which case 'one-tailed' significance (which is easier to achieve) would be sufficient.

9.4.5 Confidence intervals

While 'statistical significance' only gives us a yes/no answer about a result, the 'confidence interval' is more informative because it provides a range of scores (between two boundaries) that can be considered significant for the population. In the social sciences the usual confidence level is 95 per cent, and a 95 per cent confidence interval of a mean score can be interpreted as a range of scores that will contain the population mean with a 0.95 probability. If the mean of our specific sample falls within this range, then it can be considered significant. SPSS always supplements tests of statistical significance with confidence intervals and many researchers have recently recommended that we report such intervals more often in published studies. The Publication Manual of the American Psychological Association (APA 2001: 22), which is generally seen as the most important source of guidelines on how to present our findings in applied linguistics (see Section 12.2 on style manuals), for example states:

> The reporting of confidence intervals ... can be an extremely effective way of reporting results. Because confidence intervals combine information on location and precision and can often be directly used to infer significance levels, they are, in general, the best reporting strategy. The use of confidence intervals is therefore strongly recommended.

SPSS makes the reporting of confidence intervals easy because it provides them as part of the default output for most procedures. In spite of this, the usual practice in both applied linguistics and educational psychology has been to indicate statistical significance only without presenting the actual confidence intervals.

9.4.6 Effect size

Why do we need to bother about 'effect size' (or as it is also called, 'strength of association') if a result is statistically significant? The reason is that 'statistical significance' only means that an observed phenomenon is most probably true in the population (and not just in our sample), but what is true may not necessarily be important. For example, with very large sample sizes even tiny differences between two groups might reach statistical significance even though they may have no practical or theoretical importance whatsoever. This raises a broader issue of the overall value of significance testing and indeed the past decade has seen a heated debate over this issue. (For a recent review, see Balluerka *et al.* 2005.) As a result of this controversy, the American Psychological Association (APA) convened a committee called the 'Task Force on Statistical Inference' (TFSI), which concluded that researchers should always present effect sizes for primary outcomes (Wilkinson and TFSI 1999).

Thus, effect sizes need to be computed in order to provide information about the magnitude of an observed phenomenon, and doing so will also enable us to compare the results reported in different studies, because effect size indices are transformations onto a common scale. Indeed, Wilkinson and TFSI (1999) emphasized that scholars should report and interpret effect sizes in the context of previously reported effects, as this would make it possible to evaluate the stability of results across samples, designs, and analyses. Having said this, we must also realize the main shortcoming of effect size, namely that there are no universally accepted and straightforward indices to describe it. Instead, the calculation differs for various statistical tests and even with regard to one test we sometimes find alternative and competing effect size indicators. (For a detailed overview, see Grissom and Kim 2005.) The problem of diversity is well illustrated by the following description from the APA Publication Manual (2001: 25–6), which is likely to go over the heads of most researchers who are not statistics experts themselves:

> You can estimate the magnitude of the effect or the strength of the relationship with a number of common effect size estimates, including (but not limited to) r^2, η^2, ω^2, R^2, φ^2, Cramer's V, Kendall's W, Cohen's d and κ, Goodman-Kruskal's λ and γ, Jacobson and Truax's and Kendall's proposed measures of clinical significance, and the multivariate Roy's Θ and the Pillai-Bartlett V.

9.4.7 How much to generalize

As mentioned earlier more than once, one of the key issues in quantitative data analysis is to decide whether or not we can generalize our results to other contexts, and if so, how much. The standard advice we find in statistics texts usually amounts to the broad and rather unhelpful guideline: *do not overgeneralize!* However, research in most cases is all about the need to produce generalizable findings. After all, with the possible exception of 'action research' (see Section 8.5), applied linguists rarely investigate a sample with the sole purpose of wanting to know more only about the particular people under investigation. Instead, what we normally want to do in quantitative research is find out more about the population, that is, about all the similar people in the world. So the real question is what exactly 'over-' means in the 'do not overgeneralize' warning.

It would again be easy to give a less-than-useful, though technically correct, definition of 'overgeneralization,' namely that it occurs when we generalize the findings to a population that our sample is not representative of. (See

Section 5.1.1.) This states, in effect, that if we examine, say, primary school pupils, we should not generalize our findings to secondary or university students. There is no question about the validity of this claim, and yet it avoids the crux of the problem, which is that if we were to observe this guideline too closely, few (if any) studies in the educational psychological literature could speak about 'students' in general. It is clear that hardly any investigation is sufficiently large-scale to include representatives of every main age group, ethnicity, school type, and subject matter in a single study (just to list four key factors)—yet the discussions of the findings are rarely restricted to the particular subpopulation in question.

Having said this, I still believe that we should beware of overgeneralizations, but in the absence of hard and fast rules about what constitutes '*over*'-generalization, we need to strive to find a delicate balance between the following two considerations: on the one hand, we may wish to be able to say something of a broader relevance (since it may severely reduce our audience if we limit our discussion to very specific subgroups). On the other hand, big claims can usually be made only on the basis of big studies. Having said this, some classic studies in the research literature did confine their focus to extremely limited target issues, and some famous big claims were indeed made based on small studies.

So, the only conclusion I can offer here is that researchers need to exercise *great caution* when pitching the level of generalization in their research reports. Lazaraton (2005) warns us that using high-powered parametric procedures may easily tempt researchers to overgeneralize their results and to make grand claims regarding their findings, 'claims that far exceed what is permitted by their methodological underpinnings' (Tarone 1994, cited by Lazaraton 2005: 219). On the other hand, along with the 'Task Force on Statistical Inference' of the American Psychological Association (Wilkinson and TFSI 1999: 602), I would encourage researchers not to be afraid 'to extend your interpretations to a general class or population if you have reasons to assume that your results apply'.

9.5 Descriptive statistics

As mentioned above, descriptive statistics help us summarize findings by describing general tendencies in the data and the overall spread of the scores (i.e. how varied the scores are). Such statistics are indispensable when we share our results (for example, when we describe the participants in the methodology section of a paper) and they also form the basis of further inferential statistics. The two main categories of descriptive statistics are the 'measures of central tendency' and the 'measures of variability'.

Measures of central tendency describe the data set with a single numerical value. The three most commonly used measures are the following:

- *Mean* which is the average of the scores. This is the most common descriptive measure because it takes into account all the scores, but it has a disadvantage, namely that extreme scores skew it considerably.
- *Median* which is the 'fiftieth percentile', that is, the middle point in a set of scores that have been arranged in a rank order. This measure is not sensitive to extremes, but its actual value is only dependent on the middle scores.
- *Mode* which is the most frequently occurring score. This is a straightforward measure but it can only provide a good estimate of the central tendency of the distribution if there is a value that indeed stands out with its frequency.

'Measures of variability' provide indices of how dispersed or varied the scores are in a dataset. They include the following measures:

- *Range* which is the difference between the highest and the lowest score.
- *Variance* and its square root, the *standard deviation*, which are indicators of the average distance of the scores from the mean. They are high if the sample is heterogeneous and contains extreme scores, whereas they are low in a homogeneous sample with all the scores clustered around the mean.

Descriptive statistics can be obtained by more than one SPSS procedure, the most commonly used ones are FREQUENCIES and DESCRIPTIVES. In research articles and theses/dissertations such statistics are almost always reported in tables. Table 9.2 offers a typical sample following the APA format (which does not contain any vertical lines). As can be seen, the basic statistics that are usually provided are the mean (*M*), the standard deviation (*SD*) and the number of participants (*n*). Please note that in tables we usually omit '0' from the beginning of figures smaller than 1 (i.e. we write .80 instead of 0.80).

Language Anxiety Scores of Hungarian Secondary School Learners of Finnish, Broken Down by Proficiency Level

	Language proficiency level								
	Beginner			Intermediate			Advanced		
Sex	*M*	*SD*	*n*	*M*	*SD*	*n*	*M*	*SD*	*n*
Female	3.35	.38	353	3.20	.45	1,041	3.12	.52	274
Male	3.22	.47	257	3.04	.47	653	2.97	.52	152

Table 9.2 Sample table reporting descriptive statistics

9.6 Comparing two groups: t-tests

Comparing various groups of people is the most common statistical procedure in applied linguistic research (Lazaraton 2005). In statistics there are different methods available for such comparisons depending on the number of groups we wish to analyse. If we want to compare two groups (for example, men and women), we compute a 't-test', which is the subject of this section. The procedure to be applied with more than two groups is the 'analysis of variance' (ANOVA), which will be discussed in Section 9.7.

If we take any two sets of scores, we are bound to find some difference in the raw scores, but we cannot automatically assume that the observed difference reflects any 'real' difference; thus, we need t-test statistics to check whether we have got a generalizable result or whether the score is likely to be merely an artefact of random variation. There are two main types of t-tests:

- *Independent-samples t-tests* are for research designs where we are comparing the results of groups that are independent of each other (for example, Class 1 and Class 2).
- *Paired-samples t-tests* (also known as 'matched t-tests', 'matched-pairs t-tests' or 'pairs t-tests') are for research designs where we want to compare two sets of scores (i.e. two variables) obtained from the same group (for example, the learners' course grades in history and English) or when the same participants are measured more than once (for example, test scores before and after a course). That is, this procedure examines different results obtained from the same group.

Both types are similar in that we test whether the difference between two sets of scores is big enough to reach statistical significance. However, because the first type involves two separate groups of participants while the second involves only one group, SPSS uses different mathematical computations for them; therefore, when we run a t-test, we have to select in advance which procedure is relevant to us.

9.6.1 Illustration

SPSS provides a sample dataset for practice, containing data from the 1991 General US Social Survey. One variable in this survey involves the level of 'happiness' experienced by the respondents. Let us examine whether there was a significant difference in the US in 1991 between men and women in this respect. To do so we need to compute an independent-samples t-test. The 'syntax file' (ANALYSE → COMPARE MEANS → INDEPENDENT-SAMPLES T-TEST + PASTE) contains the following simple commands:

```
T-TEST
  GROUPS = sex (1 2)
  /MISSING = ANALYSIS
  /VARIABLES = happy
  /CRITERIA = CI (.95).
```

Table 9.3 presents the SPSS output:

T-test

Group statistics

	sex	N	Mean	Std. Deviation	Std. Error Mean
happy	1	633	1.76	.593	.024
	2	871	1.83	.632	.021

Independent Samples Test

		Levenes Test for Equality of Variances		t-test for Equality of Means						
									95% Confidence interval of the Difference	
		F	Sig.	t	df	Sig. (2-tailed)	Mean Difference	Std. Error Difference	Lower	Upper
happy	Equal variances assumed	.029	.865	-2.196	1502	.028	-.071	.032	-.134	-.008
	Equal variances not assumed			-2.219	1409.089	.027	-.071	.032	-.133	-.008

Table 9.3 Sample SPSS output reporting t-test statistics

In the first table we can see that men (indicated with '1' in the 'sex' variable) display a somewhat lower mean score for happiness than women (1.76 versus 1.83) and the key question is whether this difference reaches statistical significance. Because the probability figure—marked as 'Sig.' in the second table—is smaller than 0.05 (it is 0.028), the difference can be considered true. (Note that in the second table, because the Levene's test does not show any significant difference, we can assume equal variance in the two groups and therefore the first line of the results is relevant. If the Levene test showed a significant difference—i.e. if it was smaller than .05—this would indicate that equal variance cannot be assumed and then we would need to consider the figures in the bottom row.) We should note here that in this particular dataset the coding was such that the lower the score, the higher the level of happiness, and therefore we can conclude that in 1991 American men were reported to be happier than their female counterparts.

The most common effect size indicator for independent-samples t-tests is 'eta squared' (it can be interpreted as the percentage of the variance in the target variable explained by the grouping variable). Unfortunately, SPSS does not provide this figure but it is easy to compute using the following formula (Pallant 2005; N refers to the size of the groups):

$$\frac{t^2}{t^2 + (N1 + N2 - 2)}$$

In our current example eta squared is .003. The usual interpretation of eta squared is that .01 = small effect, .06 = moderate effect, and .14 = large effect, which means that our effect size is very small, indicating that even though the difference of happiness is significant, its magnitude is ignorable. So, in effect, American men are not happier than American women.

9.6.2 Reporting t-test results

In research articles we typically find that t-test results are reported embedded within the text rather then presented in a separate table. The following extract presents a typical result summary; it shows that we need to provide the means and standard deviations (these are sometimes presented in a table), the t-value, the degree of freedom in brackets, the probability figure, and the effect size. (The 'degree of freedom' is a statistical figure, that roughly reflects the sample size, although it does not coincide with it exactly because in this case the number of groups has been subtracted from it.)

> We have carried out an independent-samples t-test to compare the happiness scores for American men and women. There was a significant difference in scores for men ($M = 1.76$, $SD = .69$) and women ($M = 1.83$, $SD = .63$), $t(1502) = -2.20$, $p<.05$, but the magnitude of the difference in the means was very small (eta squared = .003), with sex explaining only .3 per cent of the variance in happiness.

If we have a series of t-test statistics that would make reporting them in the text confusing, we can include them in a table. Table 9.3 presents paired samples t-test statistics; for the table we need to provide the total number of participants (*n*), the means of the two variables compared (*M*), the standard deviations (*SD*), the degrees of freedom (*d*), the t-value, and the effect size. In order to save space, in tables we do not usually present separate probability values but instead indicate the level of significance by adding asterisks to the t-values that have been found statistically significant. These asterisks are always explained at the bottom of the table (as in Table 9.4).

Paired Samples T-Tests of the Students' Performance on Different Listening and Reading Tests (N=80)

	M	*SD*	*d*	*t*	Effect size[a]
Listening comprehension			79	8.57*	1.13
Test 1	87.8	13.5			
Test 2	69.6	18.2			
Reading comprehension			79	-7.21*	.83
Test 1	33.0	22.4			
Test 2	51.8	22.5			

* $p < .001$.
[a] Eta squared.

Table 9.4 Sample table reporting t-test statistics

9.7 Comparing more than two groups: analysis of variance (ANOVA)

'Analysis of variance' (more precisely, 'one-way analysis of variance', usually referred to as 'ANOVA') is very similar to the t-test but in this case we assess the significance of the differences in the means of more than two groups (for example, the mean achievement of three different class groups); we can also run ANOVA with only two groups, in which case the result will be the same as corresponding t-test statistics. In a survey of 524 empirical studies that appeared in four major applied linguistic journals between 1991 and 2001, Lazaraton (2005) found that ANOVA was the most frequently used statistical procedure, accounting for over 40 per cent of the analyses reported in the articles. As she concluded, 'one implication of this finding is that if applied linguists are to learn to carry out and/or to interpret just one statistical procedure, that procedure should be ANOVA' (p. 218). To do ANOVA, we need two variables:

- A *dependent variable* which is the target variable to be compared, such as school achievement.
- An *independent variable* (called in SPSS the 'factor'), which is the grouping variable that has as many values as the number of groups we want to compare. For example, we may have a variable called 'class group' with three values (1, 2 and 3) representing three classes, which will allow us to run ANOVA to compare these classes.

ANOVA produces multiple comparisons in two steps. First an *F* value is computed and checked for significance. If the value is significant, it means that there is at least one significant difference amongst the group means. However, because with more than two groups we have more than one contrast (i.e. with three groups—A, B, and C—we have three contrasts: between A and B, B and C, or C and A), we need a second step to determine which contrast(s) is/are significant. For this purpose we compute a *post hoc* test, which is offered by SPSS as an option for ANOVA under 'POST HOC'. Several types of *post hoc* tests are listed, typically delivering almost exactly the same results. (The most commonly used ones are LSD, S-N-K, and Tukey.) It is important to reiterate that we conduct *post hoc* tests if and only if the initial *F* value for the ANOVA was significant.

9.7.1 Illustration

Let us use again the 1991 General US Social Survey. If we look at the 'race' variable (referring to the ethnic background of the respondents), we can see that the respondents were divided into three categories: white (1), black (2), and other (3). Let us examine whether the three race types differ in terms of their happiness.

The 'syntax file' (ANALYSE → COMPARE MEANS → ONE-WAY ANOVA + PASTE) is just as straightforward as with the t-tests:

```
ONEWAY
  happy BY race
  /STATISTICS DESCRIPTIVES
  /MISSING ANALYSIS
  /POSTHOC = SNK ALPHA(.05).
```

The SPSS output is printed below in Table 9.5. As the probability figure (marked as 'Sig.' in the second table) shows, the *F* value is statistically significant at the $p < .001$ level, which is impressive. The *post hoc* test (S-N-K) reveals that the difference lies between white people and the other races (as they are presented in two different columns): white people are significantly happier than members of the non-white races (black and other), whereas the latter two groups do not differ from each other significantly and therefore must be considered equal. (We should note that the coding was such that the lower the score, the higher the level of happiness.)

Oneway

Descriptives

happy

	N	Mean	Std. Deviation	Std. Error	95% Confidence Interval for Mean Lower Bound	95% Confidence Interval for Mean Upper Bound	Minimum	Maximum
1	1256	1.77	.604	.017	1.73	1.80	1	3
2	201	1.97	.651	.046	1.87	2.06	1	3
3	47	1.94	.673	.098	1.74	2.13	1	3
Total	1504	1.80	.617	.016	1.77	1.83	1	3

ANOVA

happy

	Sum of Squares	df	Mean Square	F	Sig.
Between Groups	7.680	2	3.840	10.225	.000
Within Groups	563.679	1501	.376		
Total	571.359	1503			

Post Hoc Tests
Homogeneous Subsets

happy

Student-Newman-Keuls [a, b]

race	N	Subset for alpha = .05: 1	2
1	1256	1.77	
3	47		1.94
2	201		1.97
Sig.		1.000	.725

Means for groups in homogeneous subsets are displayed.

a. Uses Harmonic Mean Sample Size = 110.914.

b. The group sizes are unequal. The harmonic mean of the group sizes is used. Type I error levels are not guaranteed.

Table 9.5 Sample SPSS output reporting ANOVA statistics

Like with the t-test, the most common effect size indicator for ANOVA is 'eta squared' (it can be interpreted as the percentage of the variance in the target variable explained by the grouping variable). Unfortunately, SPSS does not provide this figure but it is easy to compute using the following formula (Pallant 2005):

$$\frac{\text{sum of squares between-groups}}{\text{total sum of squares}}$$

The 'sum of squares' figures can be found in the ANOVA output table; in our current example eta squared is .013. The usual interpretation of eta squared is that 0.01 = small effect, 0.06 = moderate effect, and 0.14 = large effect, which means that our effect size is rather small, indicating that even though the difference of happiness is significant, its magnitude is too small to be really meaningful.

9.7.2 Reporting ANOVA results

Similar to t-test statistics, ANOVA results are typically reported embedded within the text in research articles. The following sample shows that we need to provide the means and standard deviations, the *F*-value, the degree of freedom, and the sample size in brackets, as well as the probability figure and the effect size. If there is a significant difference then we also need to present the results of a *post hoc* test. Please note that in the following example the descriptive statistics are embedded in the text but for the sake of clarity descriptive information is often presented in a separate table.

> A one-way analysis of variance indicated that there was a significant difference in happiness amongst white people ($M = 1.77$, $SD = .60$), black people ($M = 1.97$, $SD = .65$) and other races ($M = 1.94$, $SD = .67$), F (2, 1501) = 10.23, $p < .001$. The effect size was small (eta squared = .013). S-N-K post hoc tests showed that white people were significantly happier than members of the non-white races (black and other), $p < .05$, whereas the latter two groups did not differ from each other significantly.

If we have multiple comparisons, we can report the results in a table. Table 9.6 presents sample ANOVA statistics, including descriptive statistics for the subsamples compared.

Comparison of Affective Learner Variables Across Dwelling Types

	M (SD)				
	Village (*n* = 1,555)	Town (*n* = 1,690)	City (*n* = 1,553)	F(2, 4798)	Effect size[3]
Attitudes towards tourists	3.26 (1.06)	3.22 (1.05)	3.13 (1.09)	6.28*	.003
Self-confidence	4.06 (0.75)	4.06 (0.76)	4.11 (0.70)	2.45	.001
Language learning motivation	3.16 (0.96)	3.09 (0.98)	2.98 (0.99)	13.20**	.006

*$p < .01$. **$p < .001$.
[3] Eta squared.

Table 9.6 Sample table reporting ANOVA statistics

9.7.3 Analysis of covariance (ANCOVA)

The main question that the analysis of covariance (ANCOVA) procedure answers is the same as with the t-test and ANOVA: are the mean differences observed between different groups significant, that is, true for the population? ANCOVA, however, extends ANOVA by adding a further element: before comparing the means, it statistically removes certain obscuring or confounding effects, for example, certain group differences that are related to the target (i.e. dependent) variable. For example, if we want to compare the L2 course achievement of two class groups, it may provide a fairer result if we remove statistically the language aptitude difference between the classes. Thus, when we want to compare a variable in two or more groups and suspect that the groups are not similar in terms of some important background variable that is likely to affect the target variable, we can specify this background variable as a 'covariate' and then run ANCOVA to test the group difference while controlling for this covariate. In other words, by removing the effects of certain background variables, ANCOVA in effect produces a more level playing field for the purpose of comparisons.

A special case of the use of ANCOVA occurs in quasi-experimental designs (see Section 5.3.2) when we compare the post-test scores of the control and the treatment groups while controlling for the pre-test scores as the covariate. In this case, if we find any significant difference between the post-test scores, those will be related to events that took place *after* the pre-test because the preexisting differences of the two groups have been removed by controlling for the pre-test scores.

ANCOVA can be found in SPSS under 'General Linear Models' (ANALYSIS → GENERAL LINEAR MODEL → UNIVARIATE). Although the procedure is not particularly difficult to run in SPSS, space limitations do not allow me to provide instructions here—please refer to an SPSS guide for the exact details. The good news about the SPSS output is that next to the significance value we find the 'partial eta squared' index, which is the effect size, so we do not need to calculate this manually.

9.8 Correlation

The two core purposes of statistics are to look at the *difference* between variables—discussed in Sections 9.6 and 9.7—and to examine the *relationship* between variables. The statistical procedure to achieve the second purpose is called 'correlation analysis' and it allows us to look at two variables and evaluate the strength and direction of their relationship or association with each other. To do so, we compute a 'correlation coefficient' between the two variables, which can range between -1 – +1:

- A high coefficient means a strong relationship (i.e. if an individual scores high on one variable, he/she is also likely to score high on the other); for example, students' language aptitude scores and foreign language grades tend to display a high positive correlation.
- A coefficient of 0 suggests no relationship between the two variables; for example, students' attitudes towards chocolate and the number of brothers/sisters they have are likely to have no significant correlations.
- Negative correlation coefficients suggest inverse relationships; for example, the number of days students miss school is likely to have a negative correlation with their overall school achievement.

Of course, similar to t-test and ANOVA statistics, the correlation coefficients need to be statistically significant to indicate true scores.

9.8.1 Strength of the correlation

To give an indication of the strength of the correlation coefficient, in applied linguistics research we can find meaningful correlations of as low as 0.3–0.5 (for example, between motivation and achievement) and if two tests correlate with each other in the order of 0.6, we can say that they measure more or less the same thing. Although negative correlations are preceded by a negative sign, this only indicates their direction not their strength: The coefficients of $r = 0.6$ and $r = -0.6$ are equally strong. At this point we must note that correlation coefficients only describe 'linear relationships', that is, associations between two variables that follow the 'if we score high on one, we are likely to score high on the other' principle. Thus, correlation is not appropriate to assess 'curvilinear relationships', that is, U-shaped distributions of scores (for example, the relationship between eating chocolate and enjoyment, which for most people increases up to a level but after a while can turn into slight nausea).

To make the actual strength of a correlation more tangible, it is common to square the value of the correlation coefficient, because the result thus obtained represents the proportion of the variance shared by the two variables (i.e. the variation in the score on one variable which is accounted for by the other). For example, a correlation of .60 means that 36 per cent of the variance in the scores is explained by the relationship between the two variables rather than by chance or by some other cause(s). This figure is seen as the 'effect size' of correlation.

9.8.2 Main types of correlation

The following are the four main types of correlation used in applied linguistics research (a fifth, non-parametric, version will be introduced in Section 9.9.2):

- *Pearson product–moment correlation* is the standard type, computed between two continuous variables. When we talk about 'correlation' in general, this is what we usually mean. The Pearson product-moment correlation coefficient is symbolized by the lower-case letter '*r*' (pronounced 'rho').
- *Point-biserial correlation* and *phi coefficients* Correlation coefficients can be calculated when one or both variables are dichotomous (i.e. have only two values, for example, 'gender'); fortunately, we do not need to worry about this because SPSS automatically adjusts the calculation accordingly.
- *Partial correlation* is a very useful technique, allowing us to examine the relationship between two variables after removing the correlation which is due to their mutual association with a third variable (for example, a background variable such as the learners' intelligence/aptitude, which can easily modify the scores when computing correlations between motivation and, say, achievement). This is, in a way, the correlational counterpart of ANCOVA.
- *Multiple correlation* is a technique to compute the correlation between one variable and a group of variables. This type of correlation can be used, for example, when we want to see the composite effects of a range of learner characteristics (for example, aptitude, motivation, creativity, anxiety, etc.) on achievement. It is usually symbolized by an upper-case 'R'.

9.8.3 The issue of cause–effect relations

Before we discuss various technical aspects of correlation analysis, let me highlight the greatest shortcoming of correlational research, namely that it cannot identify *cause* and *effect*. When two variables show significant positive correlation, we cannot claim that this is because one causes or influences the other. All we can say is that they are *interrelated*, since the higher one variable gets, the higher the other is likely to be. It can, for example, be the case that an observed significant association between two variables is only caused by their relationship with a third variable; for example, physical strength and language learning motivation are expected to show a significant negative correlation not because the two variables have anything to do with each other but because they are both related to the learner's sex: boys tend to be stronger and girls tend to be more motivated language learners. We must therefore exercise great caution when reporting correlational results. On the other hand, because there may be (and often is) a causal relationship between two variables that are intercorrelated, correlation analysis can suggest directions for follow-up experimental research.

9.8.4 Running correlation analysis in SPSS

Running 'ordinary' correlation (i.e. 'Pearson product-moment correlation') is straightforward: ANALYSE → CORRELATE → BIVARIATE. We need not worry about variables which have two values only—SPSS automatically adjusts the calculations accordingly. Before performing a correlation analysis, I have found that it is useful to produce a visual representation of the data distribution by generating a scatterplot (GRAPHS → SCATTER/DOT). Figure 9.2 presents a sample scatterplot of the distribution of the number of words and turns produced by 44 learners of English in an L2 communicative task. Although there are some obvious outliers (which we might want to 'deal with'—see Section 9.2.3), we can detect a 'cigar-shaped' cluster, which suggests a reasonably strong correlation (indeed, $r = .57$). If the main cluster of the points forms a curved line, then using correlation is not appropriate because correlation assumes a linear relationship.

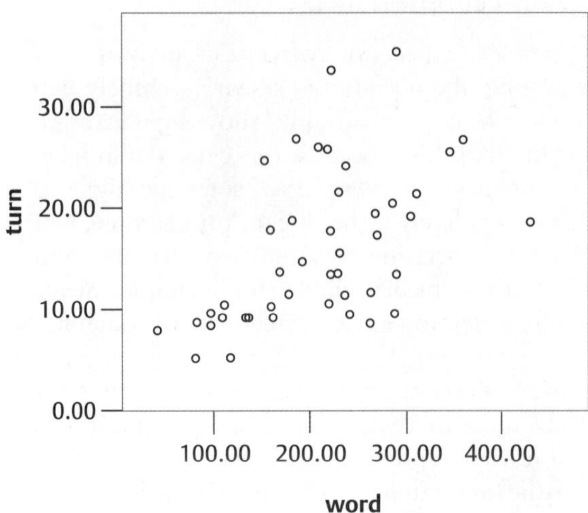

Figure 9.2 Sample scatterplot

Partial correlation is similarly straightforward: ANALYSE → CORRELATE → PARTIAL. All we have to do here is to specify an additional variable that should be controlled for.

Multiple correlation can be computed using the 'Regression' command (ANALYSE → REGRESSION), where multiple correlations are produced as part of the default output. Multiple correlation is calculated between one variable and a group of variables; in the Regression dialogue box specify the single variable as the 'Dependent' and enter the group of variables in the 'Independent(s)' box. The 'method' should be 'enter', which is the default. In the output, the multiple correlation coefficient, 'R' can be found in the 'Model summary' table and the amount of shared variance is provided under 'R Square' in the same table. The significance of R can be found in the next table, labelled 'ANOVA'.

9.8.5 Reporting correlations

In research articles correlations are typically reported in correlation tables or as they are usually referred to, 'correlation matrices'. These offer a display of the correlation coefficients for all variables in the study. Table 9.7 presents a typical example. Please note that all the abbreviations used in the table are explained in the 'Note' following the table.

Correlations Between Motivational Orientations and Achievement Measures

	Motivational orientation	
Achievement measure	Intrinsic motivation	Extrinsic motivation
GPA—Overall	.34***	-.23**
GPA—Language arts	.23***	-.17*
GPA—Mathematics	.25***	-.15*
CATS—Overall	.27**	-.32***
CATS—Reading	.21*	-.30***
CATS—Mathematics	.28**	-.28***

Note. GPA = grade point average; CATS = California Achievement Test.
*p<.05. **p<.01. ***p<.001.

Table 9.7 Sample correlation matrix

Correlation coefficients can also be reported embedded in the text. Here is an example: 'As one would expect from the extensive literature documenting the benefits of intrinsic motivation, there was a significant positive correlation between overall GPA [grade point average] and intrinsic motivation ($r = .34$, $p < .001$).' In some journals no brackets are used for presenting the figures, as in the following example: 'An analysis using Pearson's correlation coefficient supported the hypothesized relationship between GPA and intrinsic motivation, $r = .34$, $p < .001$.'

9.9 Non-parametric tests

In Section 9.4.1 we saw that there are different types of quantitative data, 'interval', 'ordinal', and 'nominal'. Interval data provides the most 'precise' information and such data—provided it is reasonably normally distributed (see Section 9.4.2)—can be processed by parametric tests, such as ANOVA or Pearson correlation. If we have less precise, ordinal data, or categorical (i.e. nominal) data or if the data is not normally distributed, parametric tests are not appropriate and we need to use non-parametric procedures. SPSS offers a wide range of such tests, with every basic parametric procedure having a non-parametric alternative.

Before I describe some concrete procedures, it is important to realize that non-parametric tests can also be used with interval data when we do not feel confident about the 'equal-intervalness' of the measurement or the normal distribution of the data. This, however, raises a question: if non-parametric tests can be selected for nominal, ordinal, and even interval data, without any worries about the normality of the distribution, why don't we simply opt for them all the time? The reason is that we want to use the most powerful procedure that we can find to test our hypotheses. ('Power' is a technical term in statistics, concerning the probability of obtaining statistically significant results.) Parametric tests utilize the most information, so they are more powerful than their non-parametric counterparts. In effect this means that when we compare, for example, two group means with a parametric test such as the t-test, we are more likely to get significant results than if we compare the same means with a non-parametric test. Therefore, parametric tests should be our first choice if we feel confident about the measurement of the variables and the distribution of the scores. Please note, however, that non-parametric tests are not necessarily second-best in this respect. In a recent study, for example, we had doubts about the intervalness of the scales and therefore replaced the parametric (Pearson) correlations with non-parametric ones (Spearman correlations—see below). We were surprised to see that in some cases the new coefficients were actually higher!

The most commonly used non-parametric test in applied linguistics is the 'Chi-square test'. After describing it I will give a brief overview of some other useful non-parametric options.

9.9.1 Chi-square test

The Chi-square procedure is valuable because it is one of the few procedures that can deal with nominal data. Recall that nominal data concern facts that can be sorted into various categories. (Typical examples of nominal data are 'L1 background', sorted into Mandarin, Hungarian, Korean, etc., or 'sex' sorted as male and female.) Let us take a learner group of 40 students (20 girls and 20 boys) who have participated in a ballot by voting 'yes' or 'no'. The frequency of the votes, broken down by sex, can be put into a 2 x 2 grid:

	Boys	Girls
Yes	4	11
No	16	9

Looking at the figures we cannot help wondering whether the students' gender influenced their choice because there seem to be very few 'yes' votes given by boys. The Chi-square procedure can tell us whether there was a significant relationship between voting orientation and gender, and if there was any, we can find out how the figures in each cell are different from the expected figure. The Chi-square test is offered as a 'Statistics' option of CROSSTABS (ANALYSE → DESCRIPTIVE STATISTICS → CROSSTABS → STATISTICS); in addition to selecting Chi-square, also select both the 'expected' and 'observed counts' and the 'unstandardized residual' in the 'Cells' option.

There is also a simplified form of the Chi-square procedure which is useful when we want to see whether the values from a variable are significantly different from expected values if we know these values. The most common example is to test whether the gender distribution of our sample is significantly different from the population, because we know that in the population the number of males and females is roughly equal. This type of Chi-square procedure is run by selecting ANALYSE → NONPARAMETRIC TESTS → CHI-SQUARE.

Illustration and reporting the results

To illustrate the first (and more common) type of Chi-square test, let us use again the 1991 General US Social Survey dataset (that we have already used in Sections 9.6.1 and 9.7.1) and examine whether the sampling of 'sex' and 'race' was independent of each other or whether there was a systematic relationship between the two categories (i.e. more males or females were selected from a particular race)—obviously, this latter case would not be desirable because it would amount to what is a gender bias. Table 9.8 presents the SPSS output.

sex * race Crosstabulation

			race			
			1	2	3	Total
sex	1	Count	545	71	20	636
		Expected count	529.9	85.5	20.5	636.0
		Residual	15.1	-14.5	-5	
	2	Count	719	133	29	881
		Expected count	734.1	188.5	28.5	881.0
		Residual	-15.1	14.5	.5	
Total		Count	1264	204	49	1517
		Expected count	1264.0	204.0	49.0	1517.0

Chi-Square Tests

	Value	df	Asymp. Sig. (2-sided)
Pearson Chi-Square	5.011[a]	2	.082
Likelihood Ratio	5.094	2	.078
Linear-by-linear Association	2.944	1	.086
N of Valid Cases	1517		

[a] 0 cells (.0%) have expected count less than 5. The minimum expected count is 20.54.

Table 9.8 Sample SPSS output reporting Chi-square statistics

In the output, first we need to look at the significance of the Pearson Chi-square value. If it is significant at the $p < .05$ level, we can claim that the two variables are not independent but are related. If so, the 'Residual' difference between the observed and the expected counts will tell us where the greatest impact occurred. In our particular example the Pearson Chi-square value is not significant, which means that the proportion of men and women in the ethnic group samples is not significantly different from each other (which is good news from the survey's point of view). Indeed, the residuals in the 'sex * race crosstabulation' table are relatively low compared to the sample size.

We could report these results as follows: 'A 2×3 Chi-square analysis revealed that there was no significant relationship between the gender and the ethnic background of the sampled participants, x^2 (2, 1517) = 5.01, $p = .082$.'

9.9.2 Non-parametric equivalents of key parametric tests

Without going into detail, let me list some other useful non-parametric tests. They are straightforward to run and their results are to be interpreted in the same way as those of the corresponding parametric tests.

- *Spearman's rank order correlation* This correlation coefficient is obtained by simply ticking the 'Spearman' box in the Pearson correlation dialogue box. (See Section 9.8.4.) As the name suggests, the correlation is based on the ranks of the data (in a rank order) rather than the actual values. It is appropriate for ordinal data or for interval data that do not satisfy the distribution normality or the equal-intervalness assumptions. If we compare the two types of correlations computed for the same variables, we can see that they are very similar but the Spearman coefficient—as expected—is usually less 'powerful' than the Pearson one; that is, it is lower and the accompanying significance figure is higher.
- *Mann-Whitney U test* This is the non-parametric alternative to the independent-samples t-test (ANALYSE → NONPARAMETRIC TESTS → 2 INDEPENDENT SAMPLES → MANN-WHITNEY U).
- *Wilcoxon signed-rank test* This is the non-parametric alternative to the paired-samples t-test (ANALYSE → NONPARAMETRIC TESTS → 2 RELATED SAMPLES → WILCOXON).
- *Kruskal-Wallis test* This is the non-parametric alternative to one-way ANOVA (ANALYSE → NONPARAMETRIC TESTS → K INDEPENDENT → KRUSKAL-WALLIS H).

9.10 Advanced statistical procedures

The previous sections have covered the basic and most often used statistical procedures. In this final section I will introduce more advanced techniques. 'Advanced' in most cases does not mean that one necessarily needs more mathematical knowledge to run these tests. In fact, the first procedure to be introduced—'two-way ANOVA'—only differs from the operations discussed before in that there are slightly more options to select from in the familiar interactive SPSS dialogue box.

The next two procedures to be presented, 'factor analysis' and 'cluster analysis', are exploratory techniques and therefore taking different options might lead to somewhat different outcomes. Thus, these techniques require a thorough understanding of the guiding principles (but not the mathematics!). Finally, I briefly introduce two procedures—'structural equation modelling' and 'meta-analysis'—that have become very popular over the past decade. They are complex in several ways and to use them one needs special software. Their description here will only offer a summary to help to understand articles using the procedures.

Although advanced statistical procedures appear to offer extended analytical opportunities, it may be worth citing here the advice of the 'Task Force on Statistical Inference' of the American Psychological Association to exercise caution not to overcomplicate the analysis (Wilkinson and TFSI 1999: 598):

> The enormous variety of modern quantitative methods leaves researchers with the nontrivial task of matching analysis and design to the research question. Although complex designs and state-of-the-art methods are sometimes necessary to address research questions effectively, simpler classical approaches often can provide elegant and sufficient answers to important questions. Do not choose an analytic method to impress your readers or to deflect criticism. If the assumptions and strength of a simpler method are reasonable for your data and research problem, use it.

9.10.1 Two-way ANOVA

'Two-way ANOVA' is similar to one-way ANOVA, which we have discussed in Section 9.7, except for one difference: instead of one independent, or grouping, variable we include two such factors. For example, if we have a dataset of school children coming from three different classes, we would use a one-way ANOVA to compare their results. But if we know that there is another relevant factor that also divides these students into other groups (for example, their sex or their level of L2 proficiency) and we want to include this factor in the paradigm as well, then we need to run a two-way ANOVA.

Mathematically the two-way ANOVA is more complex than its one-way counterpart, because here instead of one F score we need three: one for each of the independent variables and one for their interaction. The best way to understand this is by showing an example.

In a large-scale longitudinal survey of Hungarian school children's attitudes towards various foreign languages we have found (Dörnyei *et al.* 2006) that the children's attitudes towards German dropped significantly between 1993 (the first wave of data collection) and 2004 (the last wave of the data collection). We also noticed that students who were studying German at school tended to have more positive attitudes towards the language than those that were studying other languages at school, regardless of whether German was their own choice or whether they only took it because this was the only L2 offered by the school. We wanted to combine these two observations and wanted to test whether the attitudes of active learners of German dropped less over the 11-year period than the attitudes of non-learners of German. This was a typical case for a two-way ANOVA, with 'Attitudes towards German' being the dependent, and 'Time' and 'School' being the independent variables.

Two-way ANOVA can be run in SPSS by selecting GENERAL LINEAR MODELS and then UNIVARIATE. The independent, grouping variables are called 'Fixed factors'. Table 9.9 presents the SPSS output we received. We are interested in lines 3–5 in the table. Line three tells us that there is indeed a highly significant school effect (which we knew). Line four tells us that there is indeed a highly significant time effect (which we also knew). Line five reports on the interaction of the two variables as they impacted the German-related attitudes. The highly significant F value indicates that there is a 'true' combined effect.

Tests of Between-Subjects Effects

Dependent Variable: attger

Source	Type III Sum of Squares	df	Mean Square	F	Sig.
Corrected Model	649.585[a]	3	216.528	534.084	.000
Intercept	98781.531	1	98781.531	243652.7	.000
school	275.011	1	275.011	678.336	.000
time	350.540	1	350.540	864.635	.000
school*time	21.847	1	21.847	53.888	.000
Error	3875.404	9559	.405		
Total	119082.480	9563			
Corrected Total	4524.989	9562			

[a] R Squared = .144 (Adjusted R Squared = .143)

Table 9.9 Sample SPSS output reporting two-way ANOVA statistics

Often the best way of interpreting such an interaction is by a graph. An option of the Univariate procedure of SPSS is to provide a 'profile plot' (under the 'Plot' option). The line diagram in Figure 9.3 was prepared based on this output. If there had been no significant interaction between the two independent variables then we would have two roughly parallel lines in Figure 9.3. In this particular case the interaction is significant and we can easily see that this significance is caused by the fact that the attitudes of active German learners did not decrease as sharply as that of the non-learners.

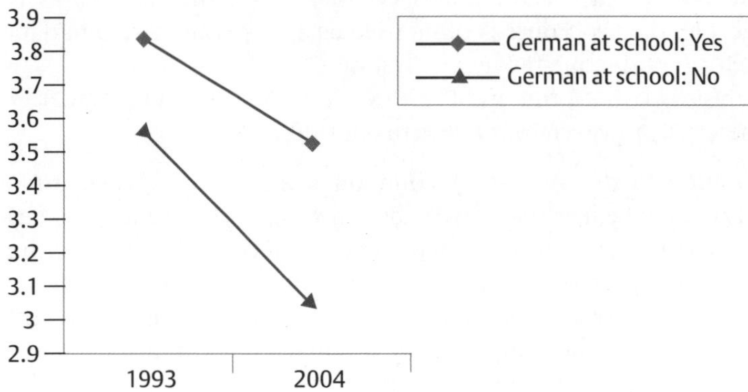

Figure 9.3 Sample diagram describing the change in L2 learners' disposition towards the L2 over time

Researchers who are not familiar with the procedure may want to start with independent variables that have only two values each (as in Figure 9.3) because the interpretation of the results is easier this way. With more than two values we need to run *post-hoc* tests (similarly to ANOVA)—these are readily available in SPSS. We can get the effect size by clicking on 'Estimates of effect size', which is an option; the effect size index, 'partial eta squared', can be interpreted in the same way as in a one-way ANOVA.

9.10.2 Factor analysis

'Factor analysis' is rather complex mathematically but fairly straightforward conceptually. In order to uncover the latent structure that underlies large datasets, it reduces the number of variables submitted to the analysis to a few values that will still contain most of the information found in the original variables. The outcome of the procedure is a small set of underlying dimensions, referred to as 'factors' or 'components'. For example, if we have collected various pieces of information about a group of children concerning their L2 proficiency (for example, test scores, course achievement, perceived competence) and their physical skills (for example, running speed, Physical Education grade, some strength index), factor analysis is likely to produce two factors, corresponding to the two areas.

As part of the factor analysis output, SPSS produces a table—the 'factor matrix'—which contains the correlations between the obtained factors and the original variables that they have been extracted from. These correlations are the 'factor loadings' and they show the extent to which each of the original variables has contributed to the resultant factors. Thus, factor analytical studies exploit the 'pattern-finding' capacity of the procedure by sampling a wide range of items and then examining their relationships with common underlying themes. Because factor analysis is useful in making large datasets more manageable, the procedure is often used as a preparatory step in data processing before conducting further analyses.

Factor analysis is easy to run on SPSS (ANALYSE → DATA REDUCTION → FACTOR). There are, however, four issues to consider:

1 *Items submitted to the analysis* A common mistake made when using factor analysis is to believe that if we submit a wide enough range of items related to a broad target domain to factor analysis, the final factor structure will provide a fair representation of the main dimensions underlying the domain. This is incorrect. The final factor structure will only represent the items submitted to the analysis. If we originally did not include in our questionnaire items concerning a key feature of the domain, that particular domain component has no chance to emerge as a statistical factor. That is, our selection of items fundamentally determines the final factor structure.

2 *Selecting the type of factor analysis (extraction and rotation)* Factor analysis employs a stepwise procedure. The first step involves 'factor extraction', that is, condensing the variables into a relatively small number of factors. The second step is 'factor rotation', that is, making the factors easier to interpret by employing mathematical techniques. There are several alternative methods for both procedures and therefore we must make a decision as to which method to employ. In practice the necessary decisions can be restricted to choosing between two extraction methods: 'principal component analysis' and 'maximum likelihood analysis'; and two rotation methods: 'orthogonal (varimax)' or 'oblique (oblimin) rotation'. These can be combined in four different ways and in the educational psychological and applied linguistic literature we can find examples of all four combinations. My personal preference is for a maximum-likelihood analysis with oblique rotation but if there is a strong multi-dimensional structure underlying the data, any method will detect it and there will be only minor variation in the individual loadings. This means that if the various methods produce essentially the same results, we can be assured that the factor structure is valid. However, if the data is such that different approaches lead to very different solutions, this should be a source of concern.

3 *Determining the number of factors to be extracted* The most difficult issue in factor analysis is to decide on the number of factors to be extracted. SPSS will provide a ready-made answer but it is not an objective solution but just a 'default' that has been artificially set. The typical default principle is that the extraction process should stop at factors which would explain less variance than each individual item submitted to the analysis (i.e. factors whose 'eigenvalue' is smaller than 1) because then, in effect, the factor is not better than a single item. This is, however, not necessarily the best solution: sometimes fewer, sometimes more factors may lead to a better result.

There is no perfect way of setting the optimal factor number, but there are several useful indicators for researchers to take into account:

- *Cattell's (1966) scree test* By plotting the variance associated with each factor (which the computer does for us), we obtain a visual representation of the steep decrease—the 'slope'—and the gradual trailing off—the 'scree'—of the factors. According to the scree test, only the factors on the 'slope' should be considered. Figure 9.4 illustrates the scree plot of the eigenvalues (which are indices of the amount of variance each factor explains) obtained by ticking 'Scree plot' under the EXTRACTION option—in this particular case we have decided that five factors offered the best solution.

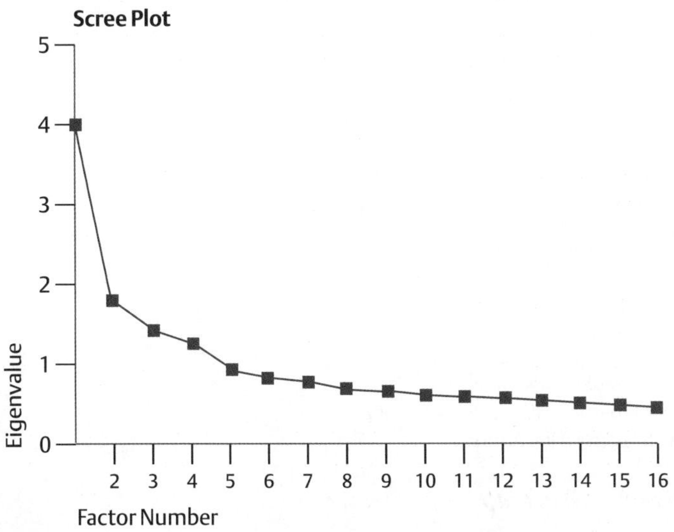

Figure 9.4 Sample SPSS output of the scree plot of factor eigenvalues

- *Aiming for a simple structure*, that is, choosing a factor solution in which each variable has salient loadings (i.e. loadings above 0.3) only on one factor (i.e. there are no cross-loadings) and each factor receives salient loadings from at least two variables (which is usually desirable to have well-defined factors). Table 9.10 presents the pattern matrix accompanying the five-factor solution represented in Figure 9.4. The solution is indeed satisfactory, but please note that such clear factor matrices can only be achieved if we select within the OPTIONS the 'Sorted by size' and 'Suppress absolute values less than .30' options. The first reorganizes the display order of the factors according to the factor grouping, the second deletes all the factor loadings that are too small to be significant and would only confuse the picture.

Pattern Matrix [a]

	Factor				
	1	2	3	4	5
ZS6A	.669				
ZS3A	.620				
ZS7A	.537				
ZS2A	.513				
ZS17U		.762			
ZS14U		.634			
ZS11U		.578			
ZS12U			.767		
ZS13U			.493		
ZS16U				.694	
ZS19U				.460	
ZS15U				.373	
ZS21U				.301	
ZS1A					.658
ZS4A					.602
ZS10A					.519

Extraction Method: Maximum Likelihood.
Rotation Method: Oblimin with Kaiser Normalization.
[a] Rotation converged in 10 iterations.

Table 9.10 Sample SPSS output of a factor matrix

4 *Identifying and naming factors* The final source of difficulty is that even if we obtain a straightforward factor solution with a clear-cut set of non-overlapping factors, it can be rather difficult to interpret and name the individual factors. Because each factor is determined by the variables that have the highest loadings on it, the task in interpreting a factor is to identify the common features among these variables, that is, to understand the theme that brought the cluster of variables together. The name of the factor, then, should reflect this common theme as closely as possible. In some cases labelling a factor is fairly straightforward but in cases where the factor receives salient loadings from seemingly different variables, the final factor label can reflect the researcher's subjectivity and, thus, can be highly contestable. Independent labelling and subsequent discussion by more than one person is an obvious way to reduce the personal biases.

9.10.3 Cluster analysis

The objective of 'cluster analysis' is to identify certain homogenous subgroups—or clusters—of participants within a given sample who share similar combinations of characteristics. There are two main types of cluster analysis, 'hierarchical' and 'non-hierarchical' clustering. In hierarchical clustering the first step involves the definition of each sample member as an individual cluster. Subsequent steps merge the closest clusters until one single cluster containing all sample members is arrived at. Non-hierarchical clustering follows a different path. During the process, sample members are put into a predefined number of clusters. As a first step, the statistical program takes the first N members of the sample (N equals the number of clusters defined prior to the analysis) and defines these as the centres of N clusters. Following this, the whole dataset is partitioned into N clusters by assigning sample members to the predefined cluster centre that they are closest to. Finally, on the basis of the position of the cluster members, new centres are identified and sample members are regrouped according to these new centres. The procedure is repeated until the centres become stable, that is, until they show no change after further regrouping.

Both hierarchical and non-hierarchical clustering techniques have their advantages and disadvantages. On the one hand, hierarchical clustering is difficult to apply if the sample size is too large. On the other hand, the results of non-hierarchical clustering are highly dependent on the initial cluster centres. To avoid these limitations, clustering is often done in two stages: first, hierarchical clustering is carried out on a smaller subsample. Based on this first step, the number of clusters and their positions (i.e. the initial cluster centres) are defined and subsequently non-hierarchical clustering is run on the whole sample by inputting the cluster centres defined previously, and the procedure of non-hierarchical clustering is iterated until stable cluster centres are received. SPSS offers both hierarchical clustering (ANALYSE → CLASSIFY → HIERARCHICAL CLUSTER) and non-hierarchical clustering (ANALYSE → CLASSIFY → K-MEANS CLUSTER). In Version 11.5 SPSS also introduced a procedure they labelled 'TwoStep Cluster Analysis', which offers a combined method. For specific details on how to run cluster analysis, please consult an SPSS guide.

It is important to point out that cluster analysis is an exploratory rather than a theory-then-research, hypothesis-testing technique (Kojic-Sabo and Lightbown 1999) whereby the computer uncovers various grouping patterns based on the mathematical configurations found in the learner data. Grouping can be based on different principles and currently cluster analysis lacks an underlying body of universally endorsed statistical theory. Thus, researchers need to make several somewhat arbitrary decisions relating to the method of calculation and these will have a strong influence on the results of the classification. Indeed, multiple cluster solutions are usually possible from a single dataset. Thus, in order to use the technique meaningfully, researchers need to be careful to keep the analysis on sound theoretical footing and to *substantiate* the emerging cluster groups by means of various validating procedures.

One procedure that is particularly appropriate to substantiate results in educational contexts involves using an external criterion variable to function as an independent indicator of cluster-group differences. Broadly speaking, if the identified subgroups perform significantly differently on the given criterion measure, this indicates that the classification resulted in meaningfully different groupings, and thus confirms the validity of the particular grouping solution. We can use a simple ANOVA to compare the criterion variable across the cluster groups.

9.10.4 Structural equation modelling

Similar to factor analysis, 'structural equation modelling' (SEM) is used to interpret the relationship among several variables within a single framework. Its big advantage over factor analysis is that an SEM model also includes directional paths between the variables and not just information about how the variables hang together. Thus, SEM makes it possible to test cause–effect relationships based on correlational data (which, as we have seen earlier, correlation analysis cannot provide), which makes SEM a powerful analytical tool as it combines the versatility of correlation analysis and the causal validity of experimental research. The structural relationships under investigation are tested by means of a series of regression equations (hence the words 'structural equation' in the name); the word 'modelling' in the name simply suggests that the structural relations can be modelled pictorially. Figure 9.5 contains a typical SEM model: the large circles indicate *latent*, theoretical components, which are defined by the *real*, observed measures (in this case composite questionnaire scales) in the rectangular boxes. The small circles indicate error variables that we should ignore at this stage (and they are often left out in SEM output figures). The arrows indicate the link between the variables and the coefficients next to the arrows can be interpreted in the same way as correlation coefficients.

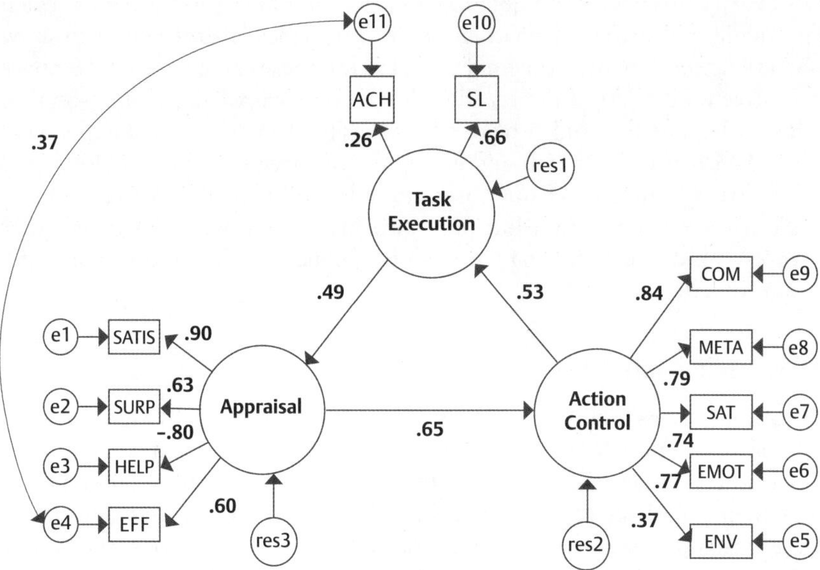

Figure 9.5 Sample SEM structural model

To start applying SEM to data, researchers need an explicitly stated theoretical model in which the main variables are quantified and their directional relationship is clearly stated. The SEM procedure is then used to confirm or reject the validity of this model—thus, SEM is not an exploratory but a *confirmatory* technique, although it is capable of suggesting certain adjustments to the model tested by providing 'modification indices'. When setting up a model, researchers need to do two things:

1 Describe the relationship between the measured variables and the hypothesized latent variables (for example, specify that the theoretical construct of 'self confidence' is measured by, say, three variables: L2 use anxiety, perceived self-competence, and a self-report confidence scale); this results in a *measurement model*. For complex studies that cover a wide range of variables, we usually have more than one measurement model.

2 Posit the causal links between all the latent (theoretical) variables under study; this results in a *full structural model*, which is, in effect, a combination of all the measurement models.

SEM then tests the adequacy of both model types, provides goodness-of-fit measures for the full (i.e. combined) structural model and produces modification indices for the purpose of improvement. As mentioned earlier, to run SEM we need special software. Currently LISREL, AMOS, and EQS are the three most popular statistical packages used for carrying out SEM, with SPSS supporting AMOS.

As every analytical technique, SEM has certain limitations, one of which in particular needs to be born in mind: SEM provides several indices to show how satisfactory the fit of the final model is and these can be used to compare alternative models and to reject ill-fitting models. However, even a solution with an adequate fit is only one of many that might fit the data equally well. Thus, SEM is not the 'be-all and end-all to research endeavours concerned with inferring causation from correlational data' (Gardner 1985: 155). It does not identify causation but only informs the researcher as to whether a hypothesized cause–effect relationship is conceivable based on the total amount of data.

9.10.5 Meta-analysis

'Meta-analysis' as a statistical term was introduced in 1976 by Gene Glass to describe a systematic approach to reviewing and synthesizing a large number of published research studies on a topic. As he defined it, 'Meta-analysis refers to the analysis of the analyses. ... It connotes a rigorous alternative to the casual, narrative discussions of research studies which typify our attempts to make sense of the rapidly expanding research literature' (p. 3). Thus, meta-analysis can be seen as a 'quantitative literature review'. It aims at determining a summary estimate of the effect sizes reported in the various studies, thus producing a combined superordinate result that synthesizes the individual studies. In Section 9.4.6 we saw that effect size provides information about the magnitude of a phenomenon observed in an investigation and that it is also useful in enabling us to compare the results reported in different studies, because effect size indicators are transformations onto a common scale. Meta-analysis capitalizes on this context-independent nature of these indices. The procedure consists of several steps:

1 Conduct a literature search to identify an extensive sample of relevant research studies. Scholars typically use electronic databases (such as ERIC or the Linguistics and Language Behaviour Abstracts) for this purpose.

2 Screen out all the studies that do not meet certain well-defined research criteria or which do not contain certain necessary technical details.

3 Identify an appropriate effect size indicator in each study. Since 1994, the APA Guidelines have encouraged researchers to report effect sizes and the *TESOL Quarterly* quantitative guidelines also require the reporting of effect size. In spite of this, as Norris and Ortega (2000) have found, many empirical studies published in applied linguistic journals still fail to provide effect size indices and therefore researchers doing a meta-analysis need to be prepared to conduct secondary analyses of the primary research data to derive appropriate effect size indices from the published details. (See Norris and Ortega's study for a number of useful formulae to be used.)

4 The final task is to calculate the summary effect. There are several ways of doing this (please consult a statistics guide), and an Internet search will also locate several free calculator software, for example Meta-Stat by Rudner, Glass, Evartt, and Emery. (See the www.edres.org/meta website for this and other software.)

Thus, meta-analysis offers a systematic way of organizing and synthesizing the rapidly expanding research literature. Nevertheless, the quality of the analysis ultimately depends on the quality of the underlying studies.

10

Qualitative data analysis

Working with naturally occurring data is inevitably a messy enterprise ... (Leung, Harris, and Rampton 2004: 242)

We saw in Chapter 2 that qualitative research is far from being a uniform approach but is characterized by diversity. As Punch (2005) points out, perhaps nowhere is that diversity more apparent than in approaches to the analysis of qualitative data. Indeed, the term 'qualitative data analysis' is used by various scholars to denote different activities from imaginative and artful speculation to following well-defined analytical moves, from deductive categorization to inductive pattern finding. In some ways, the smallest common denominator amongst the various approaches is the rejection of the use of quantitative, statistical techniques. But, of course, this is exactly at the heart of qualitative data analysis: to develop and follow certain principled analytical sequences without being tied by the constraints of the procedures and sacrificing the researcher's creative liberty of interpretation. In other words, to '[s]eek formalization and distrust it' (Miles and Huberman 1994: 310).

Having said the above, when we go beyond the philosophical discussions and look at what actually happens when we sit down in front of the qualitative data and start teasing out the hidden meaning from it, we actually find many commonalities and, as will be shown later, a great deal of the analytical process is made up of generic, method-independent procedures. Admittedly there exist certain differences in practice but even these can be summarized in terms of a few key issues and dilemmas. Thus, within the divergence of qualitative analysis there is a great deal of convergence in how scholars 'tame the data' (Richards 2005) and try to make sense of it. (For a very useful description from a second language perspective, see Richards 2003: Chapter 6.)

In the following, I first discuss four principles of qualitative data analysis that I consider central and then outline the main data analytical approaches developed over the past three decades. Of these, one approach—'grounded theory'—will be examined in more detail after presenting the generic phases of qualitative data analysis. The chapter is concluded by looking at how computers can help us with handling the data.

10.1 Main principles of qualitative data analysis

Thousands of pages have been written about the main principles of qualitative data analysis, which reflects the complexity of the question. Let us first look at four general issues that are central to the understanding of the process: (a) the language-based nature of the analysis, (b) the iterative process, (c) the tension between formalization and intuition, and (d) the tension between being methodology-bound and methodology-independent.

10.1.1 Language-based analysis

We saw in Chapter 2 that most qualitative data is transformed into a textual form—for example, interview transcriptions—and the analysis is done primarily with words. Thus, qualitative data analysis is inherently a *language-based* analysis. (In principle, it is also possible to work with images but this is far less prominent than the language-based analysis and therefore will not be discussed in this chapter.) We must realize that the language-specific nature of qualitative analysis actually favours applied linguists, because discourse analytical techniques (including conversation analysis) are part of our core discipline. As discussed in Chapter 1, this book does not cover such linguistic approaches because the applied linguistics literature contains a rich variety of specialized texts in these areas.

10.1.2 Iterative process

> *There is no particular moment when data analysis begins.*
> (Stake 1995: 71)

Quantitative analysis is orderly in a linear manner: based on the knowledge of the relevant literature we design the research instruments, then collect, process and analyse the data, and finally write up the results. Each step is well defined and builds on the previous one. In contrast, qualitative research is *iterative*, using a nonlinear, 'zigzag' pattern: we move back and forth between data collection, data analysis and data interpretation depending on the emergent results. For example, it is not at all unusual to decide well into the analytical phase that we need to collect some more data of a specific sort, or to go back to the original data transcripts to recode the text according to some newly conceived categories. That is, unlike in QUAN research, we do not need an extensive initial dataset to start QUAL data analysis because, as Hesse-Biber and Leavy (2006: 370) point out, 'A little bit of data can go a long way in gathering meaning'. In fact, these scholars warn us against being tempted to gather too much data initially because this may distract us from reflecting on the details—a common mistake with novice researchers. (See also Section 6.1.)

A key term in qualitative data analysis is 'saturation'. We have already used it with regard to qualitative sampling, referring to the point when further data does not seem to add new information, and in data analysis the term carries the same meaning, namely that the iterative process stops producing new topics, ideas, and categories, and the project 'levels off' (Richards 2005). This is the point when the researcher gains a sense of what is relevant and what falls outside the scope of the investigation. Of course, as Richards stresses, shallow data, and especially when we are not asking questions that go beyond the surface meaning, can saturate at a level of triviality—saturation only indicates that we have covered the breadth of our data with the level of analysis used.

10.1.3 Subjective intuition versus formalization

We saw in Section 6.1 that the initial raw qualitative dataset is likely to be 'messy' if not chaotic. The challenge for the analyst is to bring some insightful order to the multiple accounts of human stories and practices collected or observed. This is the point when we can resort to two fundamentally different analytical approaches: we can either rely on our *subjective intuition* to find a creative way out of the maze, or we can follow *formalized analytical procedures* that will help us to uncover the hidden meaning in a systematic, step-by-step process. Both approaches have considerable support amongst qualitative researchers.

The main argument in favour of a primarily intuitive approach has to do with the inherent importance attached to the subjective and reflexive involvement of the researcher in the analysis (see Section 2.1.4) and the need to maintain a fluid and creative analytical position that is not constrained by procedural traditions and that allows new theories to emerge freely. In fact, one of the main criticisms levelled at quantitative researchers by their qualitative colleagues is the rigidity of the analysis. In contrast, qualitative analysis needs to be flexible, data-led, and—a common term used by scholars in the intuitive camp—'artful'.

While the need for flexibility is not questioned by any qualitative researcher, there is no agreement as to what extent this 'artful fluidity' tolerates structure in the analytical process. Do we always start from scratch when we face a new dataset or can we draw on methodological knowledge in applying certain established techniques for the purpose of reaching complex hidden meaning? The most influential proponents of a more structured approach to data analysis have been Miles and Huberman (1994), who maintain that the lack of accepted analytical conventions is not a strength but a weakness of qualitative data analysis because the intuitive reflexiveness does not in itself provide any safeguards against simply *being wrong*. In addition, as Miles and Huberman argue, there are certain tasks that need to be carried out regardless of our approach; they highlight three such operations: 'data reduction', 'data display', and 'data interpretation'. As these authors claim, only by using certain systematic—that is, formalized—procedures in a transparent manner to accomplish these tasks can we convince our audiences that our conclusions are valid. (See also Section 3.1.2 on 'quality criteria in qualitative research'.)

Thus, the basic challenge of qualitative data analysis is to achieve 'rigorous flexibility' or 'disciplined artfulness' by applying procedures and frameworks that are conducive to generating new insights rather than acting as a constraining mould that does not let new results emerge. The various qualitative data analytical methods differ in the ways by which they try to standardize the process while maintaining the researcher's subjective freedom.

10.1.4 Generic analytical moves versus specific methodologies

A final area that is central to the understanding of qualitative data analysis is the tension between advocating the use of a specific and coherent methodology, such as grounded theory (see Section 10.3), or emphasizing general and generic analytical moves such as 'coding' and 'memoing' (see Sections 10.2.2 and 10.2.3). We find strong views from both sides expressed in the literature but it is my impression that the actual practice of studies published in research journals tends to favour the latter approach, and when scholars do not wish to affiliate themselves too closely with a specific methodology, they often use the broad term of 'qualitative content analysis' to characterize the collection of generic qualitative analytical moves that are applied to establish patterns in the data. In the next section (10.2) I describe in detail the most common 'pattern-finding' moves of this generic approach, and in the subsequent section (10.3) I provide a counterpoint by presenting the specific methodology of grounded theory.

10.2 Qualitative content analysis

Content analysis has recently become closely associated with qualitative research and we can therefore easily forget that it actually originates from a quantitative analytical method of examining written texts that involves the counting of instances of words, phrases, or grammatical structures that fall into specific categories. Because qualitative data is typically textual (see Section 10.1.1), QUAN content analysis has been transferred to the domain of QUAL research with one fundamental change: unlike their preconceived quantitative counterparts, the qualitative categories used in content analysis are not predetermined but are derived inductively from the data analysed. Another way of distinguishing quantitative and qualitative content analyses is by referring to the former as 'manifest level analysis', because it is an objective and descriptive account of the surface meaning of the data, and the latter as 'latent level analysis', because it concerns a second-level, interpretive analysis of the underlying deeper meaning of the data.

In this section I concentrate on latent content analysis. This type of analysis follows the very generalized sequence of coding for themes, looking for patterns, making interpretations, and building theory (Ellis and Barkhuizen 2005). To this we can add an initial phase of 'transcribing the data' because much (though not all) qualitative data consists of recorded spoken data that needs to be transcribed and, as we will see, turning recordings into transcripts already contains interpretive elements. Thus, I will centre the following discussion around four phases of the analytical process: (a) transcribing the data, (b) pre-coding and coding, (c) growing ideas—memos, vignettes, profiles, and other forms of data display, and (d) interpreting the data and drawing conclusions.

10.2.1 Transcribing the data

The first step in data analysis is to transform the recordings into a textual form. (Of course, in cases when we use written data such as documents, correspondence, or diary entires this phase may not be applicable.) This is a time-consuming process particularly if the text also needs to be translated—depending on the quality of the recording, transcribing a one-hour interview can take as much as 5–7 hours, but with very fine-tuned transcriptions in which, for example, pauses need to be measured, it can take as long as 20 hours (Duff in press). Although it is possible to work with tapes only (i.e. without a transcribed version, which is usually referred to as 'tape analysis') or with only partial transcriptions, we should resort to these labour-saving strategies only in special cases, and the default practice needs to be the preparation of full written transcripts of our recorded data. (For a more detailed discussion, see next section.)

The only good thing to say about the transcription process is that it allows us to get to know our data thoroughly, otherwise it is usually a far-too-long and less-than-enjoyable process (to say the least). It is worth buying or borrowing a transcribing machine that has a foot pedal, speed controls, and earphones because it can speed up our work considerably; alternatively, it might be worth doing the original recording digitally because there is high-quality software available to facilitate the transcription process of digital sound files. Unfortunately, mind-numbing tediousness is not the greatest problem with transcriptions—the real concern is the loss of information through the process. No matter how accurate and elaborate a transcript is, it will never capture the reality of the recorded situation. Transcriptions are, in Miller and Crabtree's (1999: 104) words, 'frozen interpretive constructs'.

The most obvious area of loss is the *nonverbal* aspects of the original communication situation such as the body language of the respondents (for example, facial expressions, gestures, or eye-movement)—given that 'actions speak louder than words', written transcriptions are seriously impoverished in this respect. It is also problematic to decide what to do with suprasegmentals, such as stress and intonation, and paralinguistic factors, such as acoustic sounds (for example, grunts) or nonvocal noises (for example, hisses). A third recurring issue is how to represent speech that is 'imperfect' in some ways, for example false starts, word repetition, stammering, or language mistakes.

For linguistic investigations such as discourse or conversation analysis it is obviously important to include as many details as possible in the transcripts and recently the use of video recordings has been increasingly advocated to supplement written corpora. (See, for example, Adolphs 2006.) On the other hand, if we are interested in the content rather than the form of the verbal data, we can decide to edit out any linguistic surface phenomena but we are not advised to make any content selection/editing at this stage because we simply cannot know what might turn out to be important. The respondent's emotional overtones can be crucial with regard to the real meaning of the message, and for this reason relevant intonational contours and emphases are often indicated in the script by using punctuation marks, upper case lettering, underlining, or emboldening.

The description so far may have given the impression that transcription is merely a technical matter. However, the issue is more complex than that because every transcription convention we use will affect the interpretation of the data. (For discussions, see, for example, Duff in press; Roberts 1997.) It is well known to applied linguists that a narrow transcription of oral discourse often appears incoherent and unsophisticated. However, the problem is more general and concerns the fact that spoken and written language are structured differently; therefore, in order to try and create the 'feel' of the oral communication in writing, we need to apply certain writing strategies (for example, polishing the text, using varied punctuation marks, dividing the speech into sentences) that will facilitate the intended kind of reading.

Thus, we should always be mindful of the fact that using different transcribing conventions to process the same recording can produce very different effects in the reader. This is why Lapadat (2000), along with many others, emphasizes that a transcript is an interpretive 'retelling' of the original communication. Or as Roberts (1997: 168) puts it, 'transcribers bring their own language ideology to the task. In other words, all transcription is representation, and there is no natural or objective way in which talk can be written'. Roberts then goes on to highlight the 'retelling' aspect of transcription by emphasizing that every decision about how to transcribe tells a story; the question, she asks, is whose story and for what purpose? The standard transcription practice in applied linguistic research on SLA has been to try and provide an elaborate representation of various interlanguage characteristics in the respondents' speech, but this has often been at the expense of foregrounding the respondents' message about their identities.

After all the considerations presented above, let me address two practical questions that every qualitative researcher must face at one point:

1 Which transcription convention shall we use?

Unfortunately, there is no 'perfect' transcription convention that we could adopt automatically. There are several widely used transcription schemes around and I would suggest following a principled 'pick-and-mix' procedure to select ideas from these. (For detailed descriptions of some conventions, see Appendix B in Schiffrin 1994: 422–34; and Chapter 18 in Wray *et al.* 1998: 201–12.) If there is a good enough reason, it may also be appropriate to invent individualized transcription rules and formats that fit our research purpose (Lapadat 2000). Thus, I fully agree with Roberts (1997) when she suggests that transcribers have to use or develop a transcription system that can best represent the interactions they have recorded. In doing so, we need to manage the tension between accuracy, readability, and the 'politics of representation'. Roberts makes certain practical recommendations to that effect:

- Use standard orthography if possible even when transcribing a nonstandard variety to avoid stigmatization and to evoke the naturalness and readability of the discourse. If appropriate, discuss with the informants how they wish the features of their speech to be represented.
- Try to find ways of contextualizing/evoking the speakers' voices.
- Consider using a layered approach to transcription, offering different versions (for example, more ethnographic and more fine-grained systems) to give different readings.

2 If transcription is as interpretive as argued above, does this mean that the researcher him/herself must transcribe rather than hire a research assistant?

Realistically, because of the demanding and time-consuming nature of the process we often need help in doing the transcriptions. However, even if we are assisted by a transcriber, we should stay as close to the data as possible. This would involve preparing detailed guidelines ('transcription protocols'), having regular debriefing discussions, and checking at least some of the transcripts. The transcription protocol should emphasize the need for confidentiality, as well as specify the extent to which the transcriber is to 'tidy up' the text and what special symbols to use (for example, for illegible parts, pauses, emphasis).

Tape analysis and partial transcription

I believe that in order to conduct a fully-fledged qualitative investigation we need to have full transcripts of the recordings that we want to analyse. However, in certain types of mixed methods research (particularly for qual → QUAN and QUAN → qual; see Section 7.3.1) where the qualitative component is of secondary importance and is mainly intended to provide additional illustration or clarification, it may not be essential to transcribe every interview and, instead, we can carry out a tape analysis. This simply means taking notes while listening to the recordings, possibly marking parts of the data (for example, the counter position of the cassette recorder or its digital equivalent) that warrant more elaborate subsequent analysis. Research methodology is often a balancing act between goals and resources and in certain situations tape analysis can be justified as a good compromise because the particular data may not deserve the huge investment of a full transcript.

In the spirit of the above, another possible compromise is to prepare a *partial transcription* of the sections that seem important. The obvious drawback of this method is that we need to make important decisions as to what to include and exclude relatively early in the analytical project, but the procedure leaves open the option to expand the transcription later. One way of improving this method is by having notes of the key points of the whole recording, indicating which parts have not been transcribed.

Computer-assisted transcription

Arksey and Knight (1999) mention an interesting technical innovation—computer-assisted transcription—that some researchers might find useful. Recent software developments have produced increasingly accurate voice recognition programs that enable the researcher to 'dictate' texts to the computer, directly into the word processor. All we need to do is listen to the recording through headphones and then repeat what we hear bit by bit. Unfortunately, even with experienced 'dictators' there will be mistakes and correcting these may still take some time, although less than transcribing the tapes ourselves. Arksey and Knight believe that with the increasing sophistication of these programs, computer-assisted transcription is likely to become a preferred way of transcribing recorded data. Indeed, Duff (in press) reports that several of her students have successfully applied this method.

Transcribing videotapes

The advantage of video recording is that it can capture information that would get lost by audio recording. This is true but how do we actually transcribe this additional information? We do not have the equivalent of 'writing' when it comes to describing body language and contextual information. Furthermore, if transcribing spoken language can carry too many subjective elements (as we have argued above), representing and interpreting body language is bound to be even more selective and open to dispute. A common practice in video transcriptions is to include a column of running commentary next to the verbal transcript, but this will multiply the costs of the transcription process. Accordingly, Arksey and Knight (1999) only recommend the transcription of videotapes in exceptional cases and with a specific focus. This, of course, raises the question of doing video recordings at all because it is my impression that untranscribed tapes will only rarely be revisited at later stages of a research project.

10.2.2 Pre-coding and coding

Most research methods texts would confirm that regardless of the specific methodology followed, qualitative data analysis invariably starts with *coding*. Yet, this statement is only partially true, because usually a considerable amount of analysis has already taken place when we begin the actual coding process. Stake (1995: 71) defines analysis as a 'matter of giving meaning to first impressions as well as to final compilations', and making sense of our first impressions is a crucial pre-coding move. It involves reading and re-reading the transcripts, reflecting on them, and noting down our thoughts in journal entries (Section 6.9) and memos (Section 10.2.3). These pre-coding reflections shape our thinking about the data and influence the way we will go about coding it. Richards (2005: 69) summarizes this question as follows:

> There is no alternative to reading and reflecting on each data record, and the sooner the better. This is purposive reading. Aim to question the record and add to it, to comment on it and to look for ideas that lead you up from the particular text to themes in the project.

Thus, the process of 'meeting the data meaningfully' during the pre-coding phase is an indispensable preparatory move. As a PhD student stated:

> If I had started with coding straight away, I think I would have just got lost in the data and perhaps would have ended up with thousands of codes that I would have never been able to integrate into a meaningful framework. (Maggie Kubanyiova, personal communication)

At one point, however, pre-coding deliberation needs to give way to a more formal and structured coding process. This can be compared to packaging vegetables in a supermarket, that is, turning the 'messy' farm products of irregular shapes, types, and sizes into distinct, sorted, and neatly wrapped up parcels that can be placed on shelves or stored piled up. After all, a 'code' is simply a label attached to a chunk of text intended to make the particular piece of information manageable and malleable. Of course, just like labels, codes can be used for many purposes, from purely descriptive (for example, 'Nottingham, 2000' on a photo) to more abstract (for example, 'The Big Moment' on a wedding photo). This is why, as Morse and Richards (2002) point out, different researchers mean several different things when they use the term 'coding'. Yet all the qualitative coding techniques are aimed at reducing or simplifying the data while highlighting special features of certain data segments in order to link them to broader topics or concepts.

In actual practice, coding involves highlighting extracts of the transcribed data and labelling these in a way that they can be easily identified, retrieved, or grouped. Traditionally, we used to use hard-copy printouts of the texts and marked these with multi-coloured highlighters but nowadays coding is increasingly done electronically. (See Section 10.4.) Whichever technique we apply, coding specifies language chunks that can range in length from a phrase to several paragraphs.

We saw in Section 10.1.2 that qualitative analysis is an iterative process and this is particularly obvious in the process of coding. Researchers usually code and recode a text several times, with the initial, usually descriptive and low-inference codes gradually being replaced or supplemented by higher-order 'pattern codes' (for example, an extract originally coded 'low salary' may be recoded later as 'source of demotivation'). As a result of revisiting the data a number of times, some salient content categories emerge, linked to various data segments. Further coding, then, aggregates these segments so that we can work with them together, 'gaining a new cut on the data' (Richards 2005: 86).

Before describing the coding process in more detail, let me point out that grounded theory, which is introduced in Section 10.3, contains an elaborate three-tier coding component, which has affected qualitative data analysis in general. Thus, there are many similarities between the generic procedures described below and the specific coding methodology suggested by grounded theory.

Initial coding

How shall we begin coding? Here is a typical recipe: first, choose a text and read it through several times to obtain a general sense of the data. Then take a highlighter (if you are working with hard copy) and start reading the text from the beginning. When you come to a passage that is relevant to your topic, simply highlight it and add an informative label on the margin. It follows from the spirit of qualitative research that at this stage you should highlight any interesting-looking passage even if it is not directly linked to your immediate focus area. This is how new insights can emerge.

Regarding the characteristics of the labels used for coding, clarity is the most important feature to aim for because it defeats the whole purpose of coding if the meaning of a code is not immediately transparent. Some researchers favour using some key words from the actual passage to make the preliminary codes more authentic (which is called 'in vivo' coding in grounded theory). It is vital that we produce explicit descriptions of the codes—Figure 10.1 presents a dialogue box of the data analytical software NVivo (see Section 10.4.2) that allows for the precise recording of code properties. Also, Lynch (2003) recommends that researchers try to arrange an external code check, that is, ask someone to look at a portion of the data and recode it using the list of codes already developed as well as possibly introducing new ones. Both the similarities and discrepancies can be enlightening, leading to a revision of the original codes.

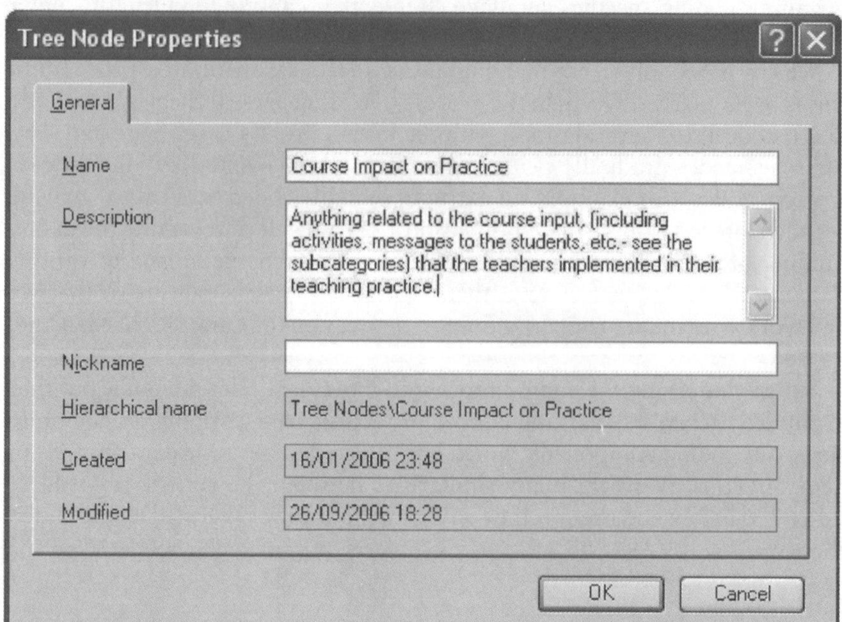

Figure 10.1 Sample NVivo dialogue box for recording code properties

Second-level coding

Every qualitative analytical method contains a second-level coding process because in most investigations we want to go beyond a mere descriptive labelling of the relevant data segments. Before long, we will have ideas that go beyond the specific account we read and we are also likely to notice patterns that emerge across the individual accounts. (For more details on these patterns, see 'axial coding' in Section 10.3.3 below.) Second-level coding intends to capture these more abstract commonalities.

One way of launching second-level coding is to go through several respondents' accounts and list all the codes that we have identified in them. There will inevitably be some similar or closely related categories, which can be clustered together under a broader label. At this point we need to look at all the specific extracts that are linked to the newly formed broader category to decide whether the new label applies to all of them or whether some may need to be recoded. If the majority of the extracts fit the new system, this can be seen as a sign of the validity of the code. Once we have finalized the revised list of codes, we may want to go back to the original transcripts and recode them according to the new categories. In some studies this process is iterated more than once.

Another useful process in second-level coding is to produce a hierarchy of codes, in the form of a tree diagram. Figure 10.2 presents part of such a 'tree' produced by the data analysis software NVivo, describing the hierarchy of codes related to 'intrinsic motivation'. Playing around with such code structures is in itself an effective analytical move because it helps to clarify how the categories are related to each other.

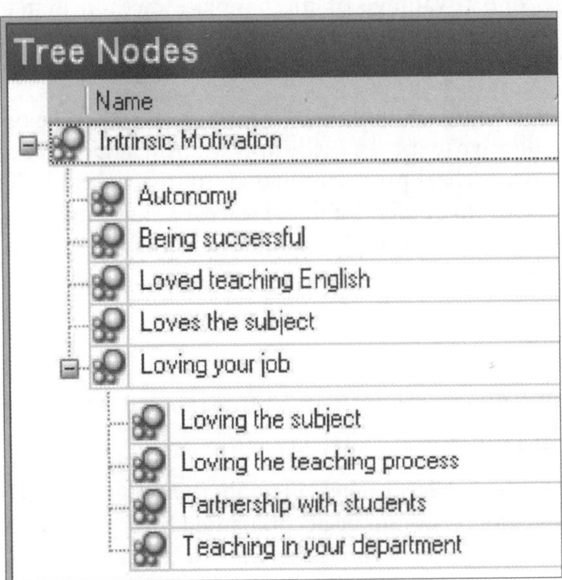

Figure 10.2 Sample NVivo output of category codes organized into a 'tree'

Using a template of codes

Crabtree and Miller (1999) describe a coding method that they called the 'template organizing style'. This is an interesting variation on the standard coding procedures in that it does not emphasize the emergent nature of the codes but, to the contrary, starts out with a template of codes. Thus, as in quantitative research, the first step of data analysis involves preparing a template, or code manual, and the transcribed texts are coded using this predetermined template. Obviously, the template method can only be used if there is sufficient background information on the topic to be able to define the template categories, although the authors also assert that the template can be prepared as a result of preliminary scanning of the data. Furthermore, the process can be made more 'qualitative' if we allow for revision or fine-tuning of the template at some point in the analytical process.

Although using preconceived categories seems to be at odds with certain qualitative principles, in effect few, if any, researchers start data analysis with no initial ideas and biases (see Section 2.3.2 on the emergent/non-emergent debate), and having a specific template of codes helps to carry out the initial coding of a large volume of text in a focused and time-efficient manner, creating links between extracts from different accounts earlier in the process. Miles and Huberman (1994) also underscore the usefulness of exploring both how to arrive at analytic categories deductively (i.e. bringing codes to the data) and getting gradually to them inductively (i.e. finding them in the data). We should note, though, that this is a contentious issue in qualitative research.

Interestingly, one advantage of the template method that Crabtree and Miller (1999) highlight is that it can make the analysis more acceptable for those sceptical of qualitative research. As they conclude:

> The interpretation of a mountain of information-rich, purposefully sampled, qualitative texts can easily appear insurmountable and quixotic, especially to researchers proficient in quantitative methods. This is reason enough to pause and briefly tremble. However, the template organizing style described in this chapter is one specific way for quantitatively trained ... researchers to take the first step into qualitative analysis. (p. 77)

10.2.3 Growing ideas: memos, vignettes, interview profiles, and forms of data display

Coding is undoubtedly a key process in qualitative content analysis, but most researchers agree that it should be accompanied by other essential analytical tools that can help to 'grow the ideas' and to develop them into the final main theme(s) of the study. These tools include preparing memos, vignettes, interview profiles, and various forms of data display, all of which are secondary (i.e. derived) data that the researcher produces as a means of structured reflection.

The most important of all these analytical tools is writing 'memos' (or 'memoing'). Researchers vary in the extent to which they use memoing during data analysis, but it is not unusual to hear claims that 'Real analysis is in the memo writing!' The process of coding actively engages analysts with the data and during this process they are to make notes of all the thoughts and ideas that come to mind. These notes are usually referred to as 'analytic memos'—they are invaluable in facilitating second-level coding and are also likely to contain the embryos of some of the main conclusions to be drawn from the study. Thus, memos are in effect explorations of ideas, hunches, and thoughts about the codes; or in Lynch's (2003: 138) words, they are 'working ideas, which may or may not pan out in the fullness of your analysis'. They can be as short as a sentence, or as long as several paragraphs, and they become part of the overall dataset. They are especially important in team projects to keep each individual researcher in the loop of collective thinking.

Figure 10.3 presents a sample analytic memo (in the form of an NVivo screen shot) that discusses the difference between two related codes (or as NVivo calls them, 'nodes'). The researcher who produced the memo comments below that this particular memo triggered off a chain of thoughts that eventually led to the conceptualization of one of the main themes of her final research report (Maggie Kubanyiova, personal communication):

> This memo, in fact, opened up a whole new theme and on re-reading the data records and my early annotations, I discovered numerous clues indicating superficial endorsement of the course content by the participants. I began to see that many of these clues pointed to what I later saw as an important theme emerging from the data: the research participants' desire to live up to the researcher's expectations. This turned out to be an important pointer towards the research participants' motivation to join the research project, which, in turn, appeared to have crucial implications for teacher change.

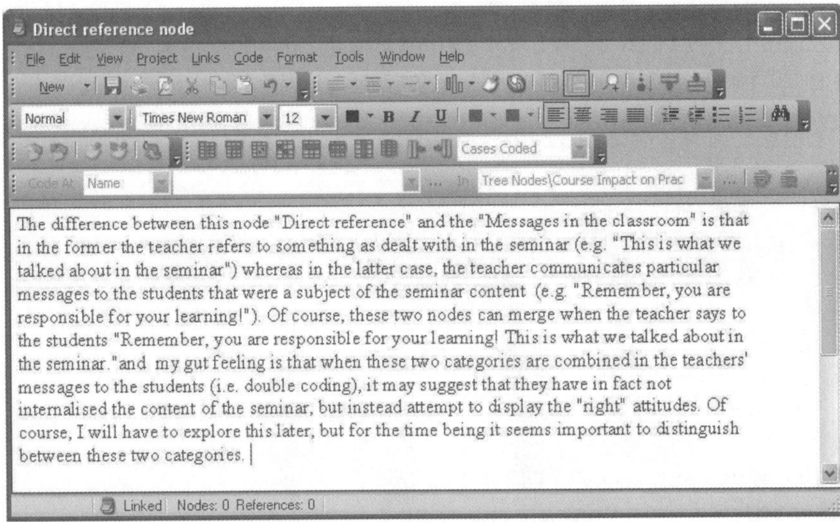

The difference between this node "Direct reference" and the "Messages in the classroom" is that in the former the teacher refers to something as dealt with in the seminar (e.g. "This is what we talked about in the seminar") whereas in the latter case, the teacher communicates particular messages to the students that were a subject of the seminar content (e.g. "Remember, you are responsible for your learning!"). Of course, these two nodes can merge when the teacher says to the students "Remember, you are responsible for your learning! This is what we talked about in the seminar."and my gut feeling is that when these two categories are combined in the teachers' messages to the students (i.e. double coding), it may suggest that they have in fact not internalised the content of the seminar, but instead attempt to display the "right" attitudes. Of course, I will have to explore this later, but for the time being it seems important to distinguish between these two categories.

Figure 10.3 Sample NVivo output of an analytic memo

In addition to writing analytic memos, many qualitative researchers prepare 'vignettes', which are short narratives that provide focused descriptions of events or participant experiences. Unlike memos, vignettes are not analytical but storylike, offering a vivid description of something that is seen as typical or representative.

A very useful method of opening up interview data to further analysis and interpretation has been suggested by Seidman (1998). He proposed the crafting of 'interview profiles', which are more substantial summaries of participant accounts than vignettes. A special feature of an interview profile is that it is primarily a compilation of the interviewee's own words, using the first-person voice of the participant, with only minimal transitional additions and clarifications by the researcher (which should be well marked in appearance). These profiles serve the same function as 'contact/document summary sheets' described by Duff (in press), which contain short summaries of an observation, interview, or document, highlighting the most salient points and themes.

So far all the analytical tools described as possible methods for developing the researcher's thinking have been verbal in nature. However, presenting and summarizing data visually is also possible, and indeed, Miles and Huberman (1994) devote a great deal of their summary of qualitative data analysis to describing methods of 'data display', defining a 'display' as 'an organized, compressed assembly of information that permits conclusion drawing and action' (p. 11). Within the category of display they discuss several types of matrices, graphs, charts, and networks that all organize and present information in a visually accessible manner, in appropriate and simplified 'gestalts or easily understood configurations' (p. 11). Such schematic representations can take a wide variety of forms, from traditional tables with regular rows and columns to flow charts, and various visual 'category maps'. (Figure 10.4 presents an example of the latter.)

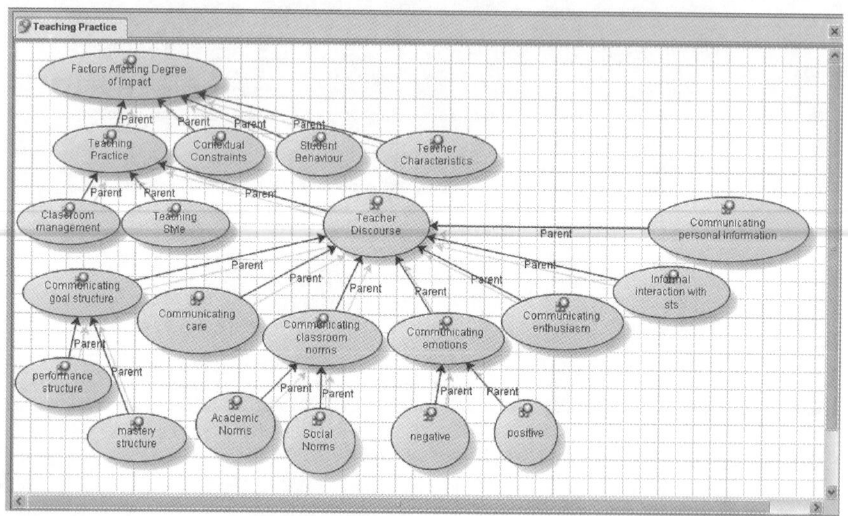

Figure 10.4 Sample computer screen shot displaying a category map

The importance of data display lies in the fact that the various visual summaries are powerful tools to help the researcher draw valid conclusions; as Miles and Huberman (1994: 11) conclude, the 'dictum "You are what you eat" might be transposed to "You know what you display"'. Onwuegbuzie and Leech (2005) also point out that it is possible for the data display to be so compelling that data interpretation can immediately begin without requiring any further analytical operations.

10.2.4 Interpreting the data and drawing conclusions

The final generic process of qualitative data analysis is interpreting the data and drawing conclusions. Strictly speaking, data interpretation happens not only near the end of a project: researchers start tentative interpreting as early as the initial coding stage when they prepare memos; in fact, the whole process of qualitative data analysis is geared to our becoming more and more familiar with the data and developing increasingly abstract analytical insights into the underlying meanings. Thus, as with so many components of qualitative research, data interpretation is also an iterative process. Yet, it is useful to distinguish the final stages of this process from the earlier, ongoing interpretation, because this is where we have to select the overarching theme or themes that the write-up will be centred around. In other words, this is where the process is turned into a product, in the form of the final conclusions.

What are these final conclusions like? To start with, they naturally build on the various interim summaries and interpretations (for example, memos, vignettes, profiles, and displays) as well as the higher-level coding categories that the researcher has developed. In qualitative research the main themes grow organically out of the foundations that were laid during the analytical process and therefore the process of drawing the final conclusions involves taking stock of what we have got, appraising the generated patterns and insights, and finally selecting a limited number of main themes or storylines to elaborate on. Selection is based on the salience of the particular concept/ process and its relationship with other important categories in the domain; ideally, the main theme(s) should serve as a focus or lens through which the whole domain can be presented.

Richards (2005) warns us that the promise of a single storyline or a 'core theme' that brings everything together can be seductive at this stage, yet it carries the danger of eliminating the subtlety of meanings that we have worked so hard to uncover. As she argues, it may often be impossible to produce a unitary account without it becoming trivial, whereas explaining divergences and the reasons why there is *no* big picture may result in a powerful understanding of the situation. In other words, drawing the final conclusion is a delicate balancing act between trying to say something of overarching significance while at the same time preserving the intricacy of situated multiple meanings.

10.3 Grounded theory

> *If you don't know what [qualitative] method you are using, it is highly unlikely to be grounded theory.*
> (Morse and Richards 2002: 56)

The term 'grounded theory' is so common in the qualitative research literature that it is often taken as a synonym for qualitative research. While grounded theory is *not* the same as qualitative research in general, it is revealing to look into the reason for this confusion. First of all, the boundaries of the term are rather fluid, particularly when it comes to actual applications: as we will see in Section 10.3.2, despite its name, 'grounded theory' is not a theory at all but rather a qualitative research method. Yet, this is still not quite correct, because in spite of the fact that grounded theory is claimed to apply to the whole research process, from participant sampling and data collection to data analysis, Charmaz (2005) points out that researchers commonly use the term to mean only a specific mode of data analysis. (See also Dey 2004, for a similar view.) As she summarizes, 'Essentially, grounded theory methods are a set of flexible analytic guidelines that enable researchers to focus their data collection and to build inductive middle-range theories through successive levels of data analysis and conceptual development' (p. 507). For this reason I discuss grounded theory in this chapter rather than in Chapter 6.

Given that grounded theory is by and large seen as a specific analytic approach, it is even more curious that its popularity (as reflected in citations in research texts) is such that it can easily be seen as a common methodological framework for qualitative research in general (Arksey and Knight 1999). Part of the explanation lies in the fact that, as we saw in Section 2.3, grounded theory offered the first conscious attempt to break the hegemony of quantitative research: it offered qualitatively inclined researchers a theoretically based, elaborate methodology. Thus, within the context of the early paradigm wars, grounded theory was the heavy artillery that qualitative researchers employed to claim legitimacy. As Charmaz (2005: 509) puts it, 'For many researchers, grounded theory methods provided a template for doing qualitative research stamped with positivist approval'. She goes on to argue that even though researchers did not always understand grounded theory methods and rarely followed them fully, they widely cited and acclaimed these methods because these justified their previously implicit practice.

Grounded theory has thus become a banner under which qualitative researchers could join forces, and this explains its pervasive influence on qualitative research methodology in general, with almost every qualitative researcher using—knowingly or unknowingly—some of its elements. It has become part of the mainstream and many of its originally unique methodological aspects have now become core issues in qualitative research. We should be careful, however, not to call our research 'grounded theory' unless at least two basic criteria are met: (a) the data analysis follows the specific sequential *coding system* advocated by grounded theory (see below), and (b) the analysis produces some *theory* as an outcome of the investigation. In the following, after providing a brief historical overview I examine these two criteria.

10.3.1 Brief historical overview

The genesis of grounded theory goes back to the 1960s when two American sociologists, Barney Glaser and Anselm Strauss, started to experiment with a new qualitative method in their investigation of interactions between health care professionals and terminal patients in hospitals. In 1967 they published a book which detailed the methodology of their, by that time highly acclaimed, 'dying studies', entitled *'The Discovery of Grounded Theory: Strategies for Qualitative Research'*. As mentioned above, grounded theory was the first qualitative approach that had been sufficiently elaborate and procedurally rigorous enough to withstand the criticisms of quantitative scholars. The method grew, therefore, from its original sociological roots to be adopted widely by researchers in a variety of fields in the social sciences, including education and psychology. It is undoubtedly one of the most influential paradigms in qualitative research today.

Ironically, it is the main strength of grounded theory, the detailed procedural guidelines for data analysis, that led to a rift between the two originators of the method. In 1992 Glaser criticized a book Strauss had written with another co-author, Juliet Corbin, for advocating the use of preconceived ideas and thus forcing research into a set framework without allowing new theories to emerge—a classic example of the tension between subjective intuition versus formalization described in Section 10.1.3. The division between Glaser and Strauss spread to the qualitative research community in general, with researchers often being expected to align themselves with one of the two competing versions of grounded theory.

Later, further chasms appeared in grounded theory (see for example, Charmaz 2005), and as a result, nowadays we cannot talk about a single, unified grounded theory methodology (Dey 2004). Several variations of the method are practised and, as already discussed, a large number of researchers utilize elements of the method (primarily the coding procedures) to carry out investigations that may or may not be true grounded theory studies (Fassinger 2005).

10.3.2 'Theory' in grounded theory

Grounded theory is not a theory, so where does the 'theory' component of the label originate? It comes from the explicit goal of the method to develop a new theory. This aim to produce new theoretical offerings, emphasized again and again in the grounded theory literature, was set by Glaser and Strauss (1967) as a reaction to the theory verification practice that dominated quantitative research in the middle of the twentieth century. Thus, the label was intended to position the approach as inductive in contrast to deductive, and the term 'grounded' indicated that the new theoretical insights were to be generated on the basis of empirical data.

The obvious question at this point is what exactly 'theory' means in grounded theory terms. We can rest assured that Glaser and Strauss did not mean by the term any 'grand theories' such as the Theory of Relativity but rather an abstract explanation of a process about a substantive topic grounded in the data (Creswell 2005). The main point about 'theory' is that researchers should go beyond merely describing or categorizing the target phenomenon and should offer some basic understanding of the principles, relationships, causes and/or motives underlying it. Fassinger (2005) points out that there is considerable controversy about what sort of product can legitimately claim to be a 'theory' proper, but if the outcome of our research articulates a coherent, contextualized explanation (rather than merely a contextual description) of an issue, possibly also outlining a (tentative) model or framework, grounded theorists would be likely to accept that as a valid theoretical offering. While defining 'theory' in such less-than-grand a manner makes sense, I believe that Seidman (1998) also has a point when he states that the frequent use of 'theory' by grounded theorists has served to inflate the term to the point that it has lost some of its usefulness.

10.3.3 Coding in grounded theory

The best-known aspect of grounded theory is the distinctions between different phases of coding the data. (See Strauss and Corbin 1998.) We saw in Section 10.2.2 that coding in qualitative research is a multi-level procedure, and grounded theory describes a logical, three-level system: first we break up the data into chunks and assign conceptual categories to the data segments ('open coding'). Second, we identify interrelationships between these categories ('axial coding'). Third, we explain these relationships at a higher level of abstraction ('selective coding'). Thus, the process appears to be sequential, moving from the descriptive to the abstract, but given the inherently iterative nature of qualitative research it should come as no surprise that the three phases occur recursively.

Open coding

'Open coding' constitutes the first level of conceptual analysis of the data. The textual data is 'broken open' into chunks whose length usually varies between a long phrase, a line, a sentence, or even a short paragraph. Each of these segments is assigned a category label, but in line with the theory-building emphasis of the method, the emphasis already at this stage is on stimulating new ideas and therefore the categories are abstract and conceptual rather than descriptive. This practice is different from other forms of qualitative analysis which usually start out with descriptive or interpretive categories; in open coding the main questions the researcher asks about each segment are of the following type: what is this piece of data an example of? What is going on? What principles underlie these actions/statements? What do they actually mean? Thus, each data segment is thoroughly 'interrogated' before assigning meaning to it, resulting in what we can call an abstracting process from data to first-order concepts.

Axial (or theoretical) coding

'Axial coding' extends the abstracting process from first-order concepts to higher-order concepts. The researcher makes connections between categories, thereby attempting to integrate them and group them into more encompassing concepts that subsume several subcategories. The word 'axial' was used by Strauss and Corbin (1998) to signify that a metaphorical axis is placed through the data to relate the categories to each other. Glaser (1992) used the more general term 'theoretical coding' to describe this stage. The relationships between the categories can be manifold, referring for example to causal conditions, consequences, and similarities as well as contextual, procedural, or strategic interdependence. These relational propositions often appear first in the researcher's memos—memoing is an integral part of grounded theory analysis and is done in the same way as described in Section 10.2.3—but sometimes the informants themselves will alert the researcher to the existence of a pattern (Ellis and Barkhuizen 2005).

We should note that by forming such relationships we are already beginning to highlight and position certain categories in the centre of the coding process—this will form the basis of the third, 'selective coding' phase. Creswell (2005) suggests that at this stage we might return to data collection or reanalyse our existing data in order to explicate or refine the newly established connections between the categories, delineating the nature of the relationships between them.

Selective coding

'Selective coding' is the final stage in grounded theory analysis, in which, as the term suggests, we need to select a 'core category' (or as Richards 2003 puts it, 'explanatory concept') to concentrate on in the rest of the analysis and the writing up of the study. This core category will be the centrepiece of the proposed new theory. Because ultimately we want to integrate much of our processed data, the central category/theme needs to be of a sufficiently high level of abstraction to be able to subsume other categories. The most common method of selecting the central concept is to further elaborate on an idea that has already been recorded in memos and which has also been explored during the axial coding stage. Obviously, the central theme needs to be central both from our own and the participants' perspective, because we need such a focal point to be able to bring together the other categories in a coherent manner. Although this final analytical stage displays great variability across studies, the outcome is typically a 'core story' with a single storyline—that is, the proposed 'theory'. This theory is also evaluated against the existing literature to enrich understanding and explanatory power (Fassinger 2005).

10.3.4 Strengths and weaknesses of grounded theory

A major strength of grounded theory is that the method offers tools for providing an in-depth analysis of a phenomenon. As Charmaz (2005: 530) concludes, 'the focused inquiry of grounded theory, with its progressive inductive analysis, moves the work theoretically and covers more empirical observations than other approaches'. The method is particularly appropriate in generating theoretical knowledge in areas where little is known about a phenomenon. The systematic and detailed procedures associated with the various grounded theory approaches (particularly with the Strauss and Corbin 1998 version) make it relatively easy for novice researchers to adopt the method, and the availability of these procedures also facilitate the transition from a quantitative research tradition to a more naturalistic paradigm.

On the other hand, to do grounded theory analysis well is a demanding and labour-intensive task, requiring highly developed analytical and conceptual skills. In my experience there is a real danger for going religiously through the time-consuming process of the coding sequences in an iterative manner and still ending up with no 'theory' or a rather trivial one. The difficulty of the grounded theory approach can be eased by utilizing computers in the analysis—as discussed in the next section, there are several computer programs that have been specifically designed to be used in grounded theory analysis.

10.4 Computer-aided qualitative data analysis (CAQDAS)

In the final section of this chapter I look at how computers can be utilized in qualitative research. In the previous chapter on quantitative data analysis, the introduction of a statistical software (SPSS) was done in the first section (9.1), and the very different positioning of the computer sections in the QUAN and QUAL chapters is telling. Whereas the use of computers by quantitative researchers has been standard practice for several decades, computer-aided qualitative data analysis (CAQDAS) software has been a relatively recent phenomenon. However, progress both in computer-literacy amongst researchers and in the quality of CAQDAS software has been so rapid over the past decade that fewer and fewer methodologists would question Richards's (2005) claim that working with computers is simply no longer a mere option for qualitative researchers: whether we like it or not, we have to accept that computers have become an integral part of qualitative data analysis. This has been recognized in the UK by the leading research funding agency in the social sciences, the Economic and Social Research Council (ESRC), when they advised in their 2001 revised guidelines for the training of graduate students that students should have skill in the use of such software packages.

As a result of this changing perspective, current discussions of CAQDAS no longer need to address the questions that used to be the crux of the matter for potential users, namely 'Will the software save me time?' or 'Is it worth the effort of learning to use it?' Instead, the new questions to ask are, 'What can the software offer qualitative researchers?' and 'How can I make the most of it for the purpose of my analysis?'

10.4.1 What does computer software offer qualitative researchers?

The most important point to stress about CAQDAS software is that these programs do not do any real analysis for us; rather, they have been designed to help researchers with the mechanisation of the clerical aspects of data management. Anybody who has done qualitative data analysis knows that sorting, organizing, and archiving hundreds of pages of rather messy interview transcripts can be a logistical nightmare, with the researcher trying to locate useful quotes hidden in the middle of thick piles and cutting out extracts to be stuck on small memo cards. This is where CAQDAS offers invaluable assistance, but—let me reiterate—this assistance is by and large *not* related to the actual analysis aspect of the research. For this reason, one of the leading experts on CAQDAS, Kelle (2004: 486), actually suggests that it would be more appropriate to refer to these programs as software for 'data administration and archiving' rather than as tools for 'data analysis'. That is, as Séror (2005) summarizes in his recent review of CAQDAS for applied linguists, what computers can offer is to replace the traditional tools of qualitative data analysis—paper, pen, scissors, and highlighter—with tools of the digital age: screen, mouse, and keyboard. In this sense, CAQDAS software is very different from the statistical packages used in quantitative research because the latter *do* carry out part of the analysis. (For an excellent summary of the functions of CAQDAS, written by one of the foremost software developers, see Richards 2005.)

In retrospect, it was inevitable that computers should become utilized in qualitative research, since they are very good at two things that are crucial for QUAL data analysis: first, computers can store large amounts of data, and given that most documents (including transcripts of recordings) are nowadays produced electronically, it would be anachronistic to print those out first and then store them as hard copies. Second, highlighting extracts in electronic texts is a simple and basic word processing task and it happens to coincide with a key component of the qualitative coding process. Thus, once the technology was available, it did not take long to develop the first software programs that allowed researchers to attach labels to the highlighted text segments so that these could be retrieved—and CAQDAS was on the march.

After this initial step about 20 years ago, scholars rapidly realized that the advantages of CAQDAS went beyond the coding, storing and retrieving functions it offered: several other word processing skills that all of us were willingly or unwillingly acquiring in the 1980s and 1990s (for example, editing and searching texts, writing and saving short memos, parallel accessing multiple texts) could also benefit qualitative data analysis. It became increasingly clear that many aspects of qualitative data analysis lend themselves to computerization, and there followed a rapid expansion in the number, capacity, flexibility, and popularity of computer programs available for both qualitative data analysis and quantitative content analysis of texts (Bazeley 2003).

Current developments in CAQDAS software involve trying to extend the programs' capabilities beyond merely functioning as a clerical tool so that they can also be used in the actual analytical process. Content analysis programs can search for and count key domain-specific words and phrases, and can even examine the co-occurrence of certain terms. They can perform 'automated' coding through text search and can produce frequency tables of target units that can be exported in a file format to a statistical package for follow-up analysis.

Further sophistication has been reached by programs that also facilitate code-based theory-building functions by allowing researchers to analyse and visually display relationships between the identified codes and organize them into hierarchically ordered 'trees'. In this way, codes may be related to superordinate themes and categories, which is a conscious attempt to make the programs appropriate for multi-level analysis such as the one involved in grounded theory. As Séror (2005) describes, the software Qualrus even uses computational strategies to suggest new codes based on the user's previous coding strategies and patterns found in the data. Miles and Huberman (1994) presented an extensive range of different data display methods for the purpose of developing concepts and theories, and we can expect new computer software to provide more and more help in producing such displays. In sum, development is fast and we are likely to see several new breakthroughs within the next decade.

10.4.2 Which software to choose?

Currently CAQDAS software development is at an expansion stage, with a number of packages competing for the highly lucrative dominant position (which SPSS has managed to take in the quantitative market). The most frequently mentioned software names in the literature include NUD*IST and its successor, NVivo, The Ethnograph, Atlas.ti, winMAX and its successor, MAXqda, Qualrus, QDA Miner, and HyperRESEARCH—Séror (2005) and Lewins and Silver (in press) offer good overviews of the various programs (for a condensed summary, see http://caqdas.soc.surrey.ac.uk), and a simple Internet search will also locate the programs' home pages as well as various review sites. My personal feeling is that one of the most serious CAQDAS software development companies in the field is the Australian QSR [Qualitative Solutions and Research] International, which produced NUD*IST in the early 1980s and then further developed it into NVivo. The popularity of NVivo is on the increase and the senior software developers in the company have also been contributing to theoretical advances in qualitative research methodology (for example, Bazeley 2003; Richards 2005).

10.4.3 Methodological merits of CAQDAS

I believe that CAQDAS is not something that we simply have to accept because of the digital age we live in. I am convinced that, as with word processors, there will be a time when we will not be able to imagine how we used to manage without qualitative data analysis software. The methodological merits of CAQDAS are manifold:

- *Speed of handling large volumes of data* The computerization of cumbersome clerical tasks results in considerable gains in efficiency. This frees up researcher time and helps to avoid data overload. In addition, the fact that computers can handle large volumes of data very quickly means that for every question or operation we can search the whole database and not just the most obvious or most accessible folders.

- *Almost unlimited storage capacity and easy indexing options* Archiving all the various data types can be done in a single storage system and the data can be preserved indefinitely. Furthermore, computer software offers easy-to-use indexing systems for identifying and retrieving any data that we have processed.

- *More sensitive second-level coding* Hammersley and Atkinson (1995) point out that computer software allows for the multiple, overlapping coding of segments, which means that we can retrieve various combinations of the coded transcript extracts in an approximation of Boolean algebra (for example, retrieve all the 'X's *and* 'Y's; or retrieve all the 'X's *but not* the 'Y's). This obviously facilitates axial coding (see Section 10.3.3) and so does the fact that we can access and review all identically coded data segments with considerable speed.

- *Potential for new analytical strategies* CAQDAS allows researchers to experiment with the data freely, without the physical and time constraints of handling hard-to-manage piles of actual transcripts. Furthermore, the recently developed analytical tools can inspire or enable completely new analytical strategies.

- *Improvement of rigour* The computerized procedures are likely to create more rigour in handling the data than the somewhat impressionistic and non-transparent way that has been typical of many so-called 'qualitative' studies.

- *Easy generation of an audit trail* We saw in section 3.1.2 that one effective way of generating confidence in qualitative inquiries is to leave an 'audit trail' that attests to the principled, well-grounded and thorough nature of the research process, including the iterative moves in data collection and analysis, the development of the coding frames, and the emergence of the main themes. Such a record can be easily generated through CAQDAS by simply saving some important screen shots or interim files. (For details, see Section 13.1.2.)

- *Increased legitimacy of qualitative research* In my experience quantitatively oriented researchers regard the use of computerized procedures as some sort of a guarantee of the quality of the project, and therefore CAQDAS can be used as an argument to claim legitimacy of qualitative inquiries.
- *Possible application in mixed methods research* Finally, because CAQDAS software can be used to quantify certain aspects of the qualitative dataset (see Section 11.1.1), making it easy to link QUAL and QUAN data concerning a particular participant, it lends itself to be applied in mixed methods research.

10.4.4 Possible dangers of CAQDAS

I know a senior colleague in our field who still writes most of his articles and books by hand sitting in a café because he finds that using a word processor distorts his thoughts—there is no doubt that the actual method of writing, or the method of analysis in our case, affects the final outcome. It is also obvious that most scholars in the past have been able to adjust to the changing technical conditions and successful academic treatises have been written both by hand and using typewriters or word processors. For this reason, I do not believe that the inevitable spread of CAQDAS will result in an overall deterioration of qualitative research outcomes that has been feared by some. (In fact, personally I am optimistic and believe that an improvement is more likely.) This does not mean, though, that we do not have to look out for potential dangers that the use of CAQDAS carries. In this final section I will draw attention to some issues that I see as potentially problematic:

- *Technological thinking* The most profound concern about CAQDAS is related to the shift it causes towards techniques and technology, which may be seen as antagonistic to the intuitive and creative process of interpretation that forms the basis of good qualitative research. No matter how complex, multi-level, nested super-coding system we use, it will not replace the researcher's thoughtful deliberation and will not compensate for the lack of any original ideas. I do not think that hi-tech 'fishing expeditions' will ever be fruitful in qualitative research.
- *The coding trap* Related to the previous point, Richards (2005) warns us of the danger of overdoing coding, especially descriptive or topic coding, when we are uncertain about what else to do and no theory seems to be emerging from the data. As she argues, more and more categories are unlikely to solve anything but will actually prevent any ideas from emerging, resulting in a 'coding trap' that may 'delay or even destroy a project' (p. 100).

- *Indirect theoretical influence* Duff (in press) emphasizes that the increasingly advanced facilities of CAQDAS software that go beyond merely offering clerical help are not theory-neutral but have 'implicit assumptions about the nature of data (for example, hierarchical conceptual relationships) that might lead researchers to view data differently than if they examined it without the constraints of an established program'.
- *Coding on screen versus coding on paper* I have found that I can never do as thorough a job proofreading a text on screen as on a paper copy, and Seidman (1998) found the same thing with regard to coding. As he argues, there is a significant difference between what one sees in a text presented on paper and the same text shown on screen, and therefore he actually recommends that we work with a paper copy first and transfer the codes to the computer later. I simply do not know how general this differential impact of the medium of screen and paper is amongst scholars, and therefore how seriously we should take this issue.
- *Decontextualized coding* If we use hard copies of the transcripts for analysis, coding is by definition contextualized within the body of the particular text. However, as Yates (2003) has experienced, the electronic coding possibilities tend to encourage increasingly fine categorizations, with the researcher working with retrieved chunks that are no longer read in context. The danger is obvious: by focusing on the trees we can lose sight of the forest.
- *Danger of losing the data* Hard copies are cumbersome but are at least *solid* whereas electronic files can be worryingly vulnerable and transient: almost everybody knows of a case when someone has accidentally deleted some important documents or has not backed up his/her data properly and after a computer crash several months' hard work has disappeared.
- *Collecting too much data* Because of the ease of handling clerical tasks through CAQDAS, there may be a danger of overdoing the data collection phase and as Richards (2005: 58) rightly concludes, 'Bulk data, especially bulk data that are not yet handled at all, can create a massive barrier to thinking'.
- *Insufficient support* Séror (2005) mentions a problem that my students and I have also experienced, namely that even today relatively few people can actually use CAQDAS software well, which makes it difficult for novice researchers to find someone to ask for help. With regard to a specific technical question, one of my research students even had to contact the company that produced the particular software we used (NVivo) to receive advice. One solution to this difficulty is to join one of the several Internet forums—the QSR forum (http://forums.qsrinternational.com), for example, offers 'question and answer' and discussion sections.

11

Data analysis in mixed methods research

> *Neither quantitative nor qualitative are monolithic* its, *but permeable domains in which many styles have emerged. Complexities in inductive and deductive iterative strategies abound and there is a renewal of interest in* both/and *rather than mono*-either/or, *so far as methods and methodology are concerned.*
> (Greene and Preston 2005: 167)

The most common perception of mixed methods research is that it is a modular process in which qualitative and quantitative components are carried out either concurrently or sequentially. Although this perception is by and large true, it also suggests that the analysis of the data should proceed independently for the QUAN and QUAL phases and mixing should occur only at the final interpretation stage. This conclusion is only partially true. While it is perfectly legitimate to leave mixing to the very final stages of the project, several scholars (for example, Caracelli and Greene 1993; Onwuegbuzie and Teddlie 2003) have argued that we can also start integrating the data at the analysis stage, resulting in what can be called 'mixed methods data analysis'. In this chapter I present specific mixed methods analytical strategies that attempt to get more out of the data than would be possible by using QUAL and QUAN techniques separately.

As a preliminary, let me address a key question: given the fundamentally different nature of QUAL and QUAN data analysis—with the former being largely iterative and inductive and the latter being sequential and deductive—is it realistic to attempt to integrate the two procedures? The answer is twofold: in many cases it may be better to keep the analyses separate and only mix the QUAL and QUAN results at a late stage to illuminate or corroborate each other. However, in some cases the inductive-deductive distinction is too black-and-white and does not reflect what is really going on at the analytical level. For example, Bazeley (2003) points out that in certain procedures the blurring of the boundaries between QUAL and QUAN data and analysis becomes markedly evident. She mentions exploratory factor analysis as an example (see Section

9.10.2), whereby arriving at a final solution in terms of extraction and rotation methods, and determining the number of factors in particular, is the result of a largely inductive process, drawing heavily on the theoretical and contextual knowledge and interpretive ability of the researcher. The same would apply to cluster analysis (Section 9.10.3) as well, and we can also find instances in qualitative research where a more deductive approach is pursued, with the template method of coding (Section 10.2.2) being a prime example. Thus, the typical association of QUAL research with an inductive logic of inquiry and QUAN research with hypothetic-deduction can often be reversed in practice, making some types of QUAL and QUAN analysis genuinely compatible with each other, sharing as they do some underlying principles.

The most common integrated analytical strategy is 'data transformation', whereby qualitative data is turned into quantitative and vice versa, so I start the discussion by addressing this issue. This is followed by describing three other broad analytical strategies: 'extreme case analysis', whereby outliers that are identified in one method are further examined using the other; 'typology/category development', whereby we define substantive categories in one method and use these to analyse the data following the other method; and 'multiple level analysis', in which we gain additional knowledge of a specific subset of participants by analysing their responses in the light of data gathered from a larger sample that these participants were part of. It must be noted here, though, that the terminology used in the literature to refer to these techniques is rather mixed, reflecting the unestablished character of the domain. The chapter is concluded with a brief discussion of how mixed methods analysis can be computerized.

11.1 Data transformation

The most obvious means by which qualitative and quantitative data can be integrated during analysis is to transform one data type into the other, thus allowing for statistical or thematic analysis of both data types together. This procedure is usually referred to as 'data transformation' (although Greene *et al.* 2005 calls it 'cross-over track analysis'), and its first proponents were Miles and Huberman (1994) and Tashakkori and Teddlie (1998). Depending on the direction of the transformation we can talk about 'quantitizing data', that is, turning QUAL data into QUAN, and 'qualitizing data', that is, turning QUAN data into QUAL. The former in particular has been common in research in the social sciences.

11.1.1 'Quantitizing' data

The technique of 'quantitizing' was first mentioned by Miles and Huberman (1994; they called it 'quantising') but in actual practice it has been commonly used by qualitative researchers who produce numerical tabulations of certain aspects of their data. The term was introduced by Tashakkori and Teddlie (1998), who considered it a key operation in mixed methods data analysis.

Quantitizing involves converting qualitative data into numerical codes that can be further processed statistically. Thus, certain salient qualitative themes are numerically represented either in *scores* (for example, frequency scores of how many times the theme is mentioned in the sample or in a single individual's responses) or *scales* (for example, evaluating the intensity or degree or weight of a narrative account such as an interviewee's description of his/her attitudes towards, say, the learning environment). A reliable way of producing scale scores of the latter type is to ask a panel of expert judges to rate the data on a continuum and then take the mean rating as the scale score.

Although, technically speaking, any qualitative theme can be quantitized by simply assigning 0 or 1 to it depending whether it appears in a specific dataset or not, already Miles and Huberman (1994) warned us that quantitizing data 'is not an operation to be taken lightly' (p. 214). Counting improves the quality of the analysis only in cases when the numeric results are used properly. For example, the common procedure of counting how many of our participants mention a certain topic and then comparing the results saying that Topic X is more important than Topic Y because more respondents mentioned it is usually erroneous because a qualitative sample is not meant to be representative and therefore subproportions of it do not reflect any real tendencies. However, if we believe that our sampling has produced a group of participants who may be seen as representative of a certain population, then we can make comparisons but we should test the significance of the results statistically, for example by employing a t-test or a Chi-square test. If we obtain a statistically significant result, that would be a powerful confirmation of the validity of our inference.

Once we have quantitized some data, we can export the numerical codes into a statistical package so that it can be submitted to various quantitative analyses, relating it to other quantitative measures. In most cases non-parametric tests (for example, Chi-square test or rank order correlation; see Section 9.9) will be more appropriate for the statistical analysis than parametric statistics because of the limited sample size that may not be normally distributed, or because the scale scores we have formed are ordinal rather than interval. (See Section 9.4.1.)

Onwuegbuzie and Leech (2005) recommend an interesting but somewhat controversial approach to processing quantitized qualitative data: they argue that if we turn each coding category into a numerical score and then factor analyse the results (see Section 9.10.2) we may obtain 'meta-themes' that subsume the original themes, thereby describing the relationship among these themes. The problem with this method is that factor analysis requires a relatively large sample size, preferably over 100 participants, which is only rarely achieved in qualitative studies due to the huge workload involved. On the other hand, as mentioned earlier, the underlying logic of factor analysis is largely inductive and therefore such an analysis would fit the overall thrust of a qualitative study. We can also consider submitting quantitized data to cluster analysis to identify subgroups in the sample who share similar combinations of some of their views or characteristics.

11.1.2 'Qualitizing' data

'Qualitizing' data, that is, interpreting quantitative data within a qualitative context, is less common in published research because quantitatively-orientated researchers rarely feel the need to add a qualitative component to their studies. However, this approach is frequent in small-scale student essays and dissertations when students collect quantitative (typically questionnaire) data but then decide to analyse the scores non-quantitatively, usually because they cannot handle statistics. This practice is, in most cases, an inappropriate use of the qualitizing process.

The two most common (and legitimate) uses of qualitized data are (a) utilizing quantitative background information in a qualitative analysis and (b) 'narrative profile formation'. A typical example of the first would involve the researcher handing out a short background questionnaire (measuring, for example, demographic information such as age and gender) to all his/her interviewees and then integrating the answers into a qualitative account to inform the interpretation of the data. The approach can be extended by including other sorts of questions about attitudes, beliefs, habits, etc. A retrospective interview (see Sections 6.6.2 and 7.3.2) focusing on questionnaire scores, in effect, provides immediate qualitizing of the questionnaire results.

'Narrative profiles' of certain participants based on quantitative information are similar to including quantitative background information in the study, but the purpose of this process is not so much the contextualization of the respondents' account (i.e. examining the data in the light of the additional quantitative information) as to develop a fuller understanding of a particular person, a group, or an institution (for example, in a case study). Profiles are an accessible and powerful means of communicating meaning, and by including qualitized summaries of several quantitative pieces of information we can make the profile more convincing and valid.

11.1.3 Data merging

A special case of data transformation is when we not only turn one data type into the other but merge together different types of data (by first converting one type) and thus create a new variable. For example, in order to define 'monitor-overusers' (Krashen 1978), that is, language learners who worry about and repair their L2 utterances too much, we can use a learning style questionnaire focusing on analytic style (QUAN), and we can combine this measure with the learners' self-reports about how they perceive and handle mistakes (QUAL). The combination can form the basis of a composite quantitative measure or a typology—see 11.3.

11.2 Extreme case analysis

We have seen in Section 9.2.3 that 'outliers', that is, extreme values that are inconsistent with the rest of the dataset, can cause havoc in statistics. However, because of their out-of-the-ordinary features, outlier participants can also be seen as particularly interesting cases whose analysis may shed light on broader issues. 'Extreme case analysis' is aimed at examining the value of such unusual cases by identifying them by one method and further examining them using the other. The usual practice involves identifying outliers in quantitative research and then submitting them to further, more intensive qualitative analysis to understand the reason for the deviance. However, we can also conceive of an analytical sequence whereby we become aware of an unusual participant during the qualitative analysis and then examine how the quantitative data available about the particular respondent furthers our understanding.

11.3 Typology/category development

In 'typology/category development' we analyse one data type and establish some substantive categories or themes. These categories are then applied in the analysis of the other type of data. We can use the categories to divide the sample into subsamples, that is, classify individuals into different types, which would be a case of 'typology development'. If the sorting category was originally qualitative, then we could see whether the grouping can be substantiated by the quantitative data and we can also identify those variables that discriminate well between the two groups. For example, based on the qualitative data we might identify two types of learners: those who pay more attention to communicative fluency than grammatical accuracy and vice versa. In the subsequent quantitative analysis we can substantiate this finding by comparing the language proficiency test scores of the learners in the two groups, and we can also examine whether the two groups show any difference on other variables, for example language aptitude or learning style.

If the sorting category is quantitative and it was derived from a statistically significant group difference, this would allow us to transfer the grouping principle to the analysis of the qualitative data and to compare the subgroups that are formed using the sorting category—something which would normally not be legitimate in qualitative research. For example, if we identified two groups of learners representing two types of motivation, we could examine how this distinction is reflected in their qualitative accounts.

Caracelli and Greene (1993) further mention that an additional important feature of the typology development strategy is its potential for iteration. As they argue, a typology could be created from one data type and applied to the analysis of the other data type, the results of which could, in turn, be used to refine and elaborate the typology. This improved typology could then be reapplied in subsequent analyses of either data type, and so forth, further explicating the initial analyses.

A variation of the typology development strategy is 'category development'. In this case, quantitative data is used to identify salient variables relevant to the target phenomenon, and these categories are used subsequently for coding the qualitative data. This strategy could work very well with the 'template approach' of coding described in the previous chapter (Section 10.2.2).

11.4 Multiple level analysis

'Multiple level analysis' is relevant if we have quantitative (for example, survey) data about a larger group and then submit a subsample of this group to further intensive qualitative investigation (for example, by means of an interview study). In this way we have two levels of embedded data which we can integrate to good effect. For example, we can use the larger sample as a norm group against which the subsample's characteristics and performance results can be evaluated. In Dörnyei *et al.* (2004), we followed this strategy by interpreting various aptitude and motivation scores of seven participants of an interview study in the light of the results of a larger survey of 70 students. To make the quantitative results more meaningful in this qualitative study, we computed standardized scores (see Section 9.2.4), which indicated how our interviewees' results differed from the mean scores obtained in the larger group. Thus, multiple level analysis combines qualitative research with quantitative measures of populations. This strategy can be used even when the qualitative component is the study of a single case to make larger claims of generalizability.

11.5 Computer-aided mixed methods data analysis

Data analysis software has traditionally focused on either quantitative or qualitative results. However, as Bazeley (2003) describes, the boundaries between numerically and textually based research are becoming less distinct and recent versions of several software packages have opened up new possibilities for working with mixed data types. Most qualitative data analysis programs can now import and incorporate quantitative data into a qualitative analysis, and many support quantitizing qualitative data and exporting it to a statistical package. Bazeley calls these procedures the 'fusing' of analysis, and this term expresses well the new quality of mixed method analysis that computer-aided analysis can offer.

Statistical packages have also responded to user demand, and even SPSS has released a text analytical add-on module, 'TextSmart', to facilitate the processing of responses to open-ended items in questionnaires. The well-known questionnaire survey software, SphinxSurvey, has also developed a 'Lexica' version which offers advanced text analysis features that include certain qualitative coding functions. Both software programs support the integrated statistical analysis of the newly formulated quantitized variables and the existing quantitative dataset.

PART FOUR

Reporting research results

12

Writing a quantitative report

Academic writing is an 'arena for struggle' in which students and researchers can find it hard to achieve personal power and voice. (Holliday 2002: 143)

Having collected and analysed the data, the researcher's job is far from being complete because the results have to be written up and disseminated. Research is inherently a social activity, and as Ortega (2005: 430) rightly points out, 'The value of research is to be judged by its social utility'. As she argues, any research field in the social sciences, including applied linguistics, has as its ultimate goal the improvement of human life and therefore the value of applied linguistics research should be judged not only by the methodological rigour it displays but also 'ultimately on the basis of its potential for positive impact on societal and educational problems' (p. 430). Given that the 'applied' nature of our field is even marked in its name, I believe that Ortega's message resonates with many scholars.

If we agree on the importance of the social value of research, we must take the next logical step and accept that sharing research results with the wider community is a central part of a researcher's job description. That is, communicating with our audience is a major facet of a researcher's responsibilities. It is for this reason that the Ethical Standards of the American Educational Research Association (AERA 2002) include amongst the researchers' responsibilities to the field that researchers should 'attempt to report their findings to all relevant stakeholders' (Guiding Standards 1/5) and that their 'reports to the public should be written straightforwardly to communicate the practical significance for policy' (Guiding Standards 1/7). This latter recommendation is later repeated: 'Educational researchers should communicate their findings and the practical significance of their research in clear, straightforward, and appropriate language to relevant research populations, institutional representatives, and other stakeholders' (Guiding Standards 11/10).

This and the next chapter discuss various aspects of the academic writing process in quantitative, qualitative, and mixed methods projects. Space constraints prevent this book from offering detailed guidelines on how to achieve good academic writing in general, but fortunately there are many useful texts for this purpose. Instead, our focus will be on highlighting those facets of academic writing that are specifically associated with the particular research approach we have adopted, that is, which show paradigmatic variation. For example, there will not be much discussion on using register-appropriate vocabulary, but we will analyse in some detail the different role of the literature review in qualitative and quantitative research.

12.1 Two functions of academic writing

The most obvious function of academic writing is to communicate our results to an audience. Accordingly, researchers need to do their best to make their reports accessible. The following three principles have guided my own writing over the years:

- *Reader-friendliness* Any writing—including quantitative research reports—should be ultimately guided by the principle of reader-friendliness, and writers need to make a conscious effort to present the content in a way that maximizes the likelihood of successful comprehension in the readers. Therefore, it is my personal belief that whenever we have a dilemma about how to present, format, or formulate something, audience-sensitivity should be our main guiding principle.
- *Accessible language and style* There is a myth amongst novice researchers that any serious academic writing is, by definition, rather convoluted language-wise. Although there is indeed a tendency in academia to try and make our work appear more scholarly by overusing jargon and using complex phrases where simple ones would do, we should note that some of the most renowned scholars in the social sciences actually write very clearly. Although sometimes we do need to express nuances in a subtle way, my personal feeling is that most cases of impenetrable language actually reflect writer uncertainties.
- *Telling a story* Telling a story is by far the most effective way of getting through to audiences and if the content of a particular work is centred around a coherent and interesting storyline, even complex material can be made enjoyable and digestible. I was pleased to find support for a vivid, personalized form of presentation in the style manual of the American Psychological Association, which is a collection of some of the most scholarly rules in academic writing:

  > Although scientific writing differs in form from literary writing, it need not and should not lack style or be dull. In describing your research, present the ideas and findings directly, but aim for an interesting and compelling manner that reflects your involvement with the problem. (APA 2001: 10)

Besides being a communicative act, academic writing also plays a second important role: it is part of the process of inquiry. We have seen in Chapter 10 (Section 10.2.3) that writing memos is an analytical tool in growing, distilling, and structuring our ideas, and I have found that the same thing is true about academic writing on a broader level: only by writing regularly can we bring our research ideas to maturity. For this reason, if we want to be good researchers we need to accept the fact that being a writer is a regular part of our professional identity. Indeed, as Creswell (2005: 13) summarizes, 'Writing exists in all phases of the creative process of planning and in conducting research'.

12.2 Style manuals

A characteristic feature of quantitative research is the desire for standardization at every level, and accordingly, the preparation of a quantitative research report is governed by the guiding principles and regulations of detailed 'style manuals'. A style manual (or 'style guide') is intended to ensure the consistency of every facet of academic writing, from the level of punctuation to the organizing structure of the manuscript. There are several competing style manuals available and journals and book publishers always require authors to submit their work following one of these manuals. The most prominent differences between the different style manuals include the way we cite references in the text (i.e. the format of the in-text citations) and prepare the final list of references in the bibliography (i.e. the format of the end-of-text references; for more details, see the next section). We also find some disparity in the format of headings/subheadings, figures and tables, as well as in the use of certain symbols, abbreviations, and other special language aspects.

Because it may be time-consuming to reformat the completed work in the last minute, it is advisable to adopt a style manual early in the writing process and then stick to it to the end. The most commonly used style manual in our field is the one offered by the American Psychological Association; it is published in a book format and the most recent edition of the 'APA style' (as is usually referred to) is the fifth edition published in 2001 (APA 2001). Many applied linguistics journals such as *Language Learning*, *The Modern Language Journal*, *TESOL Quarterly*, and *Studies in Second Language Acquisition* follow this style. With regard to book publishers, some have adopted the APA style, whereas others have developed their own style requirements over the years. The publisher of the current book, Oxford University Press, for example has its own style manual and all the books and journals published by this publisher (for example, *Applied Linguistics* and *ELT Journal*) follow this.

A useful feature of the APA style manual is that it not only offers format prescriptions but also provides elaborate guidelines on how to structure research reports and how to present and organize the content of the various parts. In the following discussion of the structure of the quantitative research report I will draw on the principles of the APA style (APA 2001: 10–30).

12.3 The structure of the quantitative research report

Regardless of the length of a quantitative research report (for example, journal article or dissertation/thesis), writing up the results is relatively straightforward because there is a well-established reporting format with conventional models and structures to guide us. The specific details of how to present our findings are usually provided by the forum to which we wish to submit the final report. These various formatting requirements are obligatory to follow and they may initially appear as a constraint in trying to communicate our message. However, I have come to appreciate the quantitative report format as being logical and reader-friendly, with everything in it being geared at the accessible presentation of the empirical results. In the following I describe the main parts of the quantitative research report, and readers can also refer to the 'Quantitative Research Guidelines' published by the journal *TESOL Quarterly* (Chapelle and Duff 2003).

12.3.1 Front matter

The 'front matter' includes the title, the abstract, and in some works, the table of contents. The importance of these rather technical parts is that they provide the initial contact point between our work and the audience.

- *Title* A good title performs two functions: on the one hand, it summarizes the main idea of the work, describing the topic and the actual variables/issues under investigation. Thus, it should be informative, particularly because in electronic abstracting and information services such as the Linguistic and Language Behaviour Abstracts (LLBA) or the ERIC (Educational Resources Information Center) database, title searches are very common. On the other hand, a good title—similar to its counterparts in creative writing—needs also to be 'catchy', that is, attract the reader's attention. For this reason, some authors include captivating phrases in their titles. Finding a balance between the two aspects is difficult and I would recommend a more conservative approach favouring an informative title over a witty one. However, I must admit that choosing a really good title—for example, *Real Men Don't Collect Soft Data* by Gherardi and Turner (1999) for a paper on the QUAL/QUAN paradigm distinction—can contribute considerably to the perception and the career of the particular work.
- *Abstract* The abstract is a hugely important paragraph at the beginning of research articles, which further pursues the 'inform-and-attract' function of the title. The APA Publication Manual (APA 2001: 12) rightly points out:

> Most people will have their first contact with an article by seeing just the abstract, usually on a computer screen with several other abstracts, as they are doing a literature search through an electronic abstract-retrieval system. Readers frequently decide on the basis of the abstract whether to read the entire article.

The abstract needs to summarize the research problem and justify why it is worth studying. It also needs to provide some information about the methodology of the study and about the most important results and implications. There is usually a strict word limit for abstracts (100-200 words is common), so the challenge is to say as much as possible in as few words as possible.

- *Table of contents* For reports that are longer than articles we also need a table of contents. Silverman (2005) emphasizes that a table of contents is not merely a trivial, technical matter. It is one of the first things a reader of a book or dissertation/thesis looks at, and thus it conveys an important message about the logical and sound nature of the material.

12.3.2 Introduction, literature review, and research questions

In the 'Introduction' we reiterate once again what we said in the title and the abstract but this time at more length. This part presents the specific topic/problem/issue under study and addresses the following questions: what is the topic and why is it important? How does the research approach of the paper relate to the issue in question? What are the theoretical implications of the study and how does the study relate to previous work in the area? That is, this section is still part of the 'selling-and-informing' phase of the report. In longer works such as dissertations and theses, the Introduction also summarizes the structure of the work by briefly outlining and justifying the content of the subsequent chapters. In article-sized reports the Introduction is sometimes merged with the literature review.

Although everybody would agree that a proper research report should contain a review of the literature, there is usually quite a bit of confusion about what sort of literature summary is needed. I believe that part of the problem stems from the ambiguous role of the literature review as it can accomplish at least four different functions: (a) it can act as the 'map of the terrain', providing a comprehensive and often historical overview of the books, articles, and other documents describing the broader domain under investigation, (b) it can provide the specific theoretical background of the empirical investigation reported, justifying the need for it, thus focusing primarily on works that have a concrete bearing on the research design or the interpretation of the results, (c) it can be used to mark out the intellectual strand/position that the author is aligning with and to generate trustworthiness in the audience by showing that the author is knowledgeable in the area, and (d) finally and related to the previous point, in university assignments (for example, dissertations and theses) it is also to prove that the author has done his/her 'homework' and has become familiar with a wide range of relevant theoretical and research approaches. A good literature review displays a bit of all the four functions, but books usually pay special attention to the first one (mapping the terrain), while articles to the second (providing specific theoretical background).

We should note here that in many research articles the literature review can be quite short, often only about 20 per cent of the total length or even less (although in some cases it can be considerably longer, taking up half of the whole paper). This is due to the space constraints of journals, with editors wanting authors to place the emphasis on the new findings reported in the article. In fact, the APA guidelines (2001: 16) state: 'Discuss the literature, but do not include an exhaustive historical review. Assume that the reader is knowledgeable about the field for which you are writing and does not require a complete digest'.

I did not mention in the above description a function that is so often cited as the main role of the literature review: to provide a 'critical analysis' of the literature. I do not think that this is a particularly helpful specification because it tends to be used to imply a number of things that, strangely enough, do not really include being 'critical' in the strict sense. In fact, it is rare and rather marked to find a literature review in a published work that is overly 'critical' in the 'criticizing' sense, and the APA guidelines (2001: 10) explicitly state that differences should be presented in a 'professional, noncombative manner'. When we talk to students about the need to be 'critical' what we really mean is that (a) there should be a personal angle, prioritization, or storyline (see Section 12.1) underlying their overview of the literature; and (b) they should not hide behind authorities (and include too many literal citations), but should also make their own voices heard.

The importance of research questions and hypotheses has been discussed in Chapter 3 (Section 3.3), and listing these questions/hypotheses is a compulsory component in a quantitative research report. The best place to do so is usually at the end of the literature review, but in longer works the writer may include a separate (short) section between the literature review and the 'Method' part to describe the research design and the guiding questions.

Internet searches and electronic databases

The use of Internet searches and electronic databases in preparing the literature review is becoming an acute issue in many postgraduate programmes so let us look at this question briefly. In the current digital age it is increasingly natural to conduct a search using an Internet search engine such as Google whenever we need some information. However, this practice should *not* be automatically transferred to our search for relevant literature. There is a lot of material on the Internet that may look relevant but is actually of questionable quality. Researchers typically want to publish their results in books and journals because only for such publications do they get official recognition. However, once a work has been published in an established forum, copyright issues usually prevent it from being made freely available on the Internet. To find quality papers related to our research topic we need to search academic databases such as the Linguistics and Language Behaviour Abstracts, the MLA International Bibliography, ERIC, or PsychInfo. These are also Internet-based but are password protected—they can be reached, for example, through university libraries. It is my personal view that only in the most exceptional cases should we include Internet sources in the literature review—of course, this restriction does not apply to articles from legitimate Internet-based electronic journals and neither does it concern previously published papers that their author has made available on the Internet for the public.

12.3.3 Method

The 'Method' section describes the technical details of how the investigation was conducted. Only on the basis of this information can readers evaluate the appropriateness of the research design and, therefore, this section is crucial in convincing the audience about the credibility of the results. It is important that this part be concise and to-the-point so that it can serve as a 'reference section' if the reader wants to look up some details. Therefore, in the Method section we should not refer to other people's work but focus entirely on our own study.

For the sake of reader-friendliness, the Method section is always further divided into labelled subsections. The conventional subheadings include 'Participants', 'Instruments/Materials/Apparatus', 'Procedures', and sometimes 'Data analysis' and 'Variables in the study':

- *Participants* The appropriate description of the research sample is critical to quantitative research because only in the light of this can we decide whether the generalization of the findings is legitimate. The exact details to be supplied depend on the focus of the study but normally include as a minimum the sample size (possibly accompanied by some justification of the sampling strategy and the total number of all the eligible people), the participants' age, gender, and ethnicity as well as any relevant grouping variable (for example, number of courses or classes they come from). If the study concerns language learners, we need to specify their level of L2 proficiency, L2 learning history, L2 teaching institution (if applicable), and the type of tuition received. Typical optional background variables include the participants' general or language aptitude (or academic ability), socio-economic status, occupation or (if the participants are students) areas of specialization, L2 class size, L2 teaching materials used, and the amount of time spent in an L2 host environment.
- *Instruments/Materials/Apparatus* In quantitative studies the design and the quality of the research instruments (typically tests and questionnaires) determine both the type and the kind of data that can be collected. There-

fore we not only have to describe the instrument accurately but have also to give a rationale for the specific content areas covered and justify leaving out some potentially important areas. We also need to supply details about the piloting of the instrument and, particularly when sensitive items are included, how anonymity and confidentially were handled. Reliability and validity data can be introduced here or later in the 'Results' section. The actual instrument is often included in an appendix.

- *Procedure* Under this subheading we describe the procedures we followed during the data collection phase, with a specific focus on how the instruments were administered, summarizing the conditions under which the measurements were taken (for example, format, time, place, and personnel who collected the data) (Wilkinson and TFSI 1999). This is where we can talk about translation issues if the instrument was in the participants' L1, as well as any complications or unexpected events during data collection.
- *Data analysis* Although the APA guidelines do not highlight 'data analysis' as an obligatory section, many studies include it because summarizing the data processing procedures in advance is a reader-friendly way of preparing the audience for what is to come, especially if some complex analytical technique is used. This section is also useful to discuss possible problem issues such as missing data, attrition, and nonresponse and how these were handled. It is important to note, however, that the Data analysis section is typically short and does *not* contain any real results, only the listing of the statistical procedures applied.
- *Variables in the study* When the data analysis concerns a large number of variables and especially when some of the variables have been derived from others (for example, composite scores), we may feel that the clarity of the report requires listing all the variables used in the study, describing how they were derived or operationalized.

In sum, there are certain compulsory subsections of the Method section and we can add to these other sections if we decide that they are essential or useful for comprehending and possibly replicating the study.

12.3.4 Results and discussion

Presenting and interpreting the findings can be done either in one combined or in two separate sections, depending on whether we prefer describing our results first and then evaluating/interpreting them or doing the two tasks in an ongoing and combined manner. If there are a lot of numerical data to present before being able to draw inferences it may be better to relegate these into an independent Results section, to be followed by a more conceptual Discussion. In most other cases I have found that the combination of the two sections works better because it allows for an ongoing commentary and theoretical framing.

With longer works such as dissertations, there are so many different types of results to report that the most reader-friendly way of dealing with them is to divide the 'Results and discussion' part into thematically labelled chapters, each containing combined results and discussion. In agreement with the APA guidelines, let me draw attention to two aspects of the discussion process that are often omitted: highlighting any theoretical consequences of the results and examining the validity of the conclusion(s).

As Sandelowski (2003) explains, in quantitative research the appeal to numbers gives studies their rhetorical power and therefore the Results and Discussion section is centred around statistics. Yet it is important to stress that this does *not* mean that this section needs to be overly technical, using statistical 'power-language' and as many complex results tables as possible. Lazaraton (2005: 218–19) expresses this very clearly:

> What are the implications of so much published applied linguistics research employing fairly sophisticated analytical procedures? One result is that a great deal of the research becomes obscure for all but the most statistically literate among us. Page after page of ANOVA tables in a results section challenges even the most determined reader, who may still give up and head right for the discussion section.

In contrast, some of the best statisticians write very clearly, emphasizing the internal logic rather than the mathematical/procedural complexity of the analyses. Also, we should use, if possible, reader-friendly data presentation methods such as tables and figures (see Section 12.4), and if we do so, we must make sure that we do not repeat verbatim the information that has already been presented in tables and figures.

12.3.5 Conclusion

Not every research article has a 'Conclusion', because if we have separate 'Results' and 'Discussion' sections, the latter can conclude the whole paper. Yet, I would generally recommend the inclusion of a short concluding section because this is a highly reader-friendly opportunity to summarize our main findings in non-technical language. As McKay (2006) sums up, the Conclusion can also include a variety of other moves in addition to the summary of the major findings, such as a call for further research on questions raised by the investigation; some discussion of the limitations of the study; an explanation of the pedagogical implications of the results; and a statement of the overall significance of the topic addressed by the study. However, we should also note the recommendations of the 'Task Force on Statistical Inference' of the American Psychological Association (Wilkinson and TFSI 1999: 602) about the content of conclusions:

> Speculation may be appropriate, but use it sparingly and explicitly. Note the shortcomings of your study. Remember, however, that acknowledging

limitations is for the purpose of qualifying results and avoiding pitfalls in future research. Confession should not have the goal of disarming criticism. Recommendations for future research should be thoughtful and grounded in present and previous findings. Gratuitous suggestions ('further research needs to be done ...') waste space.

In any case, as McKay (2006) suggests, the Conclusion should end on a 'strong note' with some general statement that leaves the reader with a 'positive sense of the article' (p. 164).

12.3.6 References or bibliography

There are two basic rules with regard to the final 'References' list (also called 'Bibliography' by some style manuals). First, all the citations in the report must appear in the reference list, and all references in the list must be cited in the text. Second, the format requirements of the presentation style of the particular publication must be adhered to rigorously. I have found that the quality and accuracy of the reference list and the way it is presented in a manuscript is an important index of the quality of the whole work.

Researchers with a publication history usually have rather unpleasant memories of the long hours (and sometimes days!) they have spent in the past reformatting references when they wanted to use them in another publication that required a different style. Fortunately, these days might be over, because recent computer software such as EndNote can help us to store all our references in a generic form, to be printed out in any format we please. This is something every novice researcher should look into (if you have not done so already).

12.3.7 Appendix

An 'Appendix' is helpful if the detailed description of certain relevant material is distracting in, or inappropriate to, the main body of the work. For example, some extensive statistical tables can be relegated to the Appendix, but only if they do not contain key results supporting the main arguments—if they do, they should be left in the main body of the text regardless of their size. The Appendix is also the place to include copies of the instruments, transcripts, and other supplementary materials for readers to have a better idea of what exactly went on; some research journals specifically require the authors to have an appendix with all of their experimental items. With dissertations and theses I tend to encourage my students to include all relevant material in the Appendices so that they do not lose them over the years.

12.4 Reader-friendly data presentation methods

There are two specific reasons why we may want to include various reader-friendly data presentation methods in quantitative research reports. First, for many people numbers and statistics are rather dry, dull, and difficult to comprehend. Second, quantitative studies can often produce complex data that needs to be presented in an effective and digestible way to maintain clarity. The most reader-friendly presentation methods are visual ones—figures (representing intricate relationships) and tables (providing complex data and sets of analyses)—whereby we can have an overview of a great deal of the results at a glance. As Wilkinson and the TFSI (1999) point out, because individuals have different preferences for processing complex information, it often helps to provide both figures and tables. On the other hand, the APA guidelines caution us not to use tables for data that can be easily presented in a few sentences in the text, partly because they take up more space and are more expensive to print.

When we use figures and tables, we must number them and give them a brief explanatory title. Then we need to mention every one of them in the text, referring the reader to the exact number (for example, 'see Figure 3') rather than saying something to the effect that 'as the table below shows'.

12.4.1 Figures

Figures are methods of visualizing various characteristics of the data. In research reports two types of figures in particular are used, charts/diagrams and schematic representations.

'Charts', or as they are also called, 'diagrams', offer a useful way of describing the size/strength of variables in relation to each other. 'Bar charts' and 'line charts' use a vertical y-axis and a horizontal x-axis to present data (see Figures 12.1 and 12.2). The vertical axis usually represents the unit of measurement (or dependent variable) and the horizontal axis the grouping (or independent) variable(s). These charts are very flexible in terms of the type of data they can display, and they can effectively demonstrate comparisons or changes over time in a way that is easy to interpret.

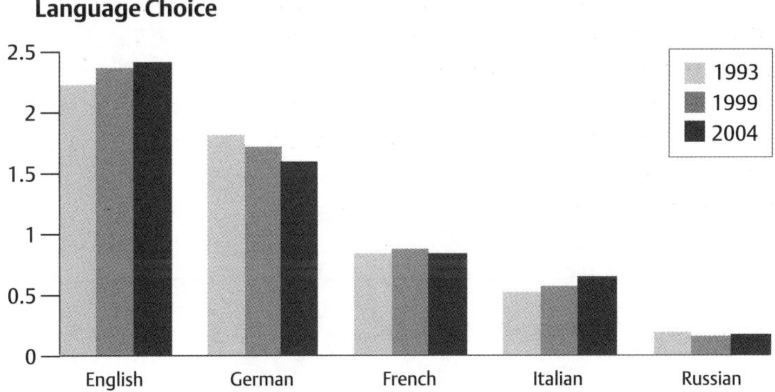

Figure 12.1 Sample bar chart/diagram

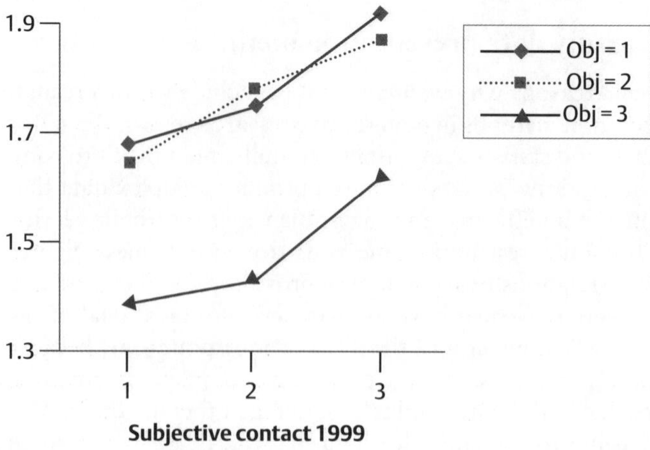

Figure 12.2 Sample line chart/diagram

'Schematic representations' offer a useful way to describe complex relationships between multiple variables, and typically utilize various boxes and arrows (see Figure 12.3). They can be used, for example, to describe the blueprint of mental processes or the componential structure of multi-level constructs.

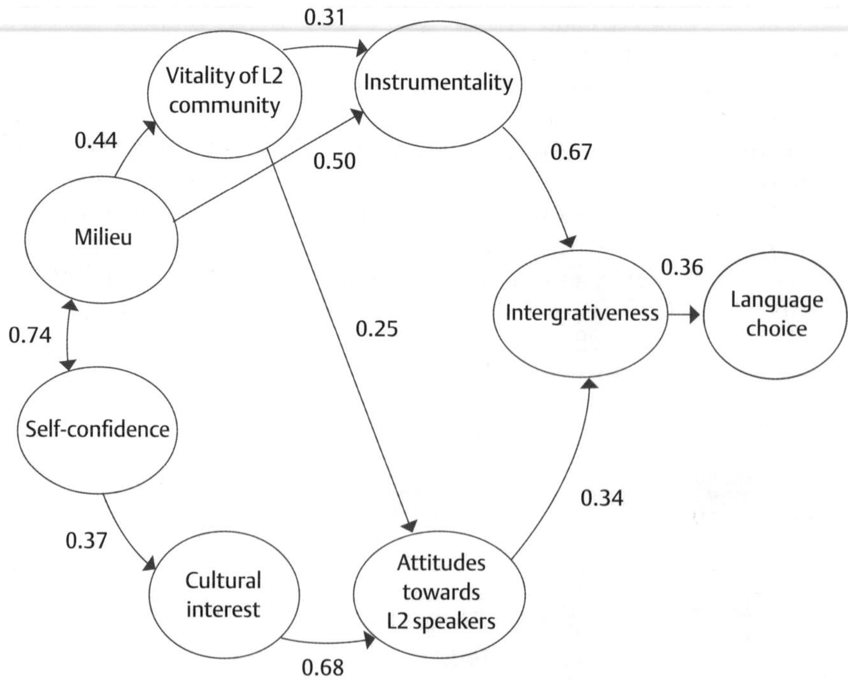

Figure 12.3 Sample schematic representation

12.4.2 Tables

Tables are used to summarize large amounts of data about the respondents and their responses, and to present the results of statistical analyses. They are typically made up of rows and columns of numbers, each marked with headings and subheadings. They can provide a more accurate and richer description than figures but they are less digestible. Tables are, therefore, more appropriate for articles in academic journals than for lectures to non-specialist audiences. Statistical results are often presented in tables and Chapter 9 contains several examples of these.

There are two points that need to be stressed about tables. First, as already mentioned in Section 12.3.4 on 'Results and discussion', if we present statistics in tables, we should *not* repeat them in the text, except for highlighting some particularly noteworthy results. Second, we should note that statistics tables have certain canonical forms (as illustrated throughout Chapter 9), both in content (i.e. what information to include) and format (for example, usually we do not use vertical lines). These need to be observed closely, which means that simply importing a table from SPSS into the manuscript is likely to be inappropriate. However, concerns for reader-friendliness, space considerations, and the particular publication's style requirements may overwrite this standard form. The best thing is to use published examples of a similar nature that follow the same style manual as models.

13 Writing qualitative and mixed methods reports

Although the previous chapter covered the writing of a research report primarily from a quantitative perspective, a great deal of what was said there also applies to qualitative or mixed methods studies. This is partly because some of the academic writing principles are universal and partly because in many ways the quantitative writing format can be seen as the default in the social sciences—an example of this is the fact that the APA style research report structure is being adopted, with modifications, by an increasing number of qualitative researchers (see below). In order to avoid any overlaps, the focus in this chapter will be on how qualitative and mixed methods reports *differ* from quantitative reports, without repeating the common features (for example, the characteristics of the title, the abstract, or the references).

13.1 Writing a qualitative report

> *An interview report should ideally be able to live up to artistic demands of expression as well as to the cross-examination of the court room.*
> (Kvale 1996: 259)

There is a wealth of literature available offering guidelines for writing up qualitative research. The fact that both authors and publishers feel that we need plenty of such advice is an accurate reflection of the problematic nature of preparing a qualitative report. We saw in the previous chapter that writing up a quantitative study is relatively straightforward, with various templates and conventions guiding our task. In contrast, similar to all other aspects of qualitative research, qualitative research writing is characterized by more freedom, diversity, and disagreement than its monolithic quantitative counterpart. This is why Davies (1995), for example, states that in her view the best way to learn how qualitative research findings are reported is to read journal articles and book chapters that model this particular genre. While I agree that following models is an effective way of being socialized into the role of the qualitative writer, in this chapter I summarize a few principles and guidelines that can facilitate and speed up this socialization process.

13.1.1 Main differences between qualitative and quantitative research reports

We do not have to conduct a thorough review of academic papers to realize that qualitative and quantitative research reports can be very different both in their organization and their style, and even in their length. Although whole books have been written on this topic, I would suggest that a great deal of this difference can be explained on the basis of the following six points.

Drawing on previous writing

In Chapter 12 (Section 12.1) I argued that being a writer is an intrinsic part of a researcher's professional identity and only by regularly writing can we take our research ideas to maturity. This is increasingly so in qualitative research where writing is seen as an indispensable means of inquiry. Qualitative researchers start writing memos, vignettes, and other forms of summaries (see Section 10.2.3) as well as personal research journals (Section 6.9) soon after beginning their projects, and keep writing, steadily and regularly, while they record and clarify their understanding of the data. Thus, as Sandelowski (2003) points out, in qualitative research the write-up is conceived less as an end product of inquiry than as an inquiry in the making because writing in order to report one's findings typically leads researchers to the generation of more ideas and subsequently more writing.

Of course, the process cannot go on forever and at one point we need to wrap it up and produce a final report. However, by that time we have accumulated a great deal of completed writing in various forms and therefore the main function of the final writing-up process is to a large extent to thread these together into a coherent order. In fact, it is difficult to imagine how any good qualitative report could emerge without drawing extensively on our previous writings.

No fixed formats or templates

How do we 'thread' the various bits and pieces together? Unfortunately for some and fortunately for others (depending on one's preference), in qualitative reporting there are no fixed formats or templates (or in Miles and Huberman's 1994: 299 words, no 'shared canons') of how our studies should be reported. This quality has a definite postmodern feel about it (and some scholars would equate qualitative writing with postmodern writing; see Hesse-Biber and Leavy 2006) but, in fact, it does not originate with postmodernism but rather with the iterative, emergent nature of the qualitative inquiry that precedes postmodernism. The canonical template of the quantitative research report is the crystallization of decades of experience on how best to present the end-product of a *linear* process. On the other hand, a qualitative investigation is often markedly *nonlinear*, and therefore imposing the template described in the last chapter on it is seen by many as counterproductive. Consequently, over the past three decades several alternative, often nonconventional, genres have been experimented with in order to fully communicate the findings of qualitative studies; these include literary modes such as novels and poems, as well as drama and dance (Sandelowski and Barroso 2002). The question of how far we can, or should, deviate from the generic norms of academic writing that originate with a different (i.e. quantitative) approach is a highly contested issue even in qualitative circles and we will come back to it in Section 13.1.2 below.

Words rather than numbers used as evidence

A common feature of any kind of primary research is that empirical data is used to support arguments and claims. In quantitative research this evidence is almost entirely number-based statistics. Although numbers can also be used in qualitative research, the dominant form of QUAL evidence involves extracts from word-based narrative accounts of either the respondents or the researcher him/herself (for example, field notes or memos). Thus, credence is achieved by illustrating and validating the researcher's inferences with a representative range of low-inference descriptors that bring the particular situation or phenomenon alive. The aim is to provide a rich and vivid description so that 'the reader can vicariously experience what it is like to be in the same situation as the research participants' (Johnson and Christensen 2004: 539).

Greater length

One good thing about numbers is that they can be summarized in a small space—we can often present all the main findings of a study in three or four tables. In contrast, words are rather 'wordy' and to provide a sufficient number of quotes takes up a lot of space, making qualitative reports usually considerably longer than their quantitative counterparts—see Magnan 2006; Gall *et al.* (2007) estimates that QUAL reports tend to be almost twice as long as QUAN reports. Thus, qualitative researchers are constantly between a rock and a hard place: on the one hand, they need to provide rich and persuasive narrative support within the fixed word limits that are imposed by almost all types of publications, and on the other hand, even by stretching the limits (and the editor's good will) to the maximum, only a tiny portion of the raw data can make it into the final report.

Telling a story

As stated in the previous chapter (Section 12.1), I am very much in favour of having a lucid storyline in any writing, including research reports, and the quantitative format makes it relatively easy to be coherent. After all, the structure itself presents an overarching process: the target issue is introduced and grounded in the literature review, then specific research questions or hypotheses are presented to which clear-cut answers are given using concise statistical support, and finally the findings are summarized. One can hardly go wrong by adhering to this template. In contrast, qualitative accounts are longer and contain far richer details, are based on an iterative and recursive data collection/analysis process, and often describe multiple meanings. The only way to present this well is by becoming *good storytellers*. 'When we cannot engage others to read our stories—our completed and complete accounts—then our efforts at descriptive research are for naught' (Wolcott 1994: 17). Thus, the success of reporting our qualitative findings depends to a large extent on how much we manage to wrap up our message in an absorbing story.

Reflexivity, style, and tone

Although quantitative research might have the edge over qualitative reports in terms of suggesting an obvious storyline, qualitative research compensates for this by allowing—in fact, encouraging—rich detail as well as a personal style and an informal tone. I argued in the previous chapter that a quantitative report does not need to be impersonal and formal (see Section 12.1), yet the fact remains that quantitative researchers often follow the style of the studies common in the natural sciences in which most of the message is conveyed by figures and facts rather than by the writer's own voice. In contrast, because the results of a qualitative study are usually seen as a co-constructed product of the participants' and the researcher's perceptions, the qualitative genre involves reflexivity, that is, including a discussion of the writer's biases, values, and assumptions in the text. As a concrete result of this, qualitative researchers tend to use the first person singular when talking about themselves rather then the impersonal 'the researcher' (which is actually becoming outdated even in quantitative reports).

Thus, with the emphasis on reflexivity and researcher involvement, qualitative research offers writers the freedom to have their own as well as their participants' voices heard, which can be turned into a powerful presentation tool. Given that the use of expressive language tends to be also highly prized among qualitative researchers (Sandelowski 2003), the qualitative writer has all the ingredients at his/her disposal to produce a vivid, detail-rich, dramatized story which can be a far better read than a report of the results of a multiple analysis of variance. Accordingly, Holliday (2002: 142) talks about the emergence of a 'new thinking, especially within progressive qualitative research, which provides scope for researchers as writers to use the conventions to establish a strong personal presence in the genre'.

13.1.2 The structure of a qualitative report

Variability and creative freedom as well as the conscious effort to avoid rigid formulae are hallmarks of qualitative inquiries at every phase of the research process, including the preparation of the research report. However, if we look at this closely, we find that the freedom of expression is not unlimited because there are certain aspects of the research project that must be covered in a report, regardless of the specific structure we use. These 'compulsory' parts include the introduction and justification of the topic; the description of the research methodology (data collection and analysis); the presentation of the findings and how they are related to other scholars' findings in the field; and finally some sort of a conclusion. Quite frankly, these components are rather similar to the main parts of the quantitative report described in the previous chapter, and even though qualitative studies may not use the conventionalized subheadings of the quantitative research report and may vary the order of the components (particularly the place of the literature review is flexible), it is fair to say that a qualitative report, in effect, covers the same ground as its quantitative counterpart.

Of course, covering the same ground does not mean that we have to do it in the same way and therefore the main question concerning qualitative writing is how much variation and at which level is desirable. Let me share at this stage my personal view: along with a number of researchers (for example, Johnson and Christensen 2004; Morrow 2005) I will advocate below a rather conservative stance, suggesting that we adopt a slightly modified version of the APA-style quantitative structuring format for qualitative reports to the extent that we even use most of the subheadings recommended by the APA style manual. The reasons for this are twofold:

1 My first reason is admittedly pragmatic: researchers do not exist in a vacuum and therefore they need to be aware of the normative influences of the research environment they work in. Thus, I would not recommend using untraditional formats simply because I have never heard of, say, a poem being accepted for a postgraduate dissertation/thesis in applied linguistics, and similarly, a researcher (and especially a non-established researcher) will stand little chance of publishing his/her results in a mainstream forum if he/she does not conform to the prevailing conventions.

2 The second reason has to do with the way 'creative freedom' is conceptualized within the research writing context. The central question is whether freedom can be exercised within a fixed framework or whether the conventional research report genre is too restrictive to allow the expression of certain meaning. The painter Vincent van Gogh is said to have complained once about the difficult situation of modern artists in the sense that there were no boundaries any more for them to stretch, whereas in the past very subtle meaning could be expressed by artists complying with and at the same time flouting the normative expectations of their age. In a similar vein, I believe that a lack of boundaries may have a detrimental effect, and adhering to a system can actually be liberating.

I would suggest, therefore, that by adopting the most recognizable academic organizing system, the APA structuring format, qualitative researchers can create a certain amount of leeway for themselves because the reader's familiarity with these conventions helps to carry, sustain, and anchor any unconventional content elements, such as a not-always-entirely-academic style. Furthermore, getting rid of traditional format conventions and setting out to report our findings in a more literary form such as a poem, for example, would be felt as inhibitive by many qualitative writers, especially by those who are new to the field. I am in agreement with Richards (2005: 187) that having no template to fill in 'is often a major obstacle to writing' and I do believe that the same idea has motivated Richardson and St. Pierre (2005: 973) when they suggested that in considering writing formats researchers should start with a 'journal article that exemplifies the mainstream writing conventions of your discipline'.

Let us now look at those aspects of the APA style quantitative research report that may require some modification to be able to accommodate the description of a qualitative inquiry. (For a list of elaborate suggestions, see the appendix of Morrow 2005.)

Introduction, literature review, and research questions

The role of the 'Introduction' is similar in qualitative and quantitative studies, except for one area, the literature review. The quantitative logic requires substantial initial coverage of the literature because the research questions, the research design, and the instruments are all justified by a priori theoretical knowledge. Qualitative studies, on the other hand are often exploratory and open-ended, and even though few qualitative researchers would adopt a 'tabula rasa' orientation, detailed background knowledge at the beginning stage is not seen as essential; in grounded theory, for example, the existing literature is only to be surveyed in the final analytical stage (i.e. in selective coding; see Section 10.3.3) to evaluate the emerging findings or 'theories' against it. Having said that, I still feel that even an exploratory, emergent qualitative study needs an initial, perhaps less substantial, literature review to provide a theoretical context for the investigation and to justify the research topic, but it might also be legitimate to introduce further literature later in the 'Discussion' section. Finally, there is another area in the Introduction where QUAL and QUAN reports differ: the characteristics of the research questions—this was discussed in Section 3.3.

Method

The main function of the 'Method' section is the same as in the APA style—namely to provide the technical information that is necessary for the evaluation of the subsequent findings and to serve as a reference section—but the different nature of qualitative and quantitative methodologies warrant certain useful additions and modifications (Morrow 2005):

- Before introducing the participants, it is useful to include a section on 'Research approach and design', describing the assumptions and principles underpinning the research and the type of qualitative methodology applied in the study.
- Because of the situated nature of qualitative research, the description of the participants needs to be particularly rich and the sampling strategy must be explicitly explained.
- Morrow (2005) suggests a useful modification whereby we merge the instruments and procedures sections under the heading of 'Sources of data', so that the various iterative steps that have been taken can be better described and explained.
- An important aspect of the 'Data analysis' is to describe how the recordings were transcribed, including the main features of the 'transcription protocol'—see Section 10.2.1. This section might also be the place to address the 'researcher-as-instrument' issue, focusing on certain characteristics of the researcher (for example, biases and disciplinary background) that may have affected the analysis. We also need to provide information on the specific approach of data analysis applied, including the nature of the various coding phases. A common shortcoming of qualitative studies is that it is not transparent how the inferences were derived from the raw data. Huberman and Miles (2002: x), for example, point out that QUAL Method sections are sometimes no more than 'shopping lists of devices commonly cited in the literature ... a sort of buzzword methodology, with scant demonstration of the processes involved in analyzing particular sets of data'. To create real transparency we need to supply key elements of an 'audit trail'. With the use of computer-aided qualitative data analysis (CAQDAS; see Section 10.4) this powerful validation strategy has become relatively easy to carry out (see below).
- *Electronic audit trail* Bringer *et al.* (2004) provide detailed guidelines on the kind of illustrations that work best in outlining the audit trail. These include screen prints of coding categories, personal journal pages, and examples from open and axial coding in a grounded theory approach. (Screen prints can be easily created by pressing the 'Print Screen' key on the keyboard and then pasting the static picture the computer has taken of the current screen into the word processor document.) In addition, examples of quotes for each main coding category provide powerful illustrations and Bringer *et al.* also suggest supplying a table that displays the number and the types of memos used and for what purpose. The particular CAQDAS software these authors used, NVivo, has special 'reporting' functions to provide category and document listings as well as more specific information such as, for example, how much of each document had been coded; these can also be used effectively to describe the development of the overall project.

- Finally, Section 3.1.2 listed a number of practical strategies to ensure validity in qualitative research. The Data analysis section should also contain some discussion of the use of such strategies in order to generate trustworthiness and eliminate or control validity threats.

Results and discussion

As explained in the previous chapter, the 'Results' section may or may not be merged with the 'Discussion' section. Morrow (2005) recommends that the two sections be kept separate in qualitative research articles to emphasize the distinction between rigorous data-based inferences and the researcher's own conclusions about the findings. In longer works such as postgraduate theses/dissertations, however, it might add to the clarity of the presentation of the findings if we divide the Results and Discussion into thematic chapters in which the various phases of the data analysis are described together. It also adds to the accessibility of the discussion (both in articles and in theses/dissertations) if we break down the text into subsections with their own subheadings. These subheadings act as reader-friendly signposts. (About the importance of signposting, see also Section 13.1.3.)

Besides the coherent storyline (which has been discussed in Section 13.1.1), the other key determinant of the effectiveness of presenting our findings is how we succeed in keeping the balance between our own interpretive commentary and the supporting evidence in the form of quotes from participants or field notes (Morrow 2005). Good qualitative reports display a smoothly flowing, natural rhythm of text and quotes—too many quotes dampen the researcher's voice and make his/her argument difficult to follow, whereas too few quotes may provide insufficient support, asking the reader, in effect, to rely heavily on the researcher's word. Morse and Richards (2002) emphasize that we should add some contextual information to the quotations concerning the social situation and the communicative context. The challenge is to achieve a thick description without the study being overly descriptive but rather analytical as a whole.

Can we edit the quotations if need be? Yes, but without distorting or misrepresenting the meaning; we need also to follow certain conventions, most importantly indicating (for example, with three dots) where something has been left out because it was redundant; briefer quotations tend to be more powerful than lengthy monologues (Morse and Richards 2002). An important purpose of the editing is to ensure the anonymity of the participants, which may require more than simply changing the names. With non-native respondents we may also edit minor linguistic inaccuracies to facilitate reading, but if we decide to do so, we should note this clearly at the first occurrence or in the Method section.

If we decide to have a separate Discussion section, this is the place to pull the various threads together and offer big-picture explanations. Some qualitative studies present an additional review of the literature at this point to evaluate the interpretations in the light of other scholars' findings.

Conclusion

Opinions about the need for a 'Conclusion' and what it should contain vary. Silverman (2005: 323), for example, argues fervently that 'you should never write a summary as your concluding chapter ... resist the temptations of a final downhill freewheel'. As he explains, by then one should have said everything in a crystal clear manner and therefore, if a reiteration of the findings is necessary, then something about the previous text is wrong. Instead of a summary, therefore, he suggests that the Conclusion should be used to reflect on the overall progression of the study from the original research question, to discuss any limitations and future research possibilities, and to communicate both the theoretical significance of the research and its practical implications for policy and practice. While I fully agree with these points, I feel that it may also be useful to recapitulate the main results in non-technical language: some readers are likely to go from the Introduction straight to the Conclusion, and will only read the rest of the study if the final claims arouse their interest.

13.1.3 Qualitative reports that don't work

It should be clear from the previous sections that preparing an effective qualitative report is no simple business and there are many areas where the writing can go wrong. To highlight some typical problem sources let us look at some examples of the how-not-to-do-it kind.

Pseudo-qualitative studies One of the inherent weaknesses of the qualitative report is that it is relatively easy to 'abuse' and call a study 'qualitative' even though it is not based on a theoretically sound, empirically grounded systematic analysis but only features a few anecdotes and vignettes (and perhaps some hand-picked interview extracts). According to Duff (in press), there are unfortunately too many of such non-scientific reports and these can discredit the scholarly image of the qualitative inquiry in general. (See also Section 3.1.2 on the danger of anecdotalism and the lack of quality safeguards.)

Long and boring We have seen that qualitative reports tend to be long narratives, without usually having tables or other kinds of summaries that help the reader digest quantitative reports. As Richardson and St. Pierre (2005) point out, qualitative work cannot be scanned but must be read fully because it carries its meaning in its entire text. Therefore, we have a major problem if the text is boring. Richardson's personal story illustrates this point well:

> A decade ago, in the first edition of this *Handbook* [*of Qualitative Research*], I confessed that for years I had yawned my way through numerous supposedly exemplary qualitative studies. Countless numbers of texts had I abandoned half read, half scanned. I would order a new book with great anticipation—the topic was one I was interested in, the author was someone I wanted to read—only to find the text boring. In 'coming out' to colleagues and students about my secret displeasure with

> much of qualitative writing, I found a community of like-minded discontents. Undergraduates, graduates, and colleagues alike said that they found much of qualitative writing to be—yes—boring. (Richardson and St. Pierre 2005: 959)

Academics are well educated and spend a great deal of their time in academia and therefore they may not realize that writing in an academic style has become second nature to them. The problem is that telling a story in a flavourless academic dialect does not work, and it works even less in qualitative narratives than it does in quantitative reports.

No signposting Qualitative accounts usually describe complex and often multiple meanings, focusing closely on several participants (except for single-case studies), alternating participant voices with the writer's own. All this results in texts of intricate tapestry. While such complex textures can be used to good effect, they also carry the danger of the reader getting lost and confused by them. Therefore, proper signposting is critical for effective qualitative reports. The signposts may include an introductory overview of the structure, various headings and subheadings, end-of-section summaries, as well as the writer's recurring commentary (as in a guided tour) on where we are in the story, how the particular part relates to what has already been said, and what is coming next.

Inaccessible language Duff (2006) mentions a further problem source that might undermine the effectiveness of a qualitative report: using inaccessible language:

> If readers are unable to easily comprehend the results and understand the chains of reasoning, the new knowledge or insights will not 'travel' or be transferable to new settings. Instead, the findings may only resonate with a small number of like-minded researchers and thus may have less impact on the field than intended or deserved. (p. 89)

On the other hand, Duff (2006) goes on to explain that qualitative research also offers potential benefits in this respect because, if done well, a qualitative report can provide concrete, situated examples of abstract phenomena and can thus communicate complex messages clearly.

More 'advanced' failures Besides the problems with style, structure, and language described above, there are some more 'advanced' ways by which a qualitative report can go wrong. Richards (2005) lists three such patterns:

- *Patchwork quilt* whereby the report is made up of a collection of long quotations, stitched together by fuzzy or superficial partial summaries. This is indeed a common mistake, especially by novice researchers, because the 'let-the-data-speak-for-itself' attitude usually covers uncertainties, or a lack of focus, or a lack of an original message.

- *Illuminated description* which offers a rich and vivid account of the situation, thus offering an enthralling presentation. What is missing is the integration of the data into a coherent argument.
- *Leap of faith* in which the writer uses an account supported with convincing evidence as a springboard to suddenly launch into moral or ideological assertions that do not follow directly from the data. Because qualitative inquiries are often motivated by ideological commitments or strivings for social justice, such a leap can be understandable but it can easily forgo the basic principle of research reports, namely that the arguments should be firmly grounded in the data.

13.2 Writing a mixed methods report

We have seen in this chapter that QUAL and QUAN research reports differ in many respects, and even amongst qualitative reports we find a great deal of divergence. Where does this leave us when we are to write up the results of a mixed methods study? The answer is a bit like the 'glass is half full/empty' metaphor because we can take both a positive and a negative view on the challenges of mixed methods writing. In the following I first discuss both the challenges and the advantages of such a project and then introduce three key principles of writing mixed methods reports. Finally, I present a number of specific recommendations to facilitate the writing process.

13.2.1 Challenges and advantages of mixed methods reports

The difference between QUAL and QUAN research reports is more than a technical one and covers both structural and terminological issues. The two types of report want to appeal to their audiences in different ways, because their audiences tend to find different things appealing (Sandelowski 2003). And given that few scholars in applied linguistics (or in the social sciences in general) are paradigmatically 'bilingual', our greatest challenge when writing a mixed methods report is that some of the material will by definition be read and evaluated by a potentially unsympathetic (or even hostile) audience. QUAL and QUAN researchers tend to find different arguments and evidence convincing and apply different quality criteria in judging the value of a study—see Chapter 3; in short, as Sandelowski concludes, they interact with the texts differently. In the light of this, is it an illusion to expect that readers will appreciate our claim that by mixing methods we can achieve a better understanding of our topic than by using a pure method?

There is also some tension at the actual level of writing because in a mixed methods report we need to use both words and numbers to support our interpretations, and although these do not exclude each other, to present them in a convincing manner and to justify the meaning inferred from them requires a different framing and formatting approach. It may indeed be the case that the different presentational modes sit awkwardly together on the page (Brannen 2005)—the dissimilarity between the personal presence and voice of the writer in QUAL on the one hand, and their absence in QUAN texts on the other, illustrates this point well. In general, QUAL and QUAN writing have a different 'look and feel' (Sandelowski 2003); this raises the question as to whether a 'hybrid' report can possibly have the same power as its monomethod counterparts.

A third problem concerns a very practical yet fundamental point: the *length* of mixed research studies. A difficult issue with qualitative studies (already mentioned) concerns the fact that because of the need for contextualization and the use of quotes rather than figures as supporting evidence they are inherently longer than quantitative research papers. However, mixed research studies involve both a QUAL and QUAN component (sometimes more than one phase of each) and therefore require even more space than their monomethod counterparts. With most journals having strict page limits, the length issue can become a serious problem when researchers working in a mixed methods paradigm attempt to publish their reports (Johnson and Christensen 2004).

On the positive side, although mixing methodologies undeniably poses challenges, using combined methods can also be turned into an advantage: after all, monomethod studies in the past have typically reached their paradigmatically selected audiences, whereas, as argued in Section 7.1.3, with mixed methods studies we have for the first time an opportunity to reach the whole research spectrum because such reports have more 'selling points'. Todd *et al.* (2004) argue that we can use the familiar component of the research to win over hostile audiences because, for example, QUAN results will appear more presentable to a QUAL audience if they are illuminated by sensitive QUAL data. That is, the QUAL data can 'authorize' the QUAN results and vice versa. In the same vein, mixed methods studies can also open up a wider range of publication venues for us because both qualitatively and quantitatively oriented journals will consider mixed methods submissions, and the paradigmatic bilingualism of mixed methods researchers may also enable them to get through to a wider audience in presentations and public lectures (Brannen 2005).

13.2.2 Key principles of writing mixed methods reports

Before addressing specific issues to facilitate the writing of mixed methods studies, let us look at three basic principles that might guide our approach. I believe that writing an effective mixed methods report requires good balancing skills and therefore the following principles are related to the writer's sensitivity to the possible impact of three key factors on the appraisal of the study: the audience, the research design, and the results.

- *Audience sensitivity* The first principle can be summarized in one sentence: if you know the paradigmatic orientation of the various decision makers and stakeholders (for example, PhD panel/examiners, journal/book editors, or conference audiences, grant application reviewers) who might be at the receiving end of your report, emphasize the aspect of the study they are more familiar with and frame the overall interpretation in the language and presentation style of the particular approach. Or as Johnson and Christensen (2004: 540) have put it, 'know your audience and write in a manner that clearly communicates to that audience'. This does not mean that we need to compromise, or change, or dumb down our message; rather we can look at this process as a translation exercise.

If we decide that the main audience is likely to be mixed, Sandelowski (2003) emphasizes that we need to permit both qualitative and quantitative readers 'access' (p. 396) to our work. Thus, writing mixed methods reports requires an understanding of the paradigmatic differences of the main characteristics of convincing write-ups in both the QUAL and QUAN traditions, and with mixed audiences that are by definition insufficiently versed in both approaches we should not take highly specialized quantitative or qualitative terms for granted. Instead, we ought to provide accessible definitions and explanations, thereby 'educating' our audience (which is, incidentally, what judges and lawyers do in court trials given that most jury members have no legal training).

- *Research design sensitivity* The paradigmatic framing of our report also depends on our research design. There is a natural tendency to write up the qualitative part of the study in a qualitative manner and the quantitative part in a quantitative manner, and do the mixing at the interpretation/discussion stages only. This may be appropriate for a 'triangulation' study where the objective is to corroborate findings as a means of validation (see Section 7.1.2), but less appropriate for a study where mixing also occurs at the analysis stage. Integrated analyses need to be written up in a more integrated manner. Sequential studies in which one research phase builds on another present yet another situation with regard to framing the report because here we also need to consider whether one of the research components has got a dominant status. In sum, the design of our study also dictates to some extent the way the report can be written up to best effect.
- *Result sensitivity* Finally, let me mention a very pragmatic principle. Deciding on the best presentation approach will also depend on what sort of results we have. If our most impressive results are quantitative, it makes sense to frame the whole report in a way so as to highlight those, whereas if the qualitative phase has generated some truly remarkable insights and we have some expressive quotes to back them up, then this would warrant a more qualitative presentation format.

13.2.3 Specific recommendations on how to write mixed methods reports

To conclude this chapter let us look at some specific mixed methods presentation techniques and issues. Although it is an option for researchers to write separate reports for the quantitative and qualitative phases of their studies that are only superficially linked, I fear that in many cases this (not uncommon) practice may actually 'short-change' our work. Therefore, my first recommendation is that if an investigation qualifies to be labelled a 'mixed methods study', we should consciously frame our report as such. In fact, Hanson *et al.* (2005) specifically recommend that researchers use the phrase 'mixed methods' in the title of their studies.

The following points are intended to help to achieve a principled presentation of methodology mixing. However, as a preliminary we can say that a mixed methods research report contains the same basic features as do most monomethod reports: there needs to be some sort of an introduction, a review of the relevant literature and a discussion of the methodology employed, followed by the presentation and analysis of the results and a conclusion.

- *Conscious accentuation of methodology mixing* Because the mixed methods approach is still an emerging field, Hanson *et al.* (2005) recommend that researchers explain in the 'Introduction' the logic, the progression and the rationale for their study—this can, in fact, serve as a 'superordinate storyline'—and include explicit purpose statements and research questions that specify the quantitative and qualitative aspects of the investigation. Because, ultimately, the value of a mixed methods study depends on its capacity to produce a more comprehensive answer to the research question than a pure method alone would, it is worth elaborating on this issue at this point. Such explanations will not only lend credence to the study but will also hopefully help to eliminate any initial orientational bias in the reader.
- *Using a modified APA style template* Similarly to my format recommendation for qualitative reports in Section 13.1.2, I would suggest that mixed methods researchers apply the APA style template for the organization of the main parts of their report. Using the familiar subheadings will help readers to orientate themselves in the overall design, which is bound to be more complex than that of a monomethod study because of the multiple research phases. We may organize the material by research question or by research paradigm. In the psychological literature it is not uncommon to report multiple investigation in a single research article, and there they are usually organized by number (for example, Study 1, Study 2, etc.).
- *Literature review* Qualitative and quantitative studies can differ considerably in the place and role they assign to the 'Literature review' (see Section 13.1.2). Therefore, depending on the sequencing of the particular mixed methods study, we may divide the Literature review into several parts, with

an initial overview in the Introduction and further, more specific discussions later where relevant. For the sake of transparency, we may signpost this division by letting readers know what to expect later.

- *Methods* Because of its reader-friendliness, I am in favour of a concise and to-the-point methodology section in any research report, and breaking it down to familiar subsections ('Participants', 'Instruments', 'Procedures', etc.) increases its usefulness for reference purposes (i.e. when someone wants to look up some factual information). However, we need to deviate on one point from the pure quantitative design, namely the inclusion of a 'Mixed research design' section, possibly at the beginning of the Methods part, in which we specify the type of design applied.
- *Contextualization* Because of the situated nature of qualitative research, QUAL studies are highly contextualized, whereas QUAN studies often require little contextualization beyond summarizing the main sample characteristics. Johnson and Christensen (2004) recommend that, even when the quantitative phase is dominant, we should always contextualize the reports. This will make it easier to relate the QUAL and QUAN components to each other, and communicating context characteristics is also necessary for the reader to appraise the validity of mixing and the generalizability of the results.
- *Tone and style* The final area to consider with regard to possible tensions between QUAL and QUAN presentation requirements concerns the overall tone and style of the writing. As argued earlier, an effective qualitative report often reads like a vivid, detail-rich, dramatized story, whereas quantitative studies tend to be more detached, formal, and matter-of-fact, devoid of 'literary frills' (Sandelowski 2003). Mixed methods researchers need to strike a balance between the two types of writing, guided by their 'audience sensitivity' described in the previous section. In addition, as already mentioned, no matter what balance we intend to achieve in a mixed methods study, we cannot rely on the authorizing force of specialized 'power-terminology' because that would inevitably alienate part of our audience.

PART FIVE
Summing up

14

How to choose the appropriate research method

> *Your research approach can be as flexible as you wish. You may, in fact, want to take a multimethod approach in your search for answers. There is never a 'one and only one' way to carry out a project.*
> (Hatch and Lazaraton 1991: 4)

Having covered the most important research issues and the main principles of data collection and analysis, it is time to address one of the most fundamental questions in research methodology: how do we decide which research method to chose for our planned investigation? Regrettably, there is no easy and universally valid answer to this question because different people choose their research methods for different reasons. In order to provide some practical guidelines for method selection, in this concluding chapter I will offer two general recommendations and summarize a number of considerations that might affect our choice.

14.1 General recommendation I: adopt a pragmatic approach

I have argued throughout this book in favour of a pragmatic approach to developing our research design; this involves, in the broadest sense, maintaining an open and flexible frame of mind and remaining as free as possible of paradigmatic dogmas. At the end of the day, research is not a philosophical exercise but an attempt to find answers to questions, and just as we can go about this in our everyday life in many different ways, the varied palette of research methodology is clear evidence for the possibility of diverse solutions in the scientific inquiry. Accordingly, my first general recommendation is indeed very general: *adopt a pragmatic approach and feel free to choose the research method that you think will work best in your inquiry.* A similar opinion was echoed by Silverman (2005: 15) when he concluded that 'it is sensible to make pragmatic choices between research methodologies according to your research problem and model'. The rest of this chapter will offer a range of different perspectives on how to make such pragmatic choices.

14.2 Research content considerations

Greene and Caracelli (2003) point out that contrary to what we might expect and what is often stated in the literature, social researchers appear to ground inquiry decisions primarily in the nature of the phenomena being investigated and the contexts in which the studies are conducted rather than in more abstract paradigm concerns. Let us start examining these specific, 'grounded' considerations by looking at the effects of the research content. In this respect, three issues in particular are relevant: (a) the research question/topic; (b) whether the investigation is exploratory or explanatory; and (c) the existing research traditions in the specific area.

- *Research question and topic* In their influential book on mixed methods research, Tashakkori and Teddlie (1998) include a whole section entitled 'The dictatorship of the research question'. In this they claim that it is the research question that ought to determine every aspect of the design of the study, and for most researchers method is secondary to the research question itself in the sense that they are ready to address their research questions with any methodological tool available, using the pragmatist credo of 'what works'. In other words, 'The best method is the one that answers the research question(s) most efficiently' (p. 167). Although I tend to agree with the thrust of this argument, it also raises a hard question: how do we know in advance what will work? In some cases there may be an obvious match between our research question and a method of inquiry, but in other (and I believe, most) cases several approaches might be suitable for exploring a problem. At times like this the 'choose-the-method-that-best-suits-the-research-question' principle does not offer much help and our choice needs to be informed by other considerations.
- *Exploratory purpose* An obvious situation when basing the method selection on our specific research question cannot work is when we do not have a specific research question. This happens, for example, when little is known about the target problem or phenomenon because it has not been studied in detail before or because previous studies have generated inadequate explanations. Such situations necessitate exploratory investigations that help us to map the terrain first and fine-tune our specific research angle later in the project. In Morse and Richards' (2002: 28) words, 'Put bluntly, if you don't know what you are likely to find, your project requires methods that will allow you to learn what the question is from the data'. As discussed in Chapter 2 (Section 2.3.3), such exploratory purposes are usually associated with a qualitative methodology.

- *Existing research tradition in the area* In some research areas there are certain dominant methods of inquiry. For example, as I explained in the Preface, when I started to investigate language learning motivation as part of my PhD studies, the available research was almost entirely quantitative, utilizing survey methodology. If we can identify such a methodological salience associated with our research problem, it makes sense to start our project by following the particular tradition. In this way we can receive guidance in the literature and our results will be directly comparable with other scholars' findings. Later, of course, we might decide to break away and try and shed new light on the area by adopting new research methods.

14.3 Audience considerations

I have argued more than once in this book that research is a social activity whereby researchers need to share their findings with the wider scholarly community. Accordingly, we need to be sensitive to the audiences to whom we report our results, whether they be university committees, dissertation/thesis examiners, journal editors, conference attendees, or colleagues in the field (Creswell 2003). Selecting a research method in a way that takes into consideration the preferences and expectations of our targeted audience is in line with such audience considerations. However, there is admittedly a fine line between such pragmatic audience-sensitivity and what Todd *et al.* (2004: 5) call 'illegitimate motives' for choosing a method based on political reasons. These may involve, for example, trying to fit the method with the most profitable research paradigm within the researcher's professional environment in order to achieve advancement.

14.4 Practical considerations

In my experience, even if we try to be principled in our selection of a research method, the final choice is likely to be a trade-off between theoretical and practical considerations. It is my impression that researchers are often ashamed of the compromises that they need to make, not realizing that making compromises is part and parcel of being a researcher. Three practical considerations are particularly relevant to novice researchers when they are to choose a method for their investigation:

- *Supervisor and other available support* Every researcher needs advice and help from time to time, and for less experienced investigators establishing some support link is vital. Therefore, one important consideration in selecting the method to be applied is to make it compatible with the expertise or research preference of people around us who may be able to offer assistance.
- *Available resources* Research methods vary in the amount of time and money they require for successful completion. Therefore, cost-effective-

ness and cost-benefit calculations always need to be seriously considered. Quantitative methods are often selected because they tend to be less time-consuming to conduct than qualitative studies (for example, compare a questionnaire survey to an interview study), but novice researchers often forget that these methods require psychometrically sound instruments and sufficient statistical expertise to process the results.

- *Available sample* The feasibility of using a particular method greatly depends on the kind of participant sample that the researcher can have access to. Reaching the most appropriate respondents can be prevented by a variety of technical, financial, logistic, or timing factors. Therefore, researchers often follow a rather opportunistic (but legitimate) approach: if they realize that they are in a position to examine a specific group of people who could provide some unique or particularly high quality data, they may tailor their method (and sometimes even their specific research topic) to the characteristics of this available sampling opportunity.

14.5 Personal considerations

At an Editorial Advisory Board meeting of *TESOL Quarterly* in the late 1990s, I had an interesting conversation with Kathy Davies (University of Hawaii) about the differences between qualitative and quantitative research. Kathy said something to the effect that qualitative and quantitative researchers tend to be 'different people', that is, they differ in some vital (research-related) personal characteristics. The more I have thought about this over the years, the more important I have come to consider this point. It seems to be the case that sometimes our research orientation is not so much related to philosophical or research-specific considerations as to who we are and what we are like. Let us look at this question in more detail.

14.5.1 Personal style and research orientation

Erzberger and Kelle (2003: 482) summarize the standard research methodological position regarding the relationship between personal preferences and method choice very clearly:

> The selection of adequate methods should not be made mainly on the basis of sympathies toward a certain methodological camp or school. Methods are tools for the answering of test questions and not vice versa. Consequently, decisions about the methods should not be made before the research questions are formulated.

While I accept that this is a rational position to take, I do have doubts about whether it is realistic to expect scholars to go against their personal tendencies and style. I stated in Section 2.5 that in my own day-to-day research activities I am more inclined towards a quantitative approach than a qualitative one, simply because I feel I am better at it and I enjoy it more. This is not unlike bilingualism. Although we can be very fluent in two languages, there are very few (if any) completely balanced bilinguals—depending on the specific language function/situation concerned most bilinguals show some language preference. I do believe that researchers should strive to become paradigmatically bilingual (or trilingual), yet I would expect that most of us are aware of which our first and which the additional research language is. Punch (2005: 240) describes this phenomenon as follows:

> Some people prefer, for a variety of reasons, one approach over the other. This may involve paradigm and philosophical issues, but there is often also a subconscious temperament factor at work. This visually comes down to different images about what a good piece of research looks like. Students will often express that by saying that they 'like this way better'.

A naturally quantitative researcher finds it exciting and intrinsically rewarding to develop neat and orderly systems of variables with firm boundaries, to explore statistics (to the extent that examining a statistical table is a pleasurable experience), and in general to uncover regularities that seem to govern certain aspects of our lives. In contrast, scholars with a qualitative orientation revel in being immersed in the 'messy' and ambiguous—often even confusing—reality of social life and have the gift of noticing patterns and teasing out underlying meanings in this 'noisy' research environment; they are less interested in broad tendencies than in the subtle perceptions, influences, and conditions that shape our idiosyncratic personalized worlds. I am not aware of any cognitive styles research into paradigmatic preferences, but it seems likely that our style characteristics (for example, global versus particular; inductive versus deductive; or synthetic versus analytic) have a strong bearing on this matter.

14.5.2 Personal training and experience

Even if we accept that many researchers have basic orientational preferences, the question is whether these are innate or learnt. I suspect that like in so many cases when the 'nature-or-nurture' question arises in the social sciences, the answer is mixed. While I believe that certain stylistic or temperamental individual difference factors may influence our methodological choices, I also consider the researcher's personal training and research experience central in this respect. Creswell (2003) rightly points out that someone trained in technical, scientific writing, and statistics (and who is also familiar with quantitative journals) would most likely choose quantitative methodology. On the other hand, the qualitative approach incorporates more of a literary form of writing—and we can add, creative writing and storytelling—as well as experience in conducting open-ended interviews and observations.

Our methodological upbringing can frame our thinking in two ways. First, once we have identified a research question, we are more likely to establish a working plan towards answering it by using methods whose capabilities we are well acquainted with. The second route is more subtle: our training and past experience in using certain methods not only act as tools but they may also shape the way we look at research problems in general. Thus, it may be the case (and I believe it often is) that the way we specify the research questions is already determined by our initial methodological orientation. Norton Peirce (1995) stresses that theory, implicitly or explicitly, informs the questions researchers ask, which in turn influence the research methods selected. While this is undoubtedly true, these considerations suggest that our experiential knowledge and skills can 'tint our lenses' over and above our theoretical orientation and actually be the starting point in the method selection chain. Lazaraton (2005: 219) even suggests that the appeal, or 'sexiness', of certain high-powered statistical procedures may lead one to ask research questions whose answers require the use of the particular procedure, which she says is an example of the 'wag the dog' syndrome.

14.5.3 Disillusionment with an approach

Finally, we might be moved towards an approach for negative reasons, that is, because we dislike or are disillusioned with the alternative methodology. For example, my own first encounter with qualitative methods was motivated by the realization of the limitations of quantitative techniques in exploring new dimensions of L2 motivation (my main research area). Indeed, according to Morse and Richards (2002), quantitative researchers often start working qualitatively because they recognize that the statistical analyses of their survey data did not seem to fit what respondents in similar situations said or what they wrote in their answers to open-ended questions.

Trying out a new approach because of an earlier disillusionment with an alternative one is a legitimate reason for method choice, but this is not the case if, as Silverman (2001) describes, we turn to qualitative research only because we cannot do statistics and cannot be bothered to learn. Morse and Richards (2002) also underscore the risks in projects where someone decides to apply qualitative methods for the wrong reason, and besides the common issue of trying to avoid statistics, they mention another interesting misconception held by some scholars, namely that quantitative research is morally/ethically inferior to the more 'humanistic' qualitative methods. As they point out, qualitative techniques can be 'most invasive, intrusive, and morally challenging; the only good reason a researcher should consider using them is that the research problem requires them' (p. 29).

14.6 General recommendation II: consider mixing methodologies

The second general recommendation I would like to make is that *it is worth considering applying a mixed methods research design in every situation.* Even if there is a good reason for opting for a specific methodology, adding a secondary component from another approach can be highly informative. I have come to see the truth in the following assertion by Greene and Caracelli (2003: 107): 'In theory, mixed methods inquiry can be a means for exploring differences; a forum for dialogue; or an opportunity to better understand different ways of seeing, knowing, and valuing'. This message is reminiscent of Miles and Huberman's (1994: 43) warning about the dangers of falling into a monomethodological 'default' mode, characterized by an 'unquestioning, partisan frame of mind'. And let me also reiterate here Lazaraton's (2005: 219) conclusion that has already been cited: 'Finally, I would also hope that we would see more studies that combine qualitative and quantitative research methods, since each highlights "reality" in a different, yet complementary, way'.

14.7 Final words

My ultimate recommendation for method selection would be for researchers to simply choose the method that they are most comfortable with. I firmly believe that we can find out valuable things about almost any topic by using research strategies associated with any of the three main methodological paradigms described in this book. That is, personally I do not think that the method itself is the decisive factor in research—it is what we do *within* the method. The real challenge may not be to find the paradigmatically best way of examining a topic of interest but rather to maintain personal freshness and creativity while pursuing a disciplined and systematic approach. I argued in Chapter 1 that the four fundamental features that can help a researcher to achieve excellence are curiosity, common sense, good ideas, and a mixture of discipline, reliability, and accountability. Methodological expertise in itself will not make us good researchers although it will help us to avoid doing bad research.

There is, of course, a decision-making level that is beyond research methodological considerations: the researcher's moral-political stance and integrity. Lourdes Ortega (2005: 438) has summarized this so well that I am happy to give the final say to her:

> I have argued that, in the ultimate analysis, it is not the methods or the epistemologies that justify the legitimacy and quality of human research, but the moral-political purposes that guide sustained research efforts.

And it is our responsibility as researchers to choose our value commitments, as it is to choose our theoretical frameworks and methodologies, and let those values inform the design, conduct, and dissemination of our studies and of the research programs they instantiate.

Afterword

While I was in the process of writing this book, I noticed at one point what should have been obvious to me a long time before, namely that what I was doing corresponded almost perfectly with the process of conducting qualitative research. Using a combination of 'typical sampling' and 'criterion sampling', the participants of my book project were the various authors of the methodology texts that I had read. The sampling procedure was 'purposive/ theoretical': I stopped collecting data for any specific topic when saturation was reached and I looked for new data (i.e. literature) to examine freshly emerging issues even at the very final stages of preparing the manuscript. Furthermore, this has undoubtedly been an extended engagement with the data—for over eight months I was immersed in the topic, day and night.

The total dataset—that is the total amount of literature I have read—amounted to tens of thousands of pages of text, and in order to process these I used a 'template approach' of coding: I started out with a broad template (the chapter headings and some subheadings) and the coding process involved selecting over a thousand quotations from the various texts under these headings. I scanned these extracts with my invaluable (and highly recommended) gadget, the 'C-Pen', which saved me the laborious task of transcription (i.e. copying). During the coding process the template (i.e. the structure of the book) was fine-tuned and modified several times and I kept going back and recoding the data accordingly.

Although the main theme of my book—the complementary values of qualitative and quantitative research and the promising possibility of combining them to best effect through mixed methods research—had been developing in my mind for several years, the final content and the specific angle of several chapters actually emerged during the analysis/writing up stage. Indeed, the table of contents submitted to Oxford University Press as part of the book proposal originally included only ten chapters, which increased in my first detailed template to sixteen, and settled in the final version to fourteen. And if I compare the subheadings in the proposal and the final version, it is in places as if I was looking at two different books.

During the data analysis process I kept writing extensive memos and I also started to prepare a first draft of the manuscript early on in the project because I found that, in line with qualitative principles, my understanding developed significantly during the writing process. Preparing the final manuscript involved drafting, redrafting, and revising the text, thus allowing the material to develop its own shape and character. I experienced directly the never-ending nature of the iterative process of the qualitative inquiry—had it not been for the publisher's deadline, I would still be refining the narrative.

As I look back, I find that my writing style was also consistent with qualitative principles. Starting in the Preface, I specified my ideological standpoint, and throughout the book I allowed my voice to be heard. However, I did not want this to go at the expense of other people's voices and I therefore included many literal quotations to convey 'insider' views. I also shared personal feelings and even certain doubts at some points but I did strive for a balanced handling of the data. As a result, this is a book which presents *my* personal take on research methodology but informed by participant meaning throughout. In sum, I realized that what I was doing was qualitative research proper! (Unfortunately, this ending reminds me so much of the joke of the little boy who claimed that he spoke French. When his friends asked him to say something in French, he said, '*Ja*'. 'But that's German!', said his friends. 'Wow!' exclaimed the little boy, 'I didn't know I could speak German too ...').

Bibliography

Abbuhl, R. and **A. Mackey.** In press. 'Second language research methods' in K. King and N. Hornberger (eds.). *Encyclopedia of Language and Education*, Vol. 10, Research Methods. New York: Springer.

Abrams, D. and **M. A. Hogg** (eds.). 1999. *Social Identity and Social Cognition.* Oxford: Blackwell.

Adolphs, S. 2006. *Introducing Electronic Text Analysis: A Practical Guide for Language and Literary Studies.* London: Routledge.

AERA. 2002. 'Ethical Standards'. http://www.aera.net/aboutaera/?id=222.

AERA, APA, and **NCME.** 1999. *Standards for Educational and Psychological Testing.* Washington, D.C.: Author.

Aiken, L. 1996. *Rating Scales and Checklists: Evaluating Behavior, Personality, and Attitudes.* New York: John Wiley.

Alderson, C. J. 2006. *Diagnosing Foreign Language Proficiency: The Interface between Assessment and Learning.* London: Continuum.

Allwright, D. 2005. 'Developing principles for practitioner research: the case of exploratory practice'. *Modern Language Journal* 89/3: 353–66.

Allwright, D. and **K. Bailey.** 1991. *Focus on the Language Classroom: An Introduction to Language Classroom Research for Language Teachers.* New York: Cambridge University Press.

Altrichter, H. and **M. L. Holly.** 2005. 'Research diaries' in B. Somekh and C. Lewin (eds.). *Research Methods in the Social Sciences.* London: Sage.

APA 2001. *Publication Manual of the American Psychological Association*, 5th Edition. Washington, D.C.: American Psychological Association.

Arksey, H. and **P. Knight.** 1999. *Interviewing for Social Scientists.* London: Sage.

Bachman, L. F. 2004a. 'Linking observations to interpretations and uses in TESOL research'. *TESOL Quarterly* 38/4: 723–8.

Bachman, L. F. 2004b. *Statistical Analyses for Language Assessment.* Cambridge: Cambridge University Press.

Bachman, L. F. 2006. 'Generalizability: a journey into the nature of empirical research in applied linguistics' in M. Chalhoub-Deville, C. A. Chapelle, and P. Duff (eds.). *Inference and Generalizability in Applied Linguistics: Multiple Perspectives.* Amsterdam: John Benjamins.

Bachman, L. F. and **A. S. Palmer.** 1996. *Language Testing in Practice.* Oxford: Oxford University Press.

Bailey, K. M. 1990. 'The use of diary studies in teacher education programmes' in J. C. Richards and D. Nunan (eds.). *Second Language Teacher Education.* Cambridge: Cambridge University Press.

Baker, C. In press. 'Survey methods in researching language and education' in K. King and N. Hornberger (eds.). *Encyclopedia of Language and Education*, Vol. 10, Research Methods. New York: Springer.

Balluerka, N., J. Gòmez, and **D. Hidalgo.** 2005. 'The controversy over null hypothesis significance testing revisited'. *Methodology* 1/2: 55–70.

Bartels, N. 2002. 'Professional preparation and action research: only for language teachers?' *TESOL Quarterly* 36/1: 71–9.

Bazeley, P. 2003. 'Computerized data analysis for mixed methods research' in A. Tashakkori and C. Teddlie (eds.). *Handbook of Mixed Methods in Social and Behavioral Research*. Thousands Oaks, Calif.: Sage.

Bell, L. 1999. 'Public and private meaning in diaries: Researching family and childcare' in A. Bryman and R. G. Burgess (eds.). *Qualitative Research*, Vol. 2. London: Sage.

Bettelheim, B. (ed.). 1987. *A Good Enough Parent*. London: Thames and Hudson.

Birnbaum, M. H. 2004. 'Human research and data collection via the Internet'. *Annual Review of Psychology* 55: 803–32.

Blatchford, P. 2005. 'A multi-method approach to the study of school class size differences'. *International Journal of Social Research Methodology* 8/3: 195–205.

Block, D. 2000. 'Problematizing interview data: voices in the mind's machine?' *TESOL Quarterly* 34/4: 757–63.

Bolger, N., A. Davis, and **E. Rafaeli.** 2003. 'Diary methods: Capturing life as it is lived'. *Annual Review of Psychology* 54: 579–616.

Brannen, J. 2005. *Mixed Methods Research: A Discussion Paper*. Southampton: ESRC National Centre for Research Methods. (Available online: http://www.ncrm.ac.uk/publications/documents/MethodsReviewPaperNCRM-005.pdf).

Brewer, J. and **A. Hunter.** 1989. *Multimethod Research : A Synthesis of Styles*. Newbury Park, Calif.: Sage.

Bringer, J. D., L. H. Johnston, and **C. H. Brackenridge.** 2004. 'Maximizing transparency in a doctoral thesis: The complexities of writing about the use of QSR*NVIVO within a grounded theory study'. *Qualitative Research* 4/2: 247–65.

Brown, J. D. 1988. *Understanding Research in Second Language Learning*. Cambridge: Cambridge University Press.

Brown, J. D. 2001. *Using Surveys in Language Programs*. Cambridge: Cambridge University Press.

Brown, J. D. 2004a. 'Research methods for applied linguistics: scope, characteristics, and standards' in A. Davis and C. Elder (eds.). *The Handbook of Applied Linguistics*. Oxford: Blackwell.

Brown, J. D. 2004b. 'Resources on quantitative/statistical research for applied linguists'. *Second Language Research* 20/4: 372–93.

Brown, J. D. 2005. *Testing in Language Programs: A Comprehensive Guide to English Language Assessment*. New York: McGraw Hill.

Brown, J. D. and **T. S. Rodgers.** 2002. *Doing Second Language Research*. Oxford: Oxford University Press.

Bryman, A. 2006. 'Integrating quantitative and qualitative research: How is it done?' *Qualitative Research* 6/1: 97–113.

Buchner, A., E. Erdfelder, and **F. Faul.** 1997. 'How to Use G*Power': http://www.psycho.uni-duesseldorf.de/aap/projects/gpower/ how_to_use_gpower.html.

Burns, A. 2005. 'Action research' in E. Hinkel (ed.). *Handbook of Research in Second Language Teaching and Learning*. Mahwah, N.J.: Lawrence Erlbaum.

Campbell, D. T. and **J. C. Stanley.** 1963. 'Experimental and quasi-experimental designs for research on teaching' in N. Gage (ed.). *Handbook of Research on Teaching*. Chicago: Rand McNally.

Campbell, D. T. and **S. W. Fiske.** 1959. 'Convergent and discriminant validation by the multitrait-multimethod matrix'. *Psychological Bulletin* 56: 81–105.

Caracelli, V. J. and **J. C. Greene.** 1993. 'Data analysis strategies for mixed-method evaluation designs'. *Educational Evaluation and Policy Analysis* 15/2: 195–207.

Carter, R., A. Goddard, D. Reah, K. Sanger, and **M. Bowring.** 2001. *Working with Texts: A Core Introduction to Language Analysis*. London: Routledge.

Cattell, R. B. 1966. 'The scree test for the number of factors'. *Multivariate Behavioral Research* 1: 245–76.

Chalhoub-Deville, M. 2006. 'Drawing the line: the generalizability and limitations of research in applied linguistics' in M. Chalhoub-Deville, C. A. Chapelle, and P. Duff (eds.). *Inference and Generalizability in Applied Linguistics: Multiple Perspectives.* Amsterdam: John Benjamins.

Chapelle, C. A. 1999. 'Validity in language assessment'. *Annual Review of Applied Linguistics* 19: 254–72.

Chapelle, C. A. and **P. Duff** (eds.). 2003. 'Some guidelines for conducting quantitative and qualitative research in TESOL'. *TESOL Quarterly* 37/1: 157–78.

Charmaz, K. 2005. 'Grounded theory in the 21st century: Applications for advancing social justice studies' in N. K. Denzin and Y. S. Lincoln (eds.). *The Sage Handbook of Qualitative Research*, 3rd Edition. Thousand Oaks, Calif.: Sage.

Chaudron, C. 1988. *Second Language Classrooms: Research on Teaching and Learning.* New York: Cambridge University Press.

Chaudron, C. 2003. 'Data collection in SLA research' in C. J. Doughty and M. H. Long (eds.). *The Handbook of Second Language Acquisition.* Oxford: Blackwell.

Cherryholmes, C. H. 1992. 'Notes on pragmatism and scientific realism'. *Educational Researcher* 21: 13–17.

Clarke, D. D. 2004. '"Structured judgement methods": The best of both worlds?' in Z. Todd, B. Nerlich, S. McKeown, and D. D. Clarke (eds.). *Mixing Methods in Psychology: The Integration of Qualitative and Quantitative Methods in Theory and Practice.* Hove, East Sussex: Psychology Press.

Cochran, W. G. 1977. *Sampling Techniques*, 3rd Edition. New York: Wiley.

Cohen, A. D. 1998. *Strategies in Learning and Using a Second Language.* Harlow: Longman.

Cohen, L., L. Manion, and **K. Morrison.** 2000. *Research Methods in Education*, 5th Edition. London: RoutledgeFalmer.

Collins, L. M. 2006. 'Analysis of longitudinal data: the integration of theoretical model, temporal design, and statistical model'. *Annual Review of Psychology* 57: 505–28.

Converse, J. M. and **S. Presser.** 1986. *Survey Questions: Handcrafting the Standardized Questionnaire.* Newbury Park, Calif.: Sage.

Cook, T. D. and **D. T. Campbell.** 1979. *Quasi-Experimentation: Design and Analysis Issues for Field Settings.* Chicago: Rand McNally.

Crabtree, B. F. and **W. L. Miller.** 1999. 'Using codes and code manuals' in B. F. Crabtree and W. L. Miller (eds.). *Doing Qualitative Research.* London: Sage.

Creswell, J. W. 1994. *Research Design: Qualitative and Quantitative Approaches.* Thousand Oaks, Calif.: Sage.

Creswell, J. W. 2003. *Research Design: Qualitative, Quantitative, and Mixed Methods Approaches.* Thousand Oaks, Calif.: Sage.

Creswell, J. W. 2005. *Planning, Conducting, and Evaluating Quantitative and Qualitative Research.* Upper Saddle River, N.J.: Pearson Prentice Hall.

Creswell, J. W., V. L. Plano Clark, M. L. Gutmann, and **W. E. Hanson.** 2003. 'Advanced mixed methods research designs' in A. Tashakkori and C. Teddlie (eds.). *Handbook of Mixed Methods in Social and Behavioral Research.* Thousands Oaks, Calif.: Sage.

Crookes, G. 1993. 'Action research for second language teachers: going beyond teacher research'. *Applied Linguistics* 14/2: 130–44.

Cryer, P. 2000. *The Research Student's Guide to Success*, 2nd Edition. Buckingham: Open University Press.

David, M. 2002. 'Problems of participation: the limits of action research'. *International Journal of Social Research Methodology* 5/1: 11–17.

Davidson, F. 1996. *Principles of Statistical Data Handling.* Thousand Oaks, Calif.: Sage.

Davies, K. A. 1995. 'Qualitative theory and methods in applied linguistics research'. *TESOL Quarterly* 29: 427-53.

Denzin, N. K. 1978. *The Research Act: A Theoretical Introduction to Sociological Methods.* Englewood Cliffs, N.J.: Prentice Hall.

Denzin, N. K. and **Y. S. Lincoln.** 2005a. 'Introduction: The discipline and practice of qualitative research' in N. K. Denzin and Y. S. Lincoln (eds.). *The Sage Handbook of Qualitative Research*, 3rd Edition. Thousand Oaks, Calif.: Sage.

Denzin, N. K. and **Y. S. Lincoln** (eds.). 2005b. *The Sage Handbook of Qualitative Research*, 3rd Edition. Thousand Oaks, Calif.: Sage.

Dey, I. 2004. 'Grounded theory' in C. Seale, G. Gobo, J. F. Gubrium, and D. Silverman (eds.). *Qualitative Research Practice*. London: Sage.

Dörnyei, Z. 2001. *Teaching and Researching Motivation*. Harlow: Longman.

Dörnyei, Z. 2003. *Questionnaires in Second Language Research: Construction, Administration, and Processing*. Mahwah, N.J.: Lawrence Erlbaum.

Dörnyei, Z. 2005. *The Psychology of the Language Learner: Individual Differences in Second Language Acquisition*. Mahwah, N.J.: Lawrence Erlbaum.

Dörnyei, Z. and **J. Kormos.** 2000. 'The role of individual and social variables in oral task performance'. *Language Teaching Research* 4: 275–300.

Dörnyei, Z. and **T. Murphey.** 2003. *Group Dynamics in the Language Classroom*. Cambridge: Cambridge University Press.

Dörnyei, Z., K. Csizér, and **N. Németh.** 2006. *Motivation, Language Attitudes and Globalisation: A Hungarian Perspective*. Clevedon, England: Multilingual Matters.

Dörnyei, Z., V. Durow, and **K. Zahran.** 2004. 'Individual differences and their effect on formulaic sequence acquisition' in N. Schmitt (ed.). *Formulaic Sequences*. Amsterdam: John Benjamins.

Duff, P. 2002. 'Research approaches in applied linguistics' in R. B. Kaplan (ed.). *The Oxford Handbook of Applied Linguistics*. New York: Oxford University Press.

Duff, P. 2006. 'Beyond generalizability: contextualization, complexity, and credibility in applied linguistics research' in M. Chalhoub-Deville, C. A. Chapelle, and P. Duff (eds.). *Inference and Generalizability in Applied Linguistics: Multiple Perspectives*. Amsterdam: John Benjamins.

Duff, P. In press. *Case Study Research in Applied Linguistics*. Mahwah, N.J.: Lawrence Erlbaum.

Duff, P. and **M. Early.** 1996. 'Problematics of classroom research across sociopolitical contexts' in J. Schachter and S. Gass (eds.). *Second Language Classroom Research: Issues and Opportunities*. Mahwah, N.J.: Lawrence Erlbaum.

Duranti, A. 1997. *Linguistic Anthropology*. Cambridge: Cambridge University Press.

Eisenhardt, K. M. 1989. 'Building theories from case study research'. *Academy of Management Review* 14/4: 532–50.

Ellis, R. and **G. Barkhuizen.** 2005. *Analysing Learner Language*. Oxford: Oxford University Press.

Ericsson, K. A. 2002. 'Towards a procedure for eliciting verbal expression of non-verbal experience without reactivity: interpreting the verbal overshadowing effect within the theoretical framework for protocol analysis'. *Applied Cognitive Psychology* 16: 981–7.

Ericsson, K. A. and **H. A. Simon.** 1987. 'Verbal reports on thinking' in C. Færch and G. Kasper (eds.). *Introspection in Second Language Research*. Clevedon, England: Multilingual Matters.

Erzberger, C. and **U. Kelle.** 2003. 'Making inferences in mixed methods: the rules of integration' in A. Tashakkori and C. Teddlie (eds.). *Handbook of Mixed Methods in Social and Behavioral Research*. Thousands Oaks, Calif.: Sage.

Færch, C. and **G. Kasper** (eds.). 1987. *Introspection in Second Language Research*. Clevedon, England: Multilingual Matters.

Fassinger, R. E. 2005. 'Paradigms, praxis, problems, and promise: Grounded theory in counseling psychology research'. *Journal of Counseling Psychology* 52/2: 156–66.

Firebaugh, G. 1997. *Analyzing Repeated Surveys*. Thousand Oaks, Calif.: Sage.

Fontana, A. and **J. H. Frey.** 2005. 'The interview' in N. K. Denzin and Y. S. Lincoln (eds.). *The Sage Handbook of Qualitative Research*, 3rd Edition. Thousand Oaks, Calif.: Sage.

Fox, J., C. Murray, and A. Warm. 2003. 'Conducting research using web-based questionnaires: practical, methodological, and ethical considerations'. *International Journal of Social Research Methodology* 6/2: 167–80.

Fulcher, G. and F. Davidson. 2006. *Language Testing and Assessment*. London: Routledge.

Gall, M. D., J. P. Gall, and W. R. Borg. 2007. *Educational Research: An Introduction*, 8th Edition. Boston, Mass.: Pearson.

Gardner, R. C. 1985. *Social Psychology and Second Language Learning: The Role of Attitudes and Motivation*. London: Edward Arnold.

Garratt, D. and Y. Li. 2005. 'The foundations of experimental/empirical research methods' in B. Somekh and C. Lewin (eds.). *Research Methods in the Social Sciences*. London: Sage.

Gass, S. M. and A. Mackey. 2000. *Stimulated Recall Methodology in Second Language Research*. Mahwah, N.J.: Lawrence Erlbaum.

Gherardi, S. and B. Turner. 1999. 'Real men don't collect soft data' in A. Bryman (ed.). *Qualitative Research*, Vol. 1. London: Sage.

Gibson, V. 1995. 'An analysis of the use of diaries as a data collection method'. *Nurse Researcher* 3/1: 66–73.

Gillham, B. 2000. *Developing a Questionnaire*. London: Continuum.

Glaser, B. G. 1992. *Basics of Grounded Theory Analysis: Emergence vs. Forcing*. Mill Valley, Calif.: Sociology Press.

Glaser, B. G. and A. L. Strauss. 1967. *The Discovery of Grounded Theory: Strategies for Qualitative Research*. New York: Aldine.

Glass, G. V. 1976. 'Primary, secondary, and meta-analysis of research'. *Educational Research* 5: 3–8.

Green, A. and J. Preston. 2005. 'Editorial: Speaking in tongues: Diversity in mixed methods research'. *International Journal of Social Research Methodology* 8/3: 167–71.

Greene, J. C. and V. J. Caracelli. 2003. 'Making paradigmatic sense of mixed methods practice' in A. Tashakkori and C. Teddlie (eds.). *Handbook of Mixed Methods in Social and Behavioral Research*. Thousands Oaks, Calif.: Sage.

Greene, J. C., H. Kreider, and E. Mayer. 2005. 'Combining qualitative and quantitative methods in social inquiry' in B. Somekh and C. Lewin (eds.). *Research Methods in the Social Sciences*. London: Sage.

Greene, J. C., V. J. Caracelli, and W. F. Graham. 1989. 'Toward a conceptual framework for mixed-method evaluation designs'. *Educational Evaluation and Policy Analysis* 11/3: 255–74.

Grissom, R. J. and J. J. Kim. 2005. *Effect Sizes for Research: A Broad Practical Approach*. Mahwah, N.J.: Lawrence Erlbaum.

Guilloteaux, M. J. and Z. Dörnyei. In press. 'Motivating language learners: a classroom-oriented investigation of the effects of motivational strategies on student motivation'. *TESOL Quarterly*.

Hammersley, M. and P. Atkinson. 1995. *Ethnography: Principles and Practice*, 2nd Edition. London: Routledge.

Hammond, C. 2005. 'The wider benefits of adult learning: An illustration of the advantages of multi-method research'. *International Journal of Social Research Methodology* 8/3: 239–55.

Hanson, W. E., J. W. Creswell, V. L. Plano Clark, K. S. Petska, and J. D. Creswell. 2005. 'Mixed methods research designs in counseling psychology'. *Journal of Counseling Psychology* 52/2: 224–35.

Harden, A. and J. Thomas. 2005. 'Methodological issues in combining diverse study types in systematic reviews'. *International Journal of Social Research Methodology* 8/3: 257–71.

Harklau, L. 2005. 'Ethnography and ethnographic research on second language teaching and learning' in E. Hinkel (ed.). *Handbook of Research in Second Language Teaching and Learning*. Mahwah, N.J.: Lawrence Erlbaum.

Hatch, E. M. and **A. Lazaraton.** 1991. *The Research Manual: Design and Statistics for Applied Linguistics*. New York: Newbury House.

Haverkamp, B. E. 2005. 'Ethical perspectives on qualitative research in applied psychology'. *Journal of Counseling Psychology* 52/2: 146–55.

Heinsman, D. T. and **W. R. Shadish.** 1996. 'Assignment methods in experimentation: when do nonrandomized experiments approximate answers from randomized experiments?' *Psychological Methods* 1/2: 154–69.

Hesse-Biber, N. S. and **P. Leavy.** 2006. *The Practice of Qualitative Research*. Thousand Oaks, Calif.: Sage.

Holliday, A. 2002. *Doing and Writing Qualitative Research*. London: Sage.

Holliday, A. 2004. 'Issues of validity in progressive paradigms of qualitative research'. *TESOL Quarterly* 38/4: 731–4.

Hornberger, N. 1994. 'Ethnography'. *TESOL Quarterly* 28/4: 688–90.

Hsieh, P., T. Acee, W-H. Chung, Y-P. Hsieh, H. Kim, G. D. Thomas, J. You, and **J. L. Levon.** 2005. 'Is educational intervention research on the decline?' *Journal of Educational Psychology* 97/4: 523–29.

Huberman, A. M. and **M. B. Miles.** 2002. 'Introduction' in A. M. Huberman and M. B. Miles (eds.). *The Qualitative Research Companion*. Thousand Oaks, Calif.: Sage.

Johnson, D. M. 1992. *Approaches to Research in Second Language Learning*. New York: Longman.

Johnson, R. B. and **L. Christensen.** 2004. *Education Research: Quantitative, Qualitative, and Mixed Approaches*, 2nd Edition. Boston: Allyn and Bacon.

Johnson, R. B. and **A. J. Onwuegbuzie.** 2004. 'Mixed methods research: a research paradigm whose time has come'. *Educational Researcher* 33/7: 14–26.

Johnson, R. B. and **L. A. Turner.** 2003. 'Data collection strategies in mixed methods research' in A. Tashakkori and C. Teddlie (eds.). *Handbook of Mixed Methods in Social and Behavioral Research*. Thousands Oaks, Calif.: Sage.

Jordan, G. 2004. *Theory Construction in Second Language Acquisition*. Amsterdam: John Benjamins.

Kasper, G. 1998. 'Analysing verbal protocols'. *TESOL Quarterly* 32: 358–62.

Keeves, J. P. 1994. 'Longitudinal research methods' in T. Husén and T. N. Postlethwaite (eds.). *The International Encyclopedia of Education*, Vol. 6, 2nd Edition. Oxford: Pergamon.

Kelle, U. 2004. 'Computer-assisted qualitative data analysis' in C. Seale, G. Gobo, J. F. Gubrium, and D. Silverman (eds.). *Qualitative Research Practice*. London: Sage.

Kemper, E. A., S. Stringfield, and **C. Teddlie.** 2003. 'Mixed methods sampling strategies in social research' in A. Tashakkori and C. Teddlie (eds.). *Handbook of Mixed Methods in Social and Behavioral Research*. Thousands Oaks, Calif.: Sage.

Kirk, J. and **M. L. Miller.** 1986. *Reliability and Validity in Qualitative Research*. Newbury Park, Calif.: Sage.

Kojic-Sabo, I. and **P. M. Lightbown.** 1999. 'Students' approaches to vocabulary learning and their relationship to success'. *Modern Language Journal* 83/2: 176–92.

Kormos, J. 1998. 'Verbal reports in L2 speech production research'. *TESOL Quarterly* 32: 353–58.

Krashen, S. 1978. 'Individual variation in the use of the monitor' in W. Ritchie (ed.). *Second Language Acquisition Research*. New York: Academic Press.

Kvale, S. 1996. *Interviews: An Introduction to Qualitative Research Interviewing*. Thousand Oaks, Calif.: Sage.

Kvale, S. 2006. 'Dominance through interviews and dialogues'. *Qualitative Inquiry* 12/3: 480–500.

Lapadat, J. C. 2000. 'Problematizing transcription: purpose, paradigm and quality'. *International Journal of Social Research Methodology* 3/3: 203–19.

Larzelere, R. E., B. R. Kuhn, and B. Johnson. 2004. 'The intervention selection bias: An underrecognized confound in intervention research'. *Psychological Bulletin* 130/2: 289–303.

Laurenceau, J-P. and N. Bolger. 2005. 'Using diary methods to study marital and family processes'. *Journal of Family Psychology* 19/1: 86–97.

Lazaraton, A. 2000. 'Current trends in research methodology and statistics in applied linguistics'. *TESOL Quarterly* 34/1: 175–81.

Lazaraton, A. 2003. 'Evaluative criteria for qualitative research in applied linguistics: Whose criteria and whose research?' *Modern Language Journal* 87/1: 1–12.

Lazaraton, A. 2005. 'Quantitative research methods' in E. Hinkel (ed.). *Handbook of Research in Second Language Teaching and Learning.* Mahwah, N.J.: Lawrence Erlbaum.

Leung, C., R. Harris, and B. Rampton. 2004. 'Living with inelegance in qualitative research on task-based learning' in B. Norton and K. Toohey (eds.). *Critical Pedagogies and Language Learning.* New York: Cambridge University Press.

Levy, P. S. and S. Lemeshow. 1999. *Sampling of Populations: Methods and Applications*, 3rd Edition. New York: John Wiley amd Sons.

Lewins, A. and C. Silver. In press. *Using Software in Qualitative Research: A Step-by-Step Guide.* London: Sage.

Lightbown, P. M. 2000. 'Classroom SLA research and second language teaching'. *Applied Linguistics* 21/4: 431–62.

Lincoln, Y. S. and E. G. Guba. 1985. *Naturalistic Enquiry.* Newbury Park, Calif.: Sage.

Liskin-Gasparro, J. E. (ed.). 2005. 'From the Associate Editor, MLJ Reviews: Presenting the Special Issue Reviews'. *Modern Language Journal* 89: 467–88.

Lynch, B. K. 2003. *Language Assessment and Programme Evaluation.* Edinburgh: Edinburgh University Press.

MacIntyre, P. D. and R. C. Gardner. 1994. 'The subtle effects of language anxiety on cognitive processing in the second language'. *Language Learning* 44: 283–305.

Mackey, A. and S. M. Gass. 2005. *Second Language Research: Methodology and Design.* Mahwah, N.J.: Lawrence Erlbaum.

Magnan, S. 2000. 'From the Editor: MLJ policies and practices: their evolution from 1916 to the year 2000'. *Modern Language Journal* 84/1: 1-4.

Magnan, S. 2006. 'From the Editor: the MLJ turns 90 in a digital age'. *Modern Language Journal* 90/1: 1–5.

Markee, N. 2001. 'Reopening the research agenda: respecifying motivation as a locally-occasioned phenomenon'. Paper presented at the annual conference of the American Association of Applied Linguistics (AAAL), St. Louis, Miss., USA.

Mason, J. 2006. 'Mixing methods in a qualitatively driven way'. *Qualitative Research* 6/1: 9–25.

Maxwell, J. A. 1992. 'Understanding the validity in qualitative research'. *Harvard Educational Review* 62/3: 279–300.

Maxwell, J. A. and D. M. Loomis. 2003. 'Mixed methods design: an alternative approach' in A. Tashakkori and C. Teddlie (eds.). *Handbook of Mixed Methods in Social and Behavioral Research.* Thousands Oaks, Calif.: Sage.

McCracken, G. 1988. *The Long Interview.* Newbury Park, Calif.: Sage.

McDonough, J. and S. McDonough. 1997. *Research Methods for English Language Teachers.* London: Arnold.

McDonough, K. 2006. 'Action research and the professional development of graduate teaching assistants'. *Modern Language Journal* 90/1: 33–47.

McKay, S. L. 2006. *Researching Second Language Classrooms.* Mahwah, N.J.: Lawrence Erlbaum.

McLeod, J. 2003. 'Why we interview now: reflexivity and perspective in a longitudinal study'. *International Journal of Social Research Methodology* 6/3: 201–11.

McNamara, T. 2006. 'Validity and values: inferences and generalizability in language testing' in M. Chalhoub-Deville, C. A. Chapelle, and P. Duff (eds.). *Inference and Generalizability in Applied Linguistics: Multiple Perspectives.* Amsterdam: John Benjamins.

Mellow, J. D., K. Reeder, and E. Forster. 1996. 'Using time-series research designs to investigate the effects of instruction on SLA'. *Studies in Second Language Acquisition* 18: 325–50.

Menard, S. 2002. *Longitudinal Research*, 2nd Edition. Thousand Oaks, Calif.: Sage.

Mertens, D. M. 2005. *Research and Evaluation in Education and Psychology: Integrating Diversity with Quantitative, Qualitative, and Mixed Methods*, 2nd Edition. Thousand Oaks, Calif.: Sage.

Miles, M. B. and A. M. Huberman. 1994. *Qualitative Data Analysis*, 2nd Edition. Thousand Oaks, Calif.: Sage.

Miller, W. L. and B. F. Crabtree. 1999. 'Depth interviewing' in B. F. Crabtree and W. L. Miller (eds.). *Doing Qualitative Research.* London: Sage.

Milroy, L. and M. Gordon. 2003. *Sociolinguistics: Method and Interpretation.* Oxford: Blackwell.

Moran-Ellis, J., V. D. Alexander, A. Cronin, M. Dickinson, J. Fielding, J. Sleney, and H. Thomas. 2006. 'Triangulation and integration: Processes, claims and implications'. *Qualitative Research* 6/1: 45–59.

Morrow, S. L. 2005. 'Quality and trustworthiness in qualitative research in counseling psychology'. *Journal of Counseling Psychology* 52/2: 250–60.

Morse, J. M. and L. Richards. 2002. *Readme First for a User's Guide to Qualitative Research.* Thousand Oaks, Calif.: Sage.

Moser, C. A. and G. Kalton. 1971. *Survey Methods in Social Investigation.* London: Heinemann.

Moskowitz, G. 1971. 'Interaction analysis: A new modern language for supervisors'. *Foreign Language Annals* 5: 211–21.

Neale, B. and J. Flowerdew 2003. 'Time, texture and childhood: the contours of longitudinal qualitative research'. *International Journal of Social Research Methodology* 6/3: 189-99.

Norris, J. and L. Ortega. 2000. 'Effectiveness of L2 instruction: A research synthesis and quantitative meta-analysis'. *Language Learning* 50/3: 417–528.

Norris, J. and L. Ortega. 2003. 'Defining and measuring SLA' in C. J. Doughty and M. H. Long (eds.). *The Handbook of Second Language Acquisition.* Oxford: Blackwell.

Norton Peirce, B. 1995. 'The theory of methodology in qualitative research'. *TESOL Quarterly* 29/3: 569–76.

Nunan, D. 1992. *Research Methods in Language Learning.* Cambridge: Cambridge University Press.

Nunan, D. 2005. 'Classroom research' in E. Hinkel (ed.). *Handbook of Research in Second Language Teaching and Learning.* Mahwah, N.J.: Lawrence Erlbaum.

O'Connor, A. and J. Sharkey. 2004. 'Defining the process of teacher-researcher collaboration'. *TESOL Quarterly* 38/2: 335–9.

Onwuegbuzie, A. J. and C. Teddlie. 2003. 'A framework for analyzing data in mixed methods research' in A. Tashakkori and C. Teddlie (eds.). *Handbook of Mixed Methods in Social and Behavioral Research.* Thousands Oaks, Calif.: Sage.

Onwuegbuzie, A. J. and N. L. Leech. 2005. 'On becoming a pragmatic researcher: the importance of combining quantitative and qualitative research methodologies'. *International Journal of Social Research Methodology* 8/5: 375–87.

Oppenheim, A. N. 1992. *Questionnaire Design, Interviewing and Attitude Measurement*, New Edition. London: Pinter.

Ortega, L. 2005. 'Methodology, epistemology, and ethics in instructed SLA research: An introduction'. *Modern Language Journal* 89/3: 317–27.

Ortega, L. and **G. Iberri-Shea.** 2005. 'Longitudinal research in second language acquisition: Recent trends and future directions'. *Annual Review of Applied Linguistics* 25: 26–45.

Pallant, J. 2005. *SPSS Survival Manual*, 2nd Edition. Maidenhead, England: Open University Press and McGraw-Hill Education.

Patton, M. Q. 2002. *Qualitative Research and Evaluation Methods*, 3rd Edition. Thousand Oaks, Calif.: Sage.

Pavlenko, A. 2002. 'Poststructuralist approaches to the study of social factors in second language learning and use' in V. Cook (ed.). *Portraits of the L2 User.* Clevedon, England: Multilingual Matters.

Pica, T. 2005. 'Classroom learning, teaching, and research: a task-based perspective'. *Modern Language Journal* 89/3: 339–52.

Polio, C. G. 1996. 'Issues and problems in reporting classroom research' in J. Schachter and S. Gass (eds.). *Second Language Classroom Research: Issues and Opportunities.* Mahwah, N.J.: Lawrence Erlbaum.

Polkinghorne, D. E. 2005. 'Language and meaning: Data collection in qualitative research'. *Journal of Counseling Psychology* 52/2: 137–45.

Punch, K. F. 2005. *Introduction to Social Research*, 2nd Edition. Thousand Oaks, Calif.: Sage.

Rampton, B. 1995. *Crossing: Language and Ethnicity among Adolescents.* Harlow: Longman.

Richards, K. 2003. *Qualitative Inquiry in TESOL.* Basingstoke: Palgrave Macmillan.

Richards, L. 2005. *Handling Qualitative Data: A Practical Guide.* London: Sage.

Richardson, L. and **E. A. St. Pierre.** 2005. 'Writing: a method of inquiry' in N. K. Denzin and Y. S. Lincoln (eds.). *The Sage Handbook of Qualitative Research*, 3rd Edition. Thousand Oaks, Calif.: Sage.

Roberts, C. 1997. 'Transcribing talk: issues of representation'. *TESOL Quarterly* 31/1: 167–72.

Roberts, C., M. Byram, A. Barro, S. Jordan, and **B. Street.** 2001. *Language Learners as Ethnographers.* Clevedon, England: Multilingual Matters.

Robson, C. 1993. *Real World Research: A Resource for Social Scientists and Practitioner-Researchers.* Oxford: Blackwell.

Robson, C. 2002. *Real World Research: A Resource for Social Scientists and Practitioner-Researchers*, 2nd Edition. Oxford: Blackwell.

Rossiter, M. J. 2001. 'The challenges of classroom-based SLA research'. *Applied Language Learning* 12/1: 31–44.

Rossman, G. B. and **B. L. Wilson.** 1985. 'Numbers and words: combining quantitative and qualitative methods in a single large-scale evaluation study'. *Evaluation Review* 9/5: 627–43.

Rounds, P. L. 1996. 'The classroom-based researcher as fieldworker: strangers in a strange land' in J. Schachter and S. Gass (eds.). *Second Language Classroom Research: Issues and Opportunities.* Mahwah, N.J.: Lawrence Erlbaum.

Rubio, O. G. 1997. 'Ethnographic interview methods in researching language and education' in N. Hornberger and D. Corson (eds.). *Encyclopedia of Language and Education*, Vol. 8, Research methods in language and education. Dordrecht, Netherlands: Kluwer.

Ruspini, E. 2002. *Introduction to Longitudinal Research.* London: Routledge.

Ryen, A. 2004. 'Ethical issues' in C. Seale, G. Gobo, J. F. Gubrium, and D. Silverman (eds.). *Qualitative Research Practice.* London: Sage.

Sandelowski, M. 2003. 'Tables of tableaux? The challenges of writing and reading mixed methods studies' in A. Tashakkori and C. Teddlie (eds.). *Handbook of Mixed Methods in Social and Behavioral Research.* Thousands Oaks, Calif.: Sage.

Sandelowski, M. and **J. Barroso.** 2002. 'Reading qualitative studies'. *International Journal of Qualitative Methods (online journal)* 1/1: Article 5.

Schachter, J. and **S. Gass.** 1996. 'Introduction' in J. Schachter and S. Gass (eds.). *Second Language Classroom Research: Issues and Opportunities.* Mahwah, N.J.: Lawrence Erlbaum.

Schieffelin, B. and **E. Ochs** (eds.). 1986. *Language Socialization across Cultures.* New York: Cambridge University Press.

Schiffrin, D. 1994. *Approaches to Discourse.* Oxford: Blackwell.

Schiffrin, D., D. Tannen, and **H. E. Hamilton** (eds.). 2003. *The Handbook of Discourse Analysis.* Oxford: Blackwell.

Schmidt, R. and **S. F. N. Frota.** 1986. 'Developing basic conversational ability in a second language: a case study of an adult learner of Portuguese' in R. Day (ed.), *Talking to Learn: A Case Study of an Adult Learner of Portuguese.* Rowley, Mass.: Newbury House.

Schwandt, T. A. 2000. 'Three epistemological stances for qualitative inquiry' in N. K. Denzin and Y. S. Lincoln (eds.). *Handbook of Qualitative Research,* 2nd Edition. Thousand Oaks, Calif.: Sage.

Seale, C., G. Gobo, J. F. Gubrium, and **D. Silverman.** 2004. 'Introduction: Inside qualitative research' in C. Seale, G. Gobo, J. F. Gubrium, and D. Silverman (eds.). *Qualitative Research Practice.* London: Sage.

Seidman, I. 1998. *Interviewing as Qualitative Research: A Guide for Researchers in Education and the Social Sciences,* 2nd Edition. New York: Teachers College Press.

Seliger, H. W. and **E. Shohamy.** 1989. *Second Language Research Methods.* Oxford: Oxford University Press.

Séror, J. 2005. 'Computers and qualitative data analysis: Paper, pens, and highlighters vs. screen, mouse, and keyboard'. *TESOL Quarterly* 39/2: 321–8.

Shavelson, R. J. and **L. Towne.** 2002. *Scientific Research in Education.* Washington, D.C.: National Academies Press.

Shohamy, E. 2004. 'Reflections on research guidelines, categories, and responsibility'. *TESOL Quarterly* 38/4: 728–31.

Silverman, D. 1997. 'The logics of qualitative research' in G. Miller and R. Dingwall (eds.). *Context and Method in Qualitative Research.* London: Sage.

Silverman, D. 2001. *Interpreting Qualitative Data: Methods for Analysing Talk, Text and Interaction,* 2nd Edition. London: Sage.

Silverman, D. 2005. *Doing Qualitative Research,* 2nd Edition. London: Sage.

Skehan, P. 1989. *Individual Differences in Second Language Learning.* London: Edward Arnold.

Smith, G. T. 2005. 'On construct validity: Issues of method and measurement'. *Psychological Assessment* 17/4: 396–408.

Smithson, J. 2000. 'Using and analysing focus groups: limitations and possibilities'. *International Journal of Social Research Methodology* 3/2: 103–19.

Spada, N. 2005. 'Conditions and challenges in developing school-based SLA research programs'. *Modern Language Journal* 89/3: 328–38.

Spada, N. and **M. Fröhlich.** 1995. *The Communicative Orientation of Language Teaching Observation Scheme: Coding Conventions and Applications.* Sydney: Macquarie University, National Centre for English Language Teaching and Research.

Spada, N., L. Ranta, and **P. M. Lightbown.** 1996. 'Working with teachers in second language acquisition research' in J. Schachter and S. Gass (eds.). *Second Language Classroom Research: Issues and Opportunities.* Mahwah, N.J.: Lawrence Erlbaum.

Stake, R. E. 1995. *The Art of Case Study Research.* Thousand Oaks, Calif.: Sage.

Stake, R. E. 2005. 'Qualitative case studies' in N. K. Denzin and Y. S. Lincoln (eds.). *The Sage Handbook of Qualitative Research,* 3rd Edition. Thousand Oaks, Calif.: Sage.

Stratman, J. F. and **L. Hamp-Lyons.** 1994. 'Reactivity in concurrent think-aloud protocols' in P. Smagorinsky (ed.). *Speaking About Writing: Reflections on Research Methodology.* Thousand Oaks, Calif.: Sage.

Strauss, A. L. and **J. Corbin.** 1998. *Basics of Qualitative Research: Techniques and Procedures for Developing Grounded Theory*, 2nd Edition. Thousand Oaks, Calif.: Sage.

Sudman, S. and **N. M. Bradburn.** 1983. *Asking Questions.* San Francisco, Calif.: Jossey-Bass.

Swain, M. 2006. 'Verbal protocols: what does it mean for research to use speaking as a data collection tool?' in M. Chalhoub-Deville, C. A. Chapelle, and P. Duff (eds.). *Inference and Generalizability in Applied Linguistics: Multiple Perspectives.* Amsterdam: John Benjamins.

Tabachnick, B. G. and **L. S. Fidell.** 2001. *Using Multivariate Statistics*, 4th Edition. Needham Heights, Mass.: Allyn and Bacon.

Taris, T. 2000. *A Primer in Longitudinal Data Analysis.* Thousand Oaks: Sage.

Tashakkori, A. and **C. Teddlie.** 1998. *Mixed Methodology: Combining Qualitative and Quantitative Approaches.* Thousand Oaks, Calif.: Sage.

Tashakkori, A. and **C. Teddlie** (eds.). 2003a. *Handbook of Mixed Methods in Social and Behavioral Research.* Thousands Oaks, Calif.: Sage.

Tashakkori, A. and **C. Teddlie.** 2003b. 'Issues and dilemmas in teaching research methods courses in social and behavioral sciences: US perspective'. *International Journal of Social Research Methodology* 6/1: 61–77.

Tashakkori, A. and **C. Teddlie.** 2003c. 'The past and future of mixed methods research: From data triangulation to mixed model designs' in A. Tashakkori and C. Teddlie (eds.). *Handbook of Mixed Methods in Social and Behavioral Research.* Thousands Oaks, Calif.: Sage.

Teddlie, C. and **A. Tashakkori.** 2003. 'Major issues and controversies in the use of mixed methods in the social and behavioral sciences' in A. Tashakkori and C. Teddlie (eds.). *Handbook of Mixed Methods in Social and Behavioral Research.* Thousands Oaks, Calif.: Sage.

Thomson, R. and **J. Holland.** 2003. 'Hindsight, foresight and insight: the challenges of longitudinal qualitative research'. *International Journal of Social Research Methodology* 6/3: 233–44.

Thomson, R., L. Plumridge, and **J. Holland.** 2003. 'Longitudinal qualitative research: A developing methodology'. *International Journal of Social Research Methodology* 6/3: 185–7.

Todd, Z., B. Nerlich, and **S. McKeown,** 2004. 'Introduction' in Z. Todd, B. Nerlich, S. McKeown, and D. D. Clarke (eds.). *Mixing Methods in Psychology: The Integration of Qualitative and Quantitative Methods in Theory and Practice.* Hove, East Sussex: Psychology Press.

Toohey, K. In press. 'Ethnography and language education' in K. King and N. Hornberger (eds.). *Encyclopedia of Language and Education*, Vol. 10, Research methods. New York: Springer.

Tseng, W-T., Z. Dörnyei, and **N. Schmitt.** 2006. 'A new approach to assessing strategic learning: The case of self-regulation in vocabulary acquisition'. *Applied Linguistics* 27/1: 78–102.

Turner, J. C. and **D. K. Meyer.** 2000. 'Studying and understanding the instructional contexts of classrooms: Using our past to forge our future'. *Educational Psychologist* 35/2: 69–85.

van Eerde, W., D. Holman, and **P. Totterdell.** 2005. 'Special section editorial'. *Journal of Occupational and Organizational Psychology* 78: 151–4.

van Lier, L. 1988. *The Classroom and the Language Learner: Ethnography and Second Language Research.* London: Longman.

van Lier, L. 2005. 'Case study' in E. Hinkel (ed.). *Handbook of Research in Second Language Teaching and Learning.* Mahwah, N.J.: Lawrence Erlbaum.

Verschuren, P. J. M. 2003. 'Case study as a research strategy: some ambiguities and opportunities'. *International Journal of Social Research Methodology* 6/2: 121–39.

Watson-Gegeo, K. A. 1988. 'Ethnography in ESL: defining the essentials'. *TESOL Quarterly* 22: 575–92.

Watson-Gegeo, K. A. 1997. 'Classroom ethnography' in N. Hornberger and D. Corson (eds.). *Encyclopedia of Language and Education*, Vol. 8, Research methods in language and education. Dordrecht, Netherlands: Kluwer.

Widdowson, H. G. 2004. *Text, Context, Pretext: Critical Issues in Discourse Analysis.* Oxford: Blackwell.

Wiles, R., S. Heath, G. Crow, and **V. Charles.** 2005. *Informed Consent in Social Research: A Literature Review.* Southampton: ESRC National Centre for Research Methods.

Wilkinson, L. and **TFSI.** 1999. 'Statistical methods in psychology journals: Guidelines and explanations'. *American Psychologist* 54/8: 594–604.

Winnicott, D. W. 1965. *The Maturational Process and the Facilitating Environment.* London: Hogarth Press.

Winter, G. 2000. 'A comparative discussion of the notion of "validity" in qualitative and quantitative research'. *Qualitative Report* 4/3 and 4/4.

Wolcott, H. F. 1994. *Transforming Qualitative Data: Description, Analysis, and Interpretation.* Thousand Oaks, Calif.: Sage.

Wong-Fillmore, L. 1979. 'Individual differences in second language acquisition' in C. J. Fillmore, W-S. Y. Wang, and D. Kempler (eds.). *Individual Differences in Language Ability and Language Behavior.* New York: Academic Press.

Wragg, E. C. 1999. *Introduction to Classroom Observation*, 2nd Edition. London: RoutledgeFalmer.

Wray, A., K. Trott, and **A. Bloomer.** 1998. *Projects in Linguistics: A Practical Guide to Researching Language.* London: Arnold.

Yates, L. 2003. 'Interpretive claims and methodological warrant in small-number qualitative, longitudinal research'. *International Journal of Social Research Methodology* 6/3: 223–32.

Zuengler, J. and **J. Mori.** 2002. 'Microanalyses of classroom discourse: a critical consideration of method—Introduction to the Special Issue'. *Applied Linguistics* 22/3: 283–8.

Zuengler, J., C. Ford, and **C. Fassnacht.** 1998. 'Analyst eyes and camera eyes: theoretical and technological considerations in "seeing" the details of classroom interaction'. Albany, N.Y.: School of Education, University at Albany.

Index

Abbuhl, R. 78
Abrams, D. 168
accelerated longitudinal design 85
Acee, T. 119
acquiescence bias 205
action research 177, 191–194
administrative panel *see* linked panel
Adolphs, S. 19, 247
AERA [American Educational Research Association] 50, 51, 67, 69, 70, 277
Aiken, L. 106
Alderson, C. J. 19
Alexander, V. D. 166
Allwright, D. 178, 179, 181, 186, 192, 193
Altrichter, H. 160, 161
AMOS 239
analysis of covariance *see* ANCOVA
analysis of variance *see* ANOVA
ANCOVA 118, 222–223, 224
anecdotalism 56
anonymity 68, 77
ANOVA 118, 215, 218–222
APA [American Psychological Association] 51, 211, 212, 278, 279, 280, 282
APA format/style 214, 279–280, 290, 294–295, 303
ARIMA analysis 91
Arksey, H. 249, 258
Atkinson, P. 11, 33, 129, 160, 265
attrition 53, 82–83
audit trail 60, 265–266, 296
authenticity 49
axial coding 261

Bachman, L. F. 19, 21, 34, 50, 51, 52
Bacon, F. 31
Bailey, K. 156, 178, 179, 181, 186, 193
Baker, C. 102
Balluerka, N. 212
Barkhuizen, G. 19, 246, 261
Barro, A. 130
Barroso, J. 54
Bartels, N. 191
Bazeley, P. 26, 264, 268, 273
Bell, L. 156
bell-shaped curve 27–28
Bettelheim, B. 10
Birnbaum, M. H. 121, 122
Blatchford, P. 171
Block, D. 134
Bloomer, A. 22
Boas, F. 36
Bolger, N. 156, 157, 158, 159
Borg, W. R. 73, 292
Bowring, M. 19
boxplot 203, 204
Brackenridge, C. H. 296
Bradburn, N. M. 75
Brannen, J. 35, 45, 167, 301
Brewer, J. 44, 63
Bringer, J. D. 296
Brown, J. D. 15, 19, 20, 21, 68, 101, 198, 202
Bryman, A. 169
Buchner, A. 100
Burns, A. 191, 193, 194
Byram, M. 130

Campbell, D. T. 43, 50, 52, 116, 117, 119, 165
CAQDAS *see* computer-aided qualitative data analysis
Caracelli, V. J. 164, 168, 268, 272, 313
Carter, R. 19
case study 36, 124, 130, 151–155
categorical data *see* nominal data
Cattell, R. B. 235
Cattell's scree test *see* scree test
census 96
chain sampling *see* snowball sampling
Chalhoub-Deville, M. 50
Chapelle, C. A. 51, 131
Charles, V. 66, 69
Charmaz, K. 258, 259, 262
chart 287–288
Chaudron, C. 19, 180, 181, 187
Cheeryholmes, C. H. 44
Chi-square test 228–230
Chicago School 36
Christensen, L. 22, 64, 65, 69, 70, 71, 73, 85, 86, 116, 118, 163, 169, 173, 174, 292, 294, 301, 302, 304

Chung, W.-H. 119
Clarke, D. D. 120
classroom observation 176, 178–186
classroom research 40, 176–194
cluster analysis 231, 237–238, 269
cluster sampling 98
Cochran, W. G. 98
code, coding 26, 57, 121, 180, 183, 186, 199–200, 245, 246, 250–254, 260–262, 263, 265, 270, 315
codebook 200
coding frame 60, 199–200, 201
coding trap 266
Cohen, A. D. 148, 151
Cohen, L. 65, 70, 71, 78, 84, 97, 132, 179
cohort effect 85
cohort study 82, 85
collective case study *see* multiple case study
Collins, L. M. 85, 90
COLT [Communication Orientation of Language Teaching] 181–182, 183
computer-aided qualitative data analysis 262–267, 296
Comte, A. 31
conceptual research 16
concurrent design 172
confidence interval 207, 210, 211
confidentiality 68–70
confirmability 57
confirmatory analysis/technique 239
Conklin, K. 11
consent *see* informed consent
construct validity 51–52
constructivist 9
content analysis 24, 245–257
content validity 51
control group 116
convenience sampling 98–99, 122, 129
conversation analysis 19
Converse, J. M. 103
Cook, T. D. 52, 116, 117
Copernicus, N. 31
Corbin, J. 43, 259, 260, 262
corpus linguistics 19
correlation 31, 223–227
correlation matrix 226–227
Crabtree, B. F. 134, 142, 246, 253, 254
credibility 49, 57
Creswell, J. D. 43, 174, 303
Creswell, J. W. 22, 42, 43, 44, 60, 70, 74, 168, 170, 171, 174, 260, 261, 279, 303, 309, 311
criterion sampling 127, 315
criterion validity 51
critical case sampling 128, 153
Cronbach, L. J. 206
Cronbach alpha 51, 206–207
Crookes, G. 193
cross-sectional research 78, 89–90
Crow, G. 66, 69
Cryer, P. 161
Csizér, K. 231
curvilinear relationship 223, 225

data cleaning 199, 202–203
data display 254, 256, 257
data merging 271
data screening 199, 202–203
data transformation 269–271
David, M. 191
Davidson, F. 19, 76, 198
Davies, K. A. 24, 290
Davis, A. 156, 157, 158, 159
DCT *see* discourse completion task
degree of freedom 217
Denzin, N. K. 22, 35, 43, 165, 310
dependability 49, 57
dependent variable 218, 222
Descartes, R. 31
descriptive statistics 207, 209
descriptive validity 68
design validity 63
deviant case sampling *see* extreme case sampling
Dewaele, J.-M. 11
Dey, I. 258
diagram *see* chart
diary study 86, 124, 156–159, 178
dimensional sampling 98
discourse analysis 19
discourse completion task [DCT] 103
Dickinson, M. 166
double-barrelled questions 109
Duff, P. 10, 11, 17, 20, 32, 36, 40, 41, 59, 62, 64, 66, 128, 130, 131, 151, 152, 153, 154, 155, 156, 160, 172, 174, 177, 184, 187, 188, 189, 190, 246, 247, 249, 255, 298, 299
Duranti, A. 139
Durow, V. 273

Early, M. 177, 187, 188, 189, 190
effect size 207, 210, 211–212, 217, 221, 224, 240
eigenvalue 234
Eisenhardt, K. M. 42, 127

Ellis, R. 19, 246, 261
emergent 37, 39, 131, 138, 253
empathetic interviewing 141
empirical research 16
empiricist 9
EQS 239
Erdfelder, E. 100
Ericsson, K. A. 147, 148, 149, 151
Erzberger, C. 43, 164, 165, 310
ethics *see* research ethics
ethnographic interview 135
ethnography 36, 124, 129–133, 178
evaluative validity 59
event sampling 180
experiment, experimental design/method 31, 33, 81, 85, 95, 115–121, 155, 173
exploratory practice 193
exploratory research 39, 171, 308
external generalizability 48
external validity 43, 46, 49, 50, 52–54, 57, 120
extreme case analysis 272
extreme case sampling 128, 153, 172

factor analysis 231, 233–236, 268
factor loading 233, 235
Færch, C. 148, 149
Fassinger, R. E. 259, 260, 261
Fassnacht, C. 184, 185
Faul, F. 100
Fidell, L. S. 23, 209
field notes 130, 132, 160
Fielding, J. 166
figure 287–288
Firebaugh, G. 82
Fisher, R. A. 31
Fiske, S. W. 43, 165
Flanders, N. A. 181
Flanders' Interaction Analysis Categories [FIAC] scheme 178, 181
Flint [Foreign Language Interaction Analysis] 181
Flowerdew, J. 80, 86, 88
focus group interview 124, 134, 144–146
follow-up study 82
Fontana, A. 141
Ford, C. 184, 185
Forster, E. 53, 80, 81, 90
Fox, J. 121, 122
Frey, J. H. 141
Fröhlich, M. 181, 182
Frota, S. F. N. 157, 160
Fulcher, G. 19

gain scores 118
Galilei, G. 31
Gall, J. P. 73, 292
Gall, M. D. 73, 292
Galton, F. 31
Gardner, R. C. 184, 206, 240
Garratt, D. 31
Gass, S. M. 21, 64, 66, 73, 147, 148, 149, 150, 151, 176, 177, 180, 181, 184, 186
generalizability, generalizable 34, 46, 50, 58–59, 61, 95, 153–154, 212–213
Gherardi, S. 40, 280
Gibson, V. 157, 158, 159
Gillham, B. 41
Glaser, B. G. 36, 37, 39, 126, 127, 259, 260, 261
Glass, G. V. 240, 241
Gobo, G. 36, 41, 55, 72
Goddard, A. 19
Gómez, J. 212
goodness of fit measure 239
Gordon, M. 22, 96
Graham, W. F. 164
Green, A. 268
Greene, J. C. 164, 166, 168, 175, 268, 269, 272, 313
Grissom, R. J. 212
grounded theory 36, 242, 257–262
groupthink 145
Guba, E. G. 49, 57–58
Gubrium, J. F. 36, 41, 55, 72
Guilloteaux, M. J. 181, 183
Gutmann, M. L. 41, 168, 170, 171

Hamilton, H. E. 19
Hammersley, M. 11, 33, 129, 160, 265
Hammond, C. 164
Hamp-Lyons, L. 151
Han, Z.-H. 154
Hanson, W. E. 41, 43, 168, 170, 171, 174, 303
Harden, A. 166
Harklau, L. 130, 133
Harris, R. 242
Hatch, E. M. 15, 21, 31, 100, 154, 159, 307
Haverkamp, B. E. 38, 67
Hawthorne effect 53, 83, 120
Heath, S. 66, 69
Heinsman, D. T. 117
Hesse-Biber, N. S. 46, 64, 243
Hidalgo, D. 212
high-inference category 180–181
histogram 203
Hogg, M. A. 168

Holland, J. 83, 86, 87
Holliday, A. 22, 35, 60, 277, 293
Holly, M. L. 160, 161
Holman, D. 158
homogeneous sampling 127
Hornberger, N. 133
Hsieh, P. 119
Hsieh, Y.-P. 119
HTML 122
Huberman, A. M. 18, 25, 29, 38, 39, 41, 42, 56, 63, 124, 129, 242, 244, 245, 254, 256, 264, 269, 270, 291, 296, 313
Hume, D. 31
Hunter, A. 44, 63
Hypertext markup language *see* HTML
hypothesis 17, 31, 72–74, 120

Iberri-Shea, G. 80, 81, 88, 90, 120
in vivo coding 251
independent variable 218
inferential statistics 81, 207, 209
informed consent 69–71
insider meaning/account 38, 131, 133, 157, 316
instrumental case study 152
internal generalizability 58
internal validity 43, 50, 52–54, 57, 120
Internet 95, 121–123
interpretist, interpretive 9, 38
interpretive validity 58
interval data 208, 227
interview 24, 124, 130, 134–144, 170–173, 178
interview guide 102, 136–138, 144
interview protocol *see* interview guide
interview schedule *see* interview guide
intrinsic case study 152
introspection 124, 134, 147–151
introspective methods *see* introspection
IRB [Institutional Review Board] 66
item analysis 113
item pool 112
iteration/iterative 126–127, 243–244, 272

Johnson, B. 120
Johnson, D. M. 21
Johnson, R. B. 22, 64, 65, 69, 70, 71, 73, 85, 86, 116, 118, 163, 167, 168, 169, 170, 173, 174, 292, 294, 301, 302, 304
Johnston, L. H. 296
Jordan, G. 31
Jordan, S. 130
journal 76, 124, 130, 159–162

Kalton, G. 115
Kasper, G. 148, 149, 150
Keeves, J. P. 84
Kelle, U. 43, 164, 165, 263, 310
Kemper, E. A. 99
Kepler, J. 31
Kim, H. 119
Kim, J. J. 212
Kirk, J. 56, 57
Knight, P. 249, 258
Kojic-Sabo, I. 237
Kolmogorov-Smirnov test 208
Kormos, J. 11, 148, 151, 175, 189
Krashen, S. 271
Kreider, H. 166, 175, 269
Kruskal-Wallis test 230
Kubanyiova, M. 11, 250
Kuhn, B. R. 120
Kvale, S. 134, 141, 143, 290

Lam, W. S. E. 154
language savant 153
Lapadat, J. C. 247, 248
Larzelere, R. E. 120
latent growth curved model 91
latent level analysis 246
Laurenceau, J.-P. 156
Lazaraton, A. 15, 21, 31, 32, 44, 100, 159, 213, 215, 285, 307, 312, 313
Lazarsfeld, P. 82
Leavy, P. 46, 64, 243
Leech, N. L. 163, 270
Lemeshow, S. 98
Leung, C. 242
Levin, K. 191
Levon, J. L. 119
Levy, P. S. 98
Lewins, A. 264
Li, Y. 31
Lightbown, P. M. 11, 178, 189, 193, 237
Likert, R. 103
Likert scale 105, 202
Lincoln, Y. S. 22, 35, 49, 57–58
linked panel 85
listwise deletion 205
LISREL 239
literature review 281–282, 295, 303–304
log/logbook *see* research log
longitudinal research 40, 62, 78–91, 154, 173
Loomis, D. M. 43, 46, 168
low-inference category 180
Lynch, B. K. 50, 51, 55, 251, 254

MacIntyre, P. D. 184
Mackey, A. 21, 64, 66, 73, 78, 147, 148, 149, 150, 151, 176, 180, 181, 184, 186
Magnan, S. 36, 44, 292
Malinowski, B. 36
manifest level analysis 245
Manion, L. 65, 70, 71, 78, 84, 97, 132, 179
Mann-Whitney U test 230
Markee, N. 19
Mason, J. 46
maturation 53
maximum variation sampling 128
Maxwell, J. A. 43, 46, 49, 58–59, 168
Mayer, E. 166, 175, 269
McCracken, G. 137, 140, 164
McDonough, J. 21, 120, 156
McDonough, K. 194
McDonough, S. 21, 120, 156
McKay, S. L. 16, 22, 154, 285, 286
McKeown, S. 166, 301, 309
McLeod, J. 86
McNamara, T. 52
mean 209, 214
measurement validity 50, 51–52
median 214
Mellow, J. D. 53, 80, 81, 90
member checking 58, 60
memo, memoing 245, 254–255, 257, 315
Menard, S. 79, 89, 118
Mertens, D. M. 164
meta-analysis 231, 240–241
'Method' section 283–284, 295–297, 304
Meyer, D. K. 186, 187
Miles, M. B. 18, 25, 29, 38, 39, 41, 42, 56, 63, 124, 129, 242, 244, 245, 253, 256, 264, 269, 270, 291, 296, 313
Miller, M. L. 56, 57
Miller, W. L. 134, 142, 246, 253, 254
Milroy, L. 22, 96
missing data 204–205
mode 214
MOLT [Motivation Orientation in Language Teaching] 183
Moran-Ellis, J. 166
Mori, J. 178
Morrison, K. 65, 70, 71, 78, 84, 97, 132, 179
Morrow, S. L. 57, 294, 295, 296, 297
Morse, J. M. 22, 46, 54, 56, 57, 77, 132, 163, 179, 250, 257, 297, 308, 312
mortality 53
Moser, C. A. 115
Moskowitz, G. 181
multi-item scale 103–104, 113, 206
multi-level analysis 45
multiple case study 152
multiple-choice items 106
multiple correlation 224
multiple level analysis 273
multitrait-multimethod research 42, 43
Murison-Bowie, S. 11
Murphey, T. 145
Murphy's Law 139, 187, 190
Murray, C. 121, 122

NCME [National Council on Measurement in Education] 51
Neale, B. 80, 86, 88
Németh, N. 231
Nerlich, B. 166, 301, 309
Newton, I. 31
Neyman, J. 31
nominal data 207, 227
non-parametric procedures/tests 208, 227–230
nonparticipant observation 130, 132, 133, 179
non-probability sampling 98–99, 122.
normal distribution 27–28, 100, 207, 208–209
Norris, J. 19, 240
Norton (Pierce), B. 154, 312
numerical rating scale *see* rating scale
Nunan, D. 22, 74, 176, 177, 186, 192
NVivo 251–255, 264, 296

observation 130, 147, 173
observation scheme 179–183, 185
observational schedule/protocol *see* observation scheme
Ochs, E. 130
O'Connor, A. 189, 192
Onwuegbuzie, A. J. 163, 167, 168, 170, 268, 270
open coding 260–261
open-ended questions 107, 112, 199
opinion poll 82, 96
Oppenheim, A. N. 111, 141
opportunistic sampling 129
opportunity sampling 98–99
ordinal data 207–208, 227
Ortega, L. 19, 80, 81, 88, 90, 120, 240, 277, 313
outliers 60, 203–204

pairwise deletion 205
Pallant, J. 22, 198, 217

Palmer, A. S. 19
panel conditioning 82–83, 86–87, 88, 150
panel study 81, 82–83, 85, 89
paradigm war 9, 28–29, 44, 163
parallel criteria 57
parametric procedures/tests 208, 227–230
partial correlation 224
partial transcription 248–249
participant meaning *see* insider meaning
participant mortality *see* mortality
participant observation 130, 131, 133, 179
Patton, M. Q. 134, 137, 138, 142
Pavlenko, A. 81
Pearson, K. 31
Pearson product-moment correlation *see* correlation
Peirce, C. 31
Petska, K. S. 43, 174, 303
Pica, T. 188
pilot study, piloting 75–76, 112–113, 150
Plano Clark, V. L. 42, 43, 168, 170, 171, 174, 303
Plumridge, L. 86
point-biserial correlation 224
Polio, C. G. 179
Polkinghorne, D. E. 126, 134
Popper, K. 31
population 83, 96–101, 212
positivism, positivist 9, 11, 258
post hoc test 219
power analysis 100
practice effect 53, 83, 150
pragmatism, pragmatist 9, 30, 44, 307
Presser, S. 103
Preston, J. 268
primary research 16
probability coefficient 210
probability sampling 97–98
probe questions, probes 137
production questionnaire discourse completion task
prospective longitudinal study 82
protocol analysis 147
psychometrics 31
Punch, K. F. 22, 38, 63, 126, 154, 170, 242, 311
purist 29
purposive sampling 126, 153, 315

qualitative data 19, 37, 124–125
qualitizing data 271
quality criteria 48–63
quantitative data 19, 32
quantitizing data 269–271
quasi-experiment, quasi-experimental design/method 32, 81, 95, 115–121, 178, 222
questionnaire 24, 31, 75, 95, 101–115, 152, 170–172
questionnaire survey *see* questionnaire
quota sampling 98, 99

Rafaeli, E. 156, 157, 158, 159
Rampton, B. 130, 242
random sampling 97
range 214
rank order correlation 228, 230
rank order items 107
Ranta, L. 189
rating scale 106, 180
Reah, D. 19
Reeder, K. 53, 80, 81, 90
regression 31, 226
reliability 49, 50–51, 56–58
repeated cross-sectional study 83–84, 85, 89
repeated measures analysis 91
repeated survey 82
reliability analysis 206–207
reliability check 60–61
representative, representativeness 96–99, 101
research ethics 48, 63–74, 190
research hypothesis *see* hypothesis
research journal *see* journal
research log 75–76, 160
research question 72–74, 281–282, 295, 308
research validity 50, 52–54
researcher effect 150, 190
retrospective interview 134, 147, 148–150, 170–171
retrospective longitudinal study 84–85, 89
Richards, K. 22, 37, 65, 72, 132, 134, 138, 140, 194, 242
Richards, L. 22, 25, 54, 56, 57, 75, 77, 125, 132, 160, 163, 179, 244, 250, 257, 262, 264, 266, 267, 295, 297, 299, 308, 312
Richardson, L. 298, 299
Roberts, C. 130, 247, 248
Robson, C. 23, 105, 142
Rodgers, T. S. 21
Rossiter, M. J. 158, 177, 187, 188, 190, 192
Rossman, G. B. 29, 30
rotating panel 85
Rounds, P. L. 189
Rubio, O. G. 134
Ruspini, E. 78, 84, 85, 89

Rutherford, E. 31
Ryen, A. 65

sample, sample size, sampling 38, 41, 56, 83, 86, 91, 95–101, 122–123, 125–129, 172, 210, 212, 237
sampling frame 97, 98
Sandelowski, M. 25, 54, 285, 291, 293, 300, 302, 304
Sanger, K. 19
Sarangi, S. 154
saturation 126–127, 244, 315
scatterplot 203, 225, 226
Schachter, J. 177
schematic representation 288
Schiefflin, B. 130
Schiffrin, D. 19, 248
Schmidt, R. 154, 157, 160
Schmitt, N. 104
Schumann, J. 154
Schwandt, T. A. 26
'scientific method' 30–31, 32
scree test 235
Seale, C. 36, 41, 55, 72
secondary research 16
segmentation 145
Seidman, I. 134, 255, 267
selective coding
self-report questionnaire *see* questionnaire
self-selection 100–101
Seliger, H. W. 22
SEM *see* structural equation modelling
semantic differential scale 105–106, 180
semi-structured interview 136
Séror, J. 263, 264, 267
Shadish, W. R. 117
Sharkey, J. 189, 192
Shavelson, R. J. 32, 72, 120
Shohamy, E. 22, 67
significance 207, 210–211
Silver, C. 264
Silverman, D. 23, 35, 41, 48, 55, 56, 57, 72, 125, 126, 160, 298, 307
Simon, H. A. 147
simultaneous cross-sectional study 84–85, 89
situationalist 30
Skehan, P. 104
Sleney, J. 166
Smith, G. T. 52
Smithson, J. 146
snowball sampling 98, 122, 129
social desirability bias 54, 115, 141
Spada, N. 181, 182, 188, 189
Spearman, C. 31
Spearman rank order correlation *see* rank order correlation
SphinxSurvey 273
split panel 85
SPSS [Statistical Package for the Social Sciences] 197–198
St. Pierre, E. A. 298, 299
Stake, R. E. 151, 152, 153, 243, 250
standard deviation 209, 214
standardized/standard score 205–206, 273
Stanley, J. C. 50, 52, 116, 119
statistical significance *see* significance
statistics 24, 27–28, 31, 33, 34, 100, 197–241
stimulated recall *see* retrospective interview
stratified random sampling 97
Stratman, J. F. 151
Strauss, A. L. 36, 37, 39, 43, 126, 127, 259, 260, 262
Street, B. 230
Stringfield, S. 99
structural equation modelling [SEM] 91, 231, 238–240
structured interview 134, 135
style manual 279–280
Sudman, S. 75
survey 31, 95, 101–115, 178
Swain, M. 150
syntax file 201
systematic sampling 97

Tabachnick, B. G. 23, 209
table 289
Tannen, D. 19
tape analysis 248–249
Taris, T. 79, 82, 83, 84, 91
Tarone, E. 213
Tashakkori, A. 10, 23, 39, 44, 62, 63, 166, 168, 169, 170, 269, 270, 308
Teddlie, C. 10, 23, 39, 44, 62, 63, 99, 166, 168, 169, 170, 268, 269, 270, 308
template of codes, template approach 253–254, 315
TextSmart 273
theoretical coding 261
theoretical sampling *see* purposive sampling
theoretical validity 58
theory 31, 258, 259–260, 261
thick description 37, 55, 60, 130, 155
think-aloud 147, 148
Thomas, G. D. 119

Thomas, H. 166
Thomas, J. 166
Thomson, R. 83, 86, 87
threats (to validity) 53–54, 59–62
time sampling 180
time-series design 80, 81, 86, 91
Todd, Z. 166, 301, 309
Toohey, K. 130, 154
Totterdell, P. 158
Towne, L. 32, 72, 120
transcribing, transcription 246–249, 315
transcription convention 248
transferability 49, 57
treatment 86, 116
trend study *see* repeated cross-sectional study
triangulation 42, 43, 45, 58, 61, 165–166, 172, 302
Trott, K. 22
true-false items 106
trustworthiness 49
Tseng, W.-T. 104
t-test 215–218
Turner, B. 40, 280
Turner, J. C. 186, 187
Turner, L. A. 167
two-tailed significance 210
two-way ANOVA 230, 231–233
typical sampling 127, 153, 172, 315
typology/category development 269, 272–273

unstructured interview 135–136

validity 45, 48–63
validity argument 52, 62
validity checks 60–61
validity threats *see* threats
value label 201
van Eerde, V. 158
van Gogh, V. 294
van Lier, L. 130, 154, 155, 178
variable 33, 201, 284
variable label 201
variance 214
verbal report/protocol 147
verbal reporting 147
Verschuren, P. J. M. 152
video recording 139, 183–185, 249
vignette 254–255, 257

Warm, A. 121, 122
Watson-Gegeo, K. A. 130, 131
Whitecross, C. 11
Widdowson, H. G. 11, 19, 133
Wilcoxon signed-rank test 230
Wiles, R. 66, 69
Wilkinson, L. 50, 212, 213, 231, 284, 285, 287
Wilson, B. L. 29, 30
Winnicott, D. W. 10
Winter, G. 58
Wolcott, H. F. 293
Wong-Fillmore, L. 153, 154
Wragg, E. C. 177, 178
Wray, A. 22

Yates, L. 41, 267
You, J. 119

Zahran, K. 273
Zuengler, J. 178, 184, 185